lonely planet

Cyprus

Paul Hellander

LONELY PLANET PUBLICATIONS
Melbourne • Oakland • London • Paris

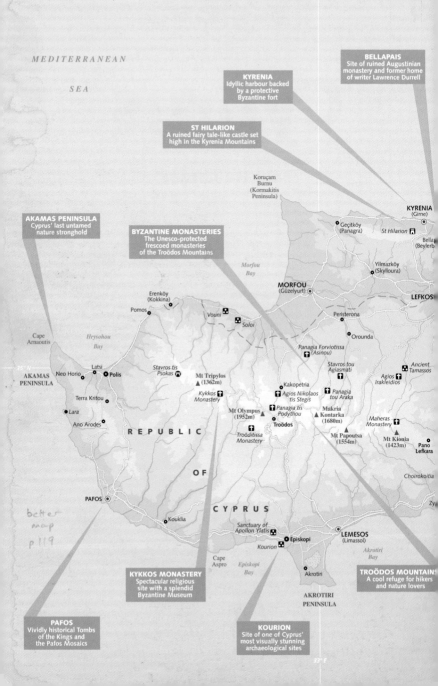

CYPRUS

MEDITERRANEAN

SEA

BELLAPAIS
Site of ruined Augustinian monastery and former home of writer Lawrence Durrell

KYRENIA
Idyllic harbour backed by a protective Byzantine fort

ST HILARION
A ruined fairy tale-like castle set high in the Kyrenia Mountains

Koruçam Burnu (Kormakitis Peninsula)

AKAMAS PENINSULA
Cyprus' last untamed nature stronghold

BYZANTINE MONASTERIES
The Unesco-protected frescoed monasteries of the Troödos Mountains

KYRENIA (Girne)

Geçitköy (Panagra)   St Hilarion

Bella (Beylerb

Morfou Bay

Yılmazköy (Skylloura)

Erenköy (Kokkina)

MORFOU (Güzelyurt)

LEFKOS

Pomos

Vouni   Soloi

Peristerona

Cape Arnaoutis

Hrysohou Bay

Panagia Forviotissa (Asinou)

Orounda

35° N

AKAMAS PENINSULA

Latsi   Polis
Neo Horio

Stavros tis Psokas

Mt Tripylos ▲(1362m)

Stavros tou Agiasmati

Ancient Tamassos

Terra Kritou

Kykkos Monastery

Kakopetria

Agios Nikolaos tis Stegis

Agios Irakleidios

Lara

Ano Arodes

Panagia tou Araka

REPUBLIC

Mt Olympus (1952m)

Panagia tis Podythou

Troödos

Makria Kontarka ▲(1680m)

Maheras Monastery

OF

Troöditissa Monastery

Mt Papoutsa ▲(1554m)

Mt Kiónia ▲(1423m)

Pano Lefkara

Choirokoitia

PAFOS

Kouklia

CYPRUS

Zy

better map p 119

Sanctuary of Apollon Ylatis

Kourion   Episkopi

LEMESOS (Limassol)

Akrotiri Bay

Cape Aspro

Episkopi Bay

Akrotiri

AKROTIRI PENINSULA

TROÖDOS MOUNTAIN
A cool refuge for hikers and nature lovers

KYKKOS MONASTERY
Spectacular religious site with a splendid Byzantine Museum

PAFOS
Vividly historical Tombs of the Kings and the Pafos Mosaics

KOURION
Site of one of Cyprus' most visually stunning archaeological sites

33° E

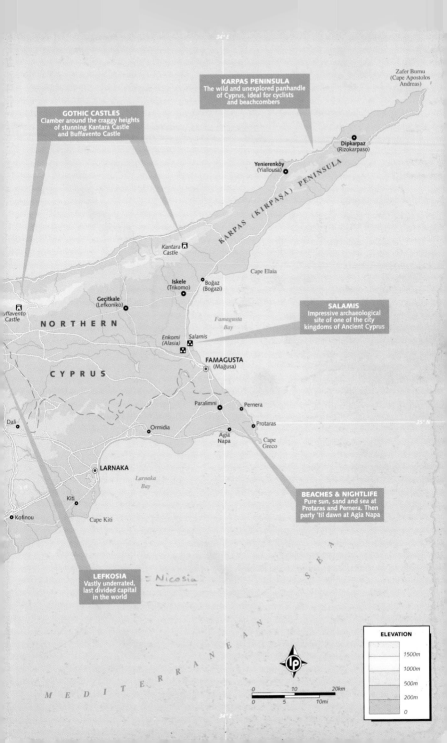

GOTHIC CASTLES
Clamber around the craggy heights of stunning Kantara Castle and Buffavento Castle

KARPAS PENINSULA
The wild and unexplored panhandle of Cyprus, ideal for cyclists and beachcombers

Zafer Burnu
(Cape Apostolos Andreas)

Dipkarpaz
(Rizokarpaso)

Yenierenköy
(Yiallousa)

KARPAS (KIRPAŞA) PENINSULA

Kantara
Castle

Cape Elaia

Iskele
(Trikomo)

Boğaz
(Bogazi)

Geçitkale
(Lefkoniko)

Buffavento
Castle

NORTHERN

Famagusta
Bay

Enkomi
(Alasia)

Salamis

SALAMIS
Impressive archaeological site of one of the city kingdoms of Ancient Cyprus

CYPRUS

FAMAGUSTA
(Mağusa)

Paralimni

Pernera

Dali

Ormidia

Protaras

Agia
Napa

Cape
Greco

BEACHES & NIGHTLIFE
Pure sun, sand and sea at Protaras and Pernera. Then party 'til dawn at Agia Napa

LARNAKA

Larnaka
Bay

Kiti

Kofinou

Cape Kiti

LEFKOSIA
Vastly underrated, last divided capital in the world

= Nicosia

M E D I T E R R A N E A N   S E A

34° E

35° N

34° E

ELEVATION

1500m
1000m
500m
200m
0

0   10   20km
0   5   10mi

Cyprus
2nd edition – June 2003
First published – May 2000

Published by
Lonely Planet Publications Pty Ltd ABN 36 005 607 983
90 Maribyrnong St, Footscray, Victoria 3011, Australia

Lonely Planet Offices
Australia Locked Bag 1, Footscray, Victoria 3011
USA 150 Linden St, Oakland, CA 94607
UK 10a Spring Place, London NW5 3BH
France 1 rue du Dahomey, 75011 Paris

Photographs
Many of the images in this guide are available for licensing from
Lonely Planet Images.
w www.lonelyplanetimages.com

Front cover photograph
Basilica ruins stand out against the blue sky at Kourion, in the Republic
of Cyprus (Paul Hellander)

Republic of Cyprus Title Page
Aphrodite Cyprus delights for sale in Geroskipou, Pafos
(Christina Dameyer)

Northern Cyprus Title Page
Patterned mosaics on the floor of the Basilica of Agia Triada in
Sipahi, Karpas (Kırpaşa) Peninula (Paul Hellander)

ISBN 1 74059 122 4

Printed through Colorcraft Ltd, Hong Kong
Printed in China

Contents – Text

1

KYRENIA & THE NORTH COAST 172

FAMAGUSTA & THE KARPAS PENINSULA 189

LANGUAGE 204

GLOSSARY 213

THANKS 215

INDEX 219

MAP LEGEND back page

METRIC CONVERSION inside back cover

Contents – Maps

MAP INDEX

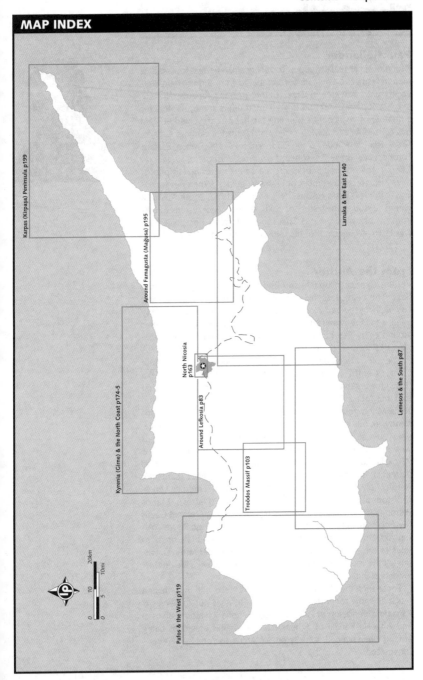

Karpas (Kírpaşa) Peninsula p199

Around Famagusta (Mağusa) p195

Lamaka & the East p140

Kyrenia (Girne) & the North Coast p174-5

North Nicosia p163

Around Lefkosia p83

Lemesos & the South p87

Troödos Massif p103

Pafos & the West p119

0   10   20km
0   5   10mi

The Author

Paul Hellander

Paul has never really stopped travelling since he first looked at a map in his native England. He graduated from Birmingham University with a degree in Greek before heading for Australia. He taught Modern Greek and trained interpreters and translators for a number of years before donning the hat of a travel writer. Paul has contributed to a wide variety of LP titles including: *Greece, Greek Islands, Rhodes & the Dodecanese, Crete, France, Eastern Europe, Israel & the Palestinian Territories, Jerusalem, Singapore, Central America* and *South America on a shoestring*. His photos have also graced a number of LP travel guides. When not travelling with his PC and Nikons, he lives in Adelaide, South Australia where he studies the history of political intelligence, listens to Californian rock music, cooks Thai food and grows hot chillies. He was last seen heading for his spiritual homeland – Greece.

From the Author

Visiting Cyprus to update the 2nd edition of this guide was a buzz. The heat, dust, flies and endless kilometres spent driving and walking the backblocks of Κύπρος–Kıbrıs were worth every minute for the hospitality found at every corner, the adventures around every bend and the sheer fun of discovering even more places to see and things to do. I would like to thank the following people who made the logistics of the operation an absolute breeze: Geoff Harvey (Driveaway, Sydney) and Peugeot Sodexa (Paris) for organizing the faultless wheels of the Peugeot 307 that took me round Cyprus and back to France without a hitch, and Tonia Marangou (Minoan Lines, Athens) who never fails to efficiently fix my always-changing ferry schedules with a big smile.

I would also like to extend my gratitude to my Cypriot friends who helped me in some way with my work: Christos Moustras (CTO, Lefkosia); Sotiris & Vasso Kokkotis (Lefkosia); Kikis Taouxis (Larnaka); Solomos Leotsakos (Protaras); Jacqui Meli (Larnaka); Antony Polycarpou (Episkopi); Giannis Kakoullis (Lemesos); Lefkos Christodoulou (Agros); Georgos Skyrianidis (Platres); Marios Petrou (Larnaka); Nikki Newhouse (North Nicosia); Mehmet Çavuş (Kyrenia); Suat Hüseyin Oğulları (Yenierenköy); Alison Dowey (Alsancak/Karavas) and all those anonymous individuals on both sides of the Attila Line who, over coffee or a beer, often unwittingly gave me clearer insights into the complexities of life on their divided island.

For sharing their homes in Cyprus and Greece with my wife and I as it all came together, my gratitude also goes out to Savvas & Panagiota Venizelou of Adelaide, Agia Marina Xyliatou (Lefkosia) and Angeliki Kanelli of Athens. Stella – thanks again for being around when needed; sons Byron & Marcus, this one is – as ever – for you too.

This Book

Paul Hellander wrote the 1st edition of *Cyprus* and also updated this edition.

From the Publisher

This edition of *Cyprus* was was produced in Lonely Planet's Melbourne office. It was commissioned by Tony Davidson and the project was managed by Andrew Weatherill with assistance from Glenn van der Knijff. Evan Jones coordinated the editing with the help of Stefanie Di Trocchio and Melanie Dankel. Jarrad Needham coordinated the mapping with assistance from Natasha Velleley, Ed Pickard, Jody Whiteoak and Mark Griffiths. Csanad Csutoros prepared the climate charts and Adrian Persoglia supplied the map legend. Birgit Jordan designed the colour pages and the images were supplied by Lonely Planet Images. Quentin Frayne compiled the Language chapter. The cover was designed by Brendan Dempsey. David Kemp was the layout designer, assisted by Sally Morgan and Jacqui Saunders. Kate McDonald and Adriana Mammarella did the layout checks. Thanks to Nick Stebbing and Mark Germanchis for providing advice during layout.

THANKS
Many thanks to the travellers who used the last edition and wrote to us with helpful hints, advice and interesting anecdotes. Your names appear in the back of this book.

Foreword

ABOUT LONELY PLANET GUIDEBOOKS

The story begins with a classic travel adventure: Tony and Maureen Wheeler's 1972 journey across Europe and Asia to Australia. There was no useful information about the overland trail then, so Tony and Maureen published the first Lonely Planet guidebook to meet a growing need.

From a kitchen table, Lonely Planet has grown to become the largest independent travel publisher in the world, with offices in Melbourne (Australia), Oakland (USA), London (UK) and Paris (France).

Today Lonely Planet guidebooks cover the globe. There is an ever-growing list of books and information in a variety of media. Some things haven't changed. The main aim is still to make it possible for adventurous travellers to get out there – to explore and better understand the world.

At Lonely Planet we believe travellers can make a positive contribution to the countries they visit – if they respect their host communities and spend their money wisely. Since 1986 a percentage of the income from each book has been donated to aid projects and human rights campaigns, and, more recently, to wildlife conservation.

Although inclusion in a guidebook usually implies a recommendation we cannot list every good place. Exclusion does not necessarily imply criticism. In fact there are a number of reasons why we might exclude a place – sometimes it is simply inappropriate to encourage an influx of travellers.

UPDATES & READER FEEDBACK

Things change – prices go up, schedules change, good places go bad and bad places go bankrupt. Nothing stays the same. So, if you find things better or worse, recently opened or long-since closed, please tell us and help make the next edition even more accurate and useful.

Lonely Planet thoroughly updates each guidebook as often as possible – usually every two years, although for some destinations the gap can be longer. Between editions, up-to-date information is available in our free, monthly email bulletin *Comet* (W www.lonelyplanet.com/newsletters). You can also check out the *Thorn Tree* bulletin board and *Postcards* section of our website, which carry unverified, but fascinating, reports from travellers.

Tell us about it! We genuinely value your feedback. A well-travelled team at Lonely Planet reads and acknowledges every email and letter we receive and ensures that every morsel of information finds its way to the relevant authors, editors and cartographers.

Everyone who writes to us will find their name listed in the next edition of the appropriate guidebook. The very best contributions will be rewarded with a free guidebook.

We may edit, reproduce and incorporate your comments in Lonely Planet products such as guidebooks, websites and digital products, so let us know if you don't want your comments reproduced or your name acknowledged.

How to contact Lonely Planet:
Online: e talk2us@lonelyplanet.com.au, W www.lonelyplanet.com
Australia: Locked Bag 1, Footscray, Victoria 3011
UK: 10a Spring Place, London NW5 3BH
USA: 150 Linden St, Oakland, CA 94607

Introduction

Independent as an integral nation for only 14 years of its long history, Cyprus today is an enigmatic and enticing destination for the traveller. Culturally European yet geographically Asian/Middle Eastern, Cyprus nonetheless shares a close history with its Levantine neighbours along the Mediterranean littoral.

Being both Turkish and Greek, and therefore Islamic and Christian, Cyprus is a bicultural nation which has often been a cause of division and strife. However, both cultures share a closer inheritance than many would care to admit, and both communities will give a friendly welcome to visitors. Cyprus is off the beaten track yet easily accessible, unless you wish to travel between the Greek and Turkish territories. Vaguely recalled school-day images of Aphrodite and the implied eroticism that accompanied her worship imbue a subtle sense of excitement in a visit to the island. Could this be why Cyprus entices so many young people to its sun-and-fun lifestyle?

While Cyprus evokes images of sun and sand to many, few realise that you can ski here in the morning and swim at one of the many beaches in the afternoon. Although the country is inextricably linked with inva-

sion and bloodshed, the tranquil valleys of the Troödos Mountains shelter humble Byzantine monasteries and churches with some of the most exquisite frescoes found in Orthodox Christendom.

The island's many invaders have left a great legacy of archaeological treasures. It was settled in Palaeolithic times and ever since has been fought over and settled by Ancient Greeks, Romans, Lusignans, Venetians, Genoese, Ottomans and the British. In more recent times, the Soviets, Greeks, Americans and Turks have all fought for control of this country with its strategic location, close to the Middle East.

Nature-lovers perhaps don't realise that Cyprus supports a rich and varied ecosystem of endemic and imported flora and fauna. The spring wild flowers of the island are a total contrast to the grey-brown aridity of its summer months.

For many visitors, though, coming to Cyprus means riotous hedonism and indulgent eating and drinking – Aphrodite would no doubt be impressed. You can partake in this scene, or avoid it altogether, depending on your tastes.

Politically, Cyprus has remained divided since 1974, when its two communities were

forcibly partitioned by outside powers. This division has been a bitter pill for its resilient people to swallow. The country entered the new millennium, with its destiny unfulfilled and uncertain, still divided by local politics and global interests. Cyprus looks set to shoulder the troubled legacy it inherited in the 20th century for the near future at least.

A small and compact country, Cyprus is smaller than the Netherlands or the US state of New Jersey. The Republic of Cyprus is an economic dynamo in the region, with one of the highest standards of living in the Mediterranean basin. In contrast, Turkish-dominated Northern Cyprus languishes in economic dependence on its sponsor and guarantor, Turkey, and is neither recognised nor seemingly wanted by the rest of the world community.

Despite its adversity and division, Cyprus is an excellent destination for independent travellers and package tourists. The infra-structure is good, English is widely spoken, the food is excellent, the Cypriots are welcoming, the climate is warm year-round – the country awaits discovery. When asked to describe his country, one proud Greek Cypriot summed it up succinctly when he said: 'Cyprus is like a Greece that works.' He was not far wrong.

Facts about Cyprus

HISTORY

Situated at the maritime crossroads of the eastern Mediterranean basin, Cyprus has a rich and varied history. Many invaders, settlers and immigrants have come here and the island has seen Greeks, Romans, Byzantines, Lusignans, Genoese, Venetians, Ottomans, British and Turks in turn seek to take a part of Cyprus for themselves.

Cypriots, whether Greek or Turkish, are rightly proud of their nation and feel a strong sense of national identity. The division of their island in 1974 is viewed by many as a temporary setback, and Cypriots look to the day when Cyprus will be a united island once again.

Neolithic & Chalcolithic Cyprus

The first evidence of human habitation can be traced back to the Aceramic Neolithic period, around 10,000 BC, with the discovery of man-made artefacts at the south-coastal site of Akrotiri Aetokremnou. These people may have brought about the extinction of the Pleistocene-era pygmy hippopotamus and dwarf elephant. By 8000 BC domesticated animals, such as cattle, pigs, sheep and goats, had been introduced into Cyprus by agro-pasturalists from the Levantine mainland. These people laid the foundations for the development of the distinctively Cypriot culture best represented at the Aceramic Neolithic settlement of Choirokoitia. Choirokoitia was an enclosed village built on the side of a hill in the southern part of the island in the 6th millennium BC. Its inhabitants lived in well-built round houses made of stone, and produced tools and containers of the same material. Other settlements of this time have been found scattered throughout Cyprus and showed evidence of contact outside the island, especially the import of obsidian from Anatolia. Choirokoitia was abandoned and there is a gap in the archaeological record until the earliest vases made of clay, which date from the 5th millennium BC.

The Ceramic Neolithic period saw a new pattern of settlement emerge, whose material culture was typified by the site of Sotira Teppes near the south coast, which has yielded abstractly painted ceramic artefacts.

Copper began to be used in the 4th millennium BC and ushered in the Chalcolithic period when copper implements were made. Among this period's most noteworthy artistic achievements was the production of cross-shaped human figurines made of picrolite, a local Cypriot stone. Around 2500 BC, a new wave of immigrants, believed to be from Anatolia, brought with them new technologies and styles and started the transition to the Bronze Age.

The Bronze Age

Implements of copper progressively replaced the old stone repertory and led to the development of the abundant copper deposits in the Troödos Mountains. At the end of the Early Bronze Age, which lasted from 2300 BC to 1950 BC, bronze objects began to be cast, using imported tin. Contacts with the outside world were otherwise few, but imaginative pottery designs flourished, which drew conspicuously on the human and animal life in and around the villages.

The Middle Bronze Age period extended from 1950 BC to 1650 BC and marked an essential continuation of the material culture of the preceding one, with the reintroduction of painted pottery on a regional basis. Settlements tended to keep to the foothills and plains and suggest a largely agrarian community. The first evidence of sustained copper mining has come from the start of this period and, by its end, Cyprus had already begun its trading relationships with the Aegean, Western Asia and Egypt, attested by its pottery exports.

The Late Bronze Age lasted from 1600 BC to 1050 BC and is considered to be one of the most important periods in the cultural and historical development of Cyprus. Extensive foreign trade with Egypt and places in the Aegean Sea characterised the era. Most importantly, writing in the form of a linear script known as Cypro-Minoan was adapted from Crete (see the boxed text 'The Cypriot Syllabary' for details). Fine jewellery, ivory carvings and delicate pottery were produced during this time and, from around 1400 BC, there was a notable increase in the amount of Mycenaean pottery imported from mainland Greece.

Greek Immigration During the Late Bronze Age new towns were established around the coast, and overseas trade in pottery containers and, later, copper ingots, expanded. Cyprus enjoyed an unprecedented level of prosperity that was accompanied by the movement of foreign goods and people into the island. Around 1200 BC the first Greek-speaking settlers arrived as part of the Sea Peoples, causing the disruption of existing Cypriot communities and led to the emergence of the city kingdoms of the Iron Age.

Archaic & Classical Cyprus

The City Kingdoms The first Greeks established a series of city kingdoms at Kourion, Pafos, Marion (Polis), Soloi, Lapithos, Tamassos and Salamis. Two more were later established at Kition and Amathous. These kingdoms enjoyed a period of advancement and increasing prosperity between 750 BC and 475 BC, as shown in evidence found at the Royal Tombs near Salamis. These extensive tombs contained sumptuous examples of wealth and also closely matched the description of Mycenaean burials described by Homer in *The Iliad*.

During this time, Cyprus was ruled in turn by Assyrians, Egyptians and Persians as the fortunes of these various empires waxed and waned.

Classical Age Cyprus' Classical Age coincides with that of mainland Greece (475–325 BC) and during this period Cypriot art came under strong Attic influence. Zenon of Kition, the founder of the Stoic philosophy movement, was born during this time. Evagoras, king of Salamis, maintained strong links with the Hellenic mainland and extended Greek influence over most of the island, despite Persian hegemony. However, he was finally overcome by the Persians in 381 BC and assassinated seven years later. His death effectively brought the Classical Age to an end.

Hellenistic & Roman Cyprus

Alexander the Great, following his victory over the last Persian ruler, Darius III, at Issus in 333 BC, took control of the city kingdoms of Cyprus and ushered in a new era. While essentially giving the kingdoms autonomy, he refuted their right to make coins. When Alexander died in 323 BC, Cyprus was ceded to Ptolemy I of Egypt who further suppressed the city kingdoms, eventually causing the last king of Salamis, Nikokreon, to commit suicide. For 250 years Cyprus remained a Ptolemaic colony, languishing under the rule of an appointed governor-general.

Cyprus was annexed by the expanding Roman Empire in 58 BC. Orator and writer

The Cypriot Syllabary

Writing came to Cyprus quite early in prehistoric times. The pre-Greek Cypriots of the Late Bronze Age in the second half of the 2nd millennium BC used the so-called Cypro-Minoan script. This was evidently derived from the Linear A script of Minoan Crete and is presumed to be syllabic. A syllabary is a set of written symbols used to represent the syllables of the words of a language – for example, *ka, ke, ki, ko* or *ku*. Syllabaries are a form of writing that bridged the gap between earlier pictographic systems and later fully alphabetic writing systems.

The Cypro-Minoan script, which has not been deciphered, consisted of about 60 symbols and occurred on clay tablets in Cyprus and at Ras Shamra on the Syrian coast. It has also been encountered on a range of other artefacts from Cyprus. The Cypro-Syllabic script almost certainly evolved from the Cypro-Minoan script, but has so far been attested in Cyprus only between the 8th and 3rd centuries BC. It undoubtedly existed earlier and consisted of about 50 separate symbols, each of which represented a different syllable.

It has been claimed that the earliest evidence for the Greek language on the island is an 11th-century-BC inscription from Kouklia. Although most Cypro-Syllabic inscriptions are in Greek, some reproduce a language that cannot yet be understood. It has been called Eteo-Cypriot by linguists and was probably the same native language as the one reproduced in the Cypro-Minoan script. The use of the Cypro-Syllabic script side by side with Greek inscriptions, hence allowing decipherment to the Greek alphabet, is unique to Cyprus.

Cicero was one of Cyprus' first proconsuls. Despite being briefly given to Cleopatra VII of Egypt and subsequently handed back to Roman control, Cyprus enjoyed some 600 years of relative peace and prosperity under Roman rule. Many public buildings and road works date from this time; noteworthy among them were the theatre at Kourion, the colonnaded gymnasium at Salamis and the Sanctuary of Apollon Ylatis.

Christianity in Cyprus It was during this period, in around AD 45, that Christianity made its early appearance on the island. Barnabas (later to become St Barnabas – Agios Varnavas in Greek), a native of Salamis, accompanied the Apostle Paul and preached on Cyprus. Among his first conversions was Sergius Paulus the Roman proconsul. Christianity flourished in Cyprus so, by the time of Constantine the Great, paganism had almost completely been supplanted on the island by Christianity.

The Byzantine Empire

In 395, the Roman Empire was divided. Its eastern variant, the Byzantine Empire, was based in Constantinople and retained hegemony over Cyprus. However, Cyprus retained a considerable degree of ecclesiastical autonomy from Constantinople and, in 488, the archbishop was granted the right to carry a sceptre instead of an archbishop's crosier, as well as the authority to write his signature in imperial purple ink. This practice is carried on to this day.

The expansion of Islam at around this time had adverse effects on Cyprus. A series of disastrous Arab raids starting in 647 caused great depredation and suffering. Salamis was sacked and never recovered, Kourion declined and coastal settlers moved inland to escape the repeated warring and pillaging. In 688 a sort of truce was called when Justinian II and the Arab caliph Abd-al-Malik signed an agreement for the joint rule of Cyprus. This agreement lasted until 965 when Emperor Nikiforos II Fokas regained Cyprus completely for the Byzantines.

Lusignan, Genoese & Venetian Cyprus

Byzantine rule might well have continued in Cyprus had renegade Governor Isaak Komninos not decided to proclaim himself Emperor of Cyprus, and in 1191 take on the might of the Crusader king Richard the Lionheart of England. Richard took possession of Cyprus and subsequently sold it to the Knights Templar. They were unable to afford the upkeep and sold it in turn to the dispossessed king of Jerusalem, Guy de Lusignan.

The French-speaking new Lord of Cyprus established a lengthy dynasty that brought mixed fortunes to the island. He invited Christian families who had lost property in the Holy Lands to settle in Cyprus, and for some time they involved themselves in the affairs of the diminished territories that still belonged to the kingdom of Jerusalem. This proved an economic strain on Cyprus until the kingdom finally fell with the fall of Acre (Akko) in 1291.

For a hundred years or so thereafter, Cyprus enjoyed a period of immense wealth and prosperity, with current-day Famagusta (Mağusa) being the centre of unrivalled commercial activity and trade. Many fine buildings and churches were completed during this period, some of which are still visible in North Nicosia (Lefkoşa), Bellapais (Beylerbeyi) and Famagusta. Cyprus' prosperity reached its zenith under King Peter I (r. 1359–69), who mounted an unsuccessful crusade in 1365 that only managed to achieve the sacking of Alexandria.

In the meantime, Orthodox Greeks, while nominally free to practise their religion independently, were becoming more and more restless at being obliged to show homage to a Latin (Roman Catholic) ecclesiastical administration. Many Greek clerics retreated to the mountains and quietly and unobtrusively built simple churches and monasteries and decorated them with some of the finest frescoes ever painted in the Orthodox world (see the boxed text 'The Frescoed Churches of Cyprus' in The Troödos Massif chapter).

The fortunes of the Lusignans were to take a turn for the worse after the accession to power of Peter I's heir and son, Peter II. Eying Cyprus' wealth and strategic position as entrepot, Genoa and Venice jostled for control. This led to Genoa seizing Famagusta, which it held for the next 100 years. The fortunes of both Famagusta and Cyprus declined as a result. The last Lusignan king was James II (1460–73). He managed to expel the Genoese from Famagusta and married a Venetian noblewoman, Caterina Cornaro, who succeeded James and became Queen of Cyprus – becoming the last royal personage of the Lusignan dynasty. Under pressure, she ceded Cyprus to Venice.

The Venetians ruled Cyprus from 1489 to 1571, but their control was characterised by indifference and torpor. Corruption and inefficiency marked the administration and the Greek peasantry fared no better under their new overlords than under their previous masters. In the meantime, the Ottoman Empire was expanding and, in anticipation of attack from the north, the Venetians fortified Lefkosia with immense circular walls and built massive fortifications around Famagusta. Neither measures held back the Ottoman onslaught and, in 1570, Lefkosia (South Nicosia) fell to the Turks. Almost a year later, after a long siege, Famagusta was taken by the Ottomans.

The Ottoman Empire

The newly arrived Ottomans suppressed the Latin Church and restored the Orthodox hierarchy. The peasantry, who had hitherto suffered under a feudal tenancy system, were given land. Taxes were initially reduced but later increased, often arbitrarily, with the Orthodox archbishop being responsible for their collection. Some 20,000 Turks were settled on Cyprus following its capture, but the island was not high in the priorities of the ruling sultans.

Indolence, corruption and sloth marked the Ottoman rule and dissent was frequently put down by oppression. In 1821 the Orthodox archbishop was hanged on suspicion of supporting the growing Greek revolution in mainland Greece. Ottoman rule lasted 300 years, until another foreign power sought influence in the region.

British Rule

In 1878 Turkey and Britain signed an agreement whereby Turkey would retain sovereignty of the languishing colony, while Britain would shoulder the responsibility for administering the island. Britain's aim was to secure a strategic outpost in the Middle East from where it could monitor military and commercial movements in the Levant and the Caucasus. As part of the agreement, Britain would protect the sultan's Asian territories from threat by Russia.

However, in 1914, the parties were at war so Britain assumed outright sovereignty of Cyprus. Turkey's recognition of the annexation of its territory was not ratified until the 1923 Treaty of Lausanne, under which it also regularised territorial claims with the newly independent Greece.

British control of Cyprus was initially welcomed by its mostly Greek population, since it was assumed that Britain would ultimately work with the Greeks to achieve *enosis,* or union with Greece. Turkish Cypriots, though, were less than enthusiastic at the prospect. The British had offered to unite Cyprus with Greece as early as 1915 on condition that Greece fulfilled its treaty obligations towards Serbia when it was attacked by Bulgaria. The Greek government refused and the offer was never repeated again.

Pro-*enosis* riots broke out in 1931, but it wasn't until the 1950s that the *enosis* movement really began to gather steam. Energy was generated by a Cypriot lieutenant colonel, Georgos 'Digenis' Grivas, who founded the Ethniki Organosi tou Kypriakou Agona (EOKA; National Organisation for the Cypriot Struggle). Between 1955 and 1958, EOKA launched a series of covert attacks on the British administration and military, and on anyone else who was seen as being against *enosis*. The British came up with various proposals for limited home rule, but all were rejected. The 17% minority Turkish Cypriots became increasingly alarmed at the prospect of being forcibly incorporated into Greece.

The respective governments in both Greece and Turkey began to take an active interest in developments in Cyprus and, as Greek Cypriots called for *enosis*, the Turkish Cypriots demanded either retrocession to Turkey, or *taksim* (partition). In 1959 Greek Cypriot ethnarch and religious leader Archbishop Makarios III and Turkish Cypriot leader Faisal Küçük met in Zurich with Greek and Turkish leaders, as well as representatives of the British government. They came to ratify a previously agreed plan whereby independence would be granted to Cyprus under conditions that would satisfy all sides. The British were to retain two bases and various other military sites as part of the agreement. Cyprus wouldn't enter into a political or economic union with Turkey or Greece, nor agree to be partitioned. Political

The Invasion of Cyprus – In a Nutshell

On 15 July 1974, a detachment of the National Guard, led by officers from mainland Greece, launched a coup aimed at assassinating Makarios and establishing *enosis*. They laid the presidential palace in ruins, but Makarios narrowly escaped. A former EOKA member, Nikos Sampson, was proclaimed president of Cyprus. Five days later, Turkish forces landed at current-day Kyrenia (Girne) to overturn Sampson's government. Despite vigorous resistance, the Turks were successful in establishing a bridgehead around Kyrenia and linking it with the Turkish sector of North Nicosia (Lefkoşa).

On 23 July Greece's junta fell and was replaced by a democratic government under Konstantinos Karamanlis. At the same time, Sampson was replaced in Cyprus by Glafkos Clerides, the president of the House of Representatives. The three guarantor powers, Britain, Greece and Turkey, as required by the treaty, met for discussions in Geneva, but it proved impossible to halt the Turkish advance until 16 August. By that time Turkey controlled the northern 37% of the island. In December, Makarios returned to resume the presidency.

power was to be shared on a proportional basis, although with less than 20% of the total population the Turkish Cypriots were granted 30% of civil service positions, 33% of seats in the House of Representatives and 40% of positions in the army.

Ominously, Britain, Turkey and Greece were to be named as 'guarantor powers' which gave any nation the right to intervene in the affairs of Cyprus should it be believed that the terms of the independence agreement were being breached in any way.

The Republic of Cyprus

The birth of the new independent Republic of Cyprus was realised on 16 August 1960. Transition from colony to an independent nation was not without growing pains and sporadic violence and agitation continued. The unrest culminated in serious sectarian violence in 1963 that further divided the Greek and Turkish communities. The Turkish Cypriots retreated to ghettos and enclaves as a means of protecting themselves against Greek harassment and aggression.

The Cold War was at its peak and Cyprus' strategic value as a radar listening post became vitally important to the British and the militarily stronger Americans. Both nations relied on Cyprus in order to monitor Soviet nuclear-missile testing in Central Asia. The British maintained an air-force garrison on its Akrotiri base that included a nuclear arsenal.

Archbishop Makarios, the President of Cyprus, played an increasingly risky game of political nonalignment while seeking arms and support from communist nations

such as the Soviet Union and Czechoslovakia. He also covertly supported further calls for *enosis* with Greece. Turkey and Turkish Cypriots became increasingly uneasy at the thought of a possible communist-dominated government in Cyprus, and the Americans and their British allies felt concern at the possibility of another Cuban crisis – this time in the Mediterranean.

Discussions on the possibility of segregation of the two communities began to take on a greater tempo. In 1967 a coup in Greece installed a right-wing military junta. Relations with Cyprus cooled while the US cosied up to the more accommodating colonels in Athens. Cyprus under Makarios became a less and less desirable option for both the Greeks and the Americans. In July 1974 a CIA-sponsored and Greek-organised coup took place in Cyprus with the intention of eliminating Makarios and installing a more pro-Western government.

Fearing *enosis* with Greece, the Turks launched a pre-emptive invasion of northern Cyprus five days later. Soon the Turkish mainland army occupied the northern 37% of the island. Cyprus was divided.

Taksim

The division of Cyprus in 1974 has remained to this day. While the arrival of the Turkish army was seen as a godsend by hitherto harried and harassed Turkish Cypriots, it was viewed as an enormous disaster by the 200,000 Greek Cypriots who then lived in the northern third of Cyprus. Many were caught up in the onslaught and killed; most were evacuated or fled to what remained of the Republic (the South). Similarly, some 100,000 Turkish Cypriots from the South fled, or were forcibly evacuated, to Northern Cyprus (the North). The economic cost to Cyprus and lack of stability brought about with division, and the number of refugees this caused, was enormous. The now-truncated Greek Republic of Cyprus was deprived of some of its best land, two major towns, its lucrative citrus industry and the bulk of its tourist infrastructure.

While the forced division of Cyprus served certain short-term military and political purposes, and Turkish Cypriots received protection from Turkey, the final result was ultimately a Pyrrhic victory for the Turks. Makarios escaped assassination by the coup plotters, the military junta collapsed and the desire for *enosis* dissipated, as Cyprus became preoccupied with its internal problems.

The declaration of a Turkish Republic of Northern Cyprus (TRNC; KKTC in Turkish) by President Rauf Denktaş in 1983 was recognised by no nation other than Turkey. The Cold War came to an end in 1990, by which time half the population of native Turkish Cypriots had fled the island for the UK, Canada and Australia.

Cyprus Today

The Greek Cypriots quickly regrouped and put their energies into rebuilding their shattered nation. Within a few years the economy was on the mend, and the Republic of Cyprus continues to enjoy international recognition as the sole legitimate representative of Cyprus. The economy is booming: the Cyprus Stock Exchange opened in mid-1999 and initially absorbed vast amounts of private funds. Later, the stock exchange took a nosedive and many Cypriots lost huge amounts of money. Tourism is generally buoyant, though 2002 saw a downward trend sparking some concern in the industry.

Known by most foreigners simply as 'Northern Cyprus' and by Greeks as the 'Occupied Territories' *(ta katehomena)*, the northern segment of Cyprus as a separate entity defies logic and it continues to survive and develop, supported in no little way by its client and sponsor nation, Turkey, while experiencing international economic sanctions.

Talks to reunite Cyprus have taken place sporadically since 1974 but little ground has been gained, both sides presenting an entrenched and uncompromising point of view. The UN has maintained peace along the Green Line (the boundary separating Greek Cypriot Lefkosia from Turkish Cypriot North Nicosia) since 1964, and in 1974 was called upon to patrol and monitor the ceasefire line, now called the Attila Line, the border which runs almost the length of the country.

With Cyprus and Turkey seeking entry to the European Union (EU), the leaders of both the South and North had thrice-weekly talks during the spring and summer of 2002 aimed at reunification, but talks became bogged down in the minutiae of the fine print. In early 2003 Kofi Annan, the UN secretary-general, tried to broker an agreement that would have allowed a referendum on reunification, but both leaders were adamant that the proposal required more concessions. While Turkey's application for admission to the EU was deferred in January 2003, Cyprus' application (with or without the North) was approved and Cyprus will be a part of the EU in May 2004. It is unclear how Turkey and the Turkish Cypriots will react if the South enters the EU on its own, but any negative reaction will impact on the likelihood of Turkey gaining EU membership.

On a more positive note, in January 2003, there was a rally of 70,000 Turkish Cypriots demanding an end to the division of the country, a remarkable event as President Denktaş has never tolerated dissent in the past. But, overall, there is only a little light at the end of a very long and dark tunnel for a solution to eventuate.

GEOGRAPHY

The saucepan shape of Cyprus reflects its geology. In the North a 100km-long mountain chain, known as the Kyrenia (Girne) Range, runs more or less parallel to the northern coastline. It is the southernmost range of the great Alpine-Himalaya chain in the Eastern Mediterranean and is made up of thrust masses of Mesozoic limestone.

South of the Kyrenia Range lies a vast plain known as the Mesaoria (or Mesarya). It stretches from Morfou (Güzelyurt) in the west to Famagusta in the east. The divided capital Lefkosia/North Nicosia lies more or less in the middle of the plain. The Mesaoria is the island's principal grain-growing

[Continued on page 17]

WILD FLOWERS OF CYPRUS

In the heat and aridity of midsummer, visitors to Cyprus could easily be forgiven for believing that the island is bereft of flora. The dry, maquis-covered and rock-strewn hills present little evidence that Cyprus is home to a wide variety of wild flowers and plants, many of which are to be found in no other country. Visitors in Cyprus during spring and late autumn, on the other hand, will be confronted by a riotous blossoming of colour, with carpets of poppies, buttercups and anemones stretching as far as the eye can see, while the Troödos Mountains and Kyrenia (Girne) Range are home to spectacular orchids and other rare endemic species.

About 45 species of orchids are to be found in Cyprus and one of these – Kotschy's bee orchid – is unique to the island. Cyprus boasts some 130 endemic plants of which 45 are found only on the high slopes of the Troödos Mountains. A further 19 endemic species are found only in North Cyprus, with Casey's Larkspur perhaps the rarest plant on the whole island.

Cyprus' Flora Profile

The country's flora profile is a result of the catastrophic ice ages when much of the flora of northern and central Europe was covered in ice sheets and glaciers, while the Mediterranean basin escaped unscathed and provided a haven for the further evolution of plant life. As an island, Cyprus became rich in endemic flora and home to a large number of varied species that are typical of the Mediterranean area as a whole.

Left: Cyprus tulip (endemic), *Tulipa cypria*

Right: St Hilarion cabbage (endemic), *Brassica Hilarionis*

Inset detail: Cyprus crocus, *Crocus cyprius* (photograph by Andreas Demetropoulos)

BOTH PHOTOGRAPHS BY HIKMET ULUÇAM

The country can be divided into six basic vegetation zones, each of which supports its own set of flowers, shrubs, bushes and trees. **Pine forests** used to cover most of Cyprus, but shipbuilding in antiquity and the unabated use of wood for charcoal has destroyed much of the original forest cover. Forests are now mainly limited to the western slopes of Mt Olympus in the Troödos Mountains. **Gariques** and **maquis** are widespread in areas of man-induced erosion where forest once stood and now only low bushes survive. **Rocky areas** comprise a variety of habitats and are commonly found in exposed mountain settings such as the Kyrenia Range. **Coastal areas** cover a narrow belt of some 50m to 100m all along the coast which, with one or two exceptions, encompass the full girt of Cyprus. **Cultivated land** includes agricultural areas as well as fallow land and constitutes the largest geographical area of the island, hosting the fewest number of flower species. **Wetlands** constitute a marginal sector of the flora distribution. They are characterised by stream beds, salt lakes, marshy areas and artificial lakes.

When & Where to Go

The best time to see Cyprus' wild flowers is in early spring (February and March) when most of the species enjoy a short period of blossoming and take advantage of the usually moist climate at this time of the year. There is a second period in late autumn (October and November) when flowers can also be enjoyed. During the arid summer months only a few hardy flowers, found chiefly in the mountain regions, and colourful thistles on the Mesaoria/Mesarya plains provide any relief from what, to the untrained eye, can seem like a botanical desert.

The main areas for flower spotting are the slopes and summit region of the Troödos Mountains, the northern aspects of the Kyrenia Range and the Akamas Peninsula. The isolated Karpas (Kırpaşa) Peninsula is also rich in specimens and the coastal strip east of Larnaka Bay is exceptional for spotting endemic flora. In order to get the best out of flower spotting, enthusiasts will need to spend plenty of time trekking and searching carefully, since many species are limited to small geographical areas, sometimes to only a few hundred square metres.

BOTH PHOTOGRAPHS BY ANDREAS DEMETROPOULOS

Left: Cyprus crocus, *Crocus cyprius*

Right: Troödos golden drop (endemic), *Onosma troodi*

What to Spot

Orchids are the most popular wild flowers for enthusiasts. The one endemic orchid, **Kotschy's bee orchid**, is an exquisite species, looking much like a bee both in its shape and patterning. It is fairly rare yet can be found in a variety of habitats all over the island. The **Troödos helleborine**, while not endemic, grows mainly on the slopes of Mt Olympus. Other orchid varieties to be found include the slender, pink-coloured **Troödos Anatolian orchid**, the cone-shaped **pyramidal orchid**, the **giant orchid** and the colourful **woodcock orchid**.

The delicate white and yellow **Cyprus crocus**, from the Iris family, is an endangered species protected by law and is found commonly at high altitudes in the Troödos Mountains. The delicate, dark-red **Cyprus tulip** is another rare species also protected by law and is today re-stricted to the Akamas and Koruçam (Kormakitis) Peninsulas and parts of the Beşparmak (Pentadaktylos) Range. A member of the borage family is the endemic **Troödos golden drop**, a small, yellow, bell-shaped flower appearing in leafy clusters. This endangered species is confined to the highest peaks of the Troödos Mountains.

Top left: Troödos Anatolian orchid, *Orchis
anatolica vat Troodi*

Top right: Pyramidal
orchid, *Anacamptis
pyramidalis*

Bottom left: Cyprus
cotton thistle (endemic),
Onopordum cyprium

Bottom right: Woodcock
orchid (endemic),
Ophrys lapethica

WILD FLOWERS OF CYPRUS

In the North, the unlikely sounding **St Hilarion cabbage** is found mainly on rocky outcrops near St Hilarion Castle. This large endemic cabbage flower grows to 1m in height and has spikes of creamy white flowers. Also found growing near St Hilarion is **Casey's larkspur**, a late-flowering species that carries a dozen or more deep-violet, long-spurred flowers atop a slender stem. Its habitat is limited to the northern extremity of one small rocky peak 1.5km southwest of St Hilarion. Less spectacular but still uniquely Cypriot flowers are the **three-coloured chamomile**, the **purple rock cress** and the hard-to-miss **Cyprus cotton thistle**, which makes its appearance during the long, hot summer months.

Tips for Spotters

While it is only possible to scratch the surface in this brief introduction, there are some good publications available for the seriously botanically minded (see following). When looking for wild flowers, travel light and on foot. Only take photos of the flowers you spot, leave the flowers themselves; their existence may be tenuous at best. Other people will no doubt want to enjoy their beauty as well.

Recommended reading: *Flora of Cyprus* by R Desmond Meikle; *The Endemic Plants of Cyprus* by Takis Tsintides & Loizos Kourtellarides; *Cyprus Trees and Shrubs* by EF Chapman; *Flowers of Cyprus* by Christos Georgiades; and *Wildflowers of Cyprus* by George Sfikas.

HIKMET ULUÇAM

HIKMET ULUÇAM

HIKMET ULUÇAM

ANDREAS DEMETROPOULOS

Top left: Kotschy's bee orchid (endemic), *Ophrys Kotschyi*

Top right: Purple rock cress (endemic), *Arabis purparea*

Bottom left: Three-coloured chamomille (endemic), *Anthemis tricolor*

Bottom right: Troödos helleborine, *Epipactis troodi*

[Continued from page 16]

area. Around half of its 188,385 hectares is irrigated; the remainder is given over to dryland farming.

The south of the island is dominated by the Troödos Massif, a vast, bulky mountain range towered over by Mt Olympus (1951m). To the east is a small, lower plateau where most of the South's tourist industry is now based.

GEOLOGY

The Troödos Massif is made up of igneous rock and was originally formed from molten rock beneath the deep ocean that once separated the continents of Eurasia and Afro-Arabia. Since antiquity the mountain range has been particularly rich in minerals, with abundant resources of copper and asbestos. Other natural resources include chromite, gypsum and iron pyrite. Marble has also been mined here since antiquity.

CLIMATE

Cyprus enjoys an intense Mediterranean climate with a typically strongly marked seasonal rhythm. Summers are hot and dry and last from June until September. Winters are changeable, with cold and warmer weather alternating, and conditions also vary with the elevation. The Troödos Mountains usually receive snow in winter. Autumn in October and spring in April and May are short and the transition between winter and summer is rapid. Rain falls mainly in autumn and winter, and outside these months precipitation is rare. Water shortages can be a real problem in Cyprus.

Average daily summer temperatures in Lefkosia are between 22°C and 37°C but often reach 40°C or more. From December to March the night temperature in the Troödos is often below freezing for several weeks.

ECOLOGY & ENVIRONMENT

Like most modern nations today, Cyprus is feeling the pinch in matters relating to urban encroachment, water and air pollution, erosion and deforestation. Significant urban encroachment took place in the South after 1974, when vast hotel complexes were built on pristine or sparsely populated coastal areas, particularly near Lemesos and Agia Napa. While many would argue that

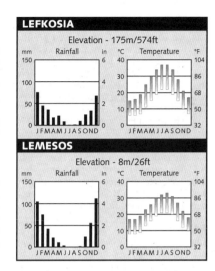

the saturation point has been reached, new hotel complexes are still being built to soak up more of the tourist dollar. These complexes use up considerable amounts of energy and, in particular, water, which is in permanent short supply.

In the North, where authorities have not yet experienced the advantages and disadvantages of mass tourism, they have had the chance to monitor encroachment more carefully. In some large areas – notably the Karpas (Kırpaşa) Peninsula – large-scale development is now banned.

Overall, authorities in the North and the South are now belatedly taking a more cautious approach on conservation issues and there are small but active conservationist groups making waves in the country. Visitors should be aware that the tourist presence does have an impact on the country and should, wherever possible, make sure that their presence is as unobtrusive as possible. (See also Responsible Tourism in the Facts for the Visitor chapter.)

FLORA

The diversity of Cyprus' flora is not immediately obvious to first-time visitors. In summer the island is arid, but spring sees an explosion of colour from its endemic flora – particularly its wild flowers. The island is home to some 1800 species and subspecies of plants, of which about 128 or 7% are indigenous to Cyprus.

Plants can be found in the five major habitats that characterise Cyprus' flora profile: pine forests, garigue and maquis, rocky areas, coastal areas and wetlands. The main areas for endemic or indigenous plant species are the Troödos Mountains and their western extension (the Pafos Forest), the Karpas Peninsula and the northern coastal strip, and the southern strip of the Cape Greco Peninsula in the southeast. (See also the special section 'Wild Flowers of Cyprus').

Serious devotees of Cypriot flora might find *Illustrated Flora of North Cyprus*, Vols 1 & 2 by Deryck Viney and published by Koeltz Scientific Books Germany very handy for extended field trips.

FAUNA

Birds travelling between Africa and Europe use Cyprus as a stepping stone on their migratory path. Bird-watchers have an excellent window onto both more exotic migratory species and local birds such as griffon vultures, falcons and kestrels. Mammals to be found on the island include fruit bats, foxes, hares and hedgehogs. There are a few snake species and, although you are unlikely to cross their paths, it is worth noting that the Montpellier snake and blunt-nosed viper are poisonous and can inflict nasty bites. Lizards are the most obvious of Cyprus' fauna species and they are everywhere. Don't be afraid of the pretty geckos in your hotel room; they come out at night to feed on insects.

A handy field companion is *Butterflies of Cyprus* by John Eddie & Wayne Jarvis, which is comprehensive guide and available quite cheaply in paperback. Birders might find *A Birdwatching Guide to Cyprus* by Jacqui Croxzier useful, while for a fuller coverage of wildlife the colourful photo guide *Collins Complete Mediterranean Wildlife* by Paul Sterry probably has the most comprehensive coverage of the region.

Endangered Species

The moufflon is Cyprus' best-known endangered species. Wide-scale shooting by farmers and hobby hunters over the years has reduced the numbers of this indigenous wild sheep drastically and now they are rarely, if ever, spotted wild in the Pafos Forest. A small herd is kept under protection at the Stavros tis Psokas forest station in the Pafos Forest. It is estimated that from near extinction in the early part of the 20th century, the current moufflon population is around 10,000. For more details see boxed text 'The Much-Maligned Cypriot Moufflon' in the Pafos & the West chapter.

Green and loggerhead turtles breed and live on the beaches. These endangered animals enjoy some protection in Cyprus, and conservation programmes in the North and the South are in place to ensure their continuing survival (see also the boxed text 'The Tale of Two Turtles' in the Famagusta & Karpas Peninsula chapter).

Another endangered species is the monk seal, which can be spotted off parts of the coastline.

NATIONAL PARKS & RESERVES

This previously neglected topic is now receiving some serious attention. In the South, the areas under study for inclusion as national parks include the Akamas Peninsula, the Akrotiri Salt Lake and Fassouri Marsh, and the Platys Valley. Two forest nature reserves have already been established at Tripylos – which includes Cedar Valley – and at Troödos. There is one marine reserve, the Lara Toxeftra Reserve on the west coast, which was established to protect marine turtles and their nesting beaches. There are also six national forest parks that have been set up in recent years.

In the North plans are afoot to declare the far eastern section of the Karpas Peninsula as a nature reserve. Marine turtles nest on beaches on the northern and southern sides of the peninsula.

GOVERNMENT & POLITICS

The partition of Cyprus has resulted in two de facto political administrations. The government of the Republic of Cyprus is recognised internationally while the government of Northern Cyprus is officially recognised only by Turkey.

MARTIN HARRIS

It's possible to spot monk seals off the coast.

Rauf Denktaş – Portrait of a Renegade

Viewed as the bane of Cypriot society by Greeks and saviour of the nation by many Turks, Rauf Denktaş provokes strong feelings among Cypriots. President of a self-proclaimed independent republic, this one-time lawyer is a mercurial character, matched in resilience and political longevity by few of his neighbouring Middle Eastern political leaders. He has used charisma and stubbornness to lead the Turkish Cypriot community from well before the forced division of Cyprus in 1974 and still shows no signs of passing on the baton of leadership, despite having heart surgery in late 2002.

Rauf Denktaş, now in his late seventies, was born near Pafos in the South and trained as a barrister in London before commencing his long political career in Cyprus. As leader of the Turkish Communal Chamber from 1960, he was in and out of the spotlight – and trouble – until 1974, whereupon he became leader of the partitioned Turkish Cypriots.

Denktaş is known for his persistence and perceived intransigence in seeking a solution for reuniting Cyprus. He dodges and weaves, teases and tests the will of both the South's political leadership and that of the intermediary nations or organisations who have vainly attempted to broker numerous peace deals.

His willingness to seek a mutually acceptable solution to the political impasse is compromised by an obdurate steadfastness and unwillingness to deviate from the long-held party line. At thrice-weekly talks held in the UN buffer zone during the spring and summer of 2002, Denktaş refused to concede any ground from the entrenched position of his party and his Turkish-mainland backers who prefer a bizonal, bicommunal state with a large degree of autonomy and separateness between the two communities. These talks sputtered on into 2003 without any progress. Only time will tell whether these talks will bear any fruit. Sceptics are weary of the stalemate and can only hope that a new leader will bring new optimism to a problem that has been unresolved for far too long.

Under the 1960 constitution, executive power is vested in the president of the Republic, elected by universal suffrage for a five-year term. The president exercises his executive power through a council of ministers appointed by him. Each minister exercises executive power over all issues within that ministry's domain. The president is both chief of state and head of government. Under the 1960 constitution, the post of vice president is allocated to a Turkish Cypriot but this post has been vacant since 1974. Tassos Papadopoulos was elected as president in February 2003, replacing Glafkos Clerides.

Parliament (House of Representatives) is currently led by the National Unity Party – a coalition of the Democratic Rally (DISY) and the Democratic Party who together hold 28 seats. Other parties in parliament include the Progressive Party of the Working People (AKEL), Communist Party with 20 seats, the Democratic Party (DIKO) holding nine seats, the Social Democrats Movement (Kisos) which holds four seats and the United Democrats Movement (EDE) with four seats. The president of the house is Spyros Kyprianou.

Presidential and parliamentary elections are held independently every five years. The next presidential elections are scheduled for 2008 and the next parliamentary elections for May 2006. For further details, look at the website of the **Public Information Office** (**w** www.pio.gov.cy).

In February 1975, Rauf Denktaş declared North Cyprus the independent Turkish Federated State of Cyprus, with himself as president. In 1983 he renamed it the Turkish Republic of Northern Cyprus (TRNC, or KKTC in Turkish). Denktaş leads a coalition of the National Unity Party (UBP) and the Demokrat Party (DP). He has been president of the Turkish Cypriot administration since 1995 with runner-up Derviş Eroğlu taking the post of prime minister in the government in 1996. A council of ministers is appointed by the president. The next presidential elections are due to be held in April 2005.

Political parties active in the North's administration are divided between right- and left-wing viewpoints. On the right are the UBP) under the leadership of Derviş Eroğlu, the DP of Sali Coşar, the National Justice

Party (MAP) and the National Resurgence Party (UDP).

On the left are the Republican Turkish Party (CTP) led by Mehmet Ali Talat, the Communal Liberation Party (TKP) led by Hüseyin Angolemli and the Patriotic Unity Party (YBH) represented by İzzet İzcan. Look at the website of the **TRNC Public Information Office** (W *www.trncpio.org)* for further information.

ECONOMY

Reflecting yet again the division that characterises present-day Cyprus, the economy of the country presents two diverse pictures. The economy of the South is generally buoyant, but highly susceptible to global events. Erratic growth rates in the 1990s reflect the economy's particular vulnerability to swings in tourist arrivals. These in turn are caused by perceived political instability as well as fluctuations in economic conditions in Western Europe. Economic policies in the South are geared to meeting the criteria laid down for accession to the EU. Other than from tourism, the South generates income from export commodities such as citrus fruits, potatoes, grapes, wine, cement, clothing and shoes.

The economy of the North hasn't fared as well as that in the South. Export commodities such as citrus fruits, potatoes and textiles supplement income generated from a modest but growing tourist industry. The economy here generates only about one-third of the per capita GDP of the South but, because the North is not recognised internationally, it has difficulties in securing foreign investment and overseas financing. The economy therefore relies heavily on the government service, which employs about 50% of the workforce, and agriculture. Difficulties are compounded by the use of the Turkish lira (TL) as legal tender, a currency that suffers repeated and almost daily inflation. Turkey ultimately provides direct and indirect aid to nearly every economic sector in order to keep the sputtering economy fuelled.

POPULATION & PEOPLE

Cyprus is primarily made up of Greek and Turkish Cypriots who together constituted a total population of 762,900 at July 2001. The Greeks are descendants of the early settlers who intermingled with the indigenous population around 1100 BC and subsequent settlers who came to Cyprus up to the 16th century AD. The Turkish Cypriots are descendants of Ottoman settlers who first arrived on Cyprus in 1570 following the Ottoman conquest of the island.

Around 18% of the population are Turkish Cypriots. Turkish immigrants from the mainland since 1974 are thought to make up to about 50% of that total. A large number of Greek Cypriots left Cyprus as refugees in 1974, but many have since chosen to return permanently to the South.

Most Cypriots in the Republic speak English and many road signs are in Greek and English. In North Cyprus this is not the case outside the tourist areas and you'll have to brush up on your Turkish. In both areas, the spelling of place and street names varies enormously.

EDUCATION

In both parts of Cyprus education is given a high priority and literacy and numeracy levels are high. Education systems in the North and the South are administered separately, but follow similar patterns. Six grades of free and compulsory education are provided for children from the age of five. At least three years of the five-year secondary-education programmes are free and all secondary education at technical schools is free. Post-secondary educational facilities include university, teacher-training colleges, technical schools, hotel and catering training, nursing and midwifery. Cyprus' university system is relatively new and still cannot absorb the demand of graduating secondary students, many of whom choose to study abroad in Greece, Turkey, the UK or the USA.

ARTS
Dance

The origin of Cypriot folk dancing dates back centuries. It may even be said to be related to shamanist ceremonies and early religious and incantational worship. Different regional characteristics may be noticed. In the Republic, musical and dance traditions also follow those of mainland Greece to some degree. One of these dances, the circular *syrtos*, is depicted on ancient Greek vases, and there are references to dances in Homer's works. Many Greek folk dances, including the *syrtos*, are performed in a circular formation; in ancient times, dancers formed a circle in order to seal themselves off from evil influences.

Many dances performed in Cyprus now are the same as those of the Greek mainland. There is of course a wide range of indigenous Cypriot dances that are only seen these days at folk festivals or specially staged dance performances. The most famous of these is the *kartzilamas*, in effect a suite of up to five different dances that usually ends with the more familiar *syrtos* dance or *zeïmbekikos*. Cypriot dances are commonly 'confronted pair' dances of two couples, or vigorous solo men's dances in which the dancer often holds an object such as a sickle, a knife, a sieve or a tumbler. Show-dances at popular tourist restaurants frequently feature a dance called *datsia* where the dancer balances a stack of glasses full of wine on a sieve. Another is a contrived dance in which diners are invited to try to light the tail – usually a rolled-up newspaper – of the solo male dancer who will attempt to dance and bob his way out of being set alight.

Dances in the North share very similar patterns of development and execution as those in the South, the only real difference being the names. Thus the *kartzilamas* is the North's *karşilama* and the *tsifteteli* is the *ciftetelli*. In addition there is the *testi*, the *kozan* and the *kaşikli oyunları* – a dance performed with wooden spoons. However, it is unlikely you will come across many occasions of Turkish dancing, unless you happen upon sporadic summer folk festivals at either Kyrenia or Famagusta, or the harvest festivals that occasionally take place in country towns and villages. Restaurants with floor shows are most likely your best opportunity to sample some of the northern variants of Cypriot dancing.

Music

Greek Cypriots have tended to follow the musical preferences of mainland Greece. Conversely, Cyprus has also produced some of its own home-grown musicians who have made a successful career in Greece as well as in their homeland.

The *bouzouki*, which you will hear all over Cyprus, is a mandolin-like instrument similar to the Turkish *saz* and *baglama*. It is one of the main instruments of *rembetika*

music – the Greek equivalent of American blues. The name *rembetika* may come from the Turkish word *rembet*, which means outlaw. Opinions differ as to the origins of *rembetika*, but it is probably a hybrid of several different types of music. One source was the music that emerged in the 1870s in the 'low-life' cafés, called *tekedes* (hashish dens), in urban areas and especially around ports such as Pireus in Greece. Another source was the Arabo-Persian music played in sophisticated Middle Eastern music cafés *(amanedes)* in the 19th century. *Rembetika* was popularised originally in Greece by the refugees from Asia Minor and was subsequently brought to Cyprus.

Today's music scene in Cyprus is a mix of old and new – traditional and modern. Young Greek Cypriots are equally as happy with *rembetika* or demotic (folk) songs as they are with contemporary Greek rock music. Among artists to look out for are Pelagia Kyriakou and in particular her contribution to two albums known as *Paralimnitika 1 & 2*, a superb collection of Cypriot demotic songs from the beginning of the 19th century and sung in the original Cypriot dialect. Mihalis Violaris is an exponent of folk and modern songs and was especially popular during the 1970s and '80s. Two popular songs he made famous (that you will inevitably hear somewhere in Cyprus) are *Ta Rialia* (Money) and *Tillyrkotissa* (Girl from Tylliria), again sung in Cypriot dialect.

Of the more modern singers, Anna Vissi sings contemporary Greek music and has appeared on albums released by top Greek singer Georgos Dalaras, and has also produced her own albums. Alkinoös Ioannides is a young Lefkosian who sings emotional ballads of his own composition, that occasionally border on rap and rock, and has released

MARGARET JUNG

The bazouki is regularly used at social events.

three excellent albums. His first, *O Dromos o Hronos kai o Ponos* (The Road, the Time and the Pain), is worth picking up for an introduction to this talented Cypriot.

Georgos Dalaras, while not a Cypriot, has devoted much time and energy to the Cypriot cause. His album *Es Gin Enalian Kypron* (To Sea-Girt Cyprus) is a poignant tribute to the trials and tribulations of modern-day Cyprus, set to the music of Cypriot composer Mihalis Hristodoulidis. Finally, Cypriot singer and lyricist Evagoras Karageorgis has produced some excellent music, best represented on a fine album that is little known outside of Cyprus called *Topi se Hroma Loulaki* (Places Painted in Violet), which is definitely worth seeking out. It is a nostalgic and painful look at the lost villages of the North sung in a mixture of Cypriot dialect and standard Greek accompanied by traditional and contemporary musical instruments.

In the North, musical trends tend to mirror those of mainland Turkey, although Greek music is still admired and quietly listened to on radio broadcasts from the South – radio thankfully knows no boundaries – and both cultures share a remarkable overlap in sounds and instrumentation. Among Turkish Cypriot musical personalities, Yıltan Taşçi has made something of a name for himself locally, and helped create and play in such bands as *Golgeler*, *Ozgurler*, *Kalender5* and *Letul*. Tasci's first recording, *Bana Seviyorum De*, came out in March 1995 and it contains seven songs that he composed and performed.

Germany-based French horn player Turgay Hilmi is originally from Northern Cyprus but now plies his trade playing classical music with renowned orchestras, such as the Nüremburg Chamber Orchestra, and contemporary material with his brass quintet. He visits Cyprus whenever he can and in 1998 participated in the first performance of the opera *Othello* in Cyprus at the Bellapais Festival.

Literature

Cyprus has produced a sprinkling of literary illuminati and the literature scene is actively promoted and encouraged by the government of the Republic with competitions and accompanying awards organised annually. Little Cypriot literature, however, is available in translation and, where it is available, its circulation is limited and usually re-stricted to Cyprus. Home-grown talent of the 20th century includes Cypriot Loukis Akritas (1932–65) who made his mark mainly in Greece as a journalist and writer, while later championing the cause of Cypriot independence through letters rather than violence. His literary works include novels, plays, short stories and essays.

Theodosis Pierides (1908–67), who wrote actively from 1928 onwards, can be considered among Cyprus' national and most respected poets. His *Cypriot Symphony* is regarded to be the 'finest most powerful epic written by a Greek poet about Cyprus', according to contemporary and fellow poet Tefkros Anthias (1903–68). Anthias himself was excommunicated by the Orthodox Church and ultimately internally exiled by the British administration in 1931 for his poetry collection *The Second Coming*. He was arrested during the liberation struggle of 1955–59 and imprisoned. While in prison he wrote a collection of poems called *The Diary of the CDP*, which was published in 1956.

The North supports a small but healthy literary scene with over 30 'name' personages. Nese Yasin (1959–) is a writer, journalist and poet and was one of the founding members of a movement known as the '74 Generation Poetry Movement. This was a post-division literary wave of writers that sought inspiration from the climate generated after Cyprus was divided. Her poems have been translated and published in magazines, newspapers, anthologies and books in Cyprus, Turkey, Greece, Yugoslavia, Hungary, the Netherlands, Germany and the UK.

Hakki Yucel (1952–) is a poet, literary researcher and eye specialist. His poems and essays have been published in magazines and newspapers in Cyprus, Turkey, the UK and Hungary. He is one of the leading members of the '74 Generation Poetry Movement and has been active in the promotion of Cypriot culture and literature in Turkey.

Painting

In the South, painting enjoys a healthy patronage and one of the more famous exponents of the art neither runs a gallery nor attends art festivals. He is Father Kallinikos Stavrovounis, the aged priest of Stavrovouni Monastery, between the cities of Lefkosia and Lemesos. Father Kallinikos is regarded as the most superb contemporary icon painter of the Orthodox Church. He has been painting Byzantine religious icons for 50 years and, despite ailing health, does not seem ready to hang up his brushes just yet. Icons are made to order and money received is ploughed back into the Orthodox Church for the upkeep of the Stavrovouni and other monasteries.

Athos Agapitos is a contemporary Greek Cypriot painter who was born in Lefkosia in 1957. His art portfolio runs the gamut from realism and naive painting to expressionism in more recent years, with a predilection for themes encompassing elements from Greek and Egyptian civilisation, mythology and mysticism. His work was exhibited at the Florence Biennale of International Contemporary Art in 1999.

Sculpture

With a small but growing pool of practitioners, sculpture is another active area of art. Among the foremost sculptors is Fylaktis Ieridis, whose talent finds its most natural expression in bronze. A chiropractor by vocation, his exposure to the human anatomy has given him an unusual insight into his subject, and his interaction with people on a day-to-day professional basis has allowed him to lend a stark realism to his works, which consist mainly of human figures. He has been commissioned to complete several busts and reliefs for heroes' monuments.

Folk Art

Cyprus is particularly well developed in the area of folk art, with lace and basketry prominent among items produced. Lefkara lace, from the village of the same name in the South Troödos foothills, is one of Cyprus' most famous folk-art export commodities. Large, woven bread baskets are on sale all over Cyprus and are characterised by their intricate and multicoloured patterns. Silver and copperware are also popular folk-art items made throughout the country and are of high quality and fine design.

The Cyprus Handicraft Service (CHS) in the South has been instrumental in promoting and preserving these arts which, without the support of the service, may well have taken the road to oblivion as have folk arts in other industrialising nations. It runs shops in the major towns and sells the wares of the artists that it supports. Look out for decorated gourd

flasks, objects that are becoming increasingly rare with the advent of modern packaging, as well as ornate bridal chests *(sendoukia)*, which are seen less and less these days at wedding celebrations. The town of Lapta (Lapithos) in the North used to be the island's centre for *sendouki*-making but that industry has taken a downturn following the events of 1974. Weaving used to be widespread throughout Cyprus, though you are unlikely to see looms, other than in remote villages or at the CHS where they are in regular use.

Pottery

Well-made and often highly decorative pottery is produced in Cyprus and is worth seeking out. You can hardly miss the enormous earthenware storage jars, called *pitharia*, which are often used as decorative plant pots outside rural houses. Originally used for storing water, oil or wine, they have fallen victim to more convenient methods of storage and packaging. Their sheer size and volume, though, render them all but impossible to take home. The village of Kornos, between Lemesos and Larnaka, is still an active pottery-making community, as is the Pafos region where, in Pafos town, you will find shops selling all kinds and sizes of multicoloured, functional as well as decorative pottery pieces.

Cinema

In Cyprus, cinema is a relatively recent phenomenon – hardly surprising perhaps, given the turbulent and disruptive nature of recent Cypriot history. At the end of the 1940s the British colonial government started to train Cypriot film makers in the Colonial Film Unit. With the impetus created by the arrival of television in 1957, the first homegrown cinema productions began. These were mainly documentaries and the first independent production was called *Roots*. The Cyprus Broadcasting Corporation sponsored most productions over the next two decades, with a 1963 production by Ninos Fenwick Mikellidis called *Cyprus, Ordained to Me* winning a prize at the Karlévy Vari Festival in Czechoslovakia. George Lanitis' film *Communication* won first prize for a short foreign film at the Thessaloniki Festival in 1970.

Further prizes were awarded in 1985 to Cypriot film makers Hristos Siopahas, at the

Moscow Film Festival for his film *The Descent of the Nine,* and Andreas Pantazis, at the Thessaloniki Film Festival for his depiction of the Turkish invasion of Cyprus entitled *The Rape of Aphrodite.* Both film makers were honoured 10 years later at the Thessaloniki Film Festival for their works *The Wing of the Fly* (by Siopahas) and *The Slaughter of the Cock* (by Pantazis), both dealing with the invasion of Cyprus.

The recent upsurge in film production in the South since 1974 is due primarily to newly found support from the state, which is keen to support young film directors. Since 1983 an enlightenment committee has been particularly active in the area of cinematography with a view to projecting the Cypriot problem to a wider international audience.

The North does not support a domestic film-making scene; its supply of cinematographic culture is supplied entirely from mainland Turkey.

Theatre

Theatre in the South is a flourishing industry, with the Cyprus University Theatre Group (Thepak) very active in the performance of Cypriot- and Greek-written works.

The biannual Kypria Festival regularly sees performances from a variety of domestic theatre groups. The Cyprus Theatre Organisation performed Aristophanes' *Peace* and the Eleftheria Theatre of Cyprus presented Euripides' *Phoenician Women* at the 2002 Kypria Festival. The stage production, choreography and music for both these plays were undertaken entirely by Cypriots.

Theatre in the North can be said to have started with the arrival of the Ottomans in 1570 and with the importation from the Turkish mainland of the *Karagöz* puppet shadow theatre. This theatre tradition is shared by the Greeks, who call it *Karagiozis.* Sadly *Karagöz* is performed rarely in the North these days (or in the South for that matter) and is relegated to television shows and live performances during feasts such as Bayram. Theatre in the modern contemporary sense started on the island with British influence after 1878, but only really took off after independence in 1960 with amateur theatre groups being established in most Turkish Cypriot communities.

A new generation of playwrights proliferated, such as Hilmi Özen, Üner Ulutug

and Ayla Haşmat. In 1964, the Department of Education provided the Atatürk Ilkokulu salon for the use of the Turkish Cypriot Theatre. The works that were performed at this venue, under the name of *First Stage,* received the admiration and support of audiences. Since then the company, now renamed the Turkish Cypriot State Theatre, has performed nearly 85 plays with success.

The Kyrenia Amateur Dramatics Society is an amateur theatre group formed by British and local residents of Kyrenia, and produces a few plays (all in English) during the year. Look around notice boards at Kyrenia for details on productions that may be on.

SOCIETY & CONDUCT

The 1974 division of Cyprus has sadly polarised Cypriot cultural life as much as it has its political scene. When asked, both Turks and Greeks will still claim to be Cypriots first and Greek or Turkish second. While the British domination of the scene was understandably rejected by Cypriots in the late 1950s, there is a lingering 'Britishness' about Cyprus in both the North and the South. This impression is reinforced by cars that drive on the left of the road and people who keep to appointed times for meetings.

Since 1974, however, there has been a creeping Turkification of the North. Greek place names have all been converted to Turkish so that anyone familiar with the previous names may find it difficult to find their way around the North without a Turkish-language map. Greek road and wall signs of any description have completely disappeared from the North and visitors cannot help but feel that they are in a district of Turkey.

Likewise there has been a near-total Hellenisation of the South. Even the former city names of Nicosia, Limassol and Paphos have been officially changed to their Greek versions, something that may catch out the unaware traveller. Other than in the UN-controlled village of Pyla (see Pyla in the Larnaka & the East chapter), where one can see Turkish and Greek Cypriots still living together, there are few signs of the Turkish language or culture anywhere in the South.

On both sides of the Green Line, though, Cypriots are friendly, hospitable and courteous. Crime rates are low. Don't listen to disparaging comments by one community about the other. While in times of war and strife many atrocities have been committed in Cyprus – and haven't they elsewhere? – Cypriots are just as eager to pursue peaceful coexistence as any other nation. Family and social unity feature very high on any Cypriot's list of priorities; strife and division are low on the list.

Traditional Culture

Despite its overt Western outlook, Cyprus is steeped in traditional customs. Name days, weddings and funerals have great significance. Weddings are highly festive occasions, with dancing, feasting and drinking sometimes continuing for days. In Cypriot villages it is common for the whole village to be invited to the wedding.

Greek Cypriots tend to be superstitious. Tuesday is considered an unlucky day because on that day the Byzantine Empire fell to the Ottomans. Many Greek Cypriots will not sign an important transaction, get married or begin a trip on a Tuesday. Greek

Cypriots also believe in the 'evil eye', a superstition prevalent in many Middle Eastern countries. If someone is the victim of the evil eye, then bad luck will befall them. The bad luck is the result of someone's envy, so one should avoid being too complimentary about things of beauty, especially newborn babies. To ward off the evil eye, Cypriots often wear a piece of blue glass, resembling an eye, on a chain around their necks.

Turkish Cypriots are noted for their seemingly excessive politeness – vestiges of a state of mind that dates back to the royal courts of the Ottoman Empires. The Turkish language has a series of rigid greeting formulas (polite phrases) that are often repeated on cue several times daily. This is simply stereotyped small talk. It might help if you go along with it, perhaps by joining in the banter with similar talk on your part.

It is considered by Greek and Turkish Cypriots as a compliment to their culture and a sign of respect if you can speak some Greek or Turkish, or at least if you make an

What's in a Name?

The issue of place names is a thorny one in Cyprus, pregnant as it is with political, cultural and linguistic overtones and potential pitfalls. To avoid treading on too many peoples' toes, we have adopted a few basic ground rules to make navigating this maze a little easier.

In general, we have adopted a bilingual approach to towns and villages that were once bicommunal, and a trilingual approach where some towns had Anglicised versions of their name. In the North, we list major tourist towns by the Anglicised names, followed by their Turkish and Greek names, while villages are listed by their Turkish name followed by the Greek name. This occurs out of a need to assist travellers to navigate Turkish-language destination signs rather than to make a political statement. Without this knowledge, and with Greek-only place names in our guide, navigating the North would be totally unfeasible. Thus Kyrenia is known as Girne in Turkish and Keryneia in Greek, Famagusta as Mağusa in Turkish and Ammohostos in Greek.

In the South, we have used the new, approved Hellenised place names for cities and towns. Thus, South Nicosia is known as Lefkosia; Limassol as Lemesos; Paphos as Pafos and Larnaca as Larnaka. Road signs these days tend to use the new names, though you will occasionally see the old names on older signs.

For the South, we list Greek versions of names and the Anglicised and Turkish ones, where appropriate. Thus Pafos is known also as Baf in Turkish, Limassol as Lemesos in Greek and Limasol in Turkish. While we acknowledge the Turkish Cypriots' right to call a town or village by a Turkish name, this can lead to problems for a publication such as this guide where many of the former Greek villages of the North are still known internationally by their Greek names and are still shown as such on many maps.

The Turkish Republic of Northern Cyprus has never been recognised by any other authority than itself and Turkey. It is not LP's intent to 'recognise' states as such and thus confer implied legality on them, but to describe a given situation as fairly as possible and allow readers to make their own conclusions. In this book we refer to Northern Cyprus as the territory currently occupied by the Turkish military, and to the Republic of Cyprus, or Southern Cyprus, as the territory not occupied by the Turkish army.

attempt to say a few phrases. Never assume that someone will speak English, though English *is* widely spoken in Cyprus.

RELIGION

About 78% of Cypriots belong to the Greek Orthodox Church, 18% are Muslims and the remaining 4% are Maronite, Armenian Apostolic and other Christian denominations. These days the Muslims live mainly in the North and the Greek Orthodox in the South. The Maronites have traditionally been centred on the village of Koruçam (Kormakitis) in the North, and there are small non-Orthodox Christian communities in both the North and the South.

The Greek Orthodox Church is closely related to the Russian Orthodox Church and together with it forms the third-largest branch of Christianity. Orthodoxy, meaning 'right belief', was founded in the 4th century by Constantine the Great, who was converted to Christianity by a vision of the Cross.

Religion is still integral to life for Greek Cypriots, and the Greek year is centred on the festivals of the church calendar. Most Greeks, when they have a problem, will go into a church and light a candle to the saint they feel is most likely to help. Sunday afternoons are popular times for visiting monasteries, and the frescoed Byzantine churches in the Troödos Mountains can often become packed with elderly weekend pilgrims.

For the most part, Turkish Cypriots are Sunni Muslims and, while religion plays an important part in Turkish Cypriot culture, the conservatism of Islamic culture elsewhere in the Middle East and rural Turkey is not so obvious in Cyprus. Alcohol, for example, is widely available and frequently consumed by Turkish Cypriots. Turkish Cypriot women dress more casually than their Turkish mainland counterparts.

Facts for the Visitor

HIGHLIGHTS
Republic of Cyprus
If it's sun, sand and fun you are looking for, there's plenty of it in the Republic of Cyprus. The economy of the South relies heavily on the tourist industry, and for the most part that means organised tourism. There are beaches, resort hotels, water sports, and wining and dining to rival the best in the world. It's well organised, easily accessible and relatively inexpensive.

If it's culture, history, archaeology, walking or cycling you prefer, the Republic caters for you too. Nine of the frescoed Byzantine churches in the Troödos Massif are on Unesco's World Heritage List, and a visit to at least some is worth the effort. Pafos is home to the Tombs of the Kings – an impressive underground necropolis dating back to the 3rd century BC – while the nearby Pafos Mosaics draw fascinated visitors who gaze upon works of art almost as fresh as the day they were created.

For hikers and cyclists, the Troödos Mountains offer cool respite from the heat of the plains and some energetic cycling circuits for those keen enough to tour the Cyprus highlands on two wheels.

Northern Cyprus
Northern Cyprus (the North) offers a refreshing antidote to the sometimes frenetic hype of the South's tourist scene. The pace is slower, people are more prepared to give you their time, the beaches are among the best in Cyprus and food and accommodation are on a par with the finest of the Mediterranean.

Kyrenia (Girne) is the North's jewel and the hub of the compact tourist industry. With its horseshoe-shaped harbour, medieval castle, waterfront restaurants, bars and sea excursions, Kyrenia is the first port of call for most visitors to the North. The proudly Greek ruins of Salamis near Famagusta (Mağusa) bear testimony to a splendid city state that flourished in Cyprus during the 11th century BC.

The almost-deserted Karpas (Kırpaşa) Peninsula, the 'panhandle' of Cyprus, tempts cyclists, walkers, lovers of solitude and beachcombers alike. The country's most magnificent beach is here and remains to-

tally unspoiled, protected as it is by a newly established national park.

SUGGESTED ITINERARIES
Depending on the length of your stay, you might want to see and do the following.

Republic of Cyprus
One week Allow two days for Lefkosia, two days for Pafos, one day for exploring the ancient

coastal sites between Pafos and Lemesos, and the rest of the time in the Troödos Mountains.

Two weeks As above but make two day trips into Northern Cyprus, add Polis and the Akamas Peninsula (beaches and walks), and have a steam bath and/or massage at the hammam in Lemesos.

Northern Cyprus

One week Allow one day for North Nicosia (Lefkoşa), one day for Famagusta, half a day for Salamis, and spend the rest staying in Kyrenia and visiting the castles in the Kyrenia (Girne) Range.

Two weeks As above but have a Turkish bath in North Nicosia, and spend some time exploring the near-deserted Karpas Peninsula and its archaeological sites.

PLANNING
When to Go

The beach-and-sea scene runs from early April to late October. At any time during this period you can be guaranteed fine weather. July and August are considerably hotter and are at the peak of Cyprus' tourist season. Avoid this period if you don't like the heat or the crowds.

October to April is the best time to see Cyprus' wild flowers, to walk either the Troödos Mountains or the Akamas Peninsula, or to cycle the Karpas Peninsula in the North. You can ski on Mt Olympus in the South from early January to mid-March.

Maps

The free country and city maps available from the Cyprus Tourism Organisation (CTO; see Tourist Offices later) for the Republic of Cyprus are quite adequate for getting around. Do check, however, the publication dates of the maps (in the lower right-hand corner). These maps are not available commercially outside Cyprus, other than from CTO offices overseas.

The North Cyprus Tourism Organisation (NCTO) also produces a few free maps – a regional map and city maps of North Nicosia, Famagusta and Kyrenia. While they are fairly skimpy and cheaply produced, they do cover a wider urban area than the equivalent city maps in this book. Similarly, these maps are only available in Northern Cyprus, or from NCTO outlets overseas (see Tourist Offices Abroad later).

Possibly the best map to cover Cyprus in general is the 1:200,000 *Cyprus Travel Map* by Insight. It's quite up-to-date and accurate and, most importantly, has both Turkish and Greek place names for North Cyprus – essential if you are going to tour the North by car where road signs list only the Turkish names of the towns and villages. The nifty, pocket-sized and laminated Insight Map, *Cyprus*, is handy for quick references and folds very easily (a boon when you are on a bus or in a taxi) but does not have Turkish place names for the North.

You might also want to look at the Kyriakou Travel Maps', *Cyprus Road & Town Maps*, which may be available in overseas bookshops. Collins' *Cyprus Holiday Map* offers less overall detail but good local maps, while the Kümmerly+Frey *Cyprus Traveller's Map* is similar to the Collins product. All of them are available internationally.

What to Bring

Bring clothes made with light-coloured and lightweight fabrics – you will not need heavier clothing or footwear unless you come in winter, or you plan to do some bush-bashing in the Troödos Mountains or Kyrenia Range. Bring a warm jacket if you plan to visit the coastal regions in winter. It can still get chilly, despite the country's southerly latitude.

Water-sports gear can be hired easily in Cyprus. Leave it at home unless you have a good reason to bring it along.

RESPONSIBLE TOURISM

Some might argue that hoteliers and tourist operators have not acted responsibly in the race to develop (in the South at least). However, there is no reason for travellers to adopt this attitude that, thankfully, with one or two notable exceptions, is beginning to wane.

Travelling light, lean and green is the way to go. Water is scarce in this country so use it sparingly, even in a big hotel. Ordinary Cypriots at home may be on water rations if a drought is biting. Take your rubbish with you when you have finished hiking the Troödos Mountains or the Karpas Peninsula. Locals take pride in their countryside so follow their example. Don't pick the wild flowers in spring; others may want to enjoy them too. Spread your spending money around; support small businesses and local artists.

Visit village tavernas, not just hotel restaurants. Get to know Cyprus – not just the facilities at your hotel.

TOURIST OFFICES
The **Cyprus Tourism Organisation** *(CTO; ☎ 2233 7715, fax 2233 4696; ⓦ www.visit cyprus.org.cy; Leoforos Lemesou 19, Lefkosia)* is the main tourist organisation in the south of the island. Its leaflets and free maps are excellent. The headquarters are in the New Town on the road to Larnaka and Lemesos. It should only be approached for written inquiries, though.

The CTO has branch offices in the major towns in Cyprus (Agia Napa, Lefkosia, Lemesos, Larnaka, Pafos, Polis and Platres) where brochures and assistance can be found easily. Their contact details are given in the regional chapters.

The main **North Cyprus Tourist Office** *(NCTO; ☎ 228 1057, fax 228 5625; ⓦ www .tourism.trnc.net; Bedrettin Demirel Caddesi)* is located in North Nicosia. There are also branch offices in North Nicosia at Kyrenia (Girne) Gate and at the Ledra Palace Hotel crossing point. It also maintains tourist offices in Famagusta, Yenierenköy (Yiallousa) and Kyrenia, which have free country and town maps, plus an increasing number of brochures.

Tourist Offices Abroad
The CTO has branches in most European countries. Apart from those listed below, there are branches in the Czech Republic, Hungary, Poland and Russia. Contact details for CTO offices include

Austria (☎ 01-513 1870, fax 513 1872; ⓔ zypern tourism@aon.at) Parkring 20, A-1010 Vienna
Belgium (☎ 02-735 0621, fax 735 6607; ⓔ cy prus@skynet.be) Rue De Crayer 2, B-1050 Brussels
France (☎ 01 42 61 42 49, fax 01 42 61 65 13; ⓔ cto.chypre.paris@wanadoo.fr) 15 Rue de la Paix, F-75002 Paris
Germany (☎ 069-251 919, fax 250 288; ⓔ cto _fra@t-online.de) An der Hautwache 7, D-60313, Frankfurt am Main
Greece (☎ 21 0361 0178, fax 21 0364 4798; ⓔ cto-athens@ath.forthnet.gr) Voukourestiou 38, GR-106 73, Athens
Israel (☎ 03-525 7442, fax 525 7443; ⓔ cto@ netvision.net.il) Top Tower, Dizengoff Centre, 14th floor, 50 Dizengoff St, Tel Aviv 64332

Italy (☎ 02 58 31 98 35, fax 02 58 30 33 75; ⓔ info@turismocipro.it) Via Santa Sofia 6, I-20122 Milano
Japan (☎ 03-3497 9329, fax 3405 0105) Palais France Bldg, 729, 1-6-1 Jingumae Shibuya-Ku, Tokyo 150-0001
Netherlands (☎ 020-624 4358, fax 638 3369; ⓔ cyprus.sun@wxs.nl) Prinsengracht 600, NL-1017 KS, Amsterdam
Sweden (☎ 08-10 50 25, fax 10 64 14; ⓔ cy pern@telia.com) Norrlandsgatan 20, S-111 43 Stockholm
Switzerland (☎ 01-262 3303, fax 251 2417; ⓔ ctozurich@bluewin.ch) Gottfried Keller Strasse 7, CH-8001 Zürich
UK (☎ 020-7569 8800, fax 7499 4935; ⓔ cto lon@ctolon.demon.co.uk) 17 Hanover St, London W1S 1YP
USA (☎ 212-683 5280, fax 683 5282; ⓔ gocy prus@aol.com) 13 East 40th St, New York, NY-10016

The NCTO can be found in the UK, Belgium, the USA, Pakistan and Turkey; otherwise inquiries are handled by Turkish tourist offices. The following two offices may provide useful information.

UK (☎ 020-7631 1930, fax 7631 1873) 29 Bedford Square, WC1B 3EG
USA (☎ 212-687 2350) 821 United Nations Plaza, 6th floor, NY 10017

VISAS & DOCUMENTS
Passport
You will need a valid passport to enter Cyprus – North or South. You will need to produce your passport or ID card every time you check into a hotel in Cyprus and to conduct banking transactions.

As a foreigner, it is best to carry your passport or ID card with you at all times; you may be stopped by the police or the military for routine checks. See Copies later for some useful hints.

Visas
In both the Republic of Cyprus and Northern Cyprus, nationals of the USA, Canada, Australia, New Zealand, Singapore and EU countries can enter and stay for up to three months without a visa. Citizens of South Africa may enter for up to 30 days without a visa.

If you have a Northern Cyprus stamp in your passport, you may have problems entering the Republic. Entry to Greece is usually less problematic. Therefore, when entering Northern Cyprus it is advisable to get immigration to stamp a separate piece of paper instead of your passport. This is a common procedure. When you enter the North from the South on day trips, Turkish Cypriot officials issue you with a day pass only and do not stamp your passport.

Travel Insurance
Don't leave home without it! Choose a policy that covers theft, loss and medical expenses. Some policies offer a range of medical-expenses options; the more expensive ones are chiefly for countries such as the USA, which have extremely high medical costs. There is a wide variety of policies available, so check the small print. Cyprus will normally be covered under 'European Countries' provisions.

Some policies specifically exclude 'dangerous activities', which can include scuba diving, motorcycling, even hiking. A locally acquired motorcycle licence is not valid under some policies.

You may prefer a policy that pays doctors or hospitals directly rather than you having to pay on the spot and claim later. If you have to claim later, make sure you keep all documentation. Some policies ask you to call (reverse charges) a centre in your home country where an immediate assessment of your problem is made.

Check that the policy covers ambulances or an emergency flight home.

Vaccination Certificates
If you are arriving from a yellow fever infected area (most of sub-Saharan Africa and parts of South America) you'll need proof of yellow fever vaccination before you will be allowed to enter Cyprus.

Driving Licence & Permits
For citizens of the EU, your home drivers licence is sufficient for use throughout Cyprus. As with your passport or ID card, keep a photocopy of the main details separate from the licence itself.

Citizens from outside the EU may not be expressly required to hold an International Driving Permit (IDP) in the North or the South, but it is a good idea to get one in any case. They are obtained easily and quickly from your home country's motoring association. You will normally need to provide only your regular drivers licence and a photo in order to obtain an IDP.

If you are driving to Cyprus through countries that do not have clearly defined agreements regarding the recognition of your home country's drivers licence, an IDP is strongly recommended. Further information on bringing a car into Cyprus and the documents required is given in the Getting There & Away chapter.

Hostel Cards
A Hostelling International (HI) card is not mandatory for a stay in any of Cyprus' youth hostels, though it may get you a 10% discount.

Student & Youth Cards
The most well-known and easily obtainable student ID card is the **International Student Identity Card** (ISIC; w www.isic.org). This is available from your home educational institution before you depart. Its only real advantage in Cyprus is to obtain student discounts for admission to museums and archaeological sites. There is no real student discount travel scene and no special student concessions on bus travel within Cyprus.

Copies
All important documents (passport data page and visa page, credit cards, travel-insurance policy, air/bus/train tickets, driving licence etc) should be photocopied before you leave home. Leave one copy with someone at home and keep another with you, separate from the originals. A copy of your birth certificate may help speed up things up if you need a replacement passport.

It's also a good idea to store details of your vital travel documents in Lonely Planet's free online Travel Vault in case you lose the photocopies or can't be bothered with them. Your password-protected Travel Vault is accessible online from anywhere in the world – create it at w www.ekno.lonelyplanet.com.

EMBASSIES & CONSULATES
Your Own Embassy
It's important to realise what your own embassy – the embassy of the country of which you are a citizen – can and can't do to help you if you get into trouble.

Generally speaking, it won't be much help in emergencies if the trouble is remotely your own fault. Remember that you are bound by the laws of the country you are visiting. Your embassy will not be sympathetic if you end up in jail after committing a crime locally, even if such actions are legal in your own country.

In genuine emergencies you might get some assistance, but only if other channels have been exhausted. For example, if you need to get home urgently, a free ticket is exceedingly unlikely – the embassy would expect you to have insurance. If you have all your money and documents stolen, it might assist with getting a new passport, but a loan for onward travel is out of the question.

Some embassies used to keep letters for travellers or have a small reading room with home newspapers, but these days the mail holding service is not common and even newspapers tend to be out of date.

Cypriot Embassies & High Commissions

The Republic of Cyprus has diplomatic representation in 26 countries, including

Australia (☎ 02-6281 0832, fax 6281 0860) 30 Beale Crescent, Deakin, ACT 2600
France (☎ 01 47 20 86 28, fax 01 40 70 13 44) 23 Rue Galillée, F-75116 Paris
Germany (☎ 030-308 6830, fax 275 1454) Wallstarsse 27, D-10179 Berlin
Greece (☎ 21 0723 2727, fax 21 0723 1927) Irodotou 16, GR-106 75, Athens
Ireland (☎ 01-676 3060, fax 676 3099) 71 Lower Leeson St, Dublin 2
Israel (☎ 03-525 0212, fax 629 0535) 50 Dizengoff St, 14th floor, Top Tower, Dizengoff Centre, 64322 Tel Aviv
Netherlands (☎ 070-346 6499, fax 392 4024) Surinamestraat 15, NL-2585 GG, Den Haag
UK (☎ 020-7499 8272, fax 7491 0691) 93 Park St, London W1Y 4ET
USA (☎ 202-462 5227, fax 483 6710) 2211 R St North West, Washington, DC 20008

The Northern Cyprus administration has offices in

Canada (☎ 905-731 4000) 328 Highway 7 East, Suite 308, Richmond Hill, Ontario L4B 3P7
France (☎ 01 40 50 01 77, fax 01 46 47 68 68) 4 Rue André Colledebousuf, F-75016 Paris
Germany (☎ 0268-332 748, fax 331 723) Auf Dem Platz 3, D-53577 Neustadt Wied-Neschen

Turkey (☎ 0312-437 6031, fax 446 5238) Rabat Sokak 20, Gaziosmanpaşa 06700, Ankara
UAR (☎ 2627 2977, fax 2627 0844) Khalifa Bin Zayad St, The Blue Tower, Suite 704-A, Abu Dhabi
UK (☎ 020-7631 1920, fax 7631 1948) 26 Bedford Square, London WC1B 3EG
USA (☎ 212-687 2350, fax 949 6872) 821 United Nations Plaza, 6th floor, New York, NY 10017

Embassies & High Commissions in Cyprus

Countries with diplomatic representation in the Republic of Cyprus include

Australia (☎ 2275 3001, fax 2276 6486) cnr Leoforos Stasinou & Annis Komninis 4, CY-1060 Lefkosia
Canada (☎ 2277 5508, fax 2277 9905) Lambousa 1, CY-1095 Lefkosia
France (☎ 2277 9910, fax 2278 1052) Ploutarhou 12, CY-2406 Engomi, Lefkosia
Germany (☎ 2245 1145, fax 2266 5694) Nikitara 10, CY-1080 Lefkosia
Greece (☎ 2268 0645, fax 2268 0649) Leoforos Lordou Vyronos 8-10, CY-1513 Lefkosia
Israel (☎ 2266 4195, fax 2266 3486) Grypari 4, CY-1307 Lefkosia
UK (☎ 2286 1100, fax 2286 1125) Alexandrou Palli St, CY-1587 Lefkosia
USA (☎ 2277 6400, fax 2278 0944) cnr Metohiou & Ploutarhou, CY-2407 Engomi, Lefkosia

Countries with diplomatic representation in Northern Cyprus include

Australia (☎ 227 7332) Güner Türkmen 20, Köşklüçiftlik, North Nicosia
Germany (☎ 227 5161) Kasım 15, North Nicosia
Turkey (☎ 227 2314, fax 228 2209) Bedrettin Demirel Caddesi, North Nicosia
UK (☎ 228 3861) Mehmet Akif Caddesi 29, Köşklüçiftlik, North Nicosia
USA (☎ 227 8295) Saran 6, Küçük Kaymaklı, North Nicosia

Mail to any of these addresses must be suffixed by 'Mersin 10, Turkey', *not* 'Northern Cyprus'.

CUSTOMS

Items that can be imported duty-free into the Republic are 250g of tobacco or the equivalent in cigarettes, 2L of wine or 1L of spirits, and one 600mL bottle of perfume. In Northern Cyprus it is 500g of tobacco or 400 cigarettes, and 1L of spirits or wine.

The importation of agricultural products, including dried nuts, seeds, bulbs and cuttings, fruit, vegetables, cut flowers etc, are subject to strict quarantine control and requires prior approval by the Ministry of Agriculture and Natural Resources.

MONEY
Currency
The Republic's unit of currency is the Cyprus pound (CY£), divided into 100 cents. There are coins of one, two, five, 10, 20 and 50 cents and notes to the value of one, five, 10 and 20 pounds. There is no limit on the amount of Cyprus pounds you can bring into the country, but foreign currency equivalent to US$1000 or above must be declared. You can leave Cyprus with CY£100 or the amount that you brought in, but exchanging Cypriot pounds into other currencies outside Cyprus may be difficult, except in Greece and perhaps neighbouring Egypt, Israel, Jordan, Lebanon and Syria, all of which have close commercial and tourist ties with Cyprus.

The unit of currency in Northern Cyprus is the Turkish lira (TL), and there are no restrictions on import or export. There are no coins and notes are issued in denominations of 100,000, 200,000, 500,000, 1 million, 5 million and 10 million Turkish lira.

Banks in Cyprus exchange all major currencies in either cash or travellers cheques. Most shops, hotels etc in Northern Cyprus accept Cyprus pounds and hard currencies such as UK pounds, US dollars and euros.

In the Republic, you can get a cash advance on Visa, MasterCard, Diners Club, Eurocard and American Express at a number of banks, and there are plenty of ATMs. In Northern Cyprus cash advances are given on Visa cards at the Vakiflar and Kooperatif banks in North Nicosia and Kyrenia; major banks (such as the İş Bank) in large towns will have ATMs.

Exchange Rates
Exchange rates for the Turkish lira are subject to fluctuations due to a high inflation rate (80% in 2002) and will most likely have changed by the time you read this. For current exchange rates refer to the website ⓦ www .oanda.com/convert/classic. All prices in this book for Northern Cyprus are either in US dollars for hotels or UK pounds for restaurants and excursions. Restaurants tend to quote in UK pounds on menus and hotels list rooms in US dollars. Museum admission and other sundry fees are given in Turkish lira.

At the time of going to print, the exchange rates for the Cyprus pound and Turkish lira were:

country	unit	Cyprus pound	Turkish lira
Australia	A$1	= 0.32	997,900
Canada	C$1	= 0.36	1.12 million
euro zone	€1	= 0.58	1.82 million
Israel	NIS1	= 0.11	341,700
New Zealand	NZ$1	= 0.29	914,500
Turkey	TL1 million	= 0.33	–
UK	UK£1	= 0.85	2.65 million
USA	US$1	= 0.53	1.65 million

Exchanging Money
Cash Having cash is always a fail-safe way to carry money around from one country to another. It is also the least safe method. Once you lose it, it's gone. It's a good idea to only carry as much cash as you need for three days or so. However, a safety stash of about €100 sewn into your backpack or suitcase will see you through a temporary cash-flow problem.

Foreign-currency notes may be OK to use in major tourist centres in Cyprus, but are not much use in Troödos Mountain villages. In the North, foreign currency is more likely to be widely accepted in lieu of Turkish lira.

Currency-exchange bureaus in tourist centres operate over extended hours and most weekends.

Travellers Cheques These are not as popular as they used to be but are a good stand-by in an emergency. Restrictions on their use are naturally greater, though many hotels and larger establishments accept them readily. Always keep the receipts listing the cheque numbers separate from the cheques themselves, and keep a list of the numbers of those you have already cashed – this will reduce problems in the event of loss or theft.

ATMs Automated teller machines (ATMs) are as popular among Cypriots as they are among international visitors. They are generally a convenient way to get cash at any time of the day and the safest way to store your hard-earned dollars, pounds or euros until you need them.

Most banks now allow you to access your regular bank account directly, though in some cases you may have to use your credit line to access cash. A good idea is to transfer money to your credit card before you leave home. Be aware, though, that your bank may levy a hefty charge each time you withdraw money from an ATM.

You will find ATMs in most towns and in most larger villages throughout the Republic of Cyprus. In the North, ATMs are currently limited to North Nicosia, Famagusta and Kyrenia.

Credit Cards Just as popular as ATMs, credit cards can be used in stores, restaurants, supermarkets and petrol stations. In the latter, you can even buy petrol after hours with your credit card from automatic dispensers.

The Republic of Cyprus is more credit card–friendly than the North, though the main restaurants, hotels and car-hire companies in the North will happily take plastic.

International Transfers If you need to access your funds, international transfers are possible from your home bank to any of Cyprus' major banks. While this method is reliable, it is usually slow – taking a week or more – and not helpful if you need a cash infusion quickly. Telegraphic transfers are nominally quicker – and cost more – but can still take up to three working days to come through.

Using private financial agencies such as Western Union is usually the best bet, as you can often obtain your transferred money the same day.

Security
As a traveller you run few risks of personal loss or harm in Cyprus, though travellers are advised to lock hotel rooms and keep personal belongings secure. The main risk here is from fellow travellers or even other foreigners.

Costs
Prices in Cyprus are reasonable in comparison to most Western European countries. The cost of tourist commodities in the North and the South tend to be similar, though the North is better value when it comes to eating out and also at the budget end of accommodation

options. Items in supermarkets, though, are probably more expensive than you will be used to paying. However, fruit and vegetables in local markets are usually considerably cheaper than at home.

Accommodation in agrotourism houses in the South can cost as little as CY£12 per person per day, and a meal with wine or beer in a local restaurant around CY£12 to CY£15. In the North, bank on around US$20 to US$30 for a single room in a mid-range hotel and around UK£5 to UK£6 for a filling meal. Accommodation and general tourist services on both sides of Cyprus increase in price in July and August.

In the South, public transport costs – bus and service taxis – are low, though taxis are not such a bargain. Access to museums and archaeological sites never exceeds CY£1.50. However, entrance to such sites in the North is comparatively more expensive with the average museum admission fee ranging from TL2 million to TL4.5 million.

Tipping & Bargaining
In both parts of the island a 10% service charge is sometimes added to a restaurant bill; if not, then a tip of a similar percentage is expected. Taxi drivers and hotel porters always appreciate a small tip. Bargaining is not normally part of the shopping scene in Cyprus – neither in the North nor the South.

Taxes & Refunds
Cyprus has a 15% value-added tax (VAT), which is automatically added to the cost of more or less all services provided. In the South you may reclaim the amount of VAT paid on goods totalling more than CY£100 as long as you are not a Cypriot passport holder and have not lived in Cyprus during the past 365 days. Refunds are made at the airport as you depart the country.

An additional tax rate of between 2% and 10% is added to goods and services in Northern Cyprus. This and the VAT are not refundable to travellers upon departure.

POST & COMMUNICATIONS
Post
Postal services on both sides of the island are generally very efficient. Post offices are located in all major towns and villages and post boxes are widely available. In the South they are yellow and in the North red.

Services are normally only related to selling stamps and some packing materials. Stamps can also be bought at newsagents and street kiosks.

In the Republic of Cyprus, postal rates for cards and letters are between CY£0.31 and CY£0.41. There are poste-restante services in Lefkosia, Larnaka, Lemesos and Pafos. Opening times (except Wednesday) are normally 7.30am to 1.30pm and 3pm to 6pm.

In Northern Cyprus, postal rates are between UK£0.26 and UK£0.32. There are poste-restante services in North Nicosia, Kyrenia and Famagusta. Opening times are normally 7.30am to 2pm and 4pm to 6pm. All mail addresses in northern Cyprus must be followed by 'Mersin 10, Turkey', *not* 'Northern Cyprus'.

Telephone

For details on ringing the North from the South, or vice versa, see the boxed text 'North–South Dialogue' later.

The South You can make overseas calls from any public telephone box. There are two types: those that accept prepaid phonecards and others that accept coins. Phonecard-operated phones have explana-

tions in English and Greek. Cards to the value of CY£3, CY£5 and CY£10 can be purchased from banks, post offices, souvenir shops, street kiosks and from Cyprus Telecommunications Authority (CYTA) offices in all towns.

At peak times, a three-minute call to the USA or the UK will cost CY£1.75, and CY£0.88 during off-peak periods (10pm to 8am Monday to Saturday and all day Sunday). Rates to Australia are approximately double.

In the South, mobile phones are popular. If you have an international GSM-equipped phone, check with your local service provider if global roaming is available. Mobile-phone numbers begin with ☎ 99. The only network is CYTA.

If you plan to spend any time in the South you may want to rent a mobile phone. CYTA's SoEasy pay-as-you-go mobile-phone plan is the only option. For around CY£28 you get a startup kit consisting of a SIM card with a new number, full connection instructions in English and Greek and a CY£5 recharge card to get you started. See ⓦ www.soeasy.cyta.com.cy for details.

The North In Northern Cyprus public telephone boxes take phonecards (TL4.75 million/UK£1.90 for a 100-unit card) bought at a Turkish Telecom administration office or at a post office. A peak, three-minute call to the UK will set you back UK£1.15 and off-peak UK£0.95. Lonely Planet's ekno service is not yet available from Northern Cyprus.

As in the South, many people in the North use mobile phones. If you have an international GSM-equipped phone, check with your local service provider if global roaming is available. Mobile-phone numbers begin with either ☎ 0542 (Telsim) or ☎ 0533 (Turkcell). To call a local number you must dial the full 11-digit number, ie, including the North Cyprus code ☎ 0392.

ekno Lonely Planet's ekno Communication Card is aimed specifically at independent travellers and provides budget international calls, a range of message services, free email and travel information. For local calls, however, you are usually better off with a local phonecard. You can get more details and join online at ⓦ www.ekno.lonelyplanet.com, or by telephone from the Republic of Cyprus by

Useful Phone Numbers

Republic of Cyprus

International access code	☎ 357
International dial-out code	☎ 00
Calling Northern Cyprus from the Republic	☎ 0139 plus local number
Domestic operator	☎ 192
International operator	☎ 194
Police	☎ 199 or 112
Ambulance	☎ 199 or 112
Fire Brigade	☎ 199 or 112

Northern Cyprus

International access code	☎ 90 392
International dial out-code	☎ 00
Calling the Republic from Northern Cyprus	☎ 0123 plus local number
Domestic operator	☎ 118
International operator	☎ 115
Police	☎ 155
Ambulance	☎ 112
Fire Brigade	☎ 199

North–South Dialogue

In a country where the northern and southern halves share only one public utility – the sewerage system – it is not hard to imagine that communication between the two sides of the Attila Line can be fraught with difficulty and frustration. This is no better illustrated than with the telephone service.

For the unknowing, calls to Northern Cyprus are usually routed through Turkey. That means you first dial Turkey (international access code ☎ 90), then the regional code for Northern Cyprus (☎ 392) and finally the local number. This can be difficult as the lines are few and far between. However, there is fortunately a back-door route via a special line through which you can talk to the North quite easily from the South. Dial ☎ 0139, wait for the dial tone and then dial the local North number. To call from North to South dial ☎ 0123 and follow the same procedure.

If you have a mobile phone brought in from outside Cyprus and have global mobile roaming activated, you should be able to tune into the GSM networks of either side.

You must also have line of sight with either Turkish Cypriot or Greek Cypriot transmission towers – this most conveniently occurs if you are in the central Mesaoria/Mesarya plain. Lefkosia/North Nicosia is the best place to make such calls. In this way a call to the North from the South in effect becomes a local mobile call within the North. The same applies with calls to the South from the North.

---

dialling ☎ 0809 6251. Once you have joined, to use ekno from the South, you need to dial ☎ 0809 6248.

Note that ekno is not available in Northern Cyprus.

Email & Internet Access

Cyprus is well connected to the Internet both for private and public users. Internet cafés abound in both the North and the South. If you plan to bring you own laptop PC, you will need to know that the phone plugs are of the flat modular kind such as those used in the UK. Adaptors are easy to find in major towns. For more information on travelling with a portable computer, see the websites ⓦ www.teleadapt.com or ⓦ www.igoproducts.com.

Your local Internet Service Provider (ISP) may well have Internet roaming agreements with Cyprus; check with them for local dialup numbers before you leave home. An easy way to connect without having to take out a local account is to use the 'Cytanet For All' service. You only pay for time connected (CY£0.20 per 10-minute block). Dial ☎ 0992 6262 from anywhere in the South; enter 'cytanetforall' as the userid and leave the password entry blank.

If you plan to spend any time in Cyprus, it may be worthwhile taking out a temporary account with one of the country's ISPs. **SpiderNet** *(☎ 2284 4844, fax 2266 9470;* ⓦ *www.spidernet.net; 4th floor, Iasonos 1, CY-1082, Lefkosia)*, in the South, can provide a temporary 'Click & Connect' account for CY£20. With this you get three-month's Internet access. Buy the CD package from any authorised dealer, or order the CD from the website.

In the North, Comtech is the main ISP. Temporary accounts can be taken out for one month (UK£9.80), three months (UK£22.80) or one year (UK£75). Dialup rates are cheap at only UK£0.13 per hour. Accounts can be opened at Kyrenia's Cafe Net Internet café (see the Kyrenia & the North Coast chapter for details).

DIGITAL RESOURCES

The World Wide Web is a rich resource for travellers. You can research your trip, hunt down bargain air fares, book hotels, check on weather conditions or chat with locals and other travellers about the best places to visit (or avoid!).

There's no better place to start your Web explorations than the Lonely Planet website (ⓦ www.lonelyplanet.com). Here you'll find succinct summaries on travelling to most places on earth, postcards from other travellers and the Thorn Tree bulletin board, where you can ask questions before you go or dispense advice when you get back. You can also find travel news and updates to many of our most popular guidebooks, and the subwwway section links you to the most useful travel resources elsewhere on the Web.

The following websites are a good starting point for information on Cyprus.

The South

Cypria.com This is a pretty up-to-date site focused on news, business and sport. There's a handy free email service as well.
  W www.cypria.com

The Cyprus Mail The daily news from the *Cyprus Mail* is presented electronically in a fairly uncluttered and basic site. It's fast and unsophisticated.
  W www.cyprus-mail.com

The Cyprus Tourist Organisation The official website of the CTO is a good first stop for any virtual visitor to the island. It's excellent on the generalities with lots of government and quasi-government data to hand, but is a bit slow and buggy at times.
  W www.visitcyprus.org.cy

The Public Information Office This is the official mouthpiece of the Government of the Republic of Cyprus. It's a rather dry and fact-driven site, but rich on useful and less-useful statistics, press releases and background material.
  W www.pio.gov.cy .

Welcome to Cyprus It's a complete guide with information ranging from doing business in Cyprus to the daily weather.
  W www.welcometocyprus.com

Window on Cyprus This is a mainly tourism-oriented site that provides information on the Republic of Cyprus, including useful leads for independent travellers.
  W www.windowoncyprus.com

The World of Cyprus The site is interesting and varied with data ranging from sport, weather, tourism, news, culture and even a Greek language course.
  W www.kypros.org

The North

Cypnet This is the official website of one of the North's ISPs. It mainly deals with telecommunications, but has a tourist link that leads to a host of useful links from education to literature, history and archaeology.
  W www.cypnet.com

Ministry of Tourism & Environment A colourful and well-presented page produced by the official tourism office, this site covers topics such as hotels, transport, culture and special-interest tourism.
  W www.tourism.trnc.net

North Cyprus Hoteliers Association Hosted by the main hotel owners body, the NCHA, this site is strong on hotels but generally average on other tourism-related topics.
  W www.northcyprus.net

TRNC President's Office This is the official mouthpiece of the office of the President of the Turkish Republic of North Cyprus (TRNC; or KKTC in Turkish). It's dry but informative and sprinkled with the occasional dose of heavy propaganda and anti-South sentiments.
  W www.trncpresidency.org

BOOKS

Most books are published in different editions by different publishers in different countries. As a result, a book might be a hardcover rarity in one country while it's readily available in paperback in another. Fortunately, bookshops and libraries search by title or author, so your local bookshop or library is best placed to advise you on the availability of the following recommendations. See also Flora and Fauna in the Facts about Cyprus chapter and also the special section 'Wild Flowers of Cyprus' for books dealing with those topics.

Lonely Planet

Lonely Planet's *Greek phrasebook* is a handy volume to help you with possible language difficulties in the South while the *Turkish phrasebook* will steer you around difficulties and perhaps open doors in the North.

The *Mediterranean Europe* guidebook covers most of the countries along the Mediterranean littoral, including a chapter on Cyprus. If you are heading further east, *Middle East* is a good general guide to the region. Individual Lonely Planet country guides exist also for *Greece*, *Turkey*, *Syria*, *Lebanon*, *Jordan*, *Egypt* and *Israel*; all these countries have direct transport links with Cyprus.

Guidebooks

The CTO produces a handy pocket-sized 150-page booklet called *Cyprus Travellers Handbook*. It is an alphabetically organised, free publication and contains a wide range of data and information on the Republic of Cyprus. It is available from any CTO office.

Walks in North Cyprus by Christina Hessenberg, Alison Dowey & Derek Dowey, is a handy guide to walking in the North. This spiral-bound booklet describes 30 walks and lists a number of good bird-watching areas. The maps are hand drawn and lack a scale, but the descriptions are quite detailed so should suffice. It's available locally in North Cyprus or by email (e adowey@iecnc.org).

Yachties might get a copy of Rod Heikell's *Turkish Waters & Cyprus Pilot*. The sixth edition has been extensively revised. It covers the coasts and islands from İstanbul, through the Sea of Marmara, the Dardanelles, the Aegean and Mediterranean coasts to the Syrian border and includes Cyprus.

Travel

Lawrence Durrell's *Bitter Lemons of Cyprus* is a great first point of call for a look at the once idyllic but later troubled Cyprus of the mid-1950s. Durrell lived in the village of Bellapais (Beylerbeyi) in Northern Cyprus and describes, in his inimitable style, life in Cyprus from the local point of view and from that of a willing expat colonial administrator.

Colin Thubron's *Journey Into Cyprus* was the last significant travelogue of the once undivided Cyprus, written following an amazing, almost-1000km walk undertaken in the spring and summer of 1972. Sprinkled with stories from the road and historical insight, this book is a must for anyone contemplating an extended visit to Cyprus.

History & Politics

The latest and best version of events on the Cyprus debacle since the 1950s up to the coup and invasion of 1974, is *The Cyprus Conspiracy* by Brendan O'Malley & Ian Craig. In this meticulously researched work the two authors shed light on the role of the British government, the CIA, Archbishop Makarios and the junta colonels of Greece in events that led to the fateful summer of 1974.

Christopher Hitchens' *Hostage to History* is another honest and at times brutally frank account of events in Cyprus' more recent history, including those leading up to partition. He argues that the intervention of Turkey, Greece, Britain and the USA turned a local dispute into a major disaster. The book was initially written in 1984, but the latest edition contains an updated preface.

A somewhat drier and more academic perspective on the whole train of events from the Turkish Cypriot viewpoint is Clemet H Dodd's *The Cyprus Imbroglio*. Compiled from a series of discussion papers written by this specialist in Middle Eastern politics, the book is a thought-provoking review of recent Cypriot politics.

Diana Weston Markides' *Cyprus: From Constitutional Conflict to Constitutional Crisis 1957–1963* is another scholarly work that dissects in detail the contributory factors that led to communal segregation in

Cyprus, and takes a sometimes stark look at the reasons for the breakdown of bicommunal society in Cyprus.

The Latin Church in Cyprus 1195–1312 by Nicholas Koureas looks at the major divisions of the Latin Church, including an examination of the Orthodox Church.

NEWSPAPERS

The Republic's English-language papers are the *Cyprus Mail* and the *Cyprus Weekly*. In Northern Cyprus look for the *Turkish Daily News* and *Cyprus Today*.

UK papers, international versions of various English-language newspapers and some German and French newspapers are widely available in the South. In the North they are almost nonexistent.

RADIO & TV

CyBC (Cyprus Broadcasting Corporation) has programmes and news bulletins in English on Radio 2 (FM 91.1) at 10am, 2pm and 8pm. BFBS 1 (British Forces Broadcasting Services) broadcasts 24 hours a day in English on 89.7 FM (Lefkosia), 92.1 FM (west Cyprus) and 99.6 FM (east Cyprus). BFBS 2 broadcasts on 89.9 FM (Lefkosia), 91.7 FM (Lemesos) and 95.3 FM (Larnaka). The BBC World Service is picked up 24 hours a day on 1323 AM.

Bayrak International is the voice of the North and has a lively and chatty English-language programme for a good part of the day. It can be picked up on 87.8 FM and 105 FM.

CyBC TV has news in English at 8pm on Channel 2. Satellite dishes are very common, so many hotels have CNN, BBC, SKY or NBC. Similar foreign-language TV stations can be picked up in the North also.

PHOTOGRAPHY & VIDEO

Cyprus is an ideal place to take pictures or make amateur videos. The weather will rarely spoil your plans. Richard I'Anson's *Travel Photography: A Guide to Taking Better Pictures* published by Lonely Planet is an excellent companion to that new camera of yours. It's full of top tips and fine photos.

Film & Equipment

All makes of cameras and film are catered for in Cyprus, though technical services may be more limited in the North. Same day or even same-hour film development of prints is available in both the North and the South; slide development will take up to three days.

The cost of a 36-exposure print film is CY£2.50 in the South and UK£2 in the North. To develop a 36-exposure print film will cost you CY£5 and UK£3.90, respectively. A better idea is to bring your own film and video tapes with you, especially if you can buy them duty free.

Cyprus uses the PAL video system.

Restrictions

In general, you can photograph anywhere in Cyprus, with some fairly obvious exceptions. You cannot normally photograph anywhere near the Attila and Green Lines. In practice, this is rarely monitored other than on both sides of the Green Line in Lefkosia, where sensitivities run high. Warning signs are normally displayed prominently so heed them.

Military camps are another no-go area and, while there are military installations in both parts of Cyprus, you will be more aware of them in the North. Do not even get a camera out if you see a warning sign, which is usually a camera with a line through it.

Airports, ports and other government installations are normally touchy photo subjects so you are advised to keep your camera out of sight near these places too.

Museums do not normally allow you to photograph exhibits unless you have written permission. Churches with icons do not allow the use of a flash and, depending on the commercial value of the photographs you take, may not allow photos at all.

TIME

Cyprus is normally two hours ahead of GMT/UTC, but has summer or daylight-saving time during the summer months. Clocks go forward one hour on the last weekend in March and back one hour on the last weekend in October.

ELECTRICITY

The current is 240V, 50Hz. Plugs are large with three square pins as in the UK. Multi-plug adaptors are widely available.

WEIGHTS & MEASURES

Cyprus uses the metric system. A standard conversion table can be found on the inside back cover of this book.

LAUNDRY

There are plenty of dry cleaners to be found in all major towns and prices are reasonable. Laundrettes are less common and can be found only in major tourist centres. Where available, laundrettes are either self-service or the service is provided for you. The latter is usually more expensive, while a self-service wash and dry will normally cost around CY£2. However, self-service laundrettes are more or less nonexistent in the North. Hotels often provide a laundry service, though prices tend to be high.

TOILETS

There are public toilets in the main towns and at tourist sites. They are almost always clean and Western sit-down style, although in Northern Cyprus you sometimes come across the squat variety. When stuck for choice, duck into a restaurant or café and discreetly use the facilities. To be polite, you could then sit down for a beer or a coffee afterwards.

HEALTH

Travel health depends on your predeparture preparations, your daily health care while travelling and how you handle any medical problem that does develop. Cyprus – both North and South – has a generally high standard of public health and public health care.

Predeparture Planning

Immunisations Before you leave, find out from your doctor, a travel health centre or an organisation such as the UK-based Medical Advisory Service for Travellers Abroad (W www.masta.org) what the current recommendations are for travel to Cyprus. Remember to leave enough time so that you can get any vaccinations you need – six weeks before travel is ideal. Discuss your requirements with your doctor, but generally it's a good idea to make sure your tetanus, diphtheria and polio vaccinations are up to date before travelling. Other vaccinations that may be recommended for travel to Cyprus include typhoid and hepatitis A. Pregnant women should make their condition known to their doctor before having any vaccinations. See Women's Health later in this section for more details.

Health Insurance Make sure that you have adequate health insurance. See Travel

Insurance under Visas & Documents earlier in this chapter for details.

Travel Health Guides *Travel with Children* by Lonely Planet includes advice on travel health for younger children.

There are also a number of excellent travel health sites on the Internet. From Lonely Planet's web page (W www.lonelyplanet.com/subwwway) you can choose the 'health and safety' option, which has links including to the World Health Organization and the US Centers for Disease Control & Prevention.

Other Preparations Make sure you're healthy before you start travelling. If you are going on a long trip make sure your teeth are OK. If you wear glasses take a spare pair and your prescription.

If you require a particular medication take an adequate supply, as it may not be available locally. Take part of the packaging showing the generic name rather than the brand, which will make getting replacements easier. It's a good idea to have a legible prescription or letter from your doctor to show that you legally use the medication to avoid any problems.

Medical Services

Emergency medical treatment and assistance is provided free of charge at government hospitals or medical institutions. However, payment of the prescribed fees is required for outpatient and inpatient treatment. Make sure your medical insurance covers any emergency.

Basic Rules

Food Take great care with shellfish such as mussels, oysters and clams and avoid undercooked meat. If a place looks clean and well run, then the food is probably safe. In general, places that are packed with travellers or locals will be fine, while empty restaurants are questionable. The food in busy restaurants is cooked and eaten quite quickly with little standing around and is probably not reheated.

Water In Cyprus water is a precious commodity, since there is not a lot to go around. In general tap water is perfectly safe to drink, though it may have a slightly salty flavour in

---

Medical Kit Check List

Following is a list of items you should consider including in your medical kit – consult your pharmacist for brands available in your country.

☐ **Aspirin or paracetamol (acetaminophen in the USA)** – for pain or fever

☐ **Antihistamine** – for allergies, eg, hay fever; to ease the itch from insect bites or stings; and to prevent motion sickness

☐ **Cold and flu tablets, throat lozenges and nasal decongestant**

☐ **Multivitamins** – consider for long trips, when dietary vitamin intake may be inadequate

☐ **Antibiotics** – consider including these if you're travelling well off the beaten track; see your doctor, as they must be prescribed, and carry the prescription with you

☐ **Loperamide or diphenoxylate** – 'blockers' for diarrhoea

☐ **Prochlorperazine or metaclopramide** – for nausea and vomiting

☐ **Rehydration mixture** – to prevent dehydration, which may occur, for example, during bouts of diarrhoea; particularly important when travelling with children

☐ **Insect repellent, sunscreen, lip balm and eye drops**

☐ **Calamine lotion, sting relief spray or aloe vera** – to ease irritation from sunburn and insect bites or stings

☐ **Antifungal cream or powder** – for fungal skin infections and thrush

☐ **Antiseptic (such as povidone-iodine)** – for cuts and grazes

☐ **Bandages, Band-Aids (plasters) and other wound dressings**

☐ **Water purification tablets or iodine**

☐ **Scissors, tweezers and a thermometer** – note that mercury thermometers are prohibited by airlines

---

some cities where the water has been reclaimed from the sea through desalination. In periods of drought – the summer of 1998 was a bad year – water supplies may be restricted, though this does not usually affect major hotels.

Bottled drinking water is widely available and very popular. The Pedoulas spring water – from the village of the same name – is among the more well-known brands. In the Troödos Mountains you will often come across people filling their empty water bottles or even large containers from roadside springs. You might wish to take advantage of free spring water to replenish your supplies.

Medical Problems & Treatment

Self-diagnosis and treatment can be risky, so you should always seek medical help. An embassy, consulate or five-star hotel can usually recommend a local doctor or clinic. Although we do give drug dosages in this section, they are for emergency use only. Correct diagnosis is vital. We have used the generic names for medications – check with a pharmacist for brands available locally.

Sunburn You can get sunburn surprisingly quickly, even through cloud, and particularly at high altitude. Use a sunscreen, hat and barrier cream for your nose and lips. Calamine lotion or a commercial after-sun preparation are good for mild sunburn. Protect your eyes with good-quality sunglasses, particularly if you will be near water, sand or snow.

Heat Exhaustion & Prickly Heat Dehydration and salt deficiency can cause heat exhaustion and can lead to severe heatstroke (see following). Take time to acclimatise to high temperatures, drink sufficient liquids such as tea and drinks rich in mineral salts (such as clear soups and fruit and vegetable juices), and do not do anything too physically demanding. Salt deficiency is characterised by fatigue, lethargy, headaches, giddiness and muscle cramps; salt tablets may help, but adding extra salt to your food is better.

Prickly heat is an itchy rash caused by excessive perspiration trapped under the skin. It usually strikes people who have just arrived in a hot climate. Keeping cool, showering often, drying the skin and using a mild talcum or prickly heat powder, wearing loose cotton clothing, or resorting to air-conditioning may help.

Heatstroke This serious, and occasionally fatal, condition can occur if the body's heat-regulating mechanism breaks down and the body temperature rises to dangerous levels. Long, continuous periods of exposure to high temperatures and insufficient fluids can leave you vulnerable to heatstroke.

The symptoms are feeling unwell, not sweating very much (or at all) and a high body temperature (39°C to 41°C or 102°F to 106°F). Where sweating has ceased, the skin becomes flushed and red. Severe, throbbing headaches and lack of coordination will also occur, and the sufferer may be confused or aggressive. If untreated, severe cases will eventually become delirious or convulse. Hospitalisation is essential, but in the interim get victims out of the sun, remove their clothing, cover them with a wet sheet or towel and then fan continually. Give fluids if they are conscious.

Infectious Diseases

Diarrhoea Simple things such as a change of water, food or climate can all cause a mild bout of diarrhoea, but a few rushed toilet trips with no other symptoms is not indicative of a major problem.

Travellers' Thrombosis

Sitting inactive for long periods of time on any form of transport (bus, train or plane), especially in cramped conditions, can give you swollen feet and ankles, and may increase the possibility of deep vein thrombosis (DVT). DVT occurs when a clot forms in the deep veins of your legs. It may be symptomless or you may get an uncomfortable ache and swelling of your calf. With a small minority of people, a piece of the clot breaks off and travels to the lungs to cause a pulmonary embolism, a very serious medical condition.

To help prevent DVT during long-haul travel, you should move around as much as possible and, while you are sitting, you should flex your calf muscles and wriggle your toes every half-hour while awake. It's also a good idea to drink plenty of water or juices during the journey to prevent dehydration, and, for the same reason, avoid drinking lots of alcohol or caffeine-containing drinks. In addition, you may want to consider wearing support stockings, especially if you have had leg swelling in the past or you are aged over 40. If you are prone to blood clotting or you are pregnant, you will need to discuss further preventive measures with your doctor before you leave.

Dehydration is the main danger with any diarrhoea, particularly in children or the elderly as dehydration can occur quite quickly. Under all circumstances *fluid replacement* (at least equal to the volume being lost) is the most important thing to remember. Weak black tea with a little sugar, soda water, or soft drinks allowed to go flat and diluted 50% with clean water are all good. With severe diarrhoea a rehydrating solution is preferable to replace minerals and salts lost. Commercially available oral rehydration salts (ORS) are very useful; add them to boiled or bottled water. In an emergency you can make up a solution of six teaspoons of sugar and a half teaspoon of salt to a litre of boiled or bottled water. Keep drinking small amounts often. Stick to a bland, fat-free diet as you recover.

Over-the-counter diarrhoea remedies such as loperamide or diphenoxylate (sold under many different brand names) can be used to bring relief from the symptoms, although they do not actually cure the problem. Only use these drugs if you do not have access to toilets, eg, if you *must* travel. Note that these drugs are not recommended for children under 12 years.

In certain situations, antibiotics may be required: severe diarrhoea, diarrhoea with blood or mucus (dysentery), any diarrhoea with fever, profuse watery diarrhoea and persistent diarrhoea not improving after 48 hours. These suggest a more serious cause of diarrhoea and in these situations over-the-counter diarrhoea remedies should be avoided.

Fungal Infections These occur more commonly in hot weather and are usually found on the scalp, between the toes (athlete's foot) or fingers, in the groin and on the body (ringworm). You get ringworm (which is a fungal infection, not a worm) from infected animals or other people. Moisture encourages these infections.

To prevent fungal infections wear loose, comfortable clothes, avoid artificial fibres, wash frequently and dry yourself carefully. If you do get an infection, wash the infected area at least daily with a disinfectant or medicated soap and water, and rinse and dry well. Apply an antifungal cream or powder. Try to expose the infected area to air or sunlight as much as possible and wash all towels and underwear in hot water, change them often and let them dry in the sun.

Hepatitis This term is a general term for inflammation of the liver. The symptoms are similar in all forms of the illness, and include fever, chills, headache, fatigue, feelings of weakness and aches and pains, followed by loss of appetite, nausea, vomiting, abdominal pain, dark urine, light-coloured faeces, jaundiced (yellow) skin and yellowing of the whites of the eyes. People who have had hepatitis should avoid alcohol for some time after the illness, as the liver needs time to recover.

Hepatitis A is transmitted by contaminated food or water. You should seek medical advice, but there is not much you can do apart from resting, drinking lots of fluids, eating lightly and avoiding fatty foods. **Hepatitis E** is transmitted in the same way as hepatitis A; it can be particularly serious in pregnant women.

Hepatitis B is spread through contact with infected blood, blood products or body fluids, for example through sexual contact, unsterilised needles and blood transfusions, or contact with blood via small breaks in the skin. Other risk situations include having a shave, tattoo or body piercing with contaminated equipment. The symptoms of hepatitis B may be more severe than type A and the disease can lead to long-term problems such as chronic liver damage, liver cancer or a long-term carrier state. **Hepatitis C and D** are spread in the same way as hepatitis B and can also lead to long-term complications.

HIV & AIDS Infection with the human immunodeficiency virus (HIV) may lead to acquired immune deficiency syndrome (AIDS), which is a fatal disease. Any exposure to blood, blood products or body fluids may put the individual at risk. The disease is often transmitted through sexual contact or dirty needles – vaccinations, acupuncture, tattooing and body piercing can be potentially as dangerous as intravenous drug use. HIV/AIDS can also be spread through infected blood transfusions; blood used for transfusions in European hospitals is screened for HIV and should be safe.

While Cyprus does not have the epidemic characteristics of some countries, AIDS is present and all precautions should be taken.

Needles in hospitals and at doctors can be assumed to be sterile so there is no need to pack your own. Cyprus' AIDS Advisory Centre can be contacted on ☎ 2230 5515.

Sexually Transmitted Infections (STIs)

HIV/AIDS and hepatitis B can be transmitted through sexual contact – see the relevant entries earlier for more details. Other STIs include gonorrhoea, herpes and syphilis: sores, blisters or rashes around the genitals and discharges or pain when urinating are common symptoms. In some STIs, such as wart virus or chlamydia, symptoms may be less marked or not observed at all, especially in women. Chlamydia infection can cause infertility in men and women before any symptoms have been noticed. Syphilis symptoms eventually disappear completely but the disease continues and can cause severe problems in later years. While abstinence from sexual contact is the only 100% effective prevention, using condoms is also effective.

Cuts, Bites & Stings

Bedbugs & Lice Bedbugs live in various places, but particularly in dirty mattresses and bedding, evidenced by spots of blood on bedclothes or on the wall. Bedbugs leave itchy bites in neat rows. Calamine lotion or a sting-relief spray may help.

All lice cause itching and discomfort. They make themselves at home in your hair (head lice), your clothing (body lice) or in your pubic hair (crabs). You catch lice through direct contact with infected people or by sharing combs, clothing and the like. Powder or shampoo treatment will kill the lice and infected clothing should then be washed in very hot, soapy water and left in the sun to dry.

Jellyfish, Sea Urchins & Weever Fish

Avoid contact with jellyfish, which have stinging tentacles – seek local advice. Stings from jellyfish in Cyprus can be very painful but are not dangerous. Dousing in vinegar will deactivate any stingers which have not 'fired'. Calamine lotion, antihistamines and analgesics may reduce the reaction and relieve the pain.

Watch out for sea urchins around rocky beaches; if you get some of their needles embedded in your skin, immersing the limb in hot water will relieve the pain (test the water temperature first!). You will then need to get a doctor to remove them in order to prevent infection. Some travellers report that using olive oil will help to loosen needles, if you try to remove them yourself.

Though instances are very rare, watch out for weever fish that bury themselves in the sea bed with just their dorsal fin showing. Stepping on the dorsal fin is very painful.

Snakes There are eight species of snakes in Cyprus, three of which are poisonous. They usually show up in spring and summer only. The most dangerous to humans is the, thankfully, rather rare blunt-nosed viper (*koufi*) recognised by its yellow, horn-like tail. The other two poisonous snakes are the cat snake and the Montpellier snake which, though they can inflict a nasty bite, are not as dangerous as the blunt-nosed viper.

To minimise your chances of being bitten, be sure to wear boots, socks and long trousers when walking through undergrowth where snakes may be present. Don't put your hands into holes and crevices, and be careful when collecting firewood.

Snake bites do not cause instantaneous death and antivenins are usually available. If bitten by a snake that could be venomous, immediately wrap the bitten limb tightly, as you would for a sprained ankle, and then attach a splint to immobilise it. Keep the victim still and seek medical help, if possible with the dead snake for identification. Don't attempt to catch the snake if there is a possibility of being bitten again. Tourniquets and sucking out the poison are now comprehensively discredited.

Women's Health

Pregnant women should take extra care when travelling, particularly in the first three months of pregnancy. Discuss with your doctor, but generally, it's best to avoid all vaccinations in those first three months as there's a theoretical risk of harm to the foetus and miscarriage. The best time to travel is during the middle three months when the risk of complications is less, the pregnancy is relatively well established and energy levels are getting back to normal. Many airlines won't allow women past 34 weeks of pregnancy to travel, in case of labour in the air. Seek medical advice from your medical practitioner before travelling.

Less-Common Diseases

The following diseases pose a small risk to travellers, and so are only mentioned in passing. Seek medical advice if you think you may have any of these diseases.

Leishmaniasis This is a group of parasitic diseases transmitted by infected sandflies, which are found in Cyprus and Turkey. Cutaneous leishmaniasis affects the skin tissue causing ulceration and disfigurement, and visceral leishmaniasis affects internal organs. Seek medical advice, as laboratory testing is required for diagnosis and treatment. Avoiding sandfly bites is the best precaution. Bites are usually painless, itchy and yet another reason to cover up and apply repellent.

Tick-Borne Diseases Lyme Disease, Tick-borne encephalitis and Typhus may be acquired in Cyprus. Seek immediate medical treatment if you believe you have any of these. **Lyme Disease** usually begins with a spreading rash at the site of the tick bite and is accompanied by fever, headache, extreme fatigue, aching joints and muscles and mild neck stiffness. **Tick-borne encephalitis** can occur in forest and rural areas. Symptoms include blotches around the bite, which is sometimes pale in the middle. Headache, stiffness and other flu-like symptoms, as well as extreme tiredness, appearing a week or two after the bite, can progress to more serious problems.

Typhus is spread by ticks, mites or lice. It begins with fever, chills, headache and muscle pains followed a few days later by a body rash. There is often a large painful sore at the site of the bite and nearby lymph nodes are swollen and painful.

Seek local advice on areas where ticks pose a danger and always check your skin carefully for ticks. An insect repellent can help, and walkers in tick-infested areas should consider having their boots and trousers impregnated with benzyl benzoate and dibutylphthalate.

Tetanus This disease is caused by a germ that lives in soil and in the faeces of horses and other animals. It enters the body via breaks in the skin. The first symptom may be discomfort in swallowing, or stiffening of the jaw and neck; this is followed by painful convulsions of the jaw and whole body. The disease can be fatal, but can be prevented by vaccination.

Typhoid This fever is a dangerous gut infection caused by contaminated water and food; medical help must be sought. In its early stages, sufferers may feel they have a bad cold or flu on the way, as initial symptoms are a headache, body aches and a fever which rises a little each day until it is around 40°C (104°F) or more. The victim's pulse is often slow relative to the degree of fever present – unlike a normal fever where the pulse increases. There may also be vomiting, abdominal pain, diarrhoea or constipation. In the second week, the high fever and slow pulse continue and a few pink spots may appear on the body. Trembling, delirium, weakness, weight loss and dehydration may occur, as may complications such as pneumonia, perforated bowel or meningitis.

SOCIAL GRACES

The Cypriot reputation for hospitality is well known. Cyprus is one of the few countries in Europe where you may be invited into a stranger's home for coffee, a meal or even to spend the night. This can often lead to a feeling of uneasiness if the host is poor, but to offer money is considered offensive. The most acceptable way of saying thank you is through a gift, perhaps to a child in the family. A similar situation arises if you go out for a meal with Cypriots; the bill is not shared as in Western European countries, but paid by the host.

When drinking wine, it is the custom to only half-fill the glass. It is impolite to empty the glass, so it must be constantly replenished. When visiting someone, you will be offered coffee and it is bad manners to refuse. You will also be given a glass of water and perhaps a small serve of preserves. It is the custom to drink the water, then eat the preserves and, after, drink the coffee.

Cypriots are a little more formal in their interpersonal relations than their mainland brethren. People are commonly addressed as Mr 'so-and-so', eg, 'Kyrie Kosta' or 'Orhan Bey', and the use of first names alone is considered to be too familiar. Appointments are usually kept to the agreed time and in the villages it is not unusual for villagers to phone each other before visiting even if they live next door to each other.

You may have come to Cyprus for sun, sand and sea, but if you want to bare all other than on a designated nude beach, remember that Cyprus is a traditional country, so take care not to offend the locals.

When visiting churches or mosques, remember that they are primarily places of worship, not tourist sights. Dress conservatively (women must cover up any exposed skin or hair to enter a mosque) and avoid prayer times or church services if possible. Don't take flash photos and if you must speak, then do so quietly. You need to take off your shoes before entering a mosque.

Some taboos to avoid in the Turkish community are pointing your finger directly at someone, showing the sole of your shoe or foot to anyone, blowing your nose loudly, picking your teeth and being overtly affectionate with someone in public.

While politics are discussed widely on both sides of the Attila Line, the 'Cypriot problem' is a very sensitive issue – particularly for Greek Cypriots – and should be approached with tact and understanding. Both Greek and Turkish Cypriots can be quite frank and forthright in discussing the issue, but it is better to let them make the running rather than for you to initiate a discussion.

Photographing People

When handled correctly, Cypriots make engaging and often very willing subjects. However, it is bad form simply to point a camera at someone without at least acknowledging your subject. A simple *'kalimera'* or *'merhaba'* or a just a smile may be all that is required to break the ice and set up a potential portrait scene.

It is not culturally appropriate to take photographs in mosques when people are praying or when a service is in progress. However, outside of these restrictions, it is usually OK to take a photograph. It is less intrusive without a flash (and draws less attention to yourself).

WOMEN TRAVELLERS

Women travellers will encounter little sexual harassment, although it is worth steering clear of any red-light areas and some of the cheaper hotels because they may double as brothels. In both parts of Cyprus, however, women may be subject to good-natured verbal sparring in the form of corny pick-up lines. This is common for both foreign and Cypriot women, though foreign women merit particular attention from these verbal Romeos. While some may find this offensive, it is part of the male culture here and is best handled good-naturedly – usually by ignoring the perpetrator.

Solo women travellers should take reasonable care at rowdy nightclub resorts, such as in Agia Napa, where inebriated foreign males may be a nuisance.

GAY & LESBIAN TRAVELLERS

Homosexuality is legal in the Republic and the **Gay Liberation Movement** (☎ 2244 3346) can be contacted at PO Box 1947, Lefkosia. You will find a useful link to gay activities in Cyprus on the Gayscape webpage ⓦ www.gayscape.com.

In the North, homosexuality is technically illegal but, in practice, police maintain a generally liberal attitude, particularly to foreigners who will not be arrested unless caught in flagrante delicto. There are no organised support groups in Northern Cyprus.

DISABLED TRAVELLERS

Any CTO can send you the *What the Disabled Visitor Needs to Know about Cyprus* factsheet, which lists some useful organisations. The Republic's airports have trucklifts to assist disabled travellers. Some of the hotels have facilities for the disabled, but there's little help at sites and museums.

Wheelchair travellers might like to check out the services offered by **GC Paraquip** (☎ 2694 9758, fax 2694 9860; ⓦ *www.paraquip.com.cy; Ahepans 1, Pafos CY-8026*). It offers a wide range of services and information on hotels, wheelchair hire and airport transfers.

In Northern Cyprus there are few facilities for the disabled visitor.

SENIOR TRAVELLERS

Older visitors will find travelling around both the Republic and Northern Cyprus fairly easy. The only real discomfort may be the usually extreme weather conditions that prevail in July and August. In general, no concessions exist for seniors.

TRAVEL WITH CHILDREN

Visiting Cyprus with junior travellers is very easy. Children are the focal point of family life for all Cypriots and will always be received very warmly. Children are welcome in restaurants and bars and can be seen running around way past midnight at the many weddings that take place around the country during the summer.

Restaurants will often have highchairs for children and hotels should be able to supply cots if requested in advance. Hotels also often provide child-minding facilities; check before you book. Hire cars will not normally supply child safety seats, so check with the company beforehand if you need one.

While large, grassy playgrounds are few and far between in the main towns, there are several water-theme parks around the country to keep kids occupied for the best part of a day and there are usually video games and rides available at most tourist centres. That said, there are always the beaches – most of them very safe with shallow water – and associated water activities to keep them amused all day.

For a rundown on how to amuse children on holiday read Cathy Lanigan's *Travel With Children*, published by Lonely Planet.

DANGERS & ANNOYANCES

In general, Cyprus is a very safe place to travel, both for locals and for tourists, and personal safety is pretty well guaranteed. The crime rate is minimal, although petty thievery and crime may be on the increase in urban centres and muggings are almost unknown – this applies equally to both the Republic and Northern Cyprus. The greatest risk will often come from fellow travellers in resorts with a high concentration of tourists, where petty theft and drunkenness by some are the most likely annoyances to be encountered.

Cypriots are very tolerant people, considering have endured occupation and colonisation for most of their history. You are unlikely to find any racial discrimination on either side of the island.

Care, however, must be exercised when travelling in the area of the Attila and Green Lines that divide the North from the South. The dividing line between the two communities is normally clearly visible and identifiable by barbed wire, sentry boxes and UN watchtowers. Despite this, there have been cases of people inadvertently straying across the Line towards the North where-

upon they have been arrested and detained. The delineation between North and South is less clearly marked within the Dekelia British Sovereign Base Area in the east where there is no UN buffer zone as such. Extra care must be exercised here.

There are occasional demonstrations and gatherings by Greek Cypriots at various points along the Attila Line and tensions can run very high. In August 1996 two Greek Cypriots were murdered by Northern Cypriot counter-demonstrators at Deryneia, close to Famagusta. At the same time, some Greek demonstrators and several foreigners were also injured by gunshots.

To avoid possible problems, travellers should not linger near military bases in the North or the South and should obey prominent signs prohibiting photography.

Greek & Turkish Travellers

If you are Greek or have a Greek surname and attempt to enter Northern Cyprus without a pre-arranged visa you will be given special attention and most likely turned back or detained. One traveller reported that even travellers with Turkish surnames may be turned back for having 'illegally' entered Cyprus from the South. For more details on travelling across the Green Line see the boxed text 'Crossing the Thin Green Line' in the Getting Around chapter.

If you make it to the North as a Greek, you will be treated with a mixture of curiosity and deference. Remember, Turkish Cypriots under the age of 25 have no experience of living with Greeks and probably do not carry the first-hand resentment towards Greeks still harboured by their elders. Some Turkish Cypriots however, particularly those who once lived in the South, will be delighted to meet you and may even speak Greek.

If you are Turkish or have a Turkish surname you will be allowed into the South and will be treated with deference and respect, though you will be an object of curiosity for some. Many Turkish Cypriots still work in construction industries in the South, crossing unhindered each day from the North via the Dekelia British Sovereign Base.

LEGAL MATTERS

The importation of drugs or any psychotropic substances is strictly forbidden. Also, the police are very vigilant on speeding and drink driving in both the South and North.

BUSINESS HOURS
The South

Shopping hours vary by season. In summer (1 June to 14 September) shops open at around 8.30am and close at around 7.30pm weekdays. In the major cities there is an afternoon break from 1pm to 4pm. In the spring/autumn periods (1 April to 31 May and 15 September to 31 October) shops close at 7pm and in the winter period (1 November to 31 March) at 6pm. On Wednesday and Saturday early closing is at 2pm, and shops do not open on Sunday.

Banks maintain somewhat shorter hours: 8.30am to 12.30pm weekdays as well as 3.15pm to 4.45pm on Monday. In July and August banks open 15 minutes earlier. Centrally positioned banks also offer afternoon tourist services; you'll see notices posted on their doors. Currency-exchange bureaus operate over more extended hours and are often open until late in the evening.

Petrol stations open at 6am and close at 7pm on weekdays (6pm from 1 October to 31 March). On Wednesday in the Lefkosia district they close early at 2pm; elsewhere early closing is 2pm on Tuesday. Saturday opening times are 6am to 3pm and on Sunday they are closed. In rural areas, many petrol stations remain open on weekends and holidays.

Out of hours, many petrol stations have automatic vending machines that take both cash and credit cards.

Public service hours are 7.30am to 3.30pm weekdays and, also, 3pm to 6pm Thursday (1 September to 30 June) and 7.30am to 2.30pm weekdays (1 July to 31 August).

The North

Banks are open 8am to noon and 2pm to 5pm weekdays from September to March, and from 8am to 1.30pm and 2.30pm to 5pm the rest of the year. Shops are open 7.30am to 2pm weekdays from May to August, and 8am to 1pm and 2pm to 5pm the rest of the year. There is also late opening on Monday from 3.30pm to 6pm.

PUBLIC HOLIDAYS & SPECIAL EVENTS

Holidays in the Republic are the same as in Greece, with the addition of Greek Cypriot Day (1 April) and Cyprus Independence Day (1 October). Greek public holidays are

New Year's Day	1 January
Epiphany	6 January
First Sunday in Lent	February
Greek Independence Day	25 March
(Orthodox) Good Friday	March/April
(Orthodox) Easter Sunday	March/April
Spring Festival/Labour Day	1 May
Kataklysmos (Deluge)	June
Feast of the Assumption	15 August
Ohi Day	28 October
Christmas Day	25 December
St Stephen's Day	26 December

Easter is the most important religious festival and just about everything stops. Fifty days before this is carnival time. A useful publication is the *Diary of Events* available from any CTO.

Northern Cyprus observes Muslim holidays, including the month of Ramadan, which means the North can sometimes shut down for up to a week. It also observes

New Year's Day	1 January
Peace & Freedom Day	20 July
Victory Day	30 August
Proclamation of the TRNC	15 November

ACTIVITIES

There are outdoor activities to suit most tastes in Cyprus. Some activities are better suited to the cooler months, including cycling, skiing and hiking. Organised water-based activities in general run from mid-March to late October, though if you have your own equipment there is nothing to prevent you from enjoying your preferred activity at any time of the year.

Cycling

The CTO produces a helpful brochure called *Cycling in Cyprus*, which lists a number of recommended mountain-bike trails utilising both regular surfaced and unsurfaced roads and off-road trails. This should be available from most CTO offices, but if it's unavailable you can obtain a copy from the CTO head office in Lefkosia. The NCTO does not yet produce a similar cycling guide.

Overall, cycling in Cyprus is quite easy and not yet overrun by long-haul cyclists due to the island's relative isolation. The distances are relatively short and quieter roads exist in parallel to the busy motorways that connect Lefkosia, Larnaka, Lemesos and eventually Pafos. Cyclists may use the wide, hard shoulder of the two-lane motorways, but the scenery of passing vehicles is less enticing than that found on the less-busy roads.

Cyclists in the Troödos Mountains in the South will find some of the most scenic areas, but bicycles with a good range of gears are necessary to cope with the long, though not necessarily steep, gradients that lead up and down the mountains. Mountain bikes can be hired in Troödos should you not relish the idea of riding your own bike uphill.

In the North, cyclists will find the relatively untrafficked roads of the Karpas Peninsula the most rewarding. Only the short-lived and narrow Kyrenia Range of mountains will provide any real obstacle to movement between the north coast and the interior plains.

Skiing

The Troödos Mountains enjoy a brief, but often vigorous, skiing season and the sport is fairly popular for those who have the equipment and energy to get up to the slopes of Mt Olympus from early January to mid-March. There are four ski runs close to Troödos and these are operated and maintained by the **Cyprus Ski Club** (☎ 2236 5340; PO Box 22185, CY-1518 Lefkosia). There are also two runs on the north face of Mt Olympus. One is 350m long and the other 500m long. There are two more 150m runs in 'Sun Valley' on the southern side of Olympus. For further information contact the Cyprus Ski Club or get the CTO leaflet Skiing in Cyprus. There is no skiing in Northern Cyprus.

Hiking

Going on hikes in Cyprus is very popular, except during July and August when the weather can get too hot. Well-marked trails have been set up and maintained by the CTO. The most popular trails are in the Troödos Mountains, which sport at least four excellent and relatively easy trails around and close to Mt Olympus.

Other trails include a series of overland hikes in the Pitsylia region immediately east of Mt Olympus. These normally require a drop-off and pick-up arrangement for hikers. The trails of the Akamas Peninsula in the far northwest are circular, as are a couple of trails in the Stavros tis Psokas park to

the immediate south of the Tyllirian wilderness in the northwest of the country. Get a copy of the CTO brochure Cyprus – Nature Trails for details on all the organised trails in the South.

The North has some excellent hiking opportunities as well, particularly in the Kyrenia Range. Local hiking operations take people on guided walks around the mountains, although armed with a walking guide (see Books earlier) you can do it easily yourself. See Kyrenia in the Kyrenia & the North Coast chapter for more details.

Windsurfing

Windsurfing is a widespread activity on both sides of Cyprus, though the area around Protaras in the South is particularly popular. Windsurfing equipment can be hired out for around CY£5 per hour for solo surfing, or for CY£5 for 30 minutes of instruction.

Boating

Boats of all kinds can be hired at the major beaches in both Northern Cyprus and the Republic. Popular spots for boating include Coral Bay near Pafos, Polis and Latsi to the north of Pafos, Geroskipou Beach near Pafos, Dasoudi Beach near Lemesos, Larnaka Public Beach and, in the north, Kyrenia. Costs range from CY£10 for 30 minutes in a 49 HP speedboat to CY£30 for 30 minutes in a 150 HP speedboat. Prices for hiring a craft in the North are somewhat cheaper.

Diving & Snorkelling

Diving is very popular in Cyprus as the island is free from seriously dangerous currents or other underwater perils. Organised subaqua clubs can be found at major tourist centres in both the North and the South, and most of them run one- to three-day training courses for novices. Do not remove antiquities or sponges from the sea bottom.

For further information contact the **Cyprus Federation of Underwater Activities** (CFUA; ☎ 2275 1757, fax 2275 5246; PO Box 21503, CY-1510 Lefkosia).

Snorkelling is as popular as organised diving in Cyprus. Masks, snorkels and flippers can all be bought or hired if you haven't brought along your own, and no special permission is required. The best area for snorkelling is probably in the less-exposed coves of eastern Cyprus, especially around

Protaras. In the North the beaches to the west of Kyrenia are probably the best bet.

Horse Riding

There is a surprisingly well-developed and organised network of horse-riding facilities, in the South at least, with at least nine major centres on offer. Rates run from CY£10 to CY£12 for either an hour's unsupervised riding or an hour's instruction. The CTO puts out a detailed flyer called *Horse Riding in Cyprus*, but for further details contact the **Cyprus Equestrian Federation** (☎ 2277 2515, fax 2235 7002; PO Box 14043, CY-2153, Aglantzia, Lefkosia).

WORK

In the Republic, work permits can only be obtained through a prospective employer applying on your behalf. The best place to look for jobs is in the *Cyprus Weekly*. During the tourist season, even if you don't have a work permit you can sometimes pick up bar or café work, and although payment is rare, bed and board may be substituted.

If you want to work in Northern Cyprus, apply to the Immigration Department of the TRNC for a work permit. Your application will be considered on its merits.

Bar Work

This is probably the best opening for casual summer work. A leisurely stroll around the bars of Agia Napa, Pafos, Kyrenia, Larnaka or Lemesos should provide you with possible opportunities. Check also the local newspapers and keep your ears tuned to the local grapevine. Bar work runs from early April to late October.

English Tutoring

In theory, it's possible to find private work tutoring English in Cyprus, but the demand – such as exists in neighbouring Greece – is not high. Check the local English-language newspapers for openings.

ACCOMMODATION
Camping

There are seven licensed camping grounds in the Republic, mostly with limited opening times. They are all equipped with hot showers, a minimarket and snack bar, and charge around CY£1.50 a day for a tent site and CY£1 per person per day. In the North there are six camping grounds, but the facilities are not as good or well developed as in the South. Costs are similar to those in the South.

Hostels

There are four Hostelling International (HI) hostels in the Republic; these are slightly cheaper if you are a member. Try contacting the **Cyprus Youth Hostel Association** (☎ 2267 0027, fax 2267 2896; e montis@logos.cy.net; PO Box 21328, CY-1506 Lefkosia). There are no HI hostels in Northern Cyprus.

Guesthouses

Domatia rooms, or rooms for rent, advertised by the word *camere*, are not common in Cyprus; in fact the practice is officially discouraged. However, in Agia Napa you will see signs advertising rooms and occasionally come across them in some of the more popular mountain resorts such as the Troödos Mountains in the South.

B&Bs & Pensions

In the Republic the B&B system is generally known as agrotourism. This is a genuinely superb and often very economical way for independent travellers to see the country. Guests stay in renovated village houses or purpose-built pensions. Most of them are self-contained and fully equipped. Rates range from CY£9 for a single room to CY£65 for a luxury studio.

With few exceptions, however, agrotourism houses and pensions are away from major centres so you will either need your own transport to get around, or will have to rely on sometimes-sketchy public transport.

For an excellent colour brochure listing all places to stay, contact **Cyprus Agrotourism Company** (☎ 2233 7715, fax 2233 9723; w www.agrotourism.net; PO Box 4535, CY-1390 Lefkosia) or check its listings online.

The North has not yet developed such a system, but a network of agrotourist houses is currently being planned.

Hotels

In the Republic, hotels are classified from one to five stars and prices for a double room range from CY£18 to over CY£200. While most hotels deal primarily with package-tour groups who pay cheaper bulk rates, individual travellers can usually find a room even in ostensibly marketed 'resort' hotels.

Quality varies markedly, though prices are strictly controlled by the CTO. The rates listed in the *Cyprus Hotel Guide* (issued free by the CTO) are *maximum* allowable prices and will only normally be applicable in high season (July to August). Outside that period, discounts of up to 50% may apply. Many hotels have email addresses so prospective guests can do some planning before arriving in Cyprus.

The quality of hotels in the North is generally good to excellent at the top end of the scale, though the supply is necessarily smaller. Package-tour visitors constitute the bulk of guests. The same principle applies to individual travellers as in the South. There will usually be a room available for walk-ins. Room rates are normally quoted in UK pounds or US dollars. In this book we give prices in UK pounds. The *North Cyprus Hotel Guide* is available from the NCTO, if you ask specifically for it.

Other Accommodation

In the Republic you can sometimes stay overnight in a monastery, ostensibly for free, but a donation is expected.

Sleeping rough, while theoretically possible, is not recommended and is frowned upon. However, you might get away with it at a deserted beach as a one-off solution.

FOOD

Cypriot food is a combination of Greek and Turkish cuisine, based primarily on meat, salad and fruit.

Local Food

The barbecue is a very popular way of cooking meat and fish, and a *mezes* is a traditional meal consisting of around 20 different small dishes. Dishes in both the North and South are very similar with a few local variants to make things interesting.

Given half a chance and at least a couple of friends or family members at hand, a Cypriot will unflinchingly order *mezes* for the main meal of the day if they are eating out. Preferably taken in the evening after a day of relative abstinence from food, a *mezes* meal can be a banquet for some and an enormous headache for others – *where is it all going to go?*

A *mezes* meal consists of three or even four rounds of dishes: dips and salads, vege-

tarian and other mixed dishes, meat dishes and fruit. The trick is to pace yourself and not overdo it on the bread and dips. Expect to pay around CY£6 to CY£8 (UK£5 to UK£6) per person for a *mezes* meal, not including drinks.

You can still order main dishes such as *mousaka/musaka* (aubergines and a cheese sauce), *kleftiko/küp kebab* (oven-baked lamb), *ofto* (similar to *kleftiko* but individually packed in foil), as well as steaks, chops and fish dishes.

The local cheese is *halumi/hellim*. Cypriots don't make a big thing out of prepared desserts, preferring instead fresh fruit of the season. Make a point of asking for prickly pears *(papoutsosyka/frenk inciri)* in August. They are a pain to pick, but devilishly delicious to eat. Watermelons, rock melons (cantaloupes), peaches and nectarines are all big summer favourites.

Fast Food

Like anywhere else in the world, fast food is finding its niche in Cyprus. Hamburgers, chicken, pizzas and sandwiches all play their role in keeping fast-moving Cypriots and travellers alike fuelled and ready.

Vegetarian

Food for vegetarians is rarely marketed as such. Even restaurants catering primarily for tourists may not make traditional (vegetarian) dishes. Instead, you can choose dishes made from vegetables or pulses, which will more often than not appear on restaurant menus anyway.

Self-Catering

Dining out every day can be expensive. In self-catering apartments or agrotourist houses you can usually cook for yourself very cheaply and easily. Supermarkets will have most of what you are familiar with back home and local fruit and vegetable markets will provide you with fresh produce. Even the smallest village will have a minimarket and grocery store.

DRINKS
Nonalcoholic Drinks

Tea and coffee are popular, though the Greek/Turkish variety of coffee – thick and strong – is more commonly consumed. Iced instant coffee *(frappé)* is gaining popularity among young Cypriots.

Alcoholic Drinks

Drinking alcohol in the dedicated pub sense – as in the UK or Australia, for example – is generally unknown in Cyprus. Alcohol is normally taken with food or at least small snacks *(mezedes)*. Local beer comes in two brands: Cypriot-made KEO and Danish-inspired but Cypriot-brewed Carlsberg. Other beers, while available, are normally more expensive. In the North you will commonly find Efes or Gold Fassl beer.

Raki (Turkish) or *zivania* (Greek) is the local firewater made from distilling the leftovers of the grape crushings. It is strong, so beware. Wine is popular on both sides of Cyprus and Commandaria from Kolossi, near Lemesos, is Cyprus' most famous export fortified wine. It dates back in popularity to the time of the Crusades.

While nominally Muslims, many Turkish Cypriots either partake of alcohol or are quite happy to let others enjoy it freely.

ENTERTAINMENT

Restaurants sometimes have live music and there are cinemas, clubs and Internet cafés open until 2am or later in most major towns and tourist areas. Bars abound in major resorts – Agia Napa having perhaps the greatest concentration of watering holes on the island. Lemesos, Larnaka, Pafos and Lefkosia all have lively night scenes, while in the North only Kyrenia has any kind of international nightlife.

Pubs & Bars

Pubs in the true British sense almost make the grade in some of the tourist enclaves in Protaras, Agia Napa and Pafos. There is a now-expected crop of Irish pubs around the South and at least one in the North. Many do have decent British or Irish beer on tap and serve pub grub, but by and large they are just overgrown bars.

There are bars aplenty and they make no pretence of being otherwise. Drinks tend to be on the pricey side – especially if the swishier establishments are mainly patronised by Cypriots – and in tourist centres they tend to be loud, cold and busy. This applies equally to both the North and the South.

Discos & Clubs

There are abundant discos in both the North and the South, with the greatest concentration being in Kyrenia and Agia Napa. There is usually a cover charge and drinks tend to be more expensive than at regular bars. They normally wind down around 1am.

Nightclubs can be found in major towns and often in resort hotels, and they take over where discos leave off. They tend to be somewhat more formal and fairly expensive; floorshows are very common. As with discos the greatest concentration is in Kyrenia and Agia Napia, with a fair few in Lefkosia.

Jazz

Lovers of jazz will have to keep their ears tuned to the grapevine for possible jazz venues or festivals. The Kourion Jazz Festival near Lemesos usually kicks in during July, but you will be hard-pressed to find anything similar in the North.

Greek Music

Summer is the best time to catch all the top-name performing musical artists from Greece. Music on offer runs the gamut from traditional demotic music to Greek rock and the quality of the artists performing is the best. You will see posters all over Cyprus each week announcing the latest act to appear. The tickets are often available from record stores or, in Lefkosia, at the box office of the **Municipal Theatre** (☎ 2246 3028; *Mouseiou 4*). Do try and catch at least one concert.

The North is not so well served, though performing artists from the Turkish mainland do appear from time to time.

Classical Music

In the South, classical-music concerts are held at various locations throughout the year. Some are held outdoors – such as at the stunning Ancient Kourion amphitheatre – while others are held in Lefkosia. Most classical concerts and other cultural events are listed in the free CTO publication *Diary of Events*, which usually covers a six-month period.

Nicosia This Month also lists concerts that may be happening and is available free from your hotel or from CTO offices.

Cinemas

Equally popular in both the North and South, cinemas abound in Cyprus. Recent releases are usually shown in the original language with subtitling in Greek or Turkish. Admission costs around TL2 million in the North and CY£3 in the South.

Theatre

Going to the theatre is certainly popular among Cypriots, though unless you speak Greek or Turkish, the entertainment value for you is likely to be very limited. Check in the local newspapers or look out for street posters advertising performances that may have some appeal for you.

SPECTATOR SPORTS

Football (soccer) is the most popular spectator sport across Cyprus with teams from a variety of leagues playing somewhere each weekend during the season (September to May). In the South, there are four national divisions each with around 14 teams. See **Takis-on-Line** (**w** *www.soccer.kypros.org*) for a full rundown including football results and standings. The most successful teams are APOEL Nicosia and Anorthosis Famagusta.

In the North, there are two leagues with about 20 teams in each. Currently the top team is OCAK from Kyrenia. Admission to a match costs TL1 million, though entry to many of the lower league games is free.

SHOPPING

Cyprus is well equipped with stores catering for all tastes and requirements. Lefkosia in particular has smart fashionable boutiques, as well as British chain stores such as Marks & Spencer and Woolworths. The North is not as well provided for when it comes to major department stores, but there is, nonetheless, a wide range of goods on display. Hypermarket-style shopping malls are beginning to take off in the South and the major cities will have at least one of these shopping centres in the suburbs somewhere.

While there are not all that many hi-tech consumer items that are specifically cheap in Cyprus, many people purchase high-grade optics such as spectacles, which are probably considerably cheaper than back home. Other good buys include leather goods, woven goods, ceramics, copperware, silverware, baskets and Lefkara lace. Local spirits such as *zivania* (*raki* in the North), brandy, Commandaria liqueur wine and other better-quality Cypriot wines are also good purchases.

Shoes and shirts and imported textiles are of high quality and most likely much cheaper than back home.

Getting There & Away

Most visitors to Cyprus arrive by air and most of them come on charter flights. Tickets on scheduled flights to Cyprus tend to be expensive, though Europe-based travellers may be able to pick up cheap, last-minute tickets with the charter companies if they shop around. This applies in practice only to travellers to the Republic of Cyprus (the South) as charter tickets to North Cyprus (the North) are rarely available. If you are already in Greece, you can pick up reasonably priced one-way or return tickets to the South from travel agents in Athens, Thessaloniki or Iraklio. The only way to arrive in the South by sea is by a cruise boat; there are no longer any passenger ferries, although vehicles may travel unaccompanied. However, there are fast and slower passenger ferries and car ferry services linking the Turkish mainland with North Cyprus.

Travellers take heed: if you have decided to visit North Cyprus first it is *not* under any circumstances possible to cross over to the South. Visitors to the South may cross to the North for up to eight hours daily only. For further information on this sensitive matter see the boxed text 'Crossing the Thin Green Line' in the Getting Around chapter.

AIR

There are scheduled and a limited amount of charter-only flights to Cyprus from most European cities and the Middle East, with discounts for students. However, they are heavily booked in the high season.

Airports

The Republic's airports are at Larnaka and Pafos, while the North is served by Ercan airport. Note that on most airline schedules Larnaka is listed as Larnaca and Pafos as Paphos. This is particularly important to know when making online bookings.

Larnaka airport was built hurriedly after the 1974 invasion and it shows. Facilities for passengers at this busy air terminal are basic and crowded and the airport is not user-friendly. The selection of car-hire outlets in the small arrivals area is somewhat over-subscribed too. There is a public bus service between the airport and Larnaka; otherwise you can take a taxi to your destination.

Pafos airport is smaller and not so frequently used by international travellers, although it is much more convenient for those heading for the Pafos coast resorts. Some Cyprus Airways flights also stop at Pafos to and from their Western European destinations. Only taxis serve Pafos airport.

Ercan airport, 14km east of North Nicosia (Lefkoşa) in North Cyprus, is not recognised by the international airline authorities, so you can't fly there direct. Airlines must touch down first in Turkey and then fly on to North Cyprus. Ercan is smaller than Pafos airport and not particularly well-equipped with arrival facilities such as baggage carts and other conveniences. Car hire must be arranged beforehand. Taxis are your only choice to and from the airport.

Tickets

If you are flying to Cyprus from outside Europe, the plane ticket will probably be the single most expensive item in your budget, and buying it can be an intimidating business. There are only a few airlines offering a scheduled service to and from North or South Cyprus so ticket pricing is controlled and is not all that cheap. You can sometimes pick up flight-only deals with package-holiday companies or find reasonable deals on the Web, but you will really have to do some homework as prices fluctuate quite illogically and depend to a large degree on the season and to a lesser degree on the day of the week or even the time you fly.

Round-the-World Tickets Neither Cyprus Airways, Olympic Airways nor Turkish Airlines are signatories to any RTW ticket agreement, but Olympic Airways does quite often have very reasonable add-on deals to its intercontinental flights to Athens. Check with your local travel agent for quotes.

Airlines

The national carrier of the Republic of Cyprus is **Cyprus Airways** (**w** www.cyprus air.com.cy). It is a small but well-appointed airline and levels of service are very good. It has destinations throughout the Middle East and Europe. The South is also served by a large number of scheduled and charter airlines.

The North is served by scheduled services from **Cyprus Turkish Airlines** (**w** www .kthy.net) and **Turkish Airlines** (**w** www .turkishairlines.com).

Charter Flights

Vacant seats on charter flights block-booked to Cyprus by package-tour companies are cheap but conditions apply on charter flights. Firstly, you can rarely get more than two weeks for your itinerary and, secondly, the departure and arrival times are quite inflexible once booked. That said, a percentage of all package-tour seats is given over to flight-only travellers, so give it a go. The travel section of major newspapers is the place to look for cheap charter deals. More information on charter flights is given later in this book under specific point-of-origin headings.

Departure Tax

Departure taxes in Cyprus are normally included in the cost of your air fare. For the record, you are paying CY£19.50 for the privilege in the Republic. From the North the equivalent fee is UK£3.50.

UK

Trailfinders (**☎** 020-7937 1234; **w** www.trail finder.co.uk; 215 Kensington High St, W8 6BD) produces a lavishly illustrated brochure that includes air fare details. **STA Travel** (**☎** 020-7361 6161; **w** www.statravel.co.uk; 86 Old Brompton Rd, SW7 3LQ) has branches in the UK. Look in the Sunday papers and *Exchange & Mart* for ads. Also look out for the free magazines and newspapers widely available in London. Those that are especially useful include *Footloose*, *Supertravel Magazine*, *TNT* and *Trailfinder*. You can pick these up outside the main train and underground stations.

Most British travel agents are registered with the Association of British Travel Agents (ABTA). If you have paid for your flight at an ABTA-registered agent that goes out of business, ABTA will guarantee a refund or an alternative. Unregistered bucket shops are riskier but also sometimes cheaper.

If you book directly with the airline companies, the best deals are with **British Airways** (in the UK **☎** 0845 722 2111), which flies to Larnaka direct daily. A return ticket will cost UK£150/215 in low/high season. **Olympic Airways** (**☎** 087 0606 0460) fly twice daily (via Athens) for UK£200/250. **Lufthansa** (**☎** 0845 773 7747) flies two to four times a week (via Frankfurt) for UK£200/300. There are some flights to Pafos but they cost around UK£300 return.

The UK office of **Cyprus Airways** (**☎** 020-8359 1333; 5 The Exchange, Brent Cross Gardens, NW4 3RJ) is based in London. Its tickets are cheaper if bought through a travel agent.

Air 2000 (**w** www.air2000.com), a budget leisure airline based in the UK, allows you to make bookings online. Sample return fares for a two-week stay range from UK£270 to UK£300.

A good website for booking your own tickets is **Travelocity** (**w** www.travelocity .co.uk). A quick search of the website brought up return fares ranging from UK£100 with Czech Airlines to UK£180 with Austrian Airlines. The **Expedia** (**w** www .expedia.co.uk) website is another good on-line booking site, but a search for return tickets to Larnaka brought up return fares including UK£139 with British Airways and UK£240 with Cyprus Airways. Another UK website, **Cheaptickets** (**w** www.cheaptickets .co.uk), brought up return fares ranging from UK£240 with Cyprus Airways to UK£560 with Lufthansa.

Return tickets to Ercan airport in North Cyprus range from UK£320 to UK£470 with **Turkish Airlines** (**☎** 020-7766 9300).

Package holidays to the Republic of Cyprus come in all shapes and sizes and range in price from UK£350 to UK£700 for one-week's accommodation with breakfast in a decent-sized hotel in Pafos. See Organised Tours at the end of this chapter for a selection of reputable package-holiday operators to both the North and South.

Continental Europe

Many European carriers fly into Larnaca airport and some also stop in Pafos, though the bulk of the traffic is made up of charter flights.

France There are regular services between France and the South with **KLM** (in France ☎ 0890 71 07 10; €339 return) and **Cyprus Airways** (☎ 01 45 01 93 38; €420-435 return). **Austrian Airlines** (☎ 0820 81 68 16; €370 return) also has daily flights to Larnaca via Vienna. **Turkish Airlines** (☎ 01 56 69 33 50; €375-485 return) links Paris with Ercan airport in Northern Cyprus daily via İstanbul.

Reliable travel agents that you can check out include

Héliades (☎ 01 42 60 87 81) 63 Rue Sainte-Anne, F-75009 Paris
Nouvelles Frontières (☎ 01 45 68 70 00, ⓦ www.nouvelles-frontieres.fr) 87 Blvd de Grenelle, F-75015 Paris
OTU Voyages (☎ 01 40 29 12 12 , ⓦ www .otu.fr) 39 Ave Georges-Bernanos
Planète Havas (☎ 01 53 29 40 00, ⓦ www .havasvoyages.fr) 26 Ave de l'Opéra, F-75001 Paris

Germany In Berlin, try **Alternativ Tours** (☎ 030-881 2089; ⓦ www.alternativ-tours .de; Wilmersdorfer Strasse 94; U-Bahn Adenauerplatz), which has discounted fares to just about anywhere in the world.

STA Travel, **SRS Studenten Reise Service** (☎ 030-2859 8264; ⓦ www.statravel.de; Gleimstrasse 28), offers special student (aged 34 or less) and youth (aged 25 or less) fares.

Travel agents that offer cheap flights advertise in Zitty, Berlin's fortnightly entertainment magazine.

In Frankfurt, try **STA Travel** (☎ 069-43 0191; ⓔ frankfurt.berger118@statravel.de; Berger Strasse 118). There is also a **Cyprus Airways** (☎ 069-695 8930; Hahnstrasse 68) office in Frankfurt.

Greece Not surprisingly, Greece is well-connected to Cyprus with up to seven flights daily to/from the South. **Olympic Airways** (reservations ☎ 0801 44444; ⓦ www.olympic -airways.gr) flies up to four times weekly from Thessaloniki and twice daily from Athens to Larnaka, while **Cyprus Airways** (☎ 21-0372 2722) flies from Athens to Larnaka up to five times daily and to Pafos twice weekly. There is an additional service from Iraklio in Crete to Larnaka three times a week. Ticket prices are reasonable though not overly cheap. Bank on around €220 to €250 for a return ticket from any of these destinations.

Despite the political odds, it is possible to fly to North Cyprus from Greece. Daily flights with Turkish Airlines from Athens to İstanbul connect with a daily evening flight to Ercan. Contact **Turkish Airlines** (☎ 21 0324 6024; Filellinon 19, Athens) for details.

Some reputable travel agents in Greece worth seeking out are **STA Travel** (☎ 21 0321 1188; ⓔ statravel@robissa.gr; Voulis 31, Athens • ☎ 231 022 1391; Tsimiski 130, Thessaloniki), **Aktina Travel Services** (☎ 21 0324 9925; ⓔ syntagma@aktinatravel.gr; Nikodimou 3, Athens) and **Prince Travel** (☎ 281 028 2706; 25 Avgoustou 30, Iraklio).

The Netherlands You can fly to Cyprus from the Netherlands any day of the week. The cheapest return deal is with Austrian Airlines (via Vienna) for €330, followed by Alitalia via Rome (€350), Lufthansa via Frankfurt or Munich (€365) and KLM (€400) direct from Amsterdam.

Travel agents in Amsterdam include

Kilroy Travels (☎ 020-524 51 00, ⓦ www .kilroytravels.com) Singel 413
Malibu Travel (☎ 020-626 32 20, ⓔ postbus@ pointtopoint.demon.nl) Prinsengracht 230
MyTravel Reiswinkels (☎ 020-692 77 88, ⓦ www.mytravel.nl) v Baerlestraat 82

USA

You can fly to Cyprus from the USA with a number of airlines, but all involve a stop and possibly a change of airline in Europe. The New York Times, the LA Times, the Chicago Tribune and the San Francisco Examiner all produce weekly travel sections in which you'll find any number of travel agents' advertisements.

Council Travel (W *www.counciltravel
.com*) and **STA Travel** (W *www.sta-travel
.com*) have offices in major cities nation-
wide. The magazine *Travel Unlimited* pub-
lishes details of the cheapest air fares and
courier possibilities for destinations all over
the world from the USA.

Among the cheaper fares offered by
travel agents are return tickets with United
Airlines and American Airlines connecting
with Cyprus Airways flights. Tickets start at
US$1515. Other permutations with British
Airways, Continental Airlines, Olympic
Airways or KLM are a little more expensive
at US$1580. Cyprus Airways in the US
is represented by **Kinisis Travel & Tours**
(☎ *718-267 6882; 34-09 Broadway, Astoria,
New York*).

You can often get cheaper deals by booking online. Check out **TRAVEL.com** (W *www
.travel.com*) for some good ticket deals. Other
sites worth checking out are **ITN** (W *www
.itn.net*), **Hotwire** (W *www.hotwire.com*) and
Travelocity (W *www.travelocity.com*).

Return tickets from these sites cost from
US$1450 from New York to Larnaka and
from US$1850 from Los Angeles or San
Francisco.

Canada

The *Vancouver Sun* and *Toronto Globe &
Mail* carry ads from travel agents. The magazine *Great Expeditions* is useful; it's available at newspaper and magazine stores.

Travel CUTS (☎ *1 866 246 9762*; W *www
.travelcuts.com*) has offices in all major cities.
Its Montreal office **Voyages Campus Travel
CUTS** (☎ *514-843 8511*) is a good place to
ask about cheap deals. You should be able to
get to Larnaka and back from Toronto, Montreal or Vancouver for C$1500.

Olympic Airways (in Toronto ☎ *905 676
484; in Montreal* ☎ *514-878 3891*) has two
flights a week from Toronto to Athens via
Montreal. From Athens you can connect
with either an Olympic Airways or Cyprus
Airways flight to Larnaka.

You can use the same online sites as for
the USA to search and book return flights
from Canada to Cyprus. Return ticket prices
include C$1420 from Toronto to Larnaka
with British Airways or Lufthansa and from
C$2800 from Vancouver to Larnaka with
various combinations of Lufthansa, Air
Canada and British Airways.

Australia

There are no direct services but Emirates allows you to fly more or less directly from
Melbourne or Perth via Singapore with a
change of aircraft in Dubai. Olympic Airways flies to Athens from Melbourne and
Sydney and can usually offer good value
add-on Cyprus legs. Singapore Airlines flies
into Athens three times a week and there
are daily connections with Cyprus Airways
and Olympic Airways. You can also fly
Malaysia Airlines from Melbourne to Beirut
via Kuala Lumpur and pick up a Royal Jor-
danian connection in Beirut to Larnaka.

Cyprus Airways is represented in Australia by **Cyprus Tourist Agency** (☎ *03-9663
3711; 237 Lonsdale St, Melbourne*).

STA Travel (☎ *1300 733 035*; W *www.sta
travel.com.au*) and **Flight Centres International** (☎ *133 133*; W *www.flightcentre.com
.au*) are major dealers in cheap air fares. Fares
are some 10% cheaper if booked online.

Axis Travel Centre (☎ *08-8331 3222, fax
8364 2922*; W *www.axistravel.com.au; 176
Glynburn Rd, Tranmere, SA 5073*) specialises
in travel to/from the Middle East, Greece
and Cyprus.

Another good website to check fares
from Australia is W www.travel.com.au.

Return ticket prices from Australia to
Cyprus range from A$2200/2835 in low/
high season. Discounted fares of around
A$1555 can also be found, but have re-
stricted conditions.

New Zealand

As in Australia, **STA Travel** (☎ *0508 782
872*; W *www.statravel.co.nz*) and **Flight Centres International** (☎ *0800 243 544*; W *www
.flightcentre.co.nz*) are popular travel agents.
Connections to Cyprus are as for Australia
with the additional cost of flying to and
from Australia.

Sample fares from the above websites for
return flights to Larnaka from Auckland
ranged from NZ$2535 with Emirates to
NZ$3950 with Qantas and British Airways.

Middle East

With Cyprus so close to the Middle East,
transport links between the countries of the
Levant and Larnaka are good but tickets are
rarely discounted. Cyprus Airways is represented in Israel by **Open Sky** (☎ *03-795
1570; Ben Yehuda 23, Tel Aviv*), in Jordan by

Petra Travel & Tourism (☎ 06-562 0115; Abdulhamid Sharaf St, Amman), in Syria by **Al Patra Travel & Tourism** (☎ 011-232 4513; 29th May St, Alani Ave, Damascus) and in Lebanon by **Cyprus Airways** (☎ 01-371 136; Starco Center Block B, Beirut Central).

A good place in Israel to buy discounted tickets is at **Israworld** (☎ 03-522 7099, fax 523 0319; ⓦ www.israworld.com; Ben Yehuda 66, Tel Aviv). It quoted US$110/150 for a one-way/return ticket to Larnaka with Cyprus Airways.

Africa

Travellers in Africa can get to Cyprus most easily via Johannesburg and Nairobi on one of Olympic Airways regular flights through Athens. An alternative route into Cyprus is from Cairo to Larnaka direct with either Egypt Air or Cyprus Airways. Both fly twice a week for US$150/200 one-way/return. Tickets are available from **Egypt Panorama Tours** (☎ 359 0200, fax 359 1199; ⓔ ept@link.net, 4 Rd 79, Maadi, Cairo). Cash payment is advisable in preference to credit cards, which may incur a 10% surcharge.

Asia

STA Travel, which is reliable throughout Asia, has branches in Hong Kong, Tokyo, Singapore, Bangkok and Kuala Lumpur. The Singapore office (☎ 6737 7188, fax 6737 2591; ⓔ retail@statravel.com.sg; 33A Cuppage Rd, Cuppage Terrace) is a good one-stop shop. Flights from Singapore to Larnaka cost S$770/950 one way/return, or S$1000/1400 one way/return with Emirates.

LAND & SEA

There are currently only passenger ferry services from Turkey to Northern Cyprus (see Overland to Cyprus following).

The Republic of Cyprus used to be connected to mainland Europe by a regular passenger- and car-ferry service between Lemesos and Piraeus, Greece. This run involved a stop in Patmos and Rhodes, or sometimes in Crete instead. Cyprus was also connected to the Middle East by an onward service to Haifa in Israel.

Unfortunately in October 2001 the two shipping companies that held the monopoly on travel to the South suspended all passenger services until further notice. Check the websites of the two shipping companies for the latest information: **Poseidon Lines** (ⓦ www.ferries.gr/poseidon) and **Salamis Lines** (ⓦ www.viamare.com). However, vehicles may travel unaccompanied (see the boxed text 'Bringing Your Car to Cyprus' for details).

Ports in the Republic

Lemesos is the main arrival and departure port in the Republic and is 3km southwest of the town centre. The port is reasonably well-equipped for sea travellers but, with the suspension of passenger ferries, the facilities are now mainly used by cruise-ship passengers. The terminal building has banks, tourist information facilities and also duty-free shops.

Overland to Cyprus

It may look a long way on the map, but it is quite feasible to get most of the way by car to Cyprus from Western Europe. The quickest way by far to the Republic of Cyprus is from Italy to Lemesos via a combination of ferries and a short land hop through Greece. Venice, or any other convenient Adriatic port such as Trieste, Ancona, Bari or Brindisi, is linked by frequent ferries to the Greek port of Patras from where it is about a four-hour drive to the port of Piraeus. From here you can ship your car to Cyprus and then fly out to meet it. From Venice you and your car could be in Lemesos in as little as four days.

The quickest way to North Cyprus is by ferry from Venice to İzmir in Turkey followed by a comfortable two-day drive to Antalya, Taşucu or Mersin, which link mainland Turkey with Kyrenia (Girne) or Famagusta (Mağusa) in North Cyprus. Both fast passenger and slower passenger and car ferry services are available. It is difficult to make reservations beforehand since the Turkish shipping companies do not maintain overseas booking agencies. Alternatively, you could also cross to one of at least three Turkish Aegean ports from three Greek islands and drive from there to the Turkish ports for North Cyprus. The crossings are Lesvos-Ayvalık, Samos-Kuşadası and Rhodes-Bodrum. However, the sometimes uncertain local politics governing these tenuous links can often mean delays or cancellations, so they may be better avoided.

Bringing Your Car to Cyprus

If you are thinking of bringing your own vehicle to Cyprus it will now require a bit of planning as there are currently no passenger/car ferries to the Republic of Cyprus. There are, however, two car-ferry services from the Turkish mainland to North Cyprus, but you will not be able to cross the UN buffer zone to visit the South.

There is currently only one company, **Salamis Lines** *(in Greece ☎ 21 0429 4325, fax 21 0452 8384; Fillelinon 12, GR-185 36 Piraeus)*, that transports vehicles to and from Piraeus in Greece and Lemesos in Southern Cyprus. The service also continues on to Haifa in Israel. After you have made a booking, present yourself at its Piraeus office on the day of your vehicle dispatch to pay for your car's passage (€135 including taxes for a small to medium-sized vehicle) and to receive your bill of lading. This procedure should not take more than half an hour.

Proceed to the company's loading wharf at Keratsini, 8km west of the main Piraeus port. You will be given instructions, but finding the wharf may be tricky as it is not signposted. Present your car papers for inspection at the wharf's small customs office. This procedure should not take more than half an hour. Take your car to the nearby vehicle ferry – Salamis Lines were using the *FB Nostos* in mid-2002 – and wait to be loaded. Once you have loaded the vehicle you are free to leave. The ferry currently departs on Tuesday and Friday.

When you arrive (by air) in Southern Cyprus, head for the Lemesos New Port area. Your vehicle will have arrived two days after departure from Keratsini. Try to be at the port to meet the ship as it will be easier to retrieve your vehicle. Call in first at the Salamis Lines counter in the main passenger terminal building with your bill of lading. After paying a port tax of CY£30 you may retrieve your car from the ship, which will be anchored nearby. You then bring your vehicle back to the passenger terminal building for a customs inspection, which is fairly thorough. Allow at least 1½ hours for this whole procedure.

The customs authorities are keen to see the vehicle registration book that clearly shows the vehicle's chassis number. Make sure you can easily link the chassis number with its identifying paperwork. The second key document the authorities will want to see is your 'Green Card' – an international extension of your home vehicle insurance policy. It must be specifically endorsed to cover the Republic of Cyprus. Make sure the CY international code for Cyprus is listed among the countries endorsed on your Green Card. If it is not listed, you will be required to purchase Cypriot insurance on-the-spot (about CY£33 for two months) before being allowed to enter. You will normally be given a three-month duty-free import permit. When all this is completed you are free to drive off. Remember to drive on the left!

On your way back, book and collect your car's ticket from the Lemesos office of Salamis Lines. On the day of departure, take your vehicle to Lemesos' New Port before midday. Check in at the Salamis Lines desk in the passenger terminal and then have your car inspected by customs. They will need the yellow form that you received when you first imported your vehicle.

When finished, drive your car to the ferry. After loading your car, head to the port gate where you can catch a local bus back to town or look for a cab.

Procedures in the North are not as stringent. If you are coming from Turkey you will have done most of the hard paperwork before entering the country. Make sure that your Green Card covers Asiatic Turkey and North Cyprus, but you will be almost certainly requested to purchase additional Northern Cyprus insurance, irrespective of what your Green Card or insurer may tell you. This currently costs around CY£3 (or equivalent in Turkish lira, UK pounds or US dollars) per day or about CY£7 for five days. On-the-spot insurance is normally available both at Kyrenia (Girne) and Famagusta (Mağusa) Ports. This applies equally to vehicles entering via the Ledra Palace Hotel land crossing in Lefkosia.

If you are a real glutton for driving you can drive all the way from Western Europe to the Turkish Mediterranean coast via the Balkans and mainland Turkey and then take a ferry to North Cyprus. Allow at least six or more days for this trip one way.

Purchase-Repurchase Scheme

If you are resident outside the European Union (EU) and you plan to make an extended visit to Cyprus, or include other nearby countries as part of your itinerary, it may be in your interest to look at possibly entering a Purchase-Repurchase scheme to meet your transport needs.

Basically you lease a brand-new car for the duration of your stay at rates considerably below daily rental rates. The two major players are Peugeot and Renault. This means that you need to pick up your car in France, or for an extra premium, from another designated European city. After, you return it to a French or European city of your choice.

Make sure that your insurance is valid for mainland Turkey or the Republic of Cyprus. You will have to purchase additional insurance at the port of entry if you take the vehicle to North Cyprus.

For further details on this excellent scheme, contact the following agents

Australia Peugeot (☎ 02-9976 3000, fax 9905 5874, W www.driveaway.com.au); Renault (☎ 02-9299 3344, 9262 4590)

Canada Peugeot (☎ 514-735 3083, fax 342 8801, W www.europauto.qc.ca); Renault (☎ 450-461 1149, fax 461 0207)

France Peugeot (☎ 01 49 04 81 56, fax 01 49 04 82 50); Renault (☎ 01 40 40 32 32, fax 01 42 41 83 47)

New Zealand Peugeot (☎ 09-914 9100, fax 379 4111); Renault (☎ 09-525 8800, fax 525 8818)

South Africa Peugeot (☎ 011-458 1600, fax 455 2818); Renault (☎ 011-325 2345, fax 325 2840)

USA Peugeot (☎ 1800 572 9655, fax 201-934 7501, W www.auto-france.com ● ☎ 1800 223 1516, fax 212-246 1458, W www.europeby car.com ● ☎ 914-825 3000, fax 835 5449, W www.kemwel.com); Renault (☎ 1800 221 1052, fax 212-725 5375)

ORGANISED TOURS

Coming on a package tour to Cyprus is easy, especially if you come from the UK, Scandinavia or Germany, which constitute the largest source countries for organised tourism to Cyprus. Package tours can't be beaten for prices and convenience, but they do restrict you timewise.

Some of the more established companies in the UK offering packaged vacations in Cyprus are

Amathus Holidays (☎ 020-7611 0901, fax 7611 0931, W www.amathusholidays.co.uk) 2 Leather Lane, London EC1N 7RA

Anatolian Sky Holidays (☎ 0121-325 5500, fax 325 5509, W www.anatolian-sky.co.uk) 1112 Stratford Rd, Hall Green, Birmingham, B28 8AE

Cyplon Holidays (☎ 020-8348 8866, fax 8348 7939, W www.cyplon-holidays.co.uk) 561–563 Green Lanes, London N8 0RL

Cyprair Holidays (☎ 020-8359 1333, fax 8359 1251, W www.cyprair.com) 5 The Exchange, Brent Cross Gardens, London NW4 3RJ

First Choice (☎ 0870 750 04 65, fax 0870 745 4533, W www.firstchoice.co.uk) Peel Cross Rd, Salford, Manchester, M4 2AN

Regent Holidays (UK) Ltd (☎ 01983-866 129, fax 864 197, e regentholidays.iow@btinternet .com) Regent House, 31A High St, Shanklin, IOW.

Sunvil Tours (☎ 020-8568 4499, fax 8568 8330, W www.sunvil.co.uk) Sunvil House, 7–8 Upper Square, Old Isleworth, Middlesex TW7 7BJ

One of the better-known cruise operators in the South is **Armata** *(☎ 2466 5408, fax 2462 7489; W www.cruisecyprus.com; Agiou Neofytou 4, Larnaka)*. Its website lists a wide range of cruise options in and out of Cyprus.

Getting Around

Cyprus is small enough for you to get around easily. Roads are good and well signposted, and traffic moves smoothly and without the excesses and unpredictability sometimes found in other countries in the Middle East or Mediterranean Europe.

Public transport is limited to buses and service taxis – stretch taxis that run on predetermined routes. There is no train network and no domestic air services in either the North or the South. Four-lane motorways link Lefkosia with Lemesos and Larnaka and this network has now been expanded west to Pafos and east to Agia Napa.

It is feasible to ride around Cyprus by bicycle along ordinary roads, which generally parallel the motorways where cycling is not allowed.

The main obstacle to obtaining a full view of Cyprus is the restriction on visits between the Republic of Cyprus and the North. For full details see the boxed text 'Crossing the Thin Green Line' later in this chapter.

Distances overall are generally short, with the longest conceivable leg in the South (Polis to Paralimni) no more than 220km. The North is equally compact, but it is quite a drive out to Zafer Burnu (Cape Apostolos Andreas) at the tip of the Karpas (Kırpaşa) panhandle from North Nicosia (Lefkoşa) or even Famagusta (Mağusa). From Morfou (Güzelyurt) to Zafer Burnu is 210km.

BUS

Buses in the South are frequent but some of the rural buses look like relics from 1950s England. However, they are comfortable, cheap and, other than services to rural areas, offer reasonably well-timed services. Some buses, usually on the main intercity routes, can transport bicycles.

Urban and long-distance buses are operated by about six private companies and run Monday to Saturday. There are no services on Sunday. Major bus companies and destinations in the South are

Alepa Ltd (☎ 9962 5027) Plateia Solomou, Lefkosia. Lefkosia to Lemesos & Pafos
Clarios Bus Co (☎ 2275 3234) Constanza Bastion, Lefkosia. Lefkosia to Troödos & Kakopetria

Eman Buses Constanza Bastion, Lefkosia. Lefkosia to Agia Napa
Intercity Buses (☎ 2266 5814) Plateia Solomou, Lefkosia. Lefkosia to Larnaka & Lemesos
Nea Amoroza Transport Co Ltd (☎ 2693 6822, 2693 6740) Plateia Solomou, Lefkosia. Lefkosia to Pafos
PEAL Bus Co (☎ 2382 1318) Stasinou 27, Lefkosia. Lefkosia to Paralimni and Deryneia

Buses in the North are a varied mix of old and newer privately owned buses too numerous to list here. See the regional chapters for more details.

Reservations

Bus reservations are not normally required in either the South or the North; the one exception being the service to some of the Troödos Mountain resorts, where phone reservations are required if you want to be picked up from either Platres or Troödos in order to return to Lefkosia.

Costs

Bus ticket prices in the South are regulated by the government and range in price between CY£1 and CY£5 for long-distance buses, while urban buses charge between CY£0.40 and CY£0.80. Bus prices in the North generally cost TL1 million or TL1.5 million for longer distances.

The following table will give you an idea of the ticket prices between major towns in the South. Where direct services are not available, the intermediate cities or towns are indicated. See the individual city and town entries for frequency and times of departures.

CAR & MOTORCYCLE

Driving or riding your way around Cyprus is the only really effective way to get around the country properly. Having your own vehicle is essential if you want to see some of the out-of-the-way places in the Troödos Mountains or the Tyllirian wilderness, where bus transport is more or less nonexistent. The scenery throughout the country is varied, petrol stations are everywhere – though there are less in remoter areas like the Troödos Mountains or the Karpas Peninsula – and facilities for bikers and motorists are very

Bus Fares in the Republic of Cyprus (CY£)

	Lefkosia	Lemesos	Pafos	Larnaka	Troödos	Agia Napa	Paralimni	Polis
Lefkosia	-	1.50	3.00	1.50	1.10	2.00	2.50	5.00
Lemesos	1.50	-	2.00	1.70	2.00 (Platres)	via Larnaka	via Larnaka	via Pafos
Larnaka	1.50	1.70	via Lemesos	-	via Lemesos	1.00	1.00	via Lemesos & Pafos
Agia Napa	2.00	via Larnaka	via Larnaka & Lemesos	1.00	via Lemesos & Larnaka	-	0.40	via Larnaka, Lemesos & Pafos
Paralimni	2.50	via Larnaka	via Lemesos & Larnaka	1.00	via Larnaka & Lemesos	0.40	-	via Larnaka, Lemesos & Pafos
Troödos	1.10	2.00 (Platres)	via Lemesos	via Lemesos	-	via Larnaka & Lemesos	via Lemesos & Larnaka	via Lemesos & Pafos
Pafos	3.00	1.50	-	via Lemesos	via Lemesos	via Larnaka & Lemesos	via Lemesos	1.00
Polis	4.00	4.00	1.00	via Lemesos & Pafos	via Lemesos	via Larnaka, Lemesos & Pafos	via Larnaka, Lemesos & Pafos	-

good. Picnic areas in the Troödos are usually only accessible if you have your own transport. Traffic is lighter in the North but roads are not as good as in the South.

For a stay of over three weeks, the high cost of bringing your own vehicle to Cyprus will be outweighed by the cost of hiring a vehicle locally. See Land & Sea in the Getting There & Away chapter for details on bringing a vehicle into Cyprus.

Parking is quite cheap, with CY£0.25 getting you two hours in central Lefkosia. Parking is free in all towns in the North. At the time of research, super and unleaded petrol cost CY£0.38 for 1L, regular was CY£0.38 and diesel just CY£0.13. In the North all petrol was priced at around TL1.35 million a litre. Diesel costs TL700,000. Both leaded and unleaded petrol are widely available.

In the South there is a **Cyprus Automobile Association** (☎ 2231 3233, fax 2231 3482; w www.cyprusaa.org; Hrysostomou Mylona 12, Lefkosia). The 24-hour emergency road assistance number is ☎ 2231 3131. There is no equivalent organisation in Northern Cyprus.

Road Rules

Traffic travels on the left in Cyprus in both the North and the South, and locally registered cars are right-hand drive. Left-hand drive cars circulating in Northern Cyprus have usually been brought over from Turkey. The speed limit on motorways in the South is 100km/h and is often rigidly enforced by speed camera–wielding police officers. The speed limit on ordinary roads is 80km/h and in built-up areas 50km/h unless otherwise indicated. There is just one short stretch of motorway in the North linking North Nicosia with Famagusta. Speed limits in the North are 100km/h on open roads and 50km/h in towns.

Front seat belts are compulsory and children under five years of age must not sit in the front seat. Driving a vehicle, motorcycle

Crossing the Thin Green Line

Which side of the Green Line you enter Cyprus will determine the areas that you can visit on your travels. The current restrictions on crossing the border are outlined below:

From the Republic to the North

Crossing to the North on a day trip is legal and is a fairly uncomplicated exercise. Visitors may cross between 8am and 1pm but must be back on the south side of the Green Line before 5pm. There are no limits to the number of times you can do this. If you are late coming home you will most likely be allowed in, but your name will be placed on the 'black list' and you will not be allowed to cross to the North again. If you are carrying a lot of luggage, border guards may not let you cross the border, believing that you may abscond to Turkey.

There is a set procedure; present yourself at the second police office by the Ledra Palace Hotel crossing and show the passport you used to enter Cyprus. Your name will be entered in a log. If you have a local contact phone number (your hotel number will do) it is good to be able to supply it. If you are travelling with your own vehicle – not Cyprus-registered or a hire car – there are no formalities at this end.

UN personnel, while maintaining a checkpoint, rarely if ever check crossing travellers. Your next stop is the Turkish Cypriot police control. Present your passport and details will be entered into a computer. You will be directed to the day-pass office. Fill in a brief form, return to the police control and surrender your pass. Keep the larger white day-pass receipt as you will need it when exiting. If you have your own vehicle you will be required to pay day insurance (CY£3 per day). If there are no queues, the whole procedure should take no more than 15 minutes. You are now free to enter the North.

This is all well and good if you are a neutral foreigner. If you are Greek, have a Greek surname or the Turkish authorities suspect that you have Greek heritage, you will have problems and you will be turned back, unless you have previously applied for a visa. If your non-Greek passport shows your place of birth as being possibly in Greece or Cyprus, it will be scrutinised.

Occasionally, travellers with Turkish surnames have been turned back for having 'illegally' entered Cyprus from the South.

From the North to the Republic

If you have entered the North from outside Cyprus, you cannot **under any circumstances** enter the South directly. Many travellers are unaware of this prohibition by the Republic of Cyprus authorities. If you are caught doing this, you will be sent back to the North and your name and passport details will be noted. It is unlikely that you will then be allowed into the South even via an indirect route.

The only indirect way you can get into the Republic of Cyprus from Northern Cyprus is to return to Turkey and then return to Cyprus via Greece. Marmaris to Rhodes is the nearest exit point and requires a ferry crossing. From here you can take a ferry to Piraeus in Greece from where you can fly to Southern Cyprus. If you have the money, you can simply fly to İstanbul, from there to Athens and from Athens to Pafos or Larnaka!

---

or even a bicycle with more than .009 milligrams of alcohol per 100 millilitres of blood is an offence.

In the Republic, car drivers must be 21 years and over, motorcycle riders 18 years and over to drive a motorcycle with an engine capacity over 50cc, or 17 years old to drive a motorcycle under 50cc. In the North you must be 18 years or over to drive a car and the same regulations apply to motorcycles as in the South.

Road distances across the country are posted in kilometres only. Road signs are in Greek and Latin script (in the Republic), while in the North, destinations are given in their Turkish version only. Destination road signs in the North are white on blue and are often indistinct or small. American and Canadian drivers need to be alerted to the differences between their own domestic road signs and those used outside of their countries.

Road Distances (km)

NORTHERN CYPRUS

	Famagusta (Mağusa)	Kyrenia (Girne)	Morfou (Güzelyurt)	North Nicosia (Lefkoşa)	Yenierenköy (Yiallousa)
Famagusta (Mağusa)	---				
Kyrenia (Girne)	87	---			
Morfou (Güzelyurt)	103	58	---		
North Nicosia (Lefkoşa)	68	29	45	---	
Yenierenköy (Yiallousa)	66	135	158	118	---

SOUTHERN CYPRUS

	Agia Napa	Larnaka	Larnaka Airport	Lefkosia	Lemesos	Pafos	Pafos Airport	Paralimni	Polis	Troödos
Agia Napa	---									
Larnaka	41	---								
Larnaka Airport	46	5	---							
Lefkosia	80	44	49	---						
Lemesos	107	66	70	82	---					
Pafos	175	134	139	150	68	---				
Pafos Airport	170	129	104	146	63	15	---			
Paralimni	5	44	48	85	111	178	178	---		
Polis	219	169	174	185	103	35	50	219	---	
Troödos	153	112	116	78	46	114	109	158	149	---

It is advisable to avoid rush hours in main cities, ie, 7am to 8.30am, 1pm to 1.30pm and also 6pm to 7pm in summer (one hour earlier in winter). When driving west in the late afternoon, be aware of sun glare, which can be very strong.

Rental

Cars and 4WDs are widely available for hire and cost between CY£14 and CY£50 a day. In some towns you can also rent motorcycles (from CY£12 to CY£20) or mopeds (CY£8). Rental cars are usually in good condition, but inspect your vehicle before you set off. Open-top jeeps are popular options; the Troödos Mountains literally swarm with them on hot weekends and they offer the option of dirt-track driving, that adventure 'look' and natural air-conditioning. If you hire a 2WD, make sure it has air-conditioning and enough power to get you up hills.

Rental cars in both the North and the South carry black on red 'Z' plates – so called because of the initial letter. Other road users normally accord a fraction more respect to 'Z' car drivers and the police are more likely to turn a blind eye for minor infractions, but don't count on it.

Purchase

Cars in Cyprus are not prohibitively expensive and there is a fairly well-organised used-car market scene. They are all right-hand drive, though, suitable only for long-term use in the UK where they are probably cheaper anyway. However, if you are planning on staying six months or more in Cyprus, the purchase and resale of a car might be cheaper than the cost of bringing your own vehicle from outside Cyprus; you will have less paperwork hassles with customs.

A typical used car in the South will cost around CY£6000 for a three- to four-year-old Toyota saloon, or about CY£5000 for a Ford Fiesta of a similar age. There is a buoyant used-car market in the North, both private and public. A basic runaround will set you back between UK£800 and UK£2500. Look in the local press or for cars bearing a Turkish 'Satilik' (For Sale) sticker.

BICYCLE

Cycling is a cheap, convenient, healthy, environmentally sound and, above all, fun way of travelling. It is advisable, though, to limit long-distance cycling trips to winter, spring or autumn as high summer temperatures will make the going tough.

It's best to stick to cycling on the ordinary roads, many of which parallel the motorways where cycling is not allowed. The roads are generally good, but there is rarely extra roadside room for cyclists, so you will have to cycle with care. You will need a bicycle with good gears to negotiate the long hauls up and around the Troödos Mountains and Kyrenia (Girne) Range.

Towns and cities in general are much more cyclist-friendly than their counterparts in other parts of the Mediterranean. In some tourist centres such as Protaras and Agia Napa there are urban bicycle paths.

The Cyprus Tourism Organisation in the South produces a very helpful brochure called *Cyprus for Cycling* that lists 19 recommended mountain bike rides around the South. These range from 2.5km to 19km from the Akamas Peninsula in the west to Cape Greco in the east.

Bringing Your Own Bike

One note of caution; before you leave home, go over your bicycle with a fine-toothed comb and fill your repair kit with every imaginable spare part. You won't necessarily be able to buy that crucial gismo for your machine when it breaks down somewhere in the back of beyond as the sun sets.

Bicycles can be brought over by plane. You can take them to pieces and put them in a bike bag or box, but it's much easier simply to wheel your bike to the check-in desk, where it should be treated as a piece of baggage. You may have to remove the pedals and turn the handlebars sideways so that it takes up less space in the hold; check all this with the airline before you make a booking.

Rental

Bicycles can be hired in most areas but particularly in the Troödos where they are usually flashy, multi-geared mountain bike types. Rates start from around CY£2.50 a day. Cycle hire is also very popular in the Agia Napa resort area.

Purchase

You can purchase a decent bicycle in the Republic if you are that keen, although you would be better off looking at one of the specialist shops in Lefkosia. Try **Zanetos Bicycles** *(☎ 2259 0945; 34 Agiou Dometiou, Strovolos)* in Lefkosia. Northern Cyprus will offer less of a choice when it comes to purchasing a bicycle. Better not count on it.

HITCHING

Hitchhiking is never entirely safe in any country in the world, and we don't recommend it. Travellers who decide to hitch should understand that they are taking a small but potentially serious risk. People who do choose to hitch will be safer if they travel in pairs and let someone know where they are planning to go.

Hitching in Cyprus is relatively easy but not very common. In rural areas where bus transport is poor, many locals hitch between their village and the city. If you do decide to hitch, stand in a prominent position with an obvious space for a ride-giver to pull in, keep your luggage to a minimum, look clean and smart and, above all, happy. A smile goes a long way.

Hitching in the North is more likely to be hampered by a lack of long-distance traffic than anything else and, in any case, public transport costs are low enough to essentially obviate the need to hitch.

LOCAL TRANSPORT

Bus

While urban bus services exist in Lefkosia, Lemesos, Larnaka and Famagusta, about the only two places where they are going to be of any practical use are in Larnaka (to get to and from the airport) and Lemesos, where buses go to and from the port (where cruises depart and dock). Distances between sights in most towns and cities are fairly short, so obviate the need to depend on the bus service. Buses also run to and from Kourion from Lemesos Fort, though these are tourist buses designed to get travellers from Lemesos out to the sights around Kourion rather than to move locals around.

Taxi

In the South, taxis are extensive and available on a 24-hour basis; they can be hailed from the street or taxi rank, or booked ahead by phone. All taxis are generally modern air-conditioned vehicles, usually comfortable Mercedes, and, apart from ones outside the major centres, are equipped with meters that drivers are obliged to use. There are two tariff periods: 6am to 8.30pm (Tariff 1) and 8.30pm to 6am (Tariff 2). Tariff 1 charges are CY£1.25 flag fall and CY£0.22 per kilometre. Tariff 2 charges are CY£1.65 flag fall and CY£0.26 per kilometre. Luggage is charged at the rate of CY£0.22 for every piece weighing more than 12kg. Extra charges of CY£0.60 per fare apply during most public holidays.

'Taxi sharing', such as is common in Greek cities such as Athens, is not permitted and taxi drivers are normally courteous and helpful.

In the North, taxis do not sport meters so agree on the fare with the driver beforehand.

As a rough guide expect to pay around TL2 million for a ride around any of the towns. A taxi ride from North Nicosia to Kyrenia (Girne) will cost around TL20 million; from North Nicosia to Famagusta TL50 million.

Service Taxi Taking up to eight people, service taxis are a useful transport option. They are run by an amalgamation of private companies called **Travel & Express** and have one national phone number (☎ 07 77 477). The individual offices can also be contacted directly: Lefkosia (☎ 2273 0888); Lemesos (☎ 2536 4114); Larnaka (☎ 2466 1010) and Pafos (☎ 2693 3181).

You can get to and from the above cities in the Republic by service taxi, but usually not directly to or from Pafos; a change in Lemesos will normally be the case. The fixed fares are competitive with bus travel. Either go to the service taxi office or phone to be picked up at your hotel. Note that pick-ups can often be up to 30 minutes later than booked, so build that into your plans if time is tight. Similarly, if you are departing from a service-taxi depot, expect to spend up to 30 minutes picking up other passengers before you actually get under way.

Northern Cyprus only has service taxis (sometimes referred to as *dolmuş*) between Kyrenia and North Nicosia, which cost TL2 million per person.

Tourist Taxis The 'tourist' taxis, that await you near the Turkish Cypriot checkpoint at the Ledra Palace Hotel, will take you anywhere you want to go around Northern Cyprus. A round-trip day tour to Kyrenia, Famagusta, Bellapais (Beylerbeyi), Buffavento and St Hilarion will cost around CY£30.

ORGANISED TOURS

Travel agencies around the South and in the North offer a wide variety of prepackaged excursions. Some reputable tour agencies in the South are

Amathus Tours (☎ 2536 9122, fax 2535 8354, ⓔ main@tourism.amathus.com.cy) Plateia Syntagmatos, Lemesos
National Tours (☎ 2236 6666, fax 2236 5230, ⓔ tourism@louisgroup.com) Leoforos Evagorou I 54–58, Lefkosia
Salamis Tours Excursions (☎ 2535 5555, fax 2536 4410) Salamis House, 28 Oktovriou, Lemesos

Land tours in the South usually run out of the main tourist centres and range from full-day tours out of Pafos to Troödos and the Kykkos Monastery for CY£15, day trips to Lefkosia from Agia Napa or Larnaka for CY£15, boat trips to Protaras from Agia Napa for CY£12 and half-day tours of Lemesos, a winery and Ancient Kourion for CY£11.

Lefkosia (South Nicosia)

ΛΕΥΚΩΣΙΑ • **Lefkoşa**
pop 47,800

The capital, known officially and to Greek speakers as Lefkosia, is often underrated and inappropriately described as boring, hot and dusty. It admittedly bears the ignominy of being the world's last divided city – split more or less evenly between the Turkish-occupied North and the Republican South. Berlin too was once divided, but eventually saw better days – a wish still fervently held by both Greek and Turkish Cypriots.

It can be searingly hot here in summer and relief by the sea is far away, but it is a lively, liveable city with fine restaurants, bars and cafés. Greek Cypriot Lefkosia (called South Nicosia by many English speakers) is sophisticated and worldly, with fine, tree-lined boulevards and an engaging mix of modern and old buildings. Turkish Cypriot North Nicosia (Lefkoşa) still retains its old-world charm and has changed very little since the city was forcibly divided in 1974. Either way, the residents of this city are not jaded by the excesses of packaged tourism and they bestow a warm welcome to visitors, whichever side of the line they live. Cyprus' capital deserves a few days of your time.

HISTORY

Lefkosia has always been the capital of Cyprus. It was established in the middle of the wide Mesaoria plain on the Pedieos River primarily for defence purposes. The city was originally known as Ledra and grew extensively during the Byzantine period. The Venetians, who briefly held Lefkosia from 1489, built the stone defensive walls around the city; however, these did little to keep the Ottomans out in 1570. Life in Lefkosia under the Ottomans saw little growth and only when the British took control in 1878 did the city begin to spread beyond the walls.

Violence inspired by the Ethniki Organosi tou Kypriakou Agona (EOKA; National Organisation for the Cypriot Struggle) against the British in the 1950s and then the Turkish Cypriots in the '60s saw considerable carnage on the streets of Lefkosia. Intercommunal disturbances between Greek and Turkish

- Explore the Venetian Ramparts that surround the Old City
- Wander along the infamous Green Line in Europe's last divided city
- Delve into the country's ancient past at the Cyprus Museum
- Take a day trip to the Mesaoria villages where living is done at a relaxed pace
- Dine in sophisticated restaurants with high-quality cuisine

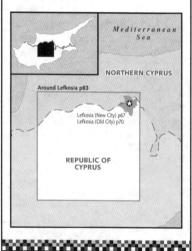

Mediterranean Sea

NORTHERN CYPRUS

Around Lefkosia p83

Lefkosia (New City) p67
Lefkosia (Old City) p70

REPUBLIC OF CYPRUS

Cypriots in 1963 brought a de facto partition of the city. The so-called 'Green Line' came into being at this time when the British military defined the Greek and Turkish areas using a green pen on a military map. The name has stuck to this day. The Turkish invasion of 1974 finally divided the city and it has remained so ever since, chaperoned by the watchful but increasingly weary eyes of UN peacekeeping forces.

ORIENTATION

The Old City is inside the 16th-century Venetian wall and is the most interesting area for visitors; the New City sprawls outwards south of the wall. Reduced in height and dissected by wide thoroughfares, the

LEFKOSIA (NEW CITY)

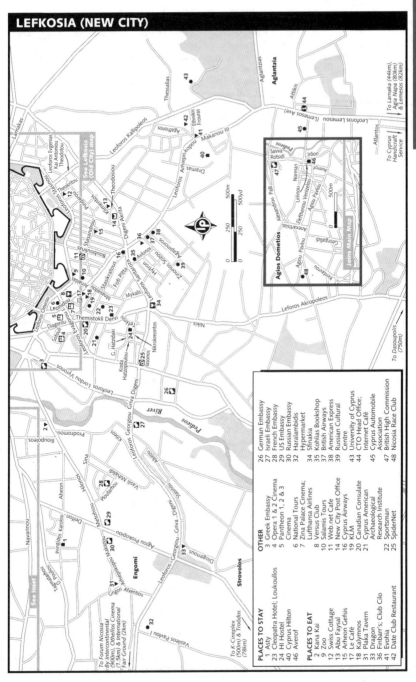

See Lefkosia (Old City) map

Joins Main Map

See Inset

PLACES TO STAY
1 Asty
23 Cleopatra Hotel; Loukoullos
24 HI Hostel
40 Cyprus Hilton
46 Averof

PLACES TO EAT
2 Kana Kai
9 Zoo
12 Swiss Cottage
13 Abu Faysal
15 Arheon Gefsis
17 Le Café
18 Kalymnos
31 Plaka Tavern
33 Dragon
36 Finbarr's; Club Clio
41 Evohia
42 Date Club Restaurant

OTHER
3 Greek Embassy
4 Opera 1 & 2 Cinema
5 Pantheon 1, 2 & 3
   Cinema
6 National Tours
7 Zina Palace Cinema;
   Lufthansa Airlines
8 Versus Club
10 Salamis Tours
11 Web.net Cafe
14 New City Post Office
16 Cyprus Airways
19 KLM
20 Canadian Consulate
21 Cyprus American
   Archaeological
   Research Institute
22 Sportsman
25 SpiderNet
26 German Embassy
27 Israeli Embassy
28 French Embassy
29 US Embassy
30 Russian Embassy
32 Haralambidis
   Hypermarket
34 Sfinakia
35 Kohlias Bookshop
37 British Airways
38 American Express
39 Russian Cultural
   Centre
43 University of Cyprus
44 CTO Head Office;
   Internet Café
45 Cyprus Automobile
   Association
47 British High Commission
48 Nicosia Race Club

wall is hardly visible in places. The town centre is Plateia Eleftherias on the south-western edge of the wall. The UN crossover point (Ledra Palace Hotel checkpoint) is at the far west and Famagusta Gate is near the Carafa Bastion to the east. At the base of the wall there are car parks and municipal gardens. See the North Nicosia (Lefkoşa) chapter for orientation tips on that half of the city.

Maps

The Cyprus Tourist Organisation (CTO; see Tourist offices later) has a fairly reasonable map of *Lefkosia City Centre* and, on the reverse side, *Major Lefkosia*. This is available free from all CTO offices. The *Street & Tourist Map of Nicosia* has a much better coverage of the outer suburbs and also has a street index. This map is available from most bookshops or stationery shops in Lefkosia or from **Selas Ltd** *(PO Box 8619, Lefkosia)*.

Some bookshops stock a street directory of sorts, but it is fairly poorly produced and not of much practical value. Public street map displays of the 'You Are Here' kind are found around central Lefkosia.

INFORMATION
Tourist Offices

The **CTO** *(☎ 2244 4264; Aristokyprou 11, Laïki Yitonia, CY-1011; open 8.30am-4pm Mon-Fri, 8.30am-2pm Sat)* is in a fairly touristy, restored area of the Old City. The CTO head office *(☎ 2233 7715, fax 331 644; Leoforos Lemesou 19)* is in the New City, though it is not really geared to handling over-the-counter queries from the public.

Money

The **Hellenic Bank** *(Solonos 1a; open 2.30pm-6.30pm Mon-Fri Sept-May, 2.30pm-8pm June-Aug)*, near the CTO, provides an afternoon tourist service.

There are a couple of ATMs at the northern end of Lidras that accept most cards, though most banks in the New City will equally accept your plastic and dispense ready cash.

The **American Express office** *(☎ 2276 5607; Agapinoros 2d; open 8.30am-5pm Mon-Fri, 9am-1.30pm Sat)* is in the New City.

Post

The central **post office** *(☎ 2230 3123; Konstantinou Paleologou; open 9am-1pm & 3pm-6pm Mon, Tues, Thur & Fri, 8.30am-1pm Sat)* is east of Plateia Eleftherias. This is where poste-restante mail comes to. There is also a small post office close to the northern end of Lidras near the Green Line lookout and another branch in the New City.

Telephone

The main telephone centre in Lefkosia is the **Cyprus Telecommunications Authority** (CYTA) close to Pafos Gate. It has some phone booths inside and outside the building. There is no real cause to go there since public phones are widely available around the city, with a large concentration on Plateia Eleftherias.

Email & Internet Access

In the New City there's **Web.net Cafe** *(☎ 2275 3345; Stasandrou 10c; open 10.30am-midnight daily)*. Access charges are CY£2.20 per hour or CY£0.50 for less than 15 minutes.

On the edge of the Old City is **Nicosia Palace Arcade** *(☎ 2266 3653; Leoforos Kostaki Pantelidi; open 10am-11pm daily)*.

In the New City is the somewhat inconveniently situated **Internet Café** *(☎ 2233 9936; Leoforos Lemesou 17a; open noon-2am Mon-Fri & 2pm-2am Sat & Sun)* near the CTO.

Travel Agencies

While there is a large number of travel agencies throughout Lefkosia, none of them is likely to offer significant price advantages over the others. **Salamis Tours Ltd** *(☎ 2276 2323, fax 2275 8337; Arnaldas 7c)* in the New City arranges airline tickets and other travel-related bookings, including cruise tickets for Salamis Lines.

Bookshops

There are only a few bookshops in Lefkosia that may be of interest to the foreign visitor. Foremost among these is the **Moufflon Bookshop** *(☎ 2266 5155, fax 2266 8703; e bookshop@moufflon.com.cy; Sofouli 1)* in the New City. This shop deals primarily in English-language titles – new and second hand – and stocks a wide range of LP guides. It has a good section of books on Cyprus both in English and in Greek.

Kohlias Bookshop *(☎ 2246 1766, fax 2244 6258; Avlonos 9)* specialises in art books and Cypriot publications, while the **Soloneion Book Centre** *(☎ 2266 6799; Vyzantiou 24,*

Strovolos), a little south of the New City, might also serve your needs. **MAM** (☎ *2275 3536;* e *mam@mam.cy.net; Konstantinou Paleologou 19)* is a leading academic bookstore that is worth seeking out.

Foreign-language newspapers and magazines can be found at either of the **Periptero Hellas** or **Miltis & Evgenis** kiosks on the west side of Plateia Eleftherias.

Libraries
At least five public or semipublic libraries in Lefkosia are open for research and reading, although you cannot take books home.

Ahilleios Library (☎ 2276 3033) Konstantinou Paleologou 30
Lefkosia Municipal Arts Centre Library (☎ 2243 2577) Apostolou Varnava 19
Makarios Cultural Foundation Library (☎ 2243 0008) Plateia Arhiepiskopou Kyprianou
Ministry of Education Library (☎ 2230 3180) Konstantinou Paleologou
Severios Library (☎ 2234 4888) Plateia Arhiepiskopou Kyprianou

Universities
The only university in the Republic of Cyprus is on the southeastern side of the New City. The **University of Cyprus** (☎ *2289 2000, fax 2289 2100;* w *www.ucy.ac.cy; Kallipoleos 75; PO Box 20537, CY-1678 Lefkosia)* was established in 1989 and admitted its first students in 1992. It currently has around 3000 undergraduate students and 500 postgraduate students.

Cultural Centres
A number of cultural centres offer a wide range of periodicals and books for reference. These include

British Council (☎ 2266 5152) Mouseiou 3
Cyprus American Archaeological Research Institute (☎ 2267 0832) Andrea Dimitriou 11
Russian Cultural Centre (☎ 2276 1607) Alasias 16

Laundry
Express Dry Cleaners *(Ippokratous 49)* in the Old City will do a service wash for you for about CY£4.

Toilets
Public toilets are scattered along the walls of the Venetian ramparts; the nearest ones to

the centre are by Plateia Eleftherias. There are also toilets in Laïki Yitonia, near the CTO office.

Medical Services
Lefkosia's **General Hospital** (☎ *2280 1400; Leoforos Nehrou)* is west of the Old City.

If you need a private doctor or pharmacy, ring ☎ 1432. Doctors' visiting hours are normally 9am to 1pm and 4pm to 7pm. Local newspapers list pharmacies, which are open during the night and on weekends and holidays, as well as the names of doctors who are on call out of normal hours.

Emergency
The **police station** (☎ *2247 7434)* in the Old City is at the northern end of Lidras, by the barrier. The general emergency numbers for police and ambulance are ☎ 199 or 112.

Dangers & Annoyances
Lefkosia is a remarkably safe city to walk around. The Old City streets, particularly near the Green Line, can appear dingy and threatening at night, though, and solo women may be best advised to avoid them. Steer clear of edgy soldiers at UN and Greek Cypriot checkpoints and keep your camera well hidden. While it is next to impossible to inadvertently stray across the Green Line in the Old City, there are still occasional reports of foreigners unwittingly (or perhaps wittingly) crossing the line at less well-guarded points in the western and eastern sectors of the New City.

WALKING TOUR
The New City is modern, clean and well-suited for shopping sprees or taking in a meal at a fine restaurant. Most of the sights, however, are within the Old City and are listed here in more or less west to east order. Allow yourself at least two days to see most of the major sights. To better orient yourself with the Old City, take one of the CTO guided walking tours, or pick up the CTO *Walking Tours* brochures and do it yourself (see boxed text 'Walking Tour of Old Lefkosia').

THINGS TO SEE & DO
Venetian Ramparts
While impressive looking, this circular defence wall that surrounds all of Old Lefkosia – North and South – failed in the

LEFKOSIA (OLD CITY)

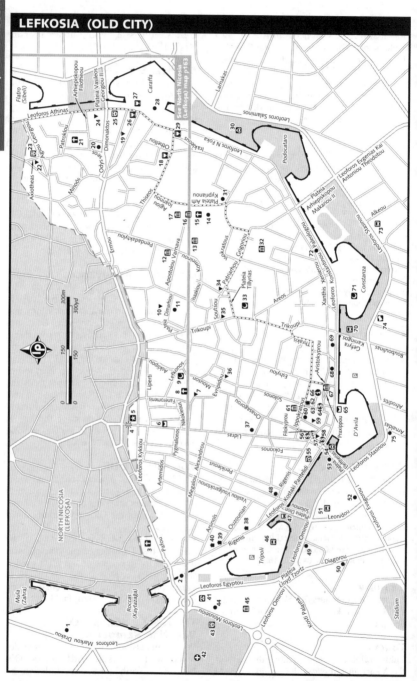

See North Nicosia (Lefkoşa) map p163

LEFKOSIA (OLD CITY)

PLACES TO STAY
38 Holiday Inn; Bonsai
39 Castelli Hotel; Pago Pago
40 Classic Hotel
62 Tony's Bed & Breakfast

PLACES TO EAT
7 To Steki tis Loxandras
10 Agios Georgios Taverna
19 Egeon
22 Taverna Axiothea
24 To Steki tis Chrysaliniotissas
34 Erodos
35 Zanettos Taverna
36 Estiatorio Savvas
57 Vasilis
59 1900 Paei Kairos

PUBS & BARS
18 Odos Othellou
26 Erotiko
27 Bastione
29 Ithaki

OTHER
1 Checkpoint (Ledra Palace Hotel)
2 Pafos Gate
3 Holy Cross Catholic Church
4 Lidras St Lookout
5 Police Station
6 Post Office
8 Faneromeni Church

9 Arablar Mosque
11 Municipal Market
12 Lefkosia Municipal Arts Centre & Library
13 Makarios Cultural Foundation & Library
14 Archbishop's Palace; Makarios III Statue
15 Agios Ioannis Church
16 Ethnographic Museum
17 National Struggle Museum
20 Chrysaliniotissa Crafts Centre
21 Panagia Hrysaliniotissa
23 University of Cyprus Workshop Theatre (thepak)
25 Theatro Ena
28 Famagusta Gate
30 Travel & Express Service Taxis
31 Severios Library
32 The House of Hatzigeorgakis Kornesios
33 Omeriye Mosque
37 Woolworths; Ledra Museum-Observatory
41 CYTA Telephone Office
42 Lefkosia General Hospital
43 Municipal Theatre and Box Office
44 British Council
45 Cyprus Museum
46 Buses to Lemesos, Pafos & Larnaka

47 Urban Bus Station; A Petsas & Sons
48 Andreas Papaeracleous Photo Store
49 Olympic Airways
50 Moufflon Bookshop
51 Buses to Pedoulas, Platres, Kambos & Kykkos
52 Alitalia
53 Periptero Hellas; Miltis & Evgenis Kiosk
54 Taxi Stand
55 Nicosia Palace Arcade
56 ATM
58 ATM
60 Express Dry Cleaners
61 Leventis Municipal Museum
63 Laïki Yitonia
64 Hellenic Bank
65 Central Post Office
66 CTO; Toilets
67 Cyprus Jewellers Museum
68 Cyprus Handicrafts Centre
69 MAM
70 Buses to Agia Napa, Troödos & Kakopetria
71 Bayraktar Mosque
72 Ahilleios Library
73 PEAL. Bus to Protaras & Paralimni
74 Australian High Commission
75 Virgin Records

purpose for which it was built. The Venetian rulers erected the wall between 1567 and 1570 with the express aim of keeping the feared Ottoman Turk invaders out of Lefkosia. The appointed engineer Ascanio Savorgnano designed the ramparts and Francesco Barbaro built the walls to specifications, while adding 11 fortifying bastions spaced equally around the ramparts for added protection. A moat was also dug, though it was apparently never intended to contain water. In July 1570 the Ottomans landed in Larnaka and three months later attacked Lefkosia, storming the fortifications.

The ramparts have remained in place more or less unchanged ever since. Five of the bastions – the **Tripoli**, **D'Avila**, **Constanza**, **Podocataro** and **Caraffa** – are still in the southern sector of Lefkosia. The **Flatro** bastion on the eastern side of the Old City is occupied by Turkish, Greek Cypriot and UN military forces, while the remaining bastions – the **Loredano** (Cevizli), **Barbaro** (Musalla), the **Quirini** (Cephane), **Mula** (Zahra) and **Roccas** (Kaytazağa) – are in North Nicosia.

The ramparts and moat in Lefkosia are in excellent condition and are used to provide car parking space and venues for outdoor concerts, strolling and relaxing. In the North, the walls are in poorer shape and have become overgrown and dilapidated in parts. Three gates originally punctured the walls: the Famagusta Gate in the east, the Pafos Gate in the west (both described later) and the **Kyrenia (Girne) Gate** in the north. Vehicle access roads at various points around the ramparts now allow regular traffic access to the Old City.

Roccas Bastion (Kaytazağa Burcu) The Roccas Bastion is unique throughout Cyprus in that it is the only place where Greek and Turkish Cypriots may eyeball each other at close quarters. It is situated about 200m south of the Ledra Palace Hotel crossing (see later) and is easily identifiable by signs prohibiting parking adjacent to the bastion walls. Look up and you will see barbed wire fencing and, more often than not, a clutch of curious Turkish Cypriot

Walking Tour of Old Lefkosia

The following will take you along some of the main streets of the Old City and past many of its museums (see individual entries later for full details).

From Plateia Eleftherias follow Lidras and turn right onto Ippokratous. At No 17 is the **Leventis Municipal Museum**, which traces the city's development from prehistoric times to the present.

Continue to the end of Ippokratous, turn left onto Thrakis and take the dogleg onto Trikoupi. Soon you'll see the **Omeriye Mosque** on your right. Turn right onto Plateia Tyllirias and shortly after you will reach Patriarhou Grigoriou. About 125m along this street on the right is the 18th-century house of **Dragoman Hatzigeorgakis**, which is now a museum.

The next left leads to Plateia Arhiepiskopou Kyprianou, dominated by the Archbishop's Palace and a colossal statue of Makarios III. Here you'll find the Makarios Cultural Foundation, comprising the **European Art Gallery**, the **Greek Independence War Gallery** and the **Byzantine Art Museum**. In the grounds of the Foundation is Agios Ioannis Church, which was built in 1662 and has the most wonderful frescoes dating from 1736. Next door is the **Ethnographic Museum**, and still nearby is the **National Struggle Museum**.

Continue north along Agiou Ioannou and turn right onto Thiseos, which leads onto Leoforos N Foka. Turn left and you'll see the imposing **Famagusta Gate**, which was once the main entrance to the city. From here it is a 400m walk past Lefkosia's trendy **night-time dining area** along Leoforos Athinas to where the street abruptly ends at the barbed wire and UN watchtowers of the **Flatro Bastion**. The most direct way back to Laïki Yitonia is to take Leoforos N Foka, following the signposts to the CTO. Check out the **Venetian ramparts** along the way.

faces looking down into what for them is forbidden territory. The UN buffer zone separating the two sides by a normally comfortable margin virtually disappears here for a stretch of about 200m, while the border of Turkish-controlled Northern Cyprus ends at the very edge of this bastion.

Most passers-by studiously avoid making eye contact with the curious onlookers on the Turkish Cypriot side, though a waved greeting will more often than not attract a smile and friendly wave in return. If you are in North Nicosia you can easily reach the Turkheld side of the Roccas Bastion. See the boxed text 'Walking Tour of Lefkoşa' in the North Nicosia (Lefkoşa) chapter for details.

Ledra Palace Hotel Crossing

People come here in droves to gawk at the only spot on the whole of the island where you may cross into the North. To the right, and just before the Greek Cypriot police checkpoints, are the remains of a ruined building, ostensibly once the **Karpasia Restaurant**, which is occasionally reincarnated and used as a summer *mezes* joint. Its roofless interior is now filled with abundant graffiti and a cement wall at the rear of the outside courtyard, covered with more graffiti, sports a couple of viewing holes where

you may observe life on the other side of the line across what used to be a sports field.

The crossing is partially blocked by a blue and white painted wall with graphic posters depicting the murder of three Greek Cypriots by Turkish counter-demonstrators near Deryneia in the eastern part of the island in 1996. On Sunday mornings Cypriot women gather to remember the 1974 invasion and hand out literature to the accompaniment of suitable songs of lamentation and protest.

While crossing to the North is legal and practised by many visitors (see the boxed text 'Crossing the Thin Green Line' in the Getting Around chapter), it is tacitly not encouraged and the Greek Cypriot police who register your departure do so with a resigned look of disapproval. The crossing itself is about 300m long and is bordered by barbed and razor wire for the entire length. To the left as you head north is the bullet-ridden former Ledra Palace Hotel, now occupied by the UN. Abandoned shops lie to the right. A white iron gate marks the entry to Turkish Cypriot–controlled territory after which lies the fairly innocuous Turkish Cypriot checkpoint building. A prominent sign welcomes you to the 'Turkish Republic of Northern Cyprus' while another sign reminds you that the 'TRNC is here to stay'.

Cyprus Museum

This museum (☎ 2286 5888; Mouseiou 1; admission CY£1.50; open 9am-5pm Mon-Sat, 10am-1pm Sun) houses the best collection of archaeological finds in Cyprus. The original building, erected in 1883, is looking tired but the collection is exemplary. It's a 10-minute walk west of Plateia Eleftherias.

Highlights include a remarkable display of **terracotta figures** found in 1929 at Agia Irini, north of Morfou (Güzelyurt) in the North. These figures are displayed as found and are presumed to have come from a warrior caste perhaps practising a fertility cult in the 7th to 6th centuries BC. All the figures are male and most have helmets. Another highlight is a collection of three **limestone lions** and **two sphinxes** found in the Tamassos necropolis south of Lefkosia. The statues show a definite Egyptian influence and were only discovered in 1997. They date from the Cypro-Archaic II period (475–400 BC).

Look out also for the famous **Aphrodite of Soli** statue marketed widely as the 'face of Cyprus' on tourist posters and also on the CY£5 banknote. An enormous bronze statue of **Emperor Septimus Severus**, found at Kythrea (Değirmenlik) in 1928, is the main exhibit in Room 6 and can hardly be overlooked. Don't miss the fascinating display of **Cypriot mining and metallurgy** history tucked away in Room 13. It makes a refreshing diversion from the abundant but often dry exhibits of bowls, craters and statuettes from Cyprus' more distant archaeological past.

Pafos Gate

This gate, known by the Venetians as the Porta Domenica, is the third of the traditional entrances to Old Lefkosia. The other two are the Famagusta Gate (see later in this chapter) and the **Kyrenia Gate** in North Nicosia. The Pafos Gate, left firmly open, guards a narrow pedestrian passage under the wall. The adjoining breach in the wall that allows traffic into the Old City is a much later addition.

Holy Cross Catholic Church

Across the road, east of the Pafos Gate on Pafou, this church carries the unfortunate status of having its rear end stuck smack bang up against the Turkish sector and it lies within the UN buffer zone. Despite this, the church still functions as a place of worship on the proviso that the back door leading onto the Turkish-controlled sector remains firmly closed. Mass times are posted inside the front door vestibule.

Faneromeni Church

This impressive structure on Faneromenis was built in 1872 on the site of an ancient orthodox nunnery and is the largest church within the city walls. The **Marble Mausoleum** on the eastern side of the church was built in memory of martyrs of the newly declared Greek War of Independence who were executed by the Turks in 1821.

The Green Line

While you can hardly miss the Green Line if you walk anywhere north in Lefkosia, in practice there is not a lot to see. UN and Greek Cypriot **bunkers** punctuate the Line across the city and you are not supposed to approach them too closely or get your camera out. The CTO signposted walking tour takes you hard up to the Line at the far eastern side of the city close to the military-controlled **Flatro Bastion**. Take the last turn left off Leoforos Athinas along Agiou Georgiou and look for the little street on the right with Taverna Axiothea (see Places to Eat later in this chapter). Walk to the end of Axiotheas and squeeze through the gap into the next street, following the walking-tour sign. You won't see a soul on the other side, but you may hear the *muezzin* (cantor who calls people to prayer) from the mosque. An area of particular desolation and destruction is towards the end of **Pendadaktylou** where it meets **Ermou**, the street that originally bisected the old city more or less equally into two. You will only meet an edgy soldier or two here.

Most visitors head for the **Lidras St lookout**. From here you can peer over a wall at a streetscape left as it was on 20 July 1974. Look for the many bullet holes and observe the Turkish and Turkish Cypriot flags fluttering no more than 100m distant. No photographs are allowed here and you are most certainly not allowed to proceed any further. Apart from possibly provoking an international incident, it is thought that many of the streets and ruined buildings are booby-trapped with mines.

Arablar Mosque

You could almost miss this tiny mosque, squirreled away as it is on Lefkosia's back-streets. In Lusignan times it was the church of the Stavros tou Misirikou. The building, which is on Lefkonos, is no longer open to the public.

Ledra Museum-Observatory

This unusual museum (☎ 2267 9396; 11th floor, Shakolas Tower, cnr Lidras & Arsinois; admission CY£0.50; open 10am-8pm Mon-Sat, 10am-6pm Sun) houses the Woolworths department store. You can use telescopes and gaze at the whole of Lefkosia from a particularly good vantage point. It is the only point where you can see over into North Nicosia to any degree.

Leventis Municipal Museum

This is a small, two-storey historical museum (☎ 2267 3375; Ippokratous 17; admission free; open 10am-4.30pm Tues-Sun) with exhibits dating from before 2000 BC to the present day. Among items on display are household equipment, traditional dress, books and prints. There is also a gift shop.

Laïki Yitonia

It's twee, fairly expensive, touristy and busy, but it looks prettier than most of old Lefkosia. Laïki Yitonia (Popular Neighbourhood) is a refurbished part of the Old City designed to catch the tourist trade with shops and restaurants. It's a bit like the Plaka district of Athens but smaller and without the backdrop of the Acropolis. You can traverse the whole area in no more than 10 minutes during which time restaurant touts will attempt to lure you into their establishments to eat. There is a wide choice of eating places, but a surprising dearth of outdoor cafeterias or bars where you can sit down and have a cold beer or an iced coffee. The CTO has an office here and you can stock up on most maps and other tourist brochures free of charge.

Cyprus Jewellers Museum

This small museum (☎ 2266 7278; Praxippou 7-9; admission free; open 10am-4pm Mon-Fri) in Laïki Yitonia presents the history of jewellery from the end of the 19th century to today. The exhibits include ornaments, religious items, silver utensils and old tools.

Cyprus Handicrafts Centre

This well-run and -presented centre (☎ 2230 5024; Athalassis 186; open 7.30am-2.30pm Mon-Fri, 3pm-6pm Thur) is a government-sponsored foundation that aims to preserve Cypriot handicrafts. Here you can watch pottery, woodwork, embroidery and other crafts being practised and nurtured. Many of the products are on sale for visitors.

Bayraktar Mosque

This prominent mosque, situated on the Constanza Bastion, marks the spot where the Venetian Walls were successfully breached by the Ottomans in 1570. The Ottoman standard bearer (for whom the mosque is named in Turkish) was immediately cut down by the defending forces but his body was subsequently recovered and buried on this spot. The mosque has been the target for terrorist activity. In the early 1960s EOKA-inspired attacks damaged the mosque and nearby tomb of the standard bearer, but it was eventually repaired and the mosque closed to the general public. In 1999 a plot was uncovered to bomb the mosque.

Omeriye Mosque

This structure (Ömeriye Camii; Trikoupi & Plateia Tyllirias; open any time prayers are not being conducted), dating from the 14th century, was originally the Augustinian Church of St Mary, which was destroyed by the Ottomans as they entered Lefkosia in 1570. The church was subsequently restored as a mosque based on a belief that this was the spot where the Muslim prophet Omer rested in the 7th century. Its rather tall minaret can be easily spotted some distance away and entrance to the mosque is from about halfway along Trikoupi. Today the mosque is used primarily as a place of worship by visiting Muslims from neighbouring Arab countries. Non-Muslims may of course visit as long you observe the general etiquette required when visiting mosques – dress conservatively, leave your shoes at the door and avoid official prayer times.

House of Hatzigeorgakis Kornesios

This well-preserved and richly restored mansion (☎ 2230 5316; Patriarhou Grigoriou 20; admission CY£0.75; open 8am-2pm Mon-Fri, 9am-1pm Sat) belonged to Kornesios, the

Great Dragoman of Cyprus from 1779 to 1809. A dragoman was an 'interpreter' (tercüman in Turkish), or liaison officer, between the Ottoman and Orthodox authorities. Kornesios was a particularly wealthy and influential dragoman, said to be the most powerful man in Cyprus at the time. His lavish excess was his undoing. A peasant revolt in 1804 forced him out of Cyprus. Returning from exile five years later he was accused of treason, beheaded and his property was confiscated. Today only one room is set up as mock living quarters and it is spread with rich floor coverings and decorations. The rest of the mansion is given over to displays of antiques and other Ottoman memorabilia.

Archbishop's Palace
This mock Venetian building on Plateia Arhiepiskopou Kyprianou was the scene of much fighting during the 1956 disturbances and during the 1974 military coup and subsequent Turkish invasion of the North. While generally closed to the public, the building is the official residence of the Archbishop of Cyprus. The present building dates from 1974 when the original palace was badly damaged by the fighting. The Palace is overshadowed by an massive and looming black statue of Archbishop Makarios III, which stares out impassively over the square.

Makarios Cultural Foundation
This complex (☎ 2243 0008; Plateia Arhiepiskopou Kyprianou; admission CY£1; open 9am-4.30pm Mon-Fri, 9am-1pm Sat) consists of three main exhibit areas. The **European Art Gallery** presents 120 oil paintings of various European schools of art from the 16th to the 19th centuries. The themes are mainly religious with works by Van Dyck, Rubens, Tintoretto, Lorraine and Delacroix.

Nearby is the **Greek Independence War Gallery**, which contains maps, copper engravings and paintings featuring persons and events from the Greek War of Independence in 1821. The **Byzantine Art Museum** has the largest collection of icons related to Cyprus. There are some 220 pieces on display, covering several periods from the 5th to the 19th centuries. Among the more interesting items on display are the icons of **Christ & the Virgin Mary** (12th century) from the Church of the Virgin Mary of Arakas at Lagoudera and the **Resurrection** (13th century) from the

Church of St John Lambadistis Monastery at Kalopanayiotis. In addition, there are six examples of the Kanakaria Mosaics, which were originally stolen from the Panagia Kanakaria (Kanakaria Church) in North Cyprus after the 1974 Turkish invasion.

Ethnographic Museum
Close to the Makarios Cultural Foundation, this small museum (☎ 2243 2578; Plateia Arhiepiskopou Kyprianou; admission CY£1; open 9am-5pm Mon-Fri, 10am-1pm Sat) is the main folk art and ethnographic museum in the country. The building dates back to the 15th century though some later additions have been made. Here you will see fine examples of embroidery, lace, costumes, pottery, metalwork, basketry, folk painting, leatherwork and woodcarving.

National Struggle Museum
This display is really for die-hard history buffs. The museum (☎ 2230 5878; Kinyras 7; admission CY£0.25; open 8am-2pm Mon-Fri, 3pm-7pm Thur) displays documents, photos and other memorabilia from the often bloody 1955–59 National Liberation Struggle against the British.

Lefkosia Arts Centre
For something a little less cerebral than the museums, duck into the little arcade to the right of the National Struggle Museum and head along Apostolou Varnava for one block to this rather avant-garde arts centre (☎ 2243 2577; Apostolou Varnava 19; admission free but donations welcome; open 10am-3pm & 5pm-11pm Tues-Sat, 10am-4pm Sun). Its air-conditioned interior contains an occasionally bizarre but mostly fascinating collection of art. The permanent collection includes paintings and sculptures and works from the Pierides Art gallery in Greece. Periodical exhibitions vary monthly. The centre also has a coffee shop and art library for visitors.

Famagusta Gate
The much-photographed Famagusta Gate (Pyli Ammohostou; open 9am-1pm & 4pm-7pm Mon-Fri) is the best preserved of the three original gates that led into the old city of Lefkosia. It's in the Caraffa Bastion off Leoforos Athinas. Its impressive wooden door and sloping facade opens out onto a tunnel that leads through the rampart wall.

The whole structure was revamped and renovated in 1981 and now serves as a concert venue and exhibition hall. Outside the tunnel and to the right is a small open-air arena where concerts by visiting artists are held, usually during the summer months. The area surrounding the gate has become a rather trendy dining and eating place for fashionable Lefkosians (see Places to Eat and also Entertainment later in this chapter).

Panagia Hrysaliniotissa

This church (Arhiepiskopou Filotheou) is dedicated to the Virgin Mary and means 'Our Lady of the Golden Flax' in Greek. It is considered to be the oldest Byzantine church in Lefkosia and was built in 1450 by Queen Helena Paleologos. It is renowned for its rich collection of old and rare icons.

Chrysaliniotissa Crafts Centre

This small arts centre (Dimonaktos 2; open 10am-1pm & 3pm-6pm Mon-Fri, 10am-1pm Sat) is worth dropping into for its display of Cypriot arts and crafts. Eight workshops and a coffee shop surround a central courtyard in a building designed on the lines of a traditional inn.

SPECIAL EVENTS

The Cyprus State Fairs Authority (☎ 2235 2918, 2235 2316; ⓦ www.csfa.org.cy; PO Box 23551, CY-1684 Lefkosia) is responsible for three annual fairs and exhibitions. The biggest is the annual Cyprus International fair that takes place between May and June; the Motorshow takes place in the first week of November; Offitec is a tech-fest of computers, office machines and telecommunications equipment. All events are held at the International Fair Grounds in the western suburb of Makedonitissa.

PLACES TO STAY – BUDGET

There is very little budget accommodation left in Lefkosia. Most of what once existed has either closed or upgraded to a mid-range category. There are a couple of options worth looking at.

HI Hostel (☎ 2267 4808, 9943 8360; Hatzidaki 5; dorm beds CY£5) is in a quiet part of the New City about six blocks from Plateia Eleftherias. Follow the signs from Tefkrou, off Themistokli Dervi. It is basic but quite reasonable for a cheap sleep.

As central as you can get is Tony's Bed & Breakfast (☎ 2266 6752, fax 2266 2225; Solonos 13; singles/doubles CY£18/28). The place is homely and friendly enough, though the rooms are a bit pokey. Nonetheless they have a fridge, TV and air-con and there's just enough room left for a bed.

PLACES TO STAY – MID-RANGE

Out on the western edge of the New City are two older hotels. The two-star Asty (☎ 2277 3030, fax 2277 3311; Pringipos Karolou 12; singles/doubles CY£38.50/63) is a pleasant and quiet hotel with comfortable rooms over in Engomi.

Closer to the Old City is the sometimes snooty Averof (☎ 2277 3447, fax 2277 3411; Averof 19; singles/doubles CY£22.50/31.50). It is near the British High Commission and in an even quieter part of Lefkosia.

Just inside the Old City are a couple of newer mid-range hotels. The three-star Classic Hotel (☎ 2266 4006, fax 2267 0072; ⓦ www.classic.com.cy; Rigenis 94; singles/doubles CY£38/48) is a member of the 'Small Luxury Hotels of the World' group. It's a neat, modernistic place with minimalist decor and smart, comfortable rooms.

Close by is the more recently opened three-star Castelli Hotel (☎ 2271 2812, fax 2268 0176; ⓔ hinnicres@cytanet.com.cy; Ouzounian 38; singles/doubles CY£72/99). Pitched mainly at the business market, the Castelli staff are subsequently rather diffident towards dishevelled looking travellers, but the rooms are unquestionably smart and comfortable with Internet ports in each room and a hotel sauna.

Equally diffident and somewhat snobbish is the four-star Cleopatra Hotel (☎ 2235 6666, fax 2235 1918; Floridis 8; ⓔ cleohotel@cleopatra.com.cy; singles/doubles CY£58/75). Again, this hotel looks to business clients for its bread and butter so travellers with scruffy bags or clothes may be frowned upon or ignored altogether. Being an older hotel, rooms aren't quite as well appointed as the other business hotels.

PLACES TO STAY – TOP END

All top-end options are in the New City and, with only one exception, are within a reasonable walking distance of the Old City.

The four-star Forum Nicosia By Intercontinental (☎ 2235 6666, fax 2235 1918;

e *forum@louishotels.com; Leoforos Georgiou Griva Digeni; singles/doubles from CY£65/ 112)* is the only one of the bunch that is a little way out of town, in the western suburb of Engomi. It has excellent rooms and facilities, and a 30% discount applies from 1 July to 31 August.

Just inside the Old City is the handy, very comfortable but somewhat overpriced four-star **Holiday Inn** *(☎ 2271 2712, fax 2267 3337;* e *hinnicres@cytanet.com.cy; Rigenis 70; singles/doubles CY£110/130).* It's pleasant, yet sterile and undistinguished from most top-end chain hotels. There's a good Japanese restaurant (see Places to Eat) an indoor pool, fitness room and sauna for guests and conference facilities for business visitors.

The five-star **Cyprus Hilton** *(☎ 2237 7777, fax 2237 7788;* w *www.hilton.com; Arhiepiskopou Makariou III; singles/doubles CY£139/156)* is Lefkosia's premier hotel with luxurious rooms, indoor and outdoor pool, tennis and squash courts and in-house restaurants. Unpublished discounts also apply from 1 July to 31 August.

PLACES TO EAT

Lefkosia offers three basic location options: eating in the Old City, the New City or the burgeoning suburbs to the east or west. While we stick mainly to options in the New and Old Cities, suburbs such as Engomi to the west or Strovolos to the south have their own culinary enclaves and a drive to either may turn up some surprise finds.

Dining in Lefkosia can be a real treat. Because the city is not a prime tourist target, it is thankfully bereft of low-quality, high-cost tourist traps that pander to foreign palates. The growing internationalism of Cyprus, coupled with the fact that many Cypriots now hanker after cuisines other than their own, means that there is a wide array of ethnic cuisines available. Chinese and Indian restaurants are among two of the main growth areas.

A word of warning: Many restaurants in Lefkosia close down for a couple of weeks in August for annual holidays. Phone beforehand to be on the safe side.

Old City

Dining here is centred on two main areas with a sprinkling of low-frills, cheap eateries scattered in between. Laïki Yitonia is

mainly popular with the lunchtime crowd of day-trippers, who then normally retreat to the coast, while the Famagusta Gate strip attracts mainly evening revellers, most of whom are locals.

Laïki Yitonia & Around It doesn't look much, but **Vasilis** *(☎ 2267 5661; Plateia Eleftherias; sandwiches CY£1.50)* is quick and cheap, and the sandwiches washed down with an icy beer after a hard day walking the streets of Lefkosia are filling and welcome.

Hidden away in the back streets of Old Lefkosia is the locals' dining strip. For a selection of Cypriot staples or a huge *mezes* spread, head for **Zanettos Taverna** *(☎ 2276 5501; Trikoupi 65; mains CY£2.50-3).* Also worth checking out is **Estiatorio Savvas** *(☎ 2276 3444; Solonos 65; open noon-4.30pm Mon-Sat).* It's unadorned, simple and basic but offers good home-cooked dishes, as does **Agios Georgios Taverna** *(☎ 2276 5971; Plateia Paliou Dimarhiou 27; grills CY£2.50-4.50)* on the northern side of the market.

1900 Paei Kairos *(☎ 2266 7668; Pasikratous 11-15; mezes CY£2.50-4.50)* is a bit of a prize for the Laïki Yitonia area. It's a neat little Greek-style *mezedopoleio*. It specialises in mix-and-match *mezedes* such as *stryftari* (a pie made up of five cheeses), eggplant stuffed with cheese in filo pastry or eggplant patties. Wash it all down with *tsipouro* (a clear, distilled spirit) or a selection of mainly Greek wines.

Another Greek-style *mezes* and steak joint is the smallish **To Steki tis Loxandras** *(☎ 2267 5757; Faneromenis 67; mezes CY£6.50; open evenings only).* It's best to book if you want a table as the demand is high on weekends. The food quality is refined and excellent.

Blink and you might just miss the atmospheric **Erodos** *(☎ 2275 2250; Patriarhou Grigoriou 1; mains CY£4-8)* nestled among leafy foliage on Plateia Tyllirias and abutting the Omeriye Mosque. Have a beer or a full meal – the *afelia* (pork cubes in red sauce) is excellent. Vegetarians could try *yemista* (stuffed tomatoes and peppers) or *koupepia* (vine leaves stuff with savoury rice).

International Cuisine Polynesia has come to Lefkosia in the **Pago Pago** *(☎ 2271 2812; Ouzounian 38; mains CY£7.50-10; open lunch & dinner)* located in Castelli Hotel (see Places to Stay). The decor is mock-Pacific, but very pleasant. Tahitian duck (CY£10) is a recommended main course. Live Cuban music is played most evenings.

The best Japanese food in town is to be found at **Bonsai** (☎ 2271 2712; *Rigenis 70; mains CY£5-9; open lunch & dinner*) tucked away deep inside the Holiday Inn (see also Places to Stay). While not cheap (Japanese cuisine rarely is), it is of high quality. Seafood lovers will head for the special *nigiri* sushi (CY£11.60) consisting of raw tuna, hamour, sword fish, omelette, salmon, mackerel, octopus, shrimp, squid and California rolls. Fried rice is CY£2.

Famagusta Gate Area This area is a popular night-time dining enclave.

A little, unassuming joint on the last street before the barricades is **Taverna Axiothea** (☎ 2243 0787; *Axiotheas 9; mains CY£3-4*). It is good for low-priced and tasty *mezedes*.

To Steki tis Chrysaliniotissas (☎ 2243 0772; *Athinas; grills CY£3-4*) is a little restaurant that spills out onto busy Athinas. Having *mezedes* is the best option here and, unlike some other restaurants that can overdo it, To Steki has just about the right balance of dishes that are both tasty and imaginative.

Open evenings only, the ever-so-discreet yet very popular **Egeon** (☎ 2243 3297; *Ektoros 40; mezes CY£7-12*) draws a faithful following of mainly local devotees. You dine in an atmospheric old house on a rich platter of imaginative *mezedes*. Bookings are essential.

New City

Cafés A bright and modern place in the heart of the New City, **Le Café** (☎ 2275 5151; *Arhiepiskopou Makariou III 16; snacks CY£2-3*) is popular with Lefkosia trendies. Pasta and salads are popular menu items, though many patrons just come to sip coffee or beer and to be seen.

Swiss Cottage (☎ 2243 3000; *Leoforos Stasinou 31; cakes CY£1.50-2*), on the corner of Theokritou close to the Old City, is great for a late-night coffee and cake. The Swiss-trained pastry chef makes some exquisite European-style tarts and flans, but prices tend to be a little steep.

Greek Cypriot Cuisine Diagonally opposite the Cyprus Hilton you'll find **Evohia** (☎ 2237 6219; *Arhiepiskopou Makariou III 99;* *buffet CY£6; open lunch & dinner*) where you dine off a rich serve-yourself buffet spread. There's a wide choice of salads, pulses and meats as well as a mouth-watering cheese-and-spinach pie. This is an ideal place for vegetarians.

Date Club Restaurant (☎ 2237 6843; *Agathonos 2; mains CY£4-6; open lunch & dinner*), also close to the Cyprus Hilton, is the place to be if you fancy rubbing your shoulders with prime ministers and presidents. Its calm, air-con interior is always busy with discerning diners. If you are going to eat here, take a friend or two and eat *mezedes*; they are tops.

Kalymnos (☎ 2247 2423; *Zinas Kanther 11; fish per kg CY£10-18*) is an unpretentious fish tavern that gets top marks from the local diner community. Fish figures prominently, though you can get most other dishes of your choice including *mezedes* and steaks. There's a little bar for a predinner drink.

Sporting chrome and steel and dishing up a modernistic dining experience, **Zoo** (☎ 2275 8262; *Stasinou 15; mains CY£3-5; open 9pm-1am*) is a popular dining venue among Lefkosian gastronomes. The menu is Mediterranean and the upstairs view of the Old City walls is unparalleled.

The management of Cleopatra Hotel may be stuffy, but it doesn't stop its in-house restaurant **Loukoullos** (☎ 2267 1000; *Florinis 8; mains CY£4-6*) from being considered one of Lefkosia's better hotel restaurants. In summer, dine on *mezedes* or European cuisine next to the pool.

For a change head on over to the west of the city centre to the **Plaka Tavern** (☎ 2244 6498; *Plateia Arhiepiskopou Makariou 8, Engomi; mezes CY£7; open Mon-Sat*) and dine at this superb little Greek-style taverna. During the summer months diners eat on the little square. The *mezedes* is the way to eat here but be warned: there are many of them and you will need a big appetite.

International Restaurants 'The root of all pleasures is the satisfaction of the stomach' said Epicurus (341–270 BC). The owners of **Arheon Gefsis** (☎ 2245 2830; *Stasandrou 29; mains CY£4-8*) have taken this to heart and offer up foods that the Ancient Greek philosopher himself may have feasted upon. Dine on dishes featuring figs, nuts, honey, beets, chickpeas and olives.

There are quite a few good Chinese restaurants in Lefkosia, many offering a takeaway service. **Dragon** (☎ 2259 1711; *Leoforos Georgiou Griva Digeni; mains CY£6-8*) is one you might like to seek out. This restaurant has a good range of dishes, all cooked by a Chinese chef.

Kana Kai (☎ 2277 3820; *Metohiou 25; set menus for 2 CY£8.80-10.80*) is a more intimate place closer to the Old City, which does a mean Peking duck. You can order takeaway chicken dishes for around CY£4.

Irish proper and Irish fusion dishes can be had at **Finbarr's** (☎ 2237 6625; *Arhiepiskopou Makariou III 52b; mains CY£5-7*). This cosy but slightly pricey restaurant/pub serves Irish staples such as beef-and-stout pie, or a jazzed up basil-and-chicken boxty.

Lebanese food comes no better than at **Abu Faysal** (☎ 2276 0353; *Klimentos 31; mezes CY£7*), three blocks south of the Constanza Bastion. The restaurant is an old house in a quiet backstreet and you dine in a leafy courtyard. Lebanese *mezedes* are the best option – ask for a bottle of Lebanese Ksara Riesling wine to wash them down.

ENTERTAINMENT

For listings, particularly for classical-music concerts and the theatre, pick up *Nicosia this Month* and the *Diary of Events* pamphlets, available from the CTO. Note that some events may not be listed in the latter publication as this goes to print several months before the events take place.

Pubs & Bars

The most popular bar strip is around the Famagusta Gate in the Old City. Places here only really get going after 10pm. **Bastione** (☎ 2243 3101; *Leoforos Athinas 6*) is a neat little bar built into the wall next to Famagusta Gate.

Ithaki (☎ 2243 4193; *N Foka 3*) is probably the most popular of the bars here and occupies a prominent corner position, straddling Athinas and Thiseos. **Odos Othellou** (*Othellou 1*), one block west and just away from the main drag, is a relaxed place for a beer or a coffee.

Also by the Gate you can't miss **Erotiko** (☎ 2234 8111; *Athinas 2-3*), a lively outdoor bar with silver chairs. It's popular with the preclub or predinner crowd.

Sfinakia (☎ 2276 6661; *Santaroza 2*), in the New City, is one of the more popular pre-clubbing bars in the city and packs in a crowd of people-watchers and poseurs. It's *not* a place for a quiet drink; be prepared for action here.

Sup Guinness and Caffrey's at **Finbarr's** (☎ 2237 6625; *Arhiepiskopou Makariou III 52b; pint of Guinness CY£2.70*) for a spot of capital craic or just to unwind with a newspaper or a magazine. Drinks are cheaper during the 'happy hour' from 4.30pm to 8pm.

Clubs

Handily next to Finbarr's Irish Pub, **Club Cilo** (☎ 2276 0061; *Arhiepiskopou Makariou III 52*) was refurbished in 2002 and is now one of the capital's 'in' clubs. Playing the best of garage on Friday and spinning house on Saturday, Club Cilo cooks.

Under the restaurant of the same name (see Places to Eat) is **Zoo** (☎ 2275 8262; *Stasinou 15*). Called Zoo presumably because people come here to look at each other (as in a zoo, right?) this trendy spot pulls in the locals and features occasional theme nights such as '70s 'flower power parties'.

Versus Club (☎ 2276 9304; w *www.versusclub.com; Capital Centre, Arhiepiskopou Makariou III 2*) keeps fans of deep, dark underground house happy several nights a week. Look out for Falling Angel nights when the club goes crazy with some weird and wonderful sound effects. VC also organises summer beach parties (entry CY£6). See the website for details.

Traditional Music

The best way to get to see and hear some traditional music is to head for any of the restaurants offering live music in Laïki Yitonia. Otherwise keep your eyes peeled for posters over the summer advertising visiting musical artists from Greece.

Concerts are commonly held at the **Skali Aglantzias** (w *www.aglantzia.com*) outdoor venue in Aglantzia and the **Scholi Tyflon** (School for the Blind) outdoor theatre near the southern suburb of Dasoupolis.

If you are keen, get in touch with promoters **Papadopoulos & Schinis Productions Ltd** (☎ 2537 2855; e *schinis@cytanet.com.cy*) for interesting upcoming events.

Classical Music

Lefkosia occasionally hosts classical music concerts and the best way to find out about them is to look in the local press. Other than this, watch for posters or drop by the Municipal Theatre box office (see Theatre following), diagonally opposite the Cyprus Museum on Mouseiou.

Cinemas

The latest and best cinema experience to hit Lefkosia is the flashy and dashy **K-Cineplex** (☎ 2235 5824; Makedonitissis 8; open 5pm-10.30pm) 2.5km out of the city in Strovolos. Sporting multiple screens, K-Cineplex runs all the latest-release movies and provides movie-goers with ample parking, a cafeteria and hi-tech sight-and-sound systems.

There are a number of other cinemas scattered around Lefkosia that show varying permutations on the latest films and sometimes reruns of English-language movies. All foreign-language films are subtitled in Greek.

Among these cinemas are **Opera 1 & 2** (☎ 2266 5305; Hristodoulou Sozou 9), **Zina Pallas** (☎ 2267 4128; Theofanous Theodotou 18), **Pantheon 1, 2 & 3** (☎ 2267 5787; Diagorou 29) and **Othellos** (☎ 2235 0579; 28 Oktovriou 1; Engomi). Admission to K-Cineplex is normally around CY£3 per person; slightly cheaper for other cinemas.

Theatre

There is a thriving local theatre scene. However, plays performed in Lefkosia are almost always in Greek.

Cyprus University Theatre Workshop (Thepak; ☎ 2243 4801) regularly puts on good-quality shows at its little theatre close to the Green Line northwest of the Famagusta Gate.

Also try **Theatro ENA** (☎ 2234 8203; Athinas 4) in the Old City for any productions that may meet your linguistic needs.

The **Municipal Theatre** (☎ 2246 3028; Mouseiou 4) is opposite the Cyprus Museum. At the handy box office you can find flyers for all upcoming events – musical as well as theatrical – and buy your tickets.

SPECTATOR SPORTS
Football

Football (soccer) is the main spectator sport in Lefkosia. The football season is from September to May. Check out w www.soccer.kypros.org/cyprus_links.htm for all the low-down on the nation's teams. The top team in 2002 was 16-times champions

APOEL Nicosia. The city also hosts Omonia and Olympiakos.

Horse Racing

The **Nicosia Race Club** (☎ 2278 2727, fax 2277 5690; w www.nicosiaraceclub.com.cy; Grigoriou Afxentiou 10-12), in the western suburb of Agios Dometios, caters for keen horse punters. Meets are normally held on Wednesday and Sunday in winter and Wednesday and Saturday in summer, starting at 4pm.

SHOPPING

The two main shopping areas are along Lidras in the Old City and Arhiepiskopou Makariou III in the New City. Tourist shops tend to be centred in the Old City. Good buys are handicrafts, Lefkara lace, jewellery, shoes and prescription eye wear.

Shoes and clothing can be found along Stasikratous and Arhiepiskopou Makariou III which run parallel to each other in the New City. Cypriot-made shoes are an especially good buy, but watch out for obvious cheaply made clones.

Lefkosia's local **Woolworths** (☎ 2244 7801; Shakolas Tower, Lidras), in the Old City, is nothing like the Woolworths you find back home. It's a classy department store selling good-quality items at fairly upmarket prices.

Virgin Records (☎ 2276 1190; Arnaldas 8) is the place music lovers might want to head for, just off Leoforos Stasinou near the D'Avila Bastion. Here you can get all the latest Greek and non-Greek releases as well as buy tickets for the many music concerts that come to Lefkosia in the summer.

In the Old City, **Andreas Papaeracleous Photo Store** (☎ 2266 6101; Rigenis 48) is a well-stocked shop catering for all photography needs. Further east along the same street is **Cyprus Handicraft & Souvenirs**.

Out in Engomi is **Haralambidis Hypermarket** (Vasileos Pavlou I). Here you can find pretty well anything you can find back home in the very well-stocked megamarket, from coconut milk to Christmas cards.

GETTING THERE & AWAY
Air

Lefkosia's international airport is in the UN buffer zone and is no longer a functioning airport. All air passengers for Lefkosia will arrive via Larnaka airport.

Most airline companies that serve Southern Cyprus have offices or representatives in Lefkosia, including

Alitalia (☎ 2267 4500, fax 2267 1894) Leoforos Evagorou I 54–58
British Airways (☎ 2276 1166, fax 2276 6017) Arhiepiskopou Makariou III 52a
Cyprus Airways (☎ 2275 1996, fax 2275 5271) Arhiepiskopou Makariou III 50
KLM (☎ 2267 1616, fax 2267 9497) Zinas Kanther 12
Lufthansa (☎ 2287 3330, fax 2267 6654) cnr Arhiepiskopou Makariou III & Evagorou I
Olympic Airways (☎ 2267 2101, fax 2266 1329) Leoforos Omirou 17

Bus

There are many private companies operating out of Lefkosia. Most buses depart from two areas: Plateia Solomou, abutting the Tripoli Bastion, and from a bus lot next to the Constanza Bastion 700m further east. Other services have their own departure points.

Agia Napa & Paralimni
Eman Buses (☎ 2372 1321) Constanza Bastion. One bus at 3pm Monday to Friday to Agia Napa (CY£2)
PEAL Bus Co (☎ 2382 1318) Stasinou 27. Runs a bus at 1.30pm Monday to Friday to Paralimni and Protaras via Agia Napa (CY£2)

Larnaka
Intercity Buses Co (☎ 2266 5814) Plateia Solomou. Six buses run Monday to Friday and two on Saturday (CY£1.50)

Lemesos
Alepa Buses (☎ 9962 5027) Plateia Solomou. Two buses run daily (2.45pm and 3.45pm) on Monday, Tuesday, Thursday and Friday and one at 12.45pm on Wednesday and Saturday (CY£2)
Intercity Buses Co (☎ 2266 5814) Plateia Solomou. Seven buses run Monday to Friday and two on Saturday (CY£1.50)

Pafos
Alepa Buses (☎ 9962 5027) Plateia Solomou. There is a service at 3.45pm on Monday, Tuesday, Thursday and Friday (CY£3) and at 12.45pm on Wednesday and Saturday (CY£3)
Nea Amoroza (☎ 2693 6822) Plateia Solomou. A bus runs at 6.30am from Monday to Friday via Lemesos and at 7am on Saturday (CY£3)
Solis (☎ 2266 6388) Plateia Solomou. A minibus runs at noon Monday to Saturday (CY£5)

Troödos
Clarios Bus Co (☎ 2275 3234) Constanza Bastion. Has a bus to Troödos at 11.30am Monday to Friday (CY£1.50) and up to 12 buses a day in summer to Kakopetria (CY£1.20)
Kambos Buses (Leonidou) Runs a bus to Kykkos Monastery at noon Monday to Saturday (CY£1.90)
Pedoulas-Platres Bus (☎ 9961 8865, 2295 2437) Leonidou 34. Runs a bus at 12.15pm Monday to Saturday to Pedoulas and Platres (CY£2). The Saturday bus doesn't continue to Platres

Car & Motorcycle

Traffic approaching Lefkosia tends to come from either the Troödos Mountains to the west, or Larnaka and Lemesos in the south. The Larnaka–Lemesos motorway ends fairly abruptly on the southern outskirts of Lefkosia about 6km south of the Old City. By following the extension of the motorway into the city centre, you will eventually reach Arhiepiskopou Makariou III, the main thoroughfare in the New City. Traffic from Troödos will enter the city along Leoforos Georgiou Griva Digeni.

Parking is most easily found at the large car parks abutting the city bastions, to the right of Arhiepiskopou Makariou III, or to your left if you approach from the Troödos. The most convenient one for new arrivals is the large lot between the D'Avila and Constanza bastions on Leoforos Stasinou. Cost is a minimum of CY£0.30 for two hours. Buy a ticket from the machine and display it on the inside of your windscreen.

Leaving Lefkosia is made easy by the prominent signs all along Leoforos Stasinou. Be wary, however, of the many one-way streets and the numerous on-street parking restrictions. Avoid the peak period of 11am to 1pm midweek when traffic can be very slow.

Service Taxi

All service-taxi destinations are now handled by *Travel & Express (☎ 07 77 474; Municipal Parking Place, Salaminos)* just next to the Podocataro Bastion. Rates are: CY£3.10 to Lemesos, CY£2.60 to Larnaka and CY£6.35 to Pafos. Although Travel & Express will pick you up at an appointed time from anywhere in urban Lefkosia, delays of up to 30 minutes are the norm. Be prepared.

Passengers boarding at the Podocatoro Bastion will usually spend up to 30 minutes picking up other passengers before actually departing Lefkosia. Service taxis do not deliver passengers to Larnaka airport.

To Northern Cyprus

Depending on prevailing politics, you're usually allowed into Northern Cyprus for a day visit. The border crossing at the Ledra Palace Hotel is open 8am to 5pm. You may cross to the North between 8am and 1pm but you must be back by 5pm. For details see the boxed text 'Crossing the Thin Green Line' in the Getting Around chapter.

GETTING AROUND

At Plateia Dionysiou Solomou is **A Petsas & Sons** (☎ 2246 2650) where you can hire cars. There are no bicycles for rent in or around the Old City.

To/From the Airport

There is no public or airline transport between Lefkosia and Larnaka or Pafos airports. If you are in a hurry, an expensive taxi (CY£14 to Larnaka, CY£30 to Pafos) is your only option. It is cheaper to take a bus or service taxi to Pafos or Larnaka and get an urban taxi from there or, in the case of Larnaka, take a local bus from there to the airport.

Bus

The urban bus station is at Plateia Solomou. **Lefkosia Buses** (☎ 2266 5814) operates numerous routes to and from the city and suburbs. Because most of the major sites and hotels are within walking distance of each other, urban buses are of limited use.

Taxi

Some local taxi companies include: **Ethniko** (☎ 2266 0880; Plateia Dionysiou Solomou), **Elpis** (☎ 2276 4966; Arhiepiskopou Makariou III 63c), and **Apostrati** (☎ 2266 3358; Plateia Eleftherias). There is a large taxi stand on Plateia Eleftherias.

Around Lefkosia

Few people make the effort to explore the area immediately to the south and west of Lefkosia. At first glance it doesn't seem to have a lot to offer visitors. The sprawling plain known as the Mesaoria looks hot and uninviting in midsummer, but it is covered with greenery in winter and spring. There are a couple of ancient archaeological sites to tempt history buffs and a sprinkling of churches and monasteries to woo the spiritually or aesthetically minded. The villages of the Troödos foothills offer a glimpse of how Cypriot life has been for ages – essentially untouched by the excesses or needs of the tourist industry.

A car will be necessary to see some of the sites listed here.

GETTING THERE & AWAY

While public buses – often colourful and old-fashioned – link most of the Mesaoria villages with Lefkosia, they are basically scheduled to service workers and schoolchildren, and not curious travellers, so will be of limited use. Ask at the villages for details including where they pick up in Lefkosia. Generally, though, you will need your own transport here, though if you have the time and patience you should be able to get around – perhaps fitfully – by hitching. Locals hitch fairly regularly and you might find it an interesting diversion to pick up someone yourself, if you have your own wheels.

Cycling in the area is easy because of the mostly gentle gradients, but the weather can get very hot in summer and the traffic on the main highways to Troödos can be heavy.

ANCIENT TAMASSOS

Homer mentioned Ancient Tamassos (admission CY£0.75; open 9am-3pm Tues-Fri, 10am-3pm Sat & Sun) in the Odyssey, where it is referred to as Temese. The goddess Athina says to Odysseas' son, Telemachos: 'We are bound for the foreign port of Temese with a cargo of gleaming iron, which we intend to trade for copper.' The site of this otherwise obscure and little-known city kingdom is on a small hillside about 17km southwest of Lefkosia next to the village of Politiko. Tamassos' main claim to fame was its seemingly endless supply of copper – the mineral from which the name of Cyprus (Kypros in Greek and Kıbrıs in Turkish) is derived. A copper-producing settlement here dates from at least the 7th century BC and production of copper ran well into the Hellenistic period. Excavations of the remains of the citadel commenced in 1889 and two tombs dating

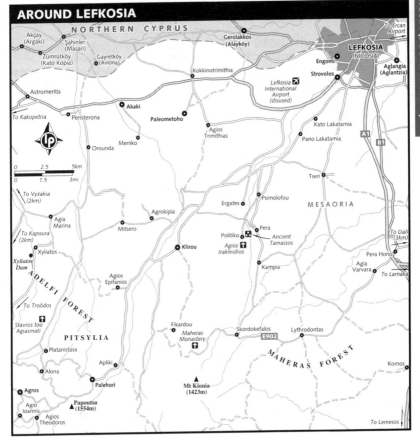

AROUND LEFKOSIA

back to the 6th century BC were discovered. Today these two tombs constitute the major attraction of the site as the citadel itself is little more than a scattering of nondescript foundations.

The tombs probably contained the remains of the kings of the citadel and, while they no doubt once held rich burial treasures, looters have long since spirited away what may have been buried with the kings. A hole in the roof of the larger tomb shows where grave robbers once broke in. The walls are unusually carved in such a way as to imitate wood – a feature that some archaeologists have linked to a possible Anatolian influence at the time of the citadel's zenith. Some theorists suggest that Tamassos was even part of the Hittite Empire.

MONASTERY OF AGIOS IRAKLEIDIOS

Easily combined with an excursion to Tamassos is a visit to the nearby Monastery of Agios Irakleidios *(open for groups only 9am-noon Mon, Tues & Thur)*. Irakleidios was born in Tamassos and guided St Paul and St Barnabas around Cyprus. He was later made the first bishop in Cyprus by Barnabas. The bishop has been subsequently attributed with bringing about many miracles, including exorcisms.

The original church was built on the present site in the 5th century AD, but the current monastic buildings date from the late 18th century. The church today boasts the usual panoply of frescoes and icons, and on a table to the eastern side of the church you can spot a reliquary containing one of the bones and skull of St Irakleidios.

THE MESAORIA VILLAGES

So called 'safari' tours often take travellers to see some of the villages of the Mesaoria (meaning 'between the mountains' in Greek) as part of a wider tour around Cyprus. In this case, Mesaoria refers to the plains lying between the Kyrenia (Girne) Range to the north and the Troödos Massif to the south. While you could rent a vehicle and randomly drive around the Mesaoria, roads tend to fan out haphazardly along roughly defined valleys and ravines and traversing from one valley to another can be slow as the roads are narrow and winding.

One of the more popular villages is **Pera** (population 1020), a couple of kilometres from Tamassos. While there are no specific sights here, Pera is nonetheless a pretty village and a stroll through the cobbled backstreets will lead photographers to some particularly captivating street scenes – old houses covered in bougainvillea, old stone jars, pretty doors and cats on walls – the stuff that postcards are made of. Visitors frequently stop at the local *kafenio* for refreshments, while the local gentry and often the village priest sip coffee and engage in gossip in a world where time means little.

The villages of **Orounda** (population 660) and **Peristerona** (population 2100), west of Lefkosia, both have interesting and photogenic churches.

From these villages, roads from the Mesaoria area all lead in various ways to the higher reaches of the Troödos, via Pitsylia, offering a slower but more scenic route into the mountains. This option is particularly useful on weekends when Lefkosians in their hundreds storm the Troödos via the main B9 road (through Astromeritis and Kakopetria) for picnics and a day out in order to escape the heat of the city.

You will find a tavern or restaurant in most villages or even in out-of-the-way places along the road. Many Lefkosians come to the country to eat on weekends and usually have their favourite haunts. Advertised widely in the area around **Agia Marina** (population 630) is **Katoï** (☎ 2285 2576; Agia Marina Xyliatou; mains CY£5-7), overlooking the village itself. Its lights are visible from afar at night and it commands a great view over the Troödos foothills and Mesaoria. The restaurant serves solid Cypriot staples and a pretty imaginative selection of *mezedes*.

Around here, you can have some pleasant picnics at picnic grounds, usually situated in cool and leafy spots. Try the **Xyliatos Dam** near the village of the same name, or **Kapoura** on a picturesque back road (the F929) linking Vyzakia with the B9, or even high up in the Maheras Forest south of Pera, at **Skordokefalos** along the E902 that leads to the Maheras Monastery. All picnic grounds have BBQ areas, tables, chairs and, most importantly, shade.

Maheras Monastery
Μονή του Μαχαιρά

It is a fair hike out to this sprawling monastery *(open 9am-noon Mon, Tues & Thur)*, perched in the foothills of the eastern spur of the Troödos Massif and under the all-seeing, enormous radar installation on Mt Kionia (1423m) to the southwest. The Maheras Monastery was founded in a similar way to the Kykkos Monastery (see the Marathasa Valley section in the Troödos Massif chapter). In about 1148 a hermit by the name of Neophytos found an icon guarded by a sword (*maheras* means knife or sword in Greek) in a cave near the site of the present monastery. The monastery developed around the icon and flourished over the years. Nothing remains of the original structures; the current building dates from around 1900.

The monastery is a popular outing for Cypriots who come as much for the cooler climate as for spiritual enlightenment. There is a small **cafeteria** in the grounds and some pilgrims may also stay overnight. One less spiritually inspired visitor was Grigoris Afxentios during the EOKA uprising of 1955–59. This fearsome EOKA leader hid out in a cave just below the monastery, but was eventually tracked down and killed by British soldiers in 1957. A huge black statue of the hero now looms over a commemorative shrine.

The monastery is open for visits by groups of parishoners only at certain times. Ask locally or perhaps at the CTO in Lefkosia on how you might join one of these groups, which will mostly consist of Cypriot pilgrims. Visits should be conducted with reverence and solemnity. The approach to the monastery is best undertaken via Klirou and Fikardou (see following) since the alternate route via Pera and the E902, while very pretty, is winding and tortuously slow.

Drivers up this way might look out for the Skordokefalos picnic area east of the Maheras Monastery.

Fikardou Village Φικάρδου
pop 3

This postcard-pretty village is close to the Maheras Monastery and visits to both are easily combined. Fikardou is the 'official' village in a clutch of preserved villages in the eastern Troödos Massif. Its Ottoman-period houses with wooden balconies are quite a visual relief after the cement structures of many modern Troödos mountain villages. That said, there is not a lot to Fikardou and few people live here permanently. The central strip is no more than a couple of hundred metres and photo opportunities are frustratingly elusive. Most visitors – many on Troödos 'safaris' – content themselves to idly sit at the village's **café-cum-restaurant** while awaiting the next move. Still, if you are in the region, a visit is recommended since there are few places left in Cyprus that retain at least a tenuous architectural link with the past.

Places to Stay

Agrotourist lodgings are the best bet in the Mesaoria, though there is really only one place serving the region. Close to the Maheras Forest, **Avli Georgallidi** (☎ 2265 5100, fax 2251 0061; ⓦ www.yourcyprus.com/agro tourism/lythrodontas.htm; Markou Drakou 3l; twin rooms CY£20, suites for up to 5 people CY£38) is in the village of Lythrodontas (population 2620), 25km south of Lefkosia. It can sleep up to 14 people in self-contained rooms and has a courtyard, phones, central heating and log fires. Lythrodontas is a cool, get-away-from-it-all kind of place.

Lemesos & the South Coast

The area south of the Troödos Mountains today constitutes the heartland, both physically and economically, of the Republic of Cyprus. Here lie Cyprus' second-largest city, its main port, some of its most important archaeological sites and medieval remains, as well as one of the most important military bases in the whole of the Mediterranean region. It is a land of rolling brown hills, where the Troödos Massif meets the sea in a series of languid bays and sandy beaches. This is a land of vigorous tourism, with choices for those who like it quiet – such as the far west of the region – and for those who like it raucous – such as the tourist strip of Lemesos.

Ancient Kourion, perched on a bluff overlooking azure Episkopi Bay west of Lemesos, was home to an advanced civilisation from as early as the 13th century BC and later played an important role in the spread of Christianity throughout the island. Ancient Amathous to the east of Lemesos was one of Cyprus' four original kingdoms and was founded 100 years before Christ. Richard the Lionheart first set foot in Cyprus in the 12th century – perhaps the island's first British colonist – and liked the country so much he kept it for himself. The English are still here and occupy the whole of the Akrotiri Peninsula, where housing estates more reminiscent of England's home counties than the eastern Mediterranean are not uncommon.

The area makes a great base for visitors wishing to be in easy touch with all of Cyprus. Take your time to explore its many facets.

Highlights

- Visit Lemesos Castle, where Richard the Lionheart married Berengaria in the 12th century
- Enjoy a concert in the amphitheatre at Ancient Kourion overlooking Episkopi Bay
- Sample Commandaria, a sweet wine first produced by the Knights Hospitaller
- Swim at Aphrodite's Rock, the spot where the goddess Aphrodite is supposed to have first arrived in Cyprus
- Dine at some fine street side restaurants in the Old City of Lemesos

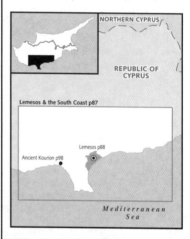

Lemesos Λεμεσός
Limasol

pop 94,600

Brash, bold and carrying the reputation as the city that never sleeps, Lemesos grew up quickly after the Turkish invasion of Cyprus in 1974, having been required to replace Famagusta (Mağusa) as the nation's main port. It was also obliged to shoulder the mantle of the country's tourist boom. Still known to many as Limassol, Lemesos is the second-largest city in Cyprus. Originally comprising what is today known as the Old City radiating out from the Old Fishing Harbour, Lemesos has outgrown its original geographic limits to now encompass a sprawling tourist suburb. The haphazard and hurried development that took place in Lemesos post-1974 is all too obvious. At first sight the city has a rough workaday appearance. The tourist centre is a riotous confusion of bars and restaurants and you could be excused for forgetting that the sea is there at all.

Still, Lemesos is a city with soul. Its Old City is experiencing a slow gentrification, with bars and restaurants appearing among run-down buildings close to what once was

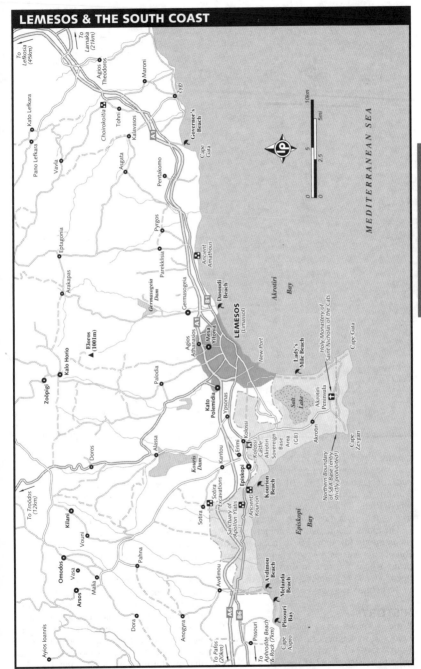

LEMESOS & THE SOUTH COAST

To Lefkosia (45km)

To Larnaka (21km)

Agios Theodoros

Maroni

Kato Lefkara

Choirokoitia

Tohni

Kalavasos

Pano Lefkara

Vavla

Asgata

Zygi

Governor's Beach

Cape Gata

Pentakomo

Eptagonia

Pyrgos

MEDITERRANEAN SEA

Arakapas

Parekklisia

Ancient Amathous

Germasogeia Dam

Germasogeia

Dasoudi Beach

Akrotiri Bay

Elaros (1001m)

Agios Athanasios

Mesa Yitonia

LEMESOS (Limassol)

Kalo Horio

Zoopigi

Palodia

New Port

Lady's Mile Beach

Holy Monastery of Saint Nicholas of the Cats

Cape Gata

Salt Lake

Akrotiri Peninsula

Kato Polemidia

Ypsonas

Doros

Alassa

Kouris Dam

Kantou

Kolossi

Erimi

Kolossi Castle

Akrotiri

Sovereign Base Area (GB)

Akrotiri

Cape Zevgari

To Troodos (12km)

Kilani

Vouni

Sotira

Episkopi

Sotira Excavations

Sanctuary of Apollon Ylatis

(Ancient) Kourion

Kourion Beach

Northern Boundary of SBA Base (entry strictly prohibited!)

Omodos

Vasa

Malia

Pahna

Avdimou

Episkopi Bay

Arsos

Dora

Avdimou Beach

Melanda Beach

Ayios Ioannis

Anogyra

Pissouri

Pissouri Bay

Cape Aspro

To Pafos (20km)

To Aphrodite Beach & Rock (7km)

10km

5mi

5

2.5

0

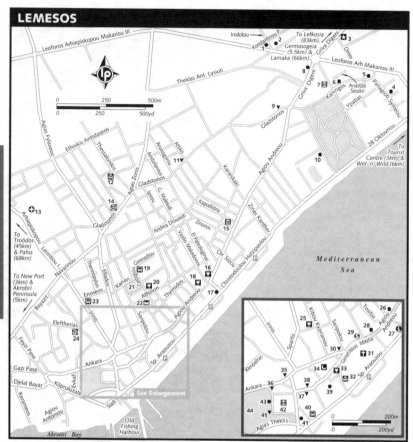

LEMESOS

the city's busy Turkish quarter. Here you can still see artisans plying their trade in the backstreets, the *muezzin* still calls the few Muslim faithful to prayer and the castle where Richard the Lionheart married Berengaria – the city's most famous landmark.

The tourist centre, with its ubiquitous and incongruous fur shops, is as popular with Russian tourists as it is with northern Europeans who come here in droves. Bars stay open late and restaurants, while not the best in the country, serve every kind of cuisine.

HISTORY

Little is known about the early history of Lemesos; its neighbour Amathous and, later, Kourion, stealing whatever limelight had hitherto existed. In 1191 the Crusader king

Richard the Lionheart put Lemesos on the map when he arrived to rescue his sister and his fiancee who had been shipwrecked and mistreated by the ruler of Cyprus, Isaac Komninos. Richard defeated Komninos in battle and took Cyprus and Lemesos for himself. The city prospered for over 200 years with a succession of Knights Hospitaller and Templar until earthquakes, marauding Genoese (1373) and Saracens (1426) reduced Lemesos' fortunes to virtually zero. Things were no better under the Ottomans, and Lawrence Durrell, writing in 1952 in *Bitter Lemons of Cyprus*, noted upon arrival in Lemesos that '...we berthed towards sunrise in a gloomy and featureless roadstead, before a town whose desolate silhouette suggested that of a tin-mining village in the Andes'.

LEMESOS

PLACES TO STAY
4 Kapetanios Hotel
6 Curium Palace
10 Chrielka
26 Metropole
28 Luxor Guest
   House

PLACES TO DRINK
16 Angel's Pub
18 Rogmes Piano Bar
20 Pieros Club
25 π
33 Alaloum

PUBS & BARS
9 Neon Phaliron
11 Antonaros Tavern

35 The Old Neighbourhood
   Taverna
36 To Frourio
37 Rizitiko Tavern
38 Porta
45 Karatello

OTHER
1 ADA Travelscope
2 Cyprus Airways
3 Police Station
5 Service Laundrette
7 Archaeological Museum
8 Quick Service Laundrette
12 Travel Express Service Taxis
13 Lemesos General Hospital
14 Explorer
15 Folk Art Museum

17 Salamis Tours
19 City Bus Station
21 Central Market
22 Main Post Office
23 Intercity Buses
24 CyberNet
27 CTO
29 Bank of Cyprus & ATM
30 Viva! Cafe
31 Church of Agia Napa
32 Acropolis Service Taxis
34 Grand Mosque (Kebir Camii)
39 Hammam
40 Panikos Kiosk (Alepa Buses)
41 Lipsos Rent-a-Car
42 Medieval Castle & Museum
43 Time Elevator
44 Turkish Quarter

ORIENTATION

Lemesos' Old City is fairly compact but the New City now extends for 12km east along the seafront encompassing the main tourist centre. Buses and taxis arrive within a short distance of each other in the Old City, though the New Port, where all ships dock, is about 3km to the west of the Old City. There is a series of handy car parks all along the waterfront abutting the Old City.

INFORMATION
Tourist Offices

The **Cyprus Tourism Organisation** (CTO; ferry terminal ☎ 2536 2756 • town centre ☎ 2557 1868, fax 2574 6596; cnr Nikolaidi & Spyrou Araouzou • tourist centre ☎ 2532 3211, fax 2531 3451; Georgiou 1, 22a; open 8.15am-2.30pm & 4pm-6.15pm Wed, Thur & Sat-Mon June-Aug) has many branches in Lemesos. Opening hours outside of summer are subject to change.

Money

You can change money on arrival at New Port, but there are some banks around the centre of the Old City equipped with ATMs for cash withdrawals. The **Bank of Cyprus** (cnr Saripolou & Agiou Andrea) is probably the most convenient to the Old City, and there are others in the tourist centre.

Post & Communications

The main **post office** (Kyprianou) is central in the Old City, a block north of the pedestrian zone. Poste-restante mail is also held here.

The city has at least four Internet cafés, though the most convenient for travellers in the Old City is **CyberNet** (Eleftherias 79; access around CY£2 per hr). On weekdays it doesn't open until 1pm.

Explorer (Agias Zonis; access around CY£2 per hour) is another Old City Internet café. Both CyberNet and Explorer open from about 10am to 11pm on weekends.

Travel Agencies

ADA Travelscope (☎ 2534 3111, fax 2534 5834; e evie@travelscope.com.cy; Konstantinou Paleologou 25b), not far from the Archaeological Museum, offers a wide variety of services and can book discounted airline tickets for most destinations.

Salamis Tours (☎ 2535 5555, fax 2536 4410; Salamis House, 28 Oktovriou) maintains its head office here, close to the CTO, and issues tickets to transport your vehicle to Greece or Israel.

Laundry

There are at least four laundrettes scattered around Lemesos. The two most central are the **Service Laundrette** (Anastasi Sioukri 20) near the Curium Palace Hotel and the **Quick Service Laundrette** (☎ 2558 7056; Griva Digeni 145). Costs range from CY£2 for a DIY service to CY£4 for a service wash done by the laundry staff.

Medical Services

Lemesos General Hospital (☎ 2533 0777; Arhiepiskopou Leontiou I) is 1km northwest of the Old Fishing Harbour. **Night pharmacy assistance** (☎ 1415) is available in Lemesos.

Emergency
There is a **police station** (cnr Griva Digeni & Omirou) on the Lefkosia road. In cases of emergency, call ☎ 199 or 122.

THINGS TO SEE & DO
Lemesos Medieval Castle & Museum
Lemesos' most famous tourist attraction is its castle and museum (Irinis; grounds admission free; open 9am-5pm Mon-Sat, 10am-1pm Sun). In attractive gardens on the west side of the Old City, the castle was built over the remains of an original Byzantine castle in the 14th century. In 1191 Richard the Lionheart married Berengaria in the chapel of the original castle, and followed that with her coronation as Queen of England. The chapel and Byzantine castle have long since gone and in its place was built the current structure.

The castle looks rather unassuming. In the gardens you will find an old **olive oil press** that dates from the 7th to 9th centuries. The press itself was found in Dounettis, while a nearby millstone was found north of Lemesos. The oil press is based on a simplified version of a Hellenistic and Roman *trapetum*, which uses only one millstone.

In order to appreciate the castle, you will have to enter the **Medieval Museum** (☎ 2533 0419; admission CY£1; open 9am-5pm Mon-Sat, 10am-1pm Sun) and browse among its varied and at times arresting collection of artefacts transferred from the original Lefkosia Medieval Museum, after the division of that city in 1974. The interior is divided into a series of rooms and chambers on varying levels. All have thematic displays of Byzantine and medieval objects of interest including Ottoman pottery, gold religious objects, tombstones, weapons and suits of armour. In the Grand Hall, to the right and on a lower level as you enter, there is a good display of black-and-white photos of Byzantine sites all over Cyprus.

You can climb up to a rooftop promenade, though the views are less than spectacular, since the castle is not all that high.

Archaeological Museum
Lemesos' Archaeological Museum (☎ 2533 0157; cnr Vyronos & Kaningos; admission CY£0.75; open 9am-5pm Mon-Sat, 10am-1pm Sun) houses a rather nondescript collection of items dating from Neolithic and Chalcolithic times, consisting primarily of shards and implements for domestic use, through to Mycenaean pottery. There is a display of classical pottery, jewellery and oil lamps as well as curiously modern-looking glass bottles and vials. The exhibits are generally pleasing only to dedicated museum heads and if you have been to the Cyprus Museum in Lefkosia, you are unlikely to be very impressed with this tired-looking collection. Still, it's worth a browse and it is at least a refreshing alternative to Lemesos' other more worldly attractions over in the tourist centre.

Folk Art Museum
This somewhat mediocre museum (☎ 2536 2303; Agiou Andreou 253; admission CY£0.50; open 8.30am-1.30pm Mon-Fri, 3pm-5.30pm Mon-Wed & Fri, 4pm-6.30pm Mon-Wed & Fri June–mid-Sept) is housed in an old mansion, not far from the city centre. It displays woodwork, traditional dress, jewellery and also traditional household utensils. There is a guidebook for sale at the ticket desk.

The Grand Mosque
The Grand Mosque (Kebir Camii; Genethliou Mitella) was once used by Lemesos' large Turkish Cypriot population and now serves the Muslims that remain and those visiting from Middle Eastern countries. As with any mosque, visitors are requested to dress conservatively, leave shoes by the door and avoid visiting at prayer times. There are no fixed opening hours as such – if the gate is open, step inside the courtyard and take a look.

The Hammam
Close by, near the mosque, is a newly restored hammam (☎ 9947 4251; Loutron 3; open 2pm-10pm daily), where you can get a steam bath and sauna or a massage for CY£5. This is not a tourist site as such, but a working steam bath and the perfect antidote to a hard day walking around in Lemesos' often humid climate. All sessions are mixed.

The Time Elevator
The latest addition to Cyprus' entertainment stable is the gee-whiz Time Elevator (☎ 2576 2828, fax 2576 2829; Vasilissis 1;

CY£7; open daily 9.30am-1pm). If you like history with the added edge of enjoying it through a virtual 'ride' then the Time Elevator is for you. Enjoy a potted history of Cyprus from 8500 BC to AD 1974 through this hi-tech experience combining gut-wrenching roller coaster effects with light-hearted historical commentary. Pregnant women and sufferers of motion sickness should watch the show from static seats, although that's like eating a hamburger without the filling. Shows start every 45 minutes.

Wet 'n' Wild
If you're young, or still aspire to be, then Lemesos has a water theme park just for you. There are actually three of them but Wet 'n' Wild *(☎ 2531 8000; W www.wetnwild.com .cy; persons 13 yrs & over/2-12 yrs/under 2 yrs CY£12.50/6.25/free; open 10am-6pm Apr-Oct)* is the most convenient and probably the best of the three. It's in the middle of the tourist centre, set back a few hundred metres from the beachfront. Boasting such attractions as raft rides, inner-tube rides, body flumes, speed slides, a lazy river, a wave pool, an activity pool, a kiddie's pool and the wet bubble, there is more than enough to keep you wet and weary for a whole day.

If you are coming to Lemesos by car, exit at the Mouttagiaka exit (junction 23) on the A1 motorway.

PLACES TO STAY
The good news is that there are plenty of hotels in Lemesos. The bad news is that they are mostly all along a 9km-long tourist centre to the northeast of the Old City and are often crowded and overpriced. The Old City offers few high quality, guest-friendly establishments, but they are more used to walk-in travellers and likely to have rooms vacant.

PLACES TO STAY – BUDGET & MID-RANGE
The cheapest hotels are clustered in the Old City, to the east of the castle.

Luxor Guest House *(☎ 2536 2265; Agiou Andreou 101; singles/doubles CY£6/12)* is a friendly, airy place with large, clean and simple rooms, most with shared bathroom.

The no-star **Metropole** *(☎ 2536 2686; Ifigenias 6; singles/doubles CY£7/10.50)* is pretty basic, but comfortable enough. Refurbished in 2001, it is located over a flash café-bar.

The three-star **Kapetanios Hotel** *(☎ 2558 6266, fax 2559 1032; e kapetdev@spidernet .com.cy; Pan. Symeou 6; singles/doubles CY£25/35)* is a little beyond the zoo on the east side of the old town but still within reasonable walking distance. All rooms have air-con, minibars, phone and satellite TV.

Another decent mid-range hotel close to the centre is **Curium Palace** *(☎ 2536 3121, fax 2535 9293; Vyronos 2; singles/doubles CY£33.50/44).* Despite its four-star status it is well priced and has plenty of facilities, including a restaurant and bar.

Best Western Pavemar *(☎ 2532 4535, fax 2558 7711; 28 Oktovriou; singles/doubles CY£37/48)* is a three-star hotel at the beginning of the tourist centre and handy to both sides of town. It offers a good range of facilities including a pool.

Overlooking the zoo and municipal park is **Chrielka** *(☎ 2535 8366, fax 2535 8279; e chrielkasuites@cytanet.com.cy; Olympion 7; 2-person suite CY£48-65),* offering business-oriented suites of a high standard. Self-cater or take breakfast downstairs. There is also a guest pool.

PLACES TO STAY – TOP END
Lemesos' really good hotels are at the far northeastern end of the tourist centre. Discounts of between 30% and 40% apply at both these hotels out of season.

Le Meridien Limassol *(☎ 2586 2000, fax 2563 4222; W www.lemeridien-cyprus.com; singles/doubles CY£120/180)* leads the pack. This five-star establishment is 12km out of the Old City. While it has escaped the crush of the central tourist centre, it's perhaps a shade too close for comfort to the Moni power station looming a couple of kilometres east. Still, you do get a luxury hotel with better distractions than a mere power station.

Amathus Beach *(☎ 2532 1152, fax 2532 7494; W www.amathushotel.com; per person from CY£84),* 3km closer to Lemesos, is another five-star high-flyer. Offering four bars and four restaurants and with rates a shade under Le Meridien's, it still offers every conceivable facility and a decent beach to match.

PLACES TO EAT
Lemesos' dining and drinking arena is quite distinctly divided between the older, more traditional local Cypriot scene in the Old City and the ritzy, glitzy scene in the tourist

centre, 3km northeast of the Old City. In between these areas and along the beachfront strip are a number of bars and restaurants that fall in between the two extremes. The best dining is to be had in the Old City

For a no-frills, genuinely Cypriot, local-style evening meal visit **Antonaros Tavern** (☎ 2537 7808; Attikis 1; mezes CY£6-6.50; open evenings only, closed Sun). Only mezedes are served here. Choose from a wide range of dishes such as snails and mussels as well as fish (CY£11 to CY£20 per kilogram). The handwritten notes on the wall are all Greek philosophical sayings.

Near the Fort and spilling out into the street at night is the locals-only **The Old Neighbourhood Taverna** (☎ 2537 6082; Ankyras 14; mezes CY£6.50). Owner Nikos Savvidis is as hospitable as his food is genuine and high quality. Evening dining is best.

To Frourio (☎ 2535 9332; Tsanakali 18; open Mon-Sat; mains CY£3-8), shoulder to shoulder with the Fort, is a little restaurant tavern housed in an 18th-century-listed building that serves excellent meat and vegetarian mezedes.

Rizitiko Tavern (☎ 2534 8769; Tzamiou 4-8; mains CY£3.50-5) is an excellent, low-key establishment, tucked away in a street close to the fort, which spills out onto the narrow street at night. The afelia (pork cooked in red wine and coriander seeds) and kleftiko (lamb or goat baked in an oven) are home-made quality and worth every cent.

In the restored Old Carob Warehouse next to the Fort you'll find the modernistic **Karatello** (☎ 2582 0464; Vasilissis 1; specialities CY£2.50-5). Create your own meal by ticking off your choices on an individual order sheet. Specialities include rabbit in yogurt with a lemon sauce and, for vegetarians, seasonal greens baked with feta cheese.

Almost hidden in a side street and sporting an enormous wooden door is **Porta** (☎ 2536 0339; Genethliou Mitella; foukouda BBQ for 2 CY£16). Originally stables, then a carob warehouse, this cosy restaurant specialises in the table BBQ called the foukouda. Wines including the organic wines Ambelida and Agravani are priced from CY£4.35 to CY£7.

For high-class gourmet dining, visit **Neon Phaliron** (☎ 2536 5768; Gladstonos 135; mains CY£7-9; open 10am-4pm & 6.30pm-midnight, closed Wed & Sun). This classy restaurant serves up eclectic Mediterranean-European fare. Head chef Haris Antoniou

Eating Meze in Cyprus

If there's one thing you are going to remember about a visit to Cyprus, it's the food. Cypriot food is not all that different to the cuisines of Greece, Turkey and the Levant, but there is one culinary speciality that has become almost institutionalised to the point where it may be regarded as the national culinary pastime – eating meze.

Meze means 'appetiser' and is the same word in Greek and Turkish. Eating meze-style means enjoying a full meal via a series of small dishes that are eaten communally and brought to the table in rounds. To really appreciate a meze meal – and most restaurants serve them – you will need at least three fellow diners with largely empty stomachs since you will be grazing on up to 30 different dishes.

The meal usually starts with a round of dips: hummus, garlic and potato dip, fish-roe salad, tahini, plus olives, bread and fresh salad to get you going. Take it easy on the bread and dips here since it is very easy to fill up prematurely. At this point you may also get octopus in wine sauce, snails in tomato sauce, pickled capers and cauliflower, rubbery halumi cheese and wild greens in oil and lemon.

A range of fish dishes normally follows these starters and these in turn are quickly followed by tasty meatballs, rissoles and sausages. If all that wasn't enough, the main dishes haven't even arrived yet! These are normally succulent kebabs, tender meat baked in a sealed oven and sizzling charcoal-grilled chicken. Dessert is usually fresh fruit.

A meze meal is a challenge as much as it is a culinary experience. The trick to successful meze eating is to eat light, or not at all at lunch (or breakfast). Pace yourself carefully and eat very slowly. Don't overdose on any particular meze dish. Remember you are supposed to be sampling the dishes, not dining on them. Some restaurants also serve vegetarian meze courses. Ask beforehand. Wash it all down with some fine Cypriot wine, enjoy yourselves and 'kali orexi' – bon appétit!

offers, among his many dishes, marinated salmon kebabs (CY£6.50) and stuffed mushrooms (CY£4). There's an extensive wine cellar for committed oenophiles.

The eastern village of Germasogeia is home to a scattering of tavernas, some with nightly music. One of the more interesting is **Lefteris Taverna** (☎ 2532 5211; Agias Christinis 4; mezes CY£7; closed Sun). Former British PM, John Major, and wife Norma once dined here. See their photo on the wall of the stone and wood interior. The food is pitched at local tastes and, while not too cheap, is well-presented and filling.

ENTERTAINMENT
Cafés
Viva! Bar-Café (Agiou Andreou 43; coffee CY£1.20-3; meals till 6.30pm) is a neat, hip little joint that offers snacks, drinks and over 10 different coffee concoctions.

π (☎ 2534 1944; Kitiou Kyprianou 27; snacks CY£2-3) is a jazzy little café to wind up your evening meal with a coffee or a brandy. Head for the cosy courtyard with candle-lit marble-topped tables for a spot of under-the-stars schmoozing.

Bars
Rogmes Piano Bar (☎ 2534 1010; Agiou Andreou 197) is a quiet, relaxed little bar, and a couple of blocks along you will find the friendly **Angel's Pub** (Agiou Andreou 219) which is a little more lively. **Alaloum** (☎ 2536 9726; Loutron 1) near the hammam is primarily a gay hang-out. **Pieros Club** (☎ 9989 5737; Georgiou Gennadiou 10) is another mainly gay joint that in practice pulls a mixed crowd.

On the tourist strip opposite the Basement and Hippodrome discos is the **Galatex Centre**, which is a conglomeration of pubs and restaurants where you can meet friends. Among pubs on tap are **Blu Bar**, **Downunder**, **Leprauchaun**, **West End**, **Lucky**, **Full Monty** and **Woody's**. Get the picture?

Clubs
In the city that never sleeps, the tourist centre offers more discos and clubs than you could ever work your way through during a two-week vacation. Start with these.

Do your thang at the **Basement Disco** (☎ 2587 3380; Potamos Germasogeias). Groove to house, trance, R'n'B, funky soul and UK

and US garage. A strict dress code applies so don your best rags and rage.

Hippodrome Disco (☎ 2532 6464; Potamos Germasogeias) is a large place with podiums, a stage and dance floor. Music runs the gamut of most popular tastes and changes according to the mood.

Close to the five-star St Raphael Resort, **Privilege** (☎ 2563 4040; Loura), at the far eastern end of the tourist centre, is an indoor and outdoor club with various bars and dance areas. The music mix is Greek and European chart sounds plus an admixture of groovy garage.

Cinemas
As in Lefkosia and Larnaka, the cinema scene is now dominated by the multi-screen **Cineplex** (☎ 2543 1955; w www.kcineplex .com; Ariadnis 8, Mouttagiaka; open 5pm-10.30pm), which features many new-release movies. It's in the middle of the tourist centre and best reached by taxi. See the website for current showings.

SHOPPING
Most of Lemesos' clothes, shoes and appliance shops are clustered along the pedestrianised streets of Agiou Andreou in central Lemesos, but also filter out through most of the backstreets of this area.

Cypriot BBQs, known as *foo-koo*, can be found in the streets leading off from the Medieval Castle area (handy for travellers who have a car). Tourist souvenir shops and fur-coat boutiques are all clustered along the length of the main drag in the tourist centre, northeast of central Lemesos.

GETTING THERE & AWAY
Air
The office of **Cyprus Airways** (☎ 2537 3787; Leoforos Arhiepiskopou Makariou 203) is a 20-minute walk northeast of the main CTO office. Lemesos is more or less equidistant from Pafos and Larnaka airports. Service or private taxis are the only way to reach either.

Bus
Intercity Buses (☎ 2266 5814; cnr Enoseos & Irinis) has frequent daily services to Lefkosia (CY£1.50) from its bus stop north of the castle. If it is still running, there is also a weekday bus at noon to Agros (CY£1) in the Troödos Mountains.

LEMESOS & THE SOUTH COAST

Intercity Buses also goes to Larnaka (CY£1.70) from the Old Fishing Harbour or from outside the CTO. Both **Alepa** (☎ 9962 5027) and **Nea Amoroza** (☎ 2693 6822) have daily buses to Pafos (CY£2). Alepa leaves from the Panikos kiosk on the promenade while Nea Amoroza leaves from the Old Fishing Harbour.

Service Taxi
Travel Express (☎ 077 7474; Thessalonikis 21) has regular service taxis to Lefkosia (CY£3.60), Larnaka (CY£3.10) and Pafos (CY£2.85). **Acropolis Service Taxis** (☎ 2536 6766; Spyrou Araouzou 65) leave regularly for the same destinations.

International Ferry
In late 2001 international passenger-ferry services from Cyprus to Israel and Greece were suspended indefinitely, making it impossible to enter the Republic of Cyprus by ferry. Travellers bringing in a vehicle to and from Cyprus must now send their vehicle independently by ship and fly to Cyprus to collect it. For details the boxed text 'Bringing Your Car to Cyprus' in the Getting There & Away chapter.

Cruises
Expensive two- and three-day cruises depart from Lemesos all year. They go to Haifa (Israel), Port Said (Egypt), a selection of Greek islands, and sometimes (in summer) to Lebanon. You can book at any travel agency, but you cannot use these cruises to exit Cyprus, unless you decide to jump ship. See Organised Tours in the Getting There & Away chapter for more details.

GETTING AROUND
The city bus station is on Georgiou Gennadiou, close to the municipal market. Bus No 1 goes to the port, bus Nos 16 and 17 to Kolossi and bus No 30 runs northeast along the seafront and passes not far from the entrance to Ancient Amathous. The CTO gives out a useful Limassol Urban Bus Routes timetable.

Buses also run at 10am, 11am and 1pm from the castle to Kourion and its beach, via Episkopi. Return times are 11.50am and 2.50pm. A one-way ticket costs CY£0.80. From April to October there's a daily Governor's Beach bus that leaves from the Old Fishing Harbour at 9.50am, making stops at about 23 locations along the seafront with the last one being at 10.02am at the Meridien Hotel. The bus returns at 4.30pm. A return ticket costs CY£2.

Lipsos Rent-a-Car (☎ 2536 5295; cnr Richard & Berengaria 6) is opposite the castle. It is the only car-rental place in the Old City. There are many more rental agencies in the tourist centre.

Around Lemesos

GETTING AROUND
For the most part it's your own transport or nothing at all. Other than Kourion/Episkopi and Ancient Amathous, which are linked with Lemesos by daily public buses, and Governor's Beach, which is served by a daily private bus, reaching any of the other places described in this section is going to require hired transport or expensive taxis. Cycling in and around Lemesos is fairly easy once you have cleared the confines of the city where traffic is intense. The terrain is reasonably flat, until you encounter the first slopes of the Troödos Mountains foothills.

BEACHES
Lemesos' city beaches, while reasonable and, to the casual observer, popular enough, are not exactly Waikiki material. You are going to have to move out of Lemesos if you want some space and freedom from the masses that congregate along the tourist centre's crowded beach scene.

Lady's Mile Beach
The nearest and easiest option is this beach, named after a horse owned by a former colonial governor who took his mare to exercise on the beach. This 7km stretch of flat, shadeless sand stretches south beyond Lemesos' New Port along the eastern side of the British-controlled Akrotiri Peninsula. On summer weekends the citizens of Lemesos flock here in large numbers to relax on its golden sand and in its rather shallow waters. A couple of beach tavernas serve the crowds and provide some shade and respite from an otherwise barren beachscape. Bring your own shade if you plan to sit on the beach all day. Unfortunately getting here requires your own transport.

Governor's Beach

Some 30km east of Lemesos, Governor's Beach is probably a better option for travellers without their own transport. A private bus commutes daily between Lemesos and this beach enclave (see Getting Around under Lemesos for more details), leaving visitors enough time to spend a relaxing day on a reasonably decent beach made up mainly of dark sand, which can get very hot in the height of summer. There are a couple of restaurants here and at least one place to stay, though the overall ambience is slightly marred by the sight of the large Vasilikos power station looming 3km to the west.

Campers could hole up here at **Governor's Beach Camping** *(☎/fax 2563 2878; tent & 1 person CY£2.50; open year-round)*. The site is OK but is more attuned to caravanners than to campers.

Kourion Beach

This beach, also reached by public transport from Lemesos, is a long stretch of mixed pebbles and sand and attracts a large number of local swimmers. Some 17km west of Lemesos and within the British Sovereign Base Area (SBA), the beach is also without shade other than that provided by the three largish beach tavernas. Locals like to drive their cars and 4WDs practically up to the water's edge. The eastern end of the beach (prominently marked) is unsafe for swimming, so head for the western end. This beach is best combined with your trip to Ancient Kourion (see later).

Avdimou Beach

Better still, but only for bathers with wheels, is this rather remote strand, a further 17km west of Kourion Beach. This low-key beach is wide and sandy with clean and usually less rough water than Kourion and has one beach taverna. However it is rather exposed and has no shade.

Kyrenia Beach Restaurant *(☎ 2521 1717)* is the only beach eatery. It is laid back and relaxing while offering a fairly predictable range of meat and fish dishes.

Melanda Beach

Close to Avdimou, but accessible only by turning inland and looking for the signposted turn-off, is this small, narrow sand and pebble beach. Due to its exposed position, there is often a fair amount of seaweed. The west side is protected by a sandstone bluff. There are windsurfers, banana rides and even jet-skis here and, like Avdimou Beach, it is favoured by RAF personnel.

Have lunch at the **Melanda Beach Restaurant** *(☎ 9956 5336; fish & chips CY£4.25)*. It's simple, plain and pitched mainly at British clientele – scampi and/or fish and chips are popular menu items.

Pissouri Bay

At Pissouri Bay, 10km west of Avdimou, you will come to this popular but still tasteful resort. The very pleasant, relaxed beach enclave pulls in a fair slice of the package-tour crowd, but it is also a good alternative base for individual travellers. A rather large number of restaurants and tavernas ply their trade here and the beach is sandy and well supplied with handy sun loungers and umbrellas.

The best choice for accommodation along the coast is here at Pissouri Bay. **Kotzias Hotel Apartments** *(☎ 2522 1014, fax 2522 2449; 1-/2-bedroom apartments in summer CY£26/32)* are an ideal mid-range option for travellers wishing to base themselves by the sea for a few days.

Among the better places to eat, **Symposio** *(☎ 2522 1158; grills CY£4-5)* is smack bang on the beach. For once, plastic fantastic misses out and diners get to sit on wooden chairs. The excellent *mousaka* is served up in a clay pot and there is a vegetarian version as well.

The **Vineleaf Tavern** *(☎ 2522 1053; mains CY£4-5)* is situated on the main road among pleasant vines, and features live music every Friday night. The menu has traditional Cypriot meat dishes as well as fish.

Set back a bit from the sea but with a good view overlooking the beach is the **Yialos Tavern** *(☎ 2522 1747; mezes CY£6)* with an upstairs balcony. The menu is pretty similar to the other places and the ambience is very pleasant.

Aphrodite's Rock & Beach

Finally, and just on the border between Lemesos and Pafos districts, is this evocative rock and accompanying beach. It is known in Greek as Petra tou Romiou (Rock of Romios) a name that has nothing to do with Aphrodite, but alludes to the Greek folk hero, Digenis Akritas. He apparently used to hurl large rocks – like this one – at his enemies.

'Romios' is another word meaning 'Greek'. However, legend has it that Aphrodite, ancient patron goddess of Cyprus, emerged from the sea at this point in a surge of sea foam. This claim is also upheld by the residents of the island of Kythira in Greece.

Most visitors either come for the usually spectacular **sunset**, best viewed from either the **Tourist Pavilion**, or from a roadside car park about 1.5km further east. Note that the actual rock is the most westerly of the sea rocks visible here. Some visitors confuse the larger fan-shaped rocks with Petra tou Romiou. There is a decent beach here, a passable cafeteria and a restaurant and gift shop at the Tourist Pavilion, which is signposted off the main road. An underground tunnel leads from the beach to the cafeteria and car park on the other side of the road.

While it is unlikely that you would make a trip just for a swim, take your swimming gear if you're heading off to see the rock anyway – it's a great place to cool off. The beach is pebbled for the most part and sits on both sides of the rock. As long as there is not a sea swell the water is calm and clean. However, this is a swimmer's rather than a paddler's beach. The beach shelves fairly quickly and there are a few tricky currents further out to be aware of.

ANCIENT AMATHOUS

This rather nondescript archaeological site 11km east of Lemesos belies its original importance. Amathous *(admission CY£0.75; open 9am-7.30pm July-Aug, 9am-5pm Sept-June)* was one of Cyprus' original four kingdoms – the others were Salamis, Pafos and Soloi. Legend has it that the city was founded by Kinyras, the son of Apollo and Pafos. It is also said that Kinyras introduced the cult of Aphrodite to Cyprus (see the boxed text 'The Cult of Aphrodite' in the Pafos chapter). Founded in about 1000 BC, the city had an unbroken history of settlement until about the 14th century, despite depredation at the hands of Corsairs during the 7th and 8th centuries. In 1191, when Richard the Lionheart appeared on the scene, the city was already on the decline. Since its harbour was silted up, King Richard was obliged to disembark on the beach to claim the once proud and wealthy city. He promptly applied the royal *coup de grace* by destroying it and Amathous was no more.

It is rather difficult to get an overview of the site without visual guidance, since much of the stone and marble has long been looted and carted away for other building projects. Most of Amathous' best treasures were removed by the infamous American consul of Larnaka, Luigi de Cesnola (see also The Pierides Foundation Museum in the Larnaka chapter). To the right as you enter the site is an explanatory pedestal with a schematic map of the area. This will help you to understand how the city was originally laid out. Excavations only started in earnest in 1980 and to date the two main visible features are an **early Christian basilica** in the so-called lower city and the remains of a sanctuary to Aphrodite on the **acropolis** immediately behind the lower city.

The full extent of the ancient city has yet to be discovered. Excavations are made difficult by the considerable growth of tourist hotels on both sides of the site. The remains of the **ancient harbour** have been found at sea. Occasional free summer concerts are held within the grounds of Amathous. Look for posters at the site or check with the CTO in Lemesos.

Local bus No 30 from Lemesos will drop you off not far from the entrance.

EPISKOPI VILLAGE
pop 3110

Instead of staying in Lemesos itself you can easily base yourself at this unassuming and rather extensive village, 14km west of Lemesos. Episkopi is served by bus from Lemesos (see Getting Around under Lemesos earlier).

Apart from being handy for the archaeological and historical sites of the area, it boasts some decent accommodation options and a couple of quite decent restaurants.

While in Episkopi you can visit the **Kourion Museum** *(☎ 2593 2453; admission CY£0.75; open 9am-2.30pm Mon-Fri, 3pm-5pm Thur Sept-June)*. The collection mainly comprises terracotta objects from Kourion and the Sanctuary of Apollo Ylatis, and is housed in what used to be the private residence of archaeologist George McFadden. The museum is signposted off the Lemesos–Kourion road as well as in Episkopi itself.

For accommodation, first try **Antony's Garden House** *(☎ 2593 2502, fax 2593 3113; e katerina.travel@cytanet.com.cy; rooms per person including breakfast CY£15-25)* is a

Vases, jasmine flowers and cobblestone streets, Pera

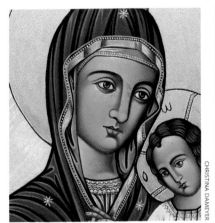

Modern painting of the Virgin and child

Fresh bread and pomegranates

Relaxing on the pebbled beach at Aphrodite's Rock, Lemesos region

PAUL HELLANDER

Another stunning sunset over Aphrodite's Rock, Lemesos region

CHRIS CHRISTO

Sanctuary of Apollon Ylatis

JON DAVISON

Street life, Lemesos

wonderful little agrotourism hotel built around a leafy and cool garden. There are beautiful double rooms and a self-contained studio. It is relatively easy to find as it is well signposted from the Lemesos side of Episkopi Village.

On the western side of the village, close to the motorway access junction, is the four-star **Episkopiana Hotel** (☎ 2593 5093, fax 2593 5094; w www.episkopiana.com; Kremastis Rd; singles/doubles CY£44/66). An LP reader recommended this hotel for its convenience as a touring base. The rooms are spacious and the hotel has a pool.

For eating try the **Episkopi Village Inn** (☎ 2523 2751; mains CY£4-5.50; open Mon-Sat), which is right next door to Antony's Garden House and is the most convenient place to eat in the village. Also recommended by the owner of Antony's Garden House, **The Old Stables** (☎ 2593 5568; kleftiko CY£4.50; open evenings only, closed Sun) is out on the Lemesos–Pafos road opposite the Mobil petrol station. The kleftiko is recommended as is the extensive array of mezedes. Takeaway is also available.

ANCIENT KOURION

This spectacular archaeological site, 19km west of Lemesos, is perhaps Cyprus' best-known tourist attraction. Kourion (☎ 2599 5048; admission CY£1; open 8am-7.30pm July-Aug, 7.30am-5pm Sept-June) attracts hordes of daily visitors, so if you wish to view it with a modicum of peace and quiet come early in the morning or late in the afternoon. These are better times for photography anyway. Ancient Kourion is close to two other attractions in the immediate vicinity, the Sanctuary of Apollon Ylatis (see following) and Kolossi Castle (see later in this chapter). All three could be combined into a day trip, followed perhaps by a swim at **Kourion Beach** spread out temptingly below the ancient site of Kourion itself (see Beaches earlier).

Ancient Kourion was settlement most likely first founded in Neolithic times, probably because of its strategic position high on a bluff overlooking the sea. It became a permanent settlement in about the 13th century BC, when Mycenaean colonisers established themselves here.

The settlement also prospered under the Ptolemies and Romans. A pre-Christian cult of Apollo was active among the inhabitants of Kourion in Roman times, as documented by the nearby Sanctuary of Apollon Ylatis. Christianity eventually supplanted Apollo worship and, despite disastrous earthquakes in the region, an **early Christian Basilica** was built in the 5th century AD, testifying to the ongoing influence of Christianity on Kourion by this time. Pirate raids 200 years later severely compromised the viability of the now-Christian bishopric and the Bishop of Kourion was obliged to move his base to a new settlement at nearby Episkopi, which means 'bishopric' in Greek. Kourion essentially declined as a settlement from that point and was not rediscovered until tentative excavations at the site began in 1876 and continued until 1933.

The site is dominated by its magnificent **amphitheatre**, which is a reconstruction of a smaller theatre that existed on the same site, high on the hill overlooking the sea, which was destroyed in earthquakes during the 3rd century. The current amphitheatre gives a good idea of how it would have been at its peak. Today it's used for cultural events such as plays, jazz festivals and music concerts by Cypriot and visiting Greek singers and bands.

Nearby is the **Annexe of Eustolios**, probably a private residence dating from the 5th century. Its colourful, Christian-influenced mosaic floors are well preserved and make minor mention of the builder Eustolios and the decidedly non-Christian patron Apollo. Look for the Christian motifs in the shape of cross-shaped ornaments and birds and fish.

The **early Christian Basilica**, perhaps built in the time of Bishop Zeno, displays all the hallmarks of an early church with foundations clearly showing the existence of a narthex, diakonikon, various rooms, baptistery and atrium. Some floor mosaics are also visible among the remains of the basilica.

Northwest is the so-called **House of the Gladiators**, thus named because of two fairly well-preserved floor mosaics depicting gladiators in combat dress. Two of these gladiators, Hellenikos and Margaritis, are depicted practising with blunt weapons.

THE SANCTUARY OF APOLLON YLATIS

This second complex (☎ 2599 5049; admission CY£0.75; open 9am-7.30pm daily May-Sept, 9am-5.30pm Oct-Apr) of the larger site

ANCIENT KOURION

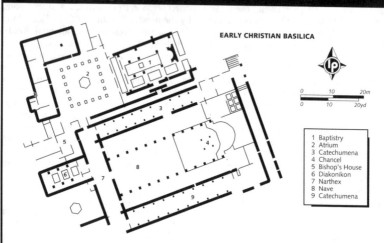

EARLY CHRISTIAN BASILICA

1	Baptistry
2	Atrium
3	Catechumena
4	Chancel
5	Bishop's House
6	Diakonikon
7	Narthex
8	Nave
9	Catechumena

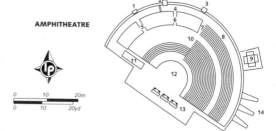

AMPHITHEATRE

1	Entrance
2	Entrance
3	Entrance
4	Vaulted Corridor
5	Corridor into Auditorium
6	Corridor into Auditorium
7	Corridor into Auditorium
8	Colonnade
9	Stair Tower
10	Auditorium Seating
11	Side Entrance
12	Orchestra
13	Scene Building area
14	Buttresses

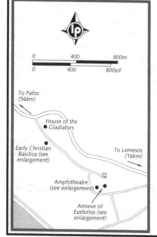

To Pafos (56km)

House of the Gladiators

Early Christian Basilica (see enlargement)

To Lemesos (16km)

Amphitheatre (see enlargement)

Annexe of Eustolios (see enlargement)

ANNEXE OF EUSTOLIOS

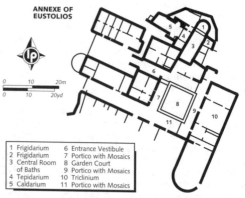

1	Frigidarium	6	Entrance Vestibule
2	Frigidarium	7	Portico with Mosaics
3	Central Room of Baths	8	Garden Court
4	Tepidarium	9	Portico with Mosaics
5	Caldarium	10	Triclinium
		11	Portico with Mosaics

of Kourion is about 2km west of Kourion and is prominently signposted off the highway. The precinct was established in the 8th century BC in honour of Apollo who was considered god of the woods; *ylatis* means 'of the woods' in Greek. The once woody site now has far less vegetation, but retains a good scattering of remains that give a reasonable idea of the layout of the original sanctuary. The remnants that you see are from buildings of the Roman era that were levelled by a large earthquake in AD 365.

The **main sanctuary** has been partly restored and the imposing standing columns mark the extent of the restoration. Also discernible is a **palaestra** (or sports arena) and **baths** for the athletes, the **priests' quarters** and a rather depleted **stadium** 500m to the east, which once seated up to 6000 spectators.

KOLOSSI CASTLE

This rather grandly labelled site (☎ 2593 4907; admission CY£0.75; open 9am-7.30pm July-Aug, 9am-5pm Sept-June) is less of a castle and more a fortified tower house, sitting incongruously between the vineyards and houses of the village that took the same name. It is nonetheless a worthwhile detour as much for its value as a reminder of the rule of the Knights of Saint John in the 13th century.

The site was known by the name Kolossi at about the time Richard the Lionheart was marrying Berengaria at nearby Lemesos, but it is not believed that a castle actually existed at the time. Lusignan king Hugh I granted the land to the Order of St John of Jerusalem, known as the Knights Hospitaller, in 1210 and it must be assumed that the first structure was built at that time. Eight years later the Knights Hospitaller formally moved their headquarters from Acre to Lemesos after their defeat in the final Crusade and Kolossi Castle took on the significance of being the focus for conventual life of the Order from 1301. In 1310 the Hospitallers transferred their headquarters yet again to Rhodes but maintained the Kolossi stronghold as a commandery.

This commandery became one of the richest possessions of the Knights, producing wine – from which the famous Cypriot wine, Commandaria, took its name – and sugar cane. However, Mameluke raids of 1425–26 compromised the prosperity of the commandery and no doubt damaged its infrastructure. The current structure dates from 1454 and was probably built over the older fortified structure by Grand Commander Louis de Magnac, whose coat of arms is visible on the east wall of the castle.

The castle is accessible by a short drawbridge that was originally defended by a machicolation high above, through which defenders would pour molten lead or boiling oil on the heads of unwanted visitors. Upon entering you come across two large chambers, one with an unusually large fireplace and a spiral staircase that leads to another two chambers on the second level. The chambers are empty so it is hard to imagine what they would have been like in their heyday. The only tangible remains of occupation is a wall painting of the crucifixion in the first-level main chamber. The spiral staircase leads to the roof where the battlements, restored in 1933, lend a final castle touch.

The basement consists of three storage vaults that were originally only accessible from above but now have a door leading out into the moat. To the east of the castle is an outbuilding, now called the **sugar factory**, where cane was processed into sugar.

AKROTIRI PENINSULA

In 1960, when Cyprus belatedly received independence from colonial administration, Britain negotiated terms that saw the new Republic of Cyprus ceding 158 sq km (99 sq miles) of its territory to its former colonial masters. This territory, now known as the Sovereign Base Areas (SBAs), is used for military purposes by the British who have a couple of well-established and solidly entrenched garrisons on the two SBAs in Cyprus. A large chunk of these areas occupies the Akrotiri Peninsula, immediately southwest of Lemesos, while the border of the Akrotiri SBA territory runs as far west as Avdimou Beach (see Beaches earlier).

The only indication that you are on 'foreign soil' is the odd sight of British SBA police patrolling the territory in special police vehicles. So, if you are booked for any traffic infringement while driving in the area you'll be booked by British military police. To the immediate west of the peninsula, along the old Lemesos–Pafos road, you will come across green playing fields, cricket pitches and housing estates more reminiscent of Aldershot than Lemesos.

LEMESOS & THE SOUTH COAST

The lower half of the peninsula is out of bounds since it is a closed **military base**, complete with its own large airfield. The village of **Akrotiri** itself is the only true settlement within the SBA (borders were set in order to exclude most settlements) and its only real claim to fame is that its inhabitants are accorded the privilege of dual citizenship. British military personnel often eat here at the several tavernas and may be seen on days off on flashy mountain bikes tackling the dirt tracks surrounding the large salt lake in the middle of the peninsula.

The only real sights are the **Fassouri plantations**, a large swathe of citrus groves across the north of the peninsula, interwoven with long, straight stretches of road overhung by tall cypress trees. They create wonderfully cool and refreshing corridors after the aridity of the southern peninsula.

Holy Monastery of Saint Nicholas of the Cats

This oddly named monastery is positioned on the edge of the salt lake with its back to the SBA base fence, and reached by a good dirt road from Akrotiri or via a not-so-obvious route west from Lady's Mile Beach. The monastery, and its original little church, were founded in 327 by the first Byzantine governor of Cyprus, Kalokeros, backed by Helen, mother of Constantine the Great. At the time, the Akrotiri Peninsula, and indeed the whole of Cyprus, was in the grip of a severe drought and was overrun with snakes, so building a monastery was fraught with practical difficulties. A large shipment of cats was subsequently brought in to combat the reptile threat and the ultimately successful felines stayed on. The peninsula was in fact known for a time as 'Cat Peninsula' before reverting to plain 'Peninsula'. There is a little renovated church that dates from the 13th century and a sprawling monastery building that received a much-needed renovation in 1983. The many cats that you'll find snoozing in the shade of the monastery colonnades far outnumber the four solitary sisters who now look after the monastery.

The Troödos Massif

The mountains of the Troödos Massif rise grandly above the scorching plains and coastal strips of Cyprus' south, culminating in Mt Olympus, the country's highest peak at 1952m. In the past the mountains have provided refuge to religious communities, colonial civil servants and the wealthy of the Levant seeking respite from the heat. These days it attracts skiers in winter and, in summer, hikers, some hardy mountain bikers and weekend picnickers who throng the spiralling mountain roads in their 4WD jeeps and recreational vehicles. Touring cyclists who wish to explore the area will need to enjoy mountain gradients. They should also try to avoid the roads when they become busy with weekenders.

Visitors to the Troödos region should allow themselves at least a week to see most of what the region has to offer. The mountains are clad in a blanket of pine trees – Aleppo pine is the predominant species – and are crisscrossed with a network of winding but good roads that link all points of habitation. Public transport to the Troödos, apart from to and from the villages of Kakopetria, Troödos, Platres and Pedoulas, is sketchy at best so this is one region where having your own transport is highly recommended. However hikers, having established themselves at one of the area's main settlements, will find plenty of activities without feeling the need to move around on wheels. The Cyprus Tourism Organisation (CTO) has sponsored a number of well-marked and well-maintained hiking trails around the mountains.

Many people come here to visit the beautiful frescoed monasteries that dot the valleys and foothills of the Troödos (see the boxed text 'The Frescoed Churches of Cyprus'). These old churches and monasteries, many dating from at least the 15th century, developed as a means of self-preservation at times when Orthodoxy was feeling the pinch at the hands of its numerous colonial rulers. The often-brilliant frescoes that decorate these churches are unique through the whole of Cyprus.

The region can be roughly divided into four sections: Central Troödos, Marathasa Valley, Solea Valley and Pitsylia.

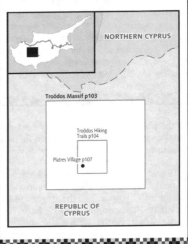

THE TROÖDOS MASSIF

Central Troödos
Κεντρικό Τρόοδος

The central region is dominated by Mt Olympus, around which are scattered settlements, ski runs, hiking trails and picnic grounds. Mt Olympus is ultimately a bit of a disappointment since you can't actually get to the summit, which is taken up by a military radar installation.

From January to the beginning of March you can usually ski on the slopes of Mt Olympus – known in Greek as Hionistra. Although it is cooler up on the Troödos than

The Frescoed Churches of Cyprus

For many people, the main reason for visiting the Troödos region is to visit a series of remarkable small churches that were built and decorated with vivid frescoes between the 11th and 15th centuries. These are the Frescoed Churches of Cyprus and 10 of them have been designated by Unesco as World Heritage sites.

By the time the French Catholic Lusignan dynasty took control in Cyprus in 1197, work on a series of small mountain churches had already begun. But it was the repression and discrimination against the Orthodox Greek Cypriots exercised by the Lusignans that prompted the Orthodox clergy, along with artisans and builders, to retreat to the northern slopes of the Troödos Mountains. Here they built and embellished their private ecclesiastical retreats where Orthodoxy could flourish undisturbed, and did so for some 300 years.

What came out of this activity were many churches built in a similar fashion. Most were little more than the size of small barns, some with domes, some without. Because of the harsh winter weather, large steeply inclined, overhanging roofs were added to protect the churches from accumulated snow. Inside, skilled fresco painters went to work producing a series of vivid images in styles that reflected changing tastes and religious fashions.

Not all churches were lavishly painted, though, but the Unesco-designated churches described in this chapter represent the finest examples. The frescoes are remarkable in the clarity of detail used and colour preserved and the later didactic-style frescoes are unusual in that they are painted almost like a 'cartoon strip', ostensibly to teach the illiterate peasants of the time the rudiments of the gospels.

You would need at least two days to visit all the churches, bearing in mind that a lot of time will be spent in tracking down caretakers with keys as a number of them are kept locked. Donations of between CY£0.50 and CY£1 are appreciated and generally expected.

on the plains, hiking is probably best undertaken in spring or autumn when there is no summer heat haze and the superb views can be better appreciated.

This area consists primarily of two settlements: Troödos itself, just below the summit of Olympus, and the larger village of Platres (sometimes Pano Platres on maps), 10km further down the southern slope. The Central Troödos can be reached by way of a reasonably fast road from Lemesos (the B8) or by its continuation (the B9) up the northern flanks from Lefkosia.

The Central Troödos can also be accessed from the east (the Pitsylia district) and from the west (Pafos and the Pafos hinterland) by good but often winding and slow roads. At peak times, such as Sunday evenings, seeking out an alternative route back to the coast or Lefkosia is advisable since traffic can be very heavy.

TROÖDOS ΤΡΟΟΔΟΣ
pop 15

At first glance there is not much to the small village of Troödos. It consists of little more than a main street, a few restaurants and some scattered public buildings. The greatest amount of current activity comes from the building of a new military base along the Lefkosia road. Yet Troödos does draw huge crowds of people who exit their coaches and hire cars to wander up and down the one main street, gawking at the few souvenir stalls. In the car park at the northern end of the main street, on any given day at least 90% of the vehicles are hire cars, identifiable by their black-on-red number plates.

Despite such potentially inauspicious initial impressions, Troödos is pleasant enough to base yourself for a few days and the hikes, or even the low-key horse riding available, will keep you active enough. If you are fit there are enough forest roads and trails to keep even the most fanatic mountain biker happy for a week. Kids are catered for with a reasonable playground adjacent to the main street. Nightlife is another matter, with none to speak of other than perhaps a drink at the bar at the one hotel. Most day visitors have long since departed by the time the sun sinks below the summit of Mt Olympus.

Orientation

From Troödos, one road leads north and downwards towards Lefkosia while another

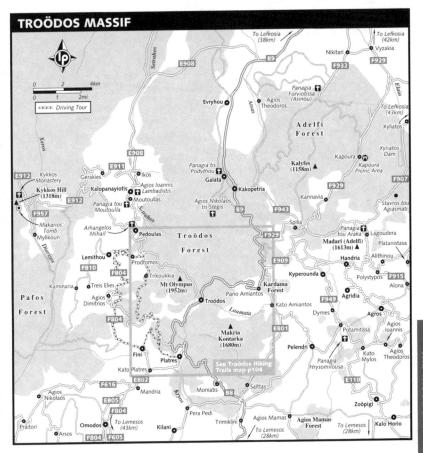

TROÖDOS MASSIF

THE TROÖDOS MASSIF

heads west to Prodromos and further afield. The approach road from Lemesos and Platres comes in directly from the south. There is a small store with a post office agency, several prominent old UK-style phone boxes and plenty of road signs – some of them totally confusing.

Information

Opened in June 2002, the **Troödos Visitor Centre** (*☎ 2542 0144; admission CY£0.50; open 10am-4pm daily*), just down from the Troödos main street, offers a comprehensive look at the fauna and flora of the Troödos National Park with a display of stuffed animals, mounted butterflies and graphic displays of the region. There is also a mini theatre where a 10-minute video is shown to

visitors. The admission fee also allows you to walk along a 300m botanical and geological trail that runs around the centre itself. You can pick information on the Troödos hiking trails (see following) here.

The Troödos Hiking Trails

The four designated trails give you a good overall picture of the flora of the Troödos. Many of the trees and plants you pass are marked with both their Latin and Greek names. There are frequent rest stops with wooden benches conveniently positioned beneath shady trees to allow you to catch your breath or simply to admire the views.

The CTO has published a fairly useful booklet called *Nature Trails of the Troödos*, which outlines all the trails and gives a

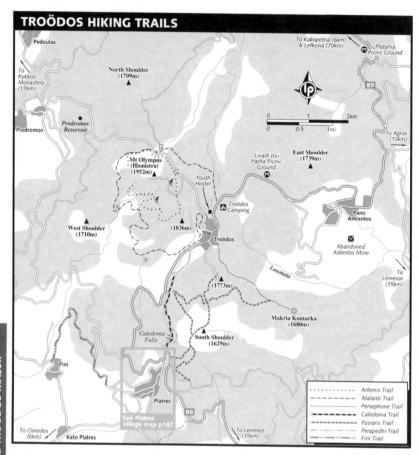

TROÖDOS HIKING TRAILS

To Kakopetria (6km)
& Lefkosia (70km)

Platania
Picnic Ground

Pedoulas

North Shoulder
(1709m)

To
Kykkos
Monastery
(17km)

B9

To Agros
(10km)

Prodromos
Reservoir

Prodromos

Mt Olympus
(Hionistra)
(1952m)

Livadi tou
Pasha Picnic
Ground

East Shoulder
(1739m)

Youth
Hostel

Troödos
Camping

Pano
Amiantos

West Shoulder
(1710m)

(1836m)

Troödos

Abandoned
Asbestos Mine

Loumata

To
Lemesos
(35km)

(1773m)

Makria Kontarka
(1680m)

Caledonia
Falls

South Shoulder
(1629m)

Fini

Platres

See Platres
Village map p107

B8

To Omodos
(6km)

Kato Platres

To Lemesos
(35km)

· · · · · · · · · · Artemis Trail
– – – – – – – Atalanti Trail
· · · · · · · · · · · Persephone Trail
▬▬▬▬▬▬ Caledonia Trail
▬ ▬ ▬ ▬ ▬ Puziaris Trail
– · – · – · – · Perapedhi Trail
· – · · – · · – Fini Trail

description of the flora and natural features to be found along the way. Detailed, though not professional, maps of the trails accompany the text.

The Artemis Trail Of the four, this is the one that you should perhaps tackle first. It is the newest of the trails and takes you around the summit of Mt Olympus in a more or less circular loop. The trailhead begins and ends at a little car park off the Mt Olympus summit road. It's better to get there by car to avoid the 1.5km walk along the often-busy highway. The trailhead sign directs you to walk clockwise though there is no reason why you should not tackle it anticlockwise. The trail end is unmarked and on the opposite side of the Olympus summit road.

The complete walk should take you no more than 2½ to 3½ hours, allowing for stops along the way. It is 7km long with very little climbing. The track runs alternately through partly shaded and open areas and the views on the south side over the foothills are indeed spectacular. Look out for signs to the **giant pine trees** and take care not to lose the trail around the ski runs on the south and north sides. There is no water along the route so take your own supplies.

The Atalanti Trail This trail is for people who like walking. It is long – about 9km – and involves a fair hike along the main Prodromos–Troödos road (or taking a 3km extension of the trail) to get back to your starting point. The Atalanti trail – named in honour of the ancient forest nymph – runs at a lower altitude than the Artemis trail but follows roughly the same route. It is relatively easy going and is well marked. There is a spring with drinking water some 3km from the trailhead at Troödos.

The views are not as spectacular as those from the Artemis trail higher up but it is a most enjoyable walk, perhaps better enjoyed by hikers with time on their hands. At the end of the trail, instead of walking back along the main road, you can head upward along a connecting track and meet up with the Artemis trail. Follow this trail clockwise until you come to the Artemis trailhead. Allow 3½ to four hours.

The Caledonia Trail The 3km Caledonia trail is perhaps the most enjoyable of the four Troödos trails. It begins about 1km or so down the hill from Troödos to near the Psilo Dendro trout farm and restaurant just outside Platres. The trail follows the course of the **Kryos River** – in reality a gurgling stream – as it winds its way down a thickly wooded and shady valley to Platres. There are many stream crossings via stepping stones and makeshift log bridges and the trail is steep in parts. It's best tackled from north to south (Troödos to Platres) as it drops some 450m throughout its course. About 1km from the southern end are the **Caledonia Falls**, a 35m drop of cascading water. The trail is shaded for the most part – great for those really scorching days – and is well marked. You can return the way you came or arrange to be picked up by car in Platres. If you have a car, leave it at the Platres end and hitch a lift up the hill to the starting point. You can also try using the local bus service (make a booking), although times may be inconvenient. Allow 1½ to two hours for a comfortable hike.

The Persephone Trail This is probably the easiest trail to undertake if you are based in Troödos without transport. Known in Greek as the **Makria Kontarka** trail, it is a simple out-and-back hike through attractive pine forest and some open areas. The trail is 3km long and should take you about 45 minutes to reach the **lookout** – the object of the walk. From here you can gaze out over the southern foothills or, if you look to your left, you will see the enormous scar caused by mining and tailings of the now

closed asbestos mine at Pano Amiantos. The marked trailhead begins opposite the Troödos police station. From the main street, walk south along the narrow road heading upward to the left and you will quickly find the trailhead after about 200m.

Horse Riding

It's hardly *Bonanza* stuff, but there is a small horse-riding outfit next to the public conveniences on the south side of the village. Short escorted rides around Troödos cost CY£3 for 15 to 20 minutes.

Picnic Grounds

Although it is easy enough to set up a picnic more or less anywhere in the Troödos, you might want to head for one of the well-organised picnic grounds on the approach roads to the Troödos summit. Bear in mind that lighting open fires anywhere is not allowed, so a picnic ground is the best solution if you wish to grill chops or spit-roast some Cypriot *kontosouvli* (large chunks of lamb). A particularly good picnic ground is the **Livadi tou Pasha**, 3km down the Troödos–Lefkosia road on the left and thankfully before the ghastly sight of the former Pano Amiantos asbestos mine. There is a BBQ area and many fixed benches and tables scattered among the pine trees.

Further along the Lefkosia road (B9) towards Kakopetria, is the very popular **Platania** (Plane Trees) picnic ground, about 8km from Troödos. This place gets inundated with weekend revellers, but is well organised and has plenty of shaded facilities including a children's adventure park. Get there early if you want to pick a good position.

Places to Stay & Eat

A kilometre or so north of Troödos along the Lefkosia road and in a pine forest, there is a reasonable **camp site** (☎ 2242 1624; tent sites CY£2; open May-Oct). There is an on-site restaurant and minimarket.

The Troödos **HI Hostel** (☎ 2542 0200; dorm beds 1st/subsequent nights CY£5/4; usually open May-Oct), with its 10 bunk beds, is the cheapest option. It's airy and clean and there's a big common area with a kitchen. If no-one's around, find a bed. Ignore the conflicting signposting in Troödos village; the hostel is set back 200m on the left as you head down the Lefkosia road.

Jubilee Hotel (☎ 2542 0107, fax 2267 3951; e jubilee@cytanet.com.cy; singles/doubles CY£27/38) is some 350m from the village along the Prodromos road. It's a laid-back place popular with school groups so peace may be at a premium here. There's a pleasant bar and lounge area and an in-house restaurant. Discounts of up to 50% are common in the off season.

Your eating choices are limited to a couple of rather Anglicised restaurants, a more up-market Cypriot taverna and a burger and hot-dog stand.

The **Half London** (hot dog CY£1.50) kebab cabin is right opposite the car park and feeds fast food to the lunch time day-trippers.

The easy-to-miss **Ben Nevis** (kebab & chips CY£2.50) is fairly low-key and unassuming, while the more popular **Fereos Restaurant** (☎ 2542 0114; full kebab CY£5), next door, does a range of Cypriot and English-style dishes.

The **Dolphin Restaurant** (☎ 2542 0215; mains CY£4-6) is signposted 100m down the hill from the main drag. It's a big Cypriot-style taverna and dishes up a wide range of Cypriot and international dishes with large buffets on weekends and public holidays.

Getting There & Away
There is a **Clarios Bus Co** (☎ 2275 3234) service that leaves the Constanza Bastion in Lefkosia at 11.30am (Monday to Friday) for Troödos via Kakopetria. It departs from Troödos for Lefkosia at about 6.30am, but only if reservations have been made in advance. A one-way ticket costs CY£1.50. Service taxis do not operate out of Troödos.

Mountain bikers have a choice of forest tracks to ride along. Bicycles can no longer be hired here.

PLATRES ΠΛΑΤΡΕΣ
pop 280

«Τ' αηδόνια δε σ' αφήνουνε να κοιμηθείς στις Πλάτρες.» (The nightingales won't let you sleep in Platres.)

Georgos Seferis, *Eleni*, 1953

In the 'good old colonial' days, Platres was *the* mountain vacation resort for the well heeled and well connected. This included such luminaries as King Farouk of Egypt and Nobel Prize–winning Greek poet, Georgos

Seferis. This was, of course, long before beach vacations had become *de rigueur* among the burgeoning classes of sun worshippers who fled en masse to the beaches of Cyprus' North and South. Platres was modelled after colonial hill stations in India and offered all the trappings of a cool mountain retreat: forest walks, gurgling streams, relief from the searing heat of the plains and gins and tonic to be taken on the balconies of old-world hotels catering for their guests' every wish.

Those days are more or less gone and today Platres caters for hikers, retirees, travellers who still prefer the hills to the beaches, and the purely curious who either make the drive up in rented cars, or as part of Troödos 'safaris' in long wheelbase Land Rovers. Most easily accessible from Lemesos, Platres is still a fine place for a day or two of indolence coupled with a hike or two and perhaps followed by lingering sunset cocktails.

Orientation
Platres is, at first sight, confusingly strung out around a series of snaking roads, just off the main Lemesos–Troödos highway. All public transport arrives at and departs from the area adjoining the CTO office. The police station and post office are also here. Platres basically consists of the upper road, which is home to a number of hotels, and the lower road, which is home to its restaurants, shops, bars and three swimming pools. The service-taxi rank is next to the CTO office.

Information
The **CTO office** (☎ 2542 1316; e platresinfo@cto.org.cy; open 9am-3.30pm Mon-Fri, 9am-2.30pm Sat, closes 30 minutes earlier July & Aug) is well stocked with brochures on the Troödos hiking trails as well as on the rest of Cyprus, and the staff are very willing to help with queries.

There are ATMs at the **Bank of Cyprus** and the **Laïki Bank**, close to each other on Platres' main street.

The Platres hospital is about 600m south of the village centre just off the main road to Kato Platres and Omodos. Some English-language newspapers may be purchased at the little shop opposite the Bank of Cyprus or at the Cherryland Supermarket on Leoforos Makariou. Call ☎ 1407 to report a forest fire.

Things to See & Do

Apart from succumbing to the temptation to brandy sours in the company of a good novel around one of Platres' three outdoors **swimming pools**, Platres lends itself ideally to a relaxing break away from the torrid heat of summer or, in winter, to engaging in **skiing** or sitting around a roaring log fire.

Hiking Four hiking trails have been described previously (see Troödos earlier). Other options may include hikes from Platres to Fini (a longish 9km downhill route to the west perhaps requiring a taxi or lift back), Platres to Perapedhi (slightly shorter at 7km) or Platres to Pouziaris (shorter at only 3km, but uphill). These hikes and others are described in greater detail in the CTO brochure *Platres,* which also contains a map of the village.

Places to Stay

Accommodation options in Platres are decidedly more favourable than uphill in Troödos. Discounts apply to all these hotels out of high season.

The central **Lantern Hotel** (☎ 9945 2307; Makariou 6; singles/doubles CY£12/18) is an excellent budget choice. It's clean and unpretentious and most rooms have bathrooms.

The cosy **Minerva Hotel** (☎ 2542 1731, fax 421 075; e minerva@globalsoftmail.com; Kaledonion 6; singles/doubles including breakfast CY£18/28) is probably the best choice for first-timers to Platres. It's a very comfortable and tasteful two-star hotel with spotless rooms in the older part of the hotel, or even better mini-suites in the newer annexe at the rear. Each room has a bathroom and a phone, and off-street parking is available.

The **Petit Palais** (☎ 2542 1723, fax 2542 1065; e petitpalais@spidernet.com.cy; singles/doubles including breakfast CY£32/36), a Swiss-looking two-star hotel, is as central as you can get and offers smallish rooms with en-suite that have good views.

Pendeli Hotel (☎ 2542 1736, fax 2542 1808; e pendeli@cylink.com.cy; Makariou; singles/doubles including breakfast CY£40/55) is a three-star place that is another notch up. It has a cool welcoming lobby and inviting swimming pool. Modern, fan-cooled rooms are available.

The three-star **New Helvetia Hotel** (☎ 2542 1348, fax 2542 2148; e helvetia@

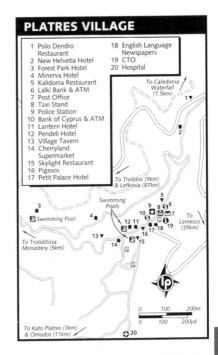

PLATRES VILLAGE

1 Psilo Dendro Restaurant
2 New Helvetia Hotel
3 Forest Park Hotel
4 Minerva Hotel
5 Kalidonia Restaurant
6 Laïki Bank & ATM
7 Post Office
8 Taxi Stand
9 Police Station
10 Bank of Cyprus & ATM
11 Lantern Hotel
12 Pendeli Hotel
13 Village Tavern
14 Cherryland Supermarket
15 Skylight Restaurant
16 Pigasos
17 Petit Palace Hotel
18 English Language Newspapers
19 CTO
20 Hospital

To Caledonia Waterfall (1.5km)
To Troödos (9km) & Lefkosia (87km)
Swimming Pools
Swimming Pool
To Troöditissa Monastery (5km)
To Lemesos (39km)
To Kato Platres (3km) & Omodos (11km)

spidernet.com.cy; Elvetias 6; singles/doubles CY£38/50) is at the northeastern end of the village near the main highway. Its comfortable rooms all have TV, phones and small balconies.

Forest Park Hotel (☎ 2542 1751, fax 2542 1875; w www.forestparkhotel.com.cy; singles/doubles CY£49/78) is a four-star hotel. In the past it has hosted such luminaries as Greek and British royalty; Indian Prime Minister Indira Ghandi; West German Chancellor Willy Brandt; and East German leader Erich Honnecker. It's set among pine trees and conspicuously apart on the west side of the main village centre. Accommodation comes with all the creature comforts.

Places to Eat

There is a cluster of restaurants and cafeterias close to the main drag.

For a quick snack and a cold beer the **Pigasos** (☎ 2542 1744; Faneromenis 1; sandwich CY£2; open lunch only), right in the centre, is great for *halumi* (firm goat's or ewe's milk cheese) and *lountza* (smoked loin of pork) sandwich concoctions, or *lahmajoun* – pitta bread stuffed with spicy mince.

Brandy Sour & the Royal Connection

A visit to Cyprus without tasting a brandy sour would be like eating cake without icing. Touted as Cyprus' national cocktail, a brandy sour goes down just perfectly after a hard day on the beach or hiking through the forests. Its origins, like so many weird and wacky alcoholic concoctions, have a story behind them.

One of the regular visitors to Cyprus in the 1930s was the young King Farouk of Egypt. He liked to stay at the then-new and fashionable Forest Park Hotel in Platres. Following a state visit to the UK, he stopped off on his way home at Platres where he was due to meet a delegation of Cypriot VIPs and foreign dignitaries. Being a Western-educated and rather worldly royal, Farouk was not averse to the odd tipple or two. Not wishing to cause a scene by appearing to drink alcohol in public (Farouk being Muslim of course) he had his aide instruct the head barman at the Forest Park, a chap by the name of Stelios, to whip up a cocktail that looked like iced tea.

Without batting his shaker an inch out of sync, Stelios proceeded to mix two parts of the best Cypriot brandy with one part of fine lemon squash. He then added two drops of Angostura bitters and poured it all over ice cubes, then topping the mixture up with soda water. A slice of lemon completed the illusion. King Farouk got his tipple, the dignitaries were none the wiser and the Cypriot brandy sour was born. Cheers!

An excellent place for a romantic evening meal is the **Village Tavern** (☎ 2542 2777; Makariou; mains CY£4-5) where the succulent *stifado* (beef and onion stew) and *kleftiko* (oven-baked lamb) are absolutely mouth-watering. The excellent red house wine is also recommended.

Also good is the **Skylight Restaurant** (☎ 2542 2244; mezes CY£6.75), which has a pool. Enjoy a swim before a filling jacket potato lunch (CY£2.75 to CY£3.50). Non-diners pay CY£2 to use the pool.

Often crowded, the **Kalidonia Restaurant** (☎ 2542 1404; Olympou 41; mains CY£4.50-7) is very popular among local Cypriot diners; the food is of a high quality.

Psilo Dendro Restaurant (☎ 2542 1350; Aïdonion 13; trout CY£5.75; open 11am-5pm) is the place for trout as the restaurant is also a trout farm. Set back from a bend in the road above Platres, you could be forgiven for assuming that there was no restaurant as it is hidden behind an inconspicuous house.

Getting There & Away
Check with the CTO as to whether buses between Lemesos and Platres are still operating. There is also a very early morning bus to and from Lefkosia Monday to Friday (CY£2) via Pedoulas and Troödos. You'll need to make a reservation.

Service taxis (☎ 2542 1346) regularly run between Platres and Lemesos for CY£2 per person.

AROUND PLATRES
Using Platres as a base, you can make a series of easy half-day tours of the surrounding mountain slopes, or the sunny villages of the southern Troödos range known locally as the *krasohoria* – the wine villages. Being exposed to the southerly sun, vines grow here in abundance and many wineries have taken the opportunity to produce some of Cyprus' best wines, including the famous, rich, red desert wine, Commandaria. You can visit a number of these wineries and sample their product.

You will need your own transport to explore this area.

Mountain Village Driving Tour
With a vehicle you can make a leisurely loop driving around some of the villages that dot the western flanks of Mt Olympus. An easy and picturesque anticlockwise loop can be made from Platres following the narrow the F804 roads that form an elongated circle on the west side of Mt Olympus.

The first point of interest along this route is the 13th-century **Troöditissa Monastery** (open 6am-noon & 2pm-8pm daily). The monastery is primarily a working religious establishment and is not too inclined to receive curious onlookers. Nonetheless, it is in a beautiful setting and is open for suitably pious visitors. It was founded on the basis of a miraculous icon discovered in a nearby cave which had been guarded by two hermits until their death. At this point, the potential significance of the icon was recognised and the monastery was established.

Continue along the very pretty mountain road passing a couple of idyllic and shaded **picnic areas** in cool pine forests until you reach the village of **Prodromos** (population 150). This small village to the west of Troödos used to have a sizable hill-station clientele, but has not weathered the changes as well as Troödos and Platres. The main claim to fame of this quiet little backwater is that it is officially Cyprus' highest village at 1400m elevation.

Loop back and down at this point following signs to **Paleomylos** (population 30), **Agios Dimitrios** (population 55) and **Fini** (population 445). The first two of these villages are timeless places barely touched by tourism and are almost buried beneath the greenery of fruit trees and grapevines. Fini is a more popular destination and is famous for its hand-made **pottery**. It's a good stop for lunch or even an excursion for an evening meal. Try the untouristy and genuine Cypriot **Fini Taverna** (☎ 2542 1828; mains CY£5-10.50) here – a neat little place. Dine on a vine-covered balcony overlooking a verdant valley. The house speciality is the enormous *tournado* (special steak for CY£10.50). There's a wide selection of Cypriot wines (CY£4.50 to CY£7) to wash it down with. Try the rich red *Othello 1992*.

Head back to Platres by one of two signposted routes uphill.

Omodos & the Krasohoria

Ομοδος κατ τα Κρασοχώρια

An excellent half-day tour can be made to **Omodos** (population 310), on the southwest flank of Troödos Central. This pretty village is Cyprus' wine capital and is very attractively situated amid sprawling vineyards. Traditional stone houses punctuate its winding streets. The central area is paved over with cobbled stones and is accessible to pedestrians only.

Unusually, Omodos is built around a monastery, the Byzantine **Moni Timiou Stavrou** (Monastery of the Holy Cross), which was originally built in around 1150 and was extended and extensively remodelled in the 19th century.

Also of interest is the **Socrates Traditional House** (admission free; open 9.30am-

7pm), signposted prominently in and around the back streets. Wander in and admire the ornaments, photos, wedding attire, wine and *zivania* (strong Cypriot spirit) presses, loom, hand corn mill and other items of rural life. Taste the home-made Commandaria wine and take home a bottle for CY£2.

Worth a visit is the **Pitsylia Winery**, (☎ 2537 2928; e tsiakkas@swaypage.com), between the villages of Platres and Pelendri on the southeastern side of the Troödos. This small winery welcomes visitors for a tour and tasting. Wines here are made from the local grapes *Mavro Ambelissimo*, *Xynisteri*, *Ofthalmo* and *Pambatzies*, which are pretty palatable red, whites and rosés. Visiting times are fairly loose, but it's probably a good idea to ring beforehand.

To reach the Pitsylia Winery from Trimiklini village, go right onto the E806 the winery is just before Pelendri village. If coming from Platres, you will need to turn left before you get to Trimiklini .

Places to Stay & Eat

To Katoï (☎ 2542 1230; 3-4 person apartment Nov-Apr only CY£15-20; snacks CY£1.20-3.50; open 11am-4pm, 7.30pm-midnight) is a pleasant little stone and wood-clad taverna in the back streets of Omodos (look for signs). Try the hearty village sausages or the garlic mushrooms and wash it down with a bottle of the smooth local red wine (CY£2). There are also some spacious apartments for rent.

Giannis Agathokleous (☎ 2542 1376; Omodos; apartment CY£30), close by, also has a large apartment for rent that can take up to eight persons. It is open year-round.

Troödos wineries welcome visitors.

The Marathasa Valley Κοιλάδα Μαραθάσας

The beautiful Marathasa Valley extends from Pedoulas (famous for its spring waters) at its southern end, to the plains that open out onto Northern Cyprus. The Setrahos River flows through the valley and empties into Morfou Bay in the North.

The trip up the valley from the north is particularly impressive, especially the final winding climb up to the amphitheatrically displayed village of Pedoulas that lies at the head of the valley. Pilgrims heading for the Kykkos Monastery from Lefkosia used to transit the valley, but now take a newly improved side road via Gerakies. While not physically within the confines of the Marathasa Valley – it is actually out on the edge of the Tyllirian wilderness – we include the Kykkos Monastery in this section for convenience.

The valley is home to a couple of frescoed churches worth visiting and is probably best visited in the spring when the wild flowers and cherry trees are in bloom and the whole valley is imbued with riotous colour.

The main centre is Pedoulas. Lower down the valley, the villages of Kalopanayiotis and Moutoulas are colourful, though less touristy.

GETTING THERE & AWAY

There is a daily bus from Lefkosia to Pedoulas via Kalopanayiotis at 12.15pm Monday to Saturday (CY£2), which continues to Platres (except Saturday) via Troödos village. The bus returns to Lefkosia from Pedoulas the following morning at 6am. For information ring ☎ 2295 2437 or ☎ 9961 8865.

PEDOULAS ΠΕΔΟΥΛΑΣ
pop 190

Pedoulas, at the southern end of the valley before the rise over the Troödos ridge, is the main settlement and tourist centre in the Marathasa Valley and has banks and a post office. It is well known for its cool air, bracing climate and bottled spring water, which can be found on sale all over Cyprus.

There are more than enough accommodation options to absorb most visitors. However, Pedoulas can be busy with day-trippers,

either in hire cars or in buses that ply the often winding routes of the Troödos Valley.

The gable-roofed church of **Arhangelos Mihail**, one of the ten Unesco-listed churches of Cyprus, is in the lower part of Pedoulas village. It dates from 1474 and visitors can see restored **frescoes** depicting the Archangel Michael, the Sacrifice of Abraham, the Virgin and Christ, Pontius Pilate and the Denial of Christ. If there is no-one in the church, seek out the village priest by asking in the local café.

There are a few basic but comfortable places to stay in and around Pedoulas.

Rooms to Rent (☎ 2295 2321; doubles around CY£10) on the south side of the village has comfortable doubles.

The **Central** (☎ 2295 2457, fax 2295 3324; singles/doubles CY£20/35) is a pleasant and newish B&B option in the upper part of the village.

Mountain Rose (☎ 2295 2727, fax 2295 2555; singles/doubles CY£20/32) is a big and airy hotel at the southern end of the village on the main through road.

Treetops (☎ 2295 2200, fax 2295 2230; singles/doubles CY£23/34) is good if you have a car and fancy a view. It's a two-star place on the northwest road out of town to Gerakies and Kykkos, and is good value.

Pedoulas also has the best choice of places to eat in the valley, and the **Mountain Rose** (☎ 2295 2727; mains CY£3-4), part of the hotel is the easiest to find. For a relaxed lunch at a very reasonable price, **Platanos** (☎ 2295 2518; mains CY£2-4), in the centre of the village, offers pleasant dining under a large plane tree.

KALOPANAYIOTIS
ΚΑΛΟΠΑΝΑΓΙΩΤΗΣ
pop 290

The village of Kalopanayiotis does not offer the same variety of accommodation and eating options as Pedoulas, but is nonetheless a useful stopover point along the valley. It is home to at least one impressive Byzantine church and visitors to Kykkos can save some time by taking the newly upgraded road from Kalopanayiotis to Kykkos, via Gerakies.

Still, Kalopanayiotis is typical of the mountain villages of the Troödos Valley and its more down-to-earth ambience may appeal to travellers looking for a quieter and perhaps more genuine item.

The no-frills **Kastalia** (☎ 2295 2455, fax 2235 1288; singles/doubles CY£14/28) is the cheapest place to stay in the village.

The much better **Olga's Katoï** (☎ 2295 2432, fax 2235 1305; doubles CY£35) consists of a traditional main house and 10 attached rooms all enjoying superb views over the Marathasa Valley. Rooms all have heating and phones.

Polyxeni's House (☎ 2249 7509, fax 2235 4030; 4-bed house CY£40) is on the Lefkosia side of the village. The two-bedroom house accommodates up to four people and has a kitchenette, large bathroom and a quiet courtyard where guests can relax and wine and dine in peace.

AROUND KALOPANAYIOTIS
Agios Ioannis Lambadistis
Αγιος Ιωάννης Λαμπαδιστής
This Unesco-listed church (admission free but donations encouraged; open 8am-noon & 1.30pm-6pm daily May-Sept) is signposted from the long main street of Kalopanayiotis and is reached by following a road downwards and then upwards again at the opposite side of the valley. Built in the traditional Troödos style with a large barn-like roof, it is actually three churches in one, built side-on to one another over 400 years from the 11th to the 15th centuries. The original **Orthodox church** has a double nave, to which has been added a narthex and a Latin chapel.

This composite church is one of the better preserved of the Troödos churches and visitors come for its intricate and colourful frescoes. The best **frescoes** are the 13th-century works in the main domed Orthodox church, especially those dedicated to Agios Irakleidios, the Entry into Jerusalem, the Raising of Lazarus, the Crucifixion and the Ascension. The vivid colour scheme suggests that the artists hailed from Constantinople.

More frescoes can be viewed in the narthex and Latin chapel and date from the 15th to the 16th centuries. In the Latin chapel the scenes depict the **Akathistos** hymn, which praises the Virgin Mary, while the **Arrival of the Magi** represents the Magi on horseback in a style less Byzantine in its execution than the earlier frescoes in the Orthodox section of the church.

From October to April you will have to seek out the village priest to open the church up for you. Photographs are not allowed.

Panagia of Kykkos Monastery
Μονή Παναγίας Κύκκου
This richest and most famous of Cyprus' religious institutions had humble, if rather odd, beginnings. The founder of the monastery (open dawn-dusk year-round) was a hermit called Isaiah, who lived in a cave near the monastery's site in the 11th century. One day, while out hunting, the Byzantine administrator of Cyprus, Manouil Voutomytis, crossed paths and had words with Isaiah. Because of his self-imposed ascetic lifestyle, Isaiah refused to talk to the self-important Voutomytis who promptly beat up the hermit.

Later, while suffering an incurable illness in Lefkosia, Voutomytis remembered how he had mistreated Isaiah and asked for him to be sent for in order that he might ask for forgiveness on the off-chance that his act of charitable penance might also restore his failing health. In the meantime, God had already appeared to Isaiah and asked him to request Voutomytis to bring the icon of the Virgin Mary to Cyprus from Constantinople. This icon had been painted by Luke the Apostle (St Luke).

After much delay and soul searching by Voutomytis, the icon was brought to Cyprus with the blessing of the Byzantine emperor, Alexios I Komninos. The Emperor's own daughter developed the same illness that had afflicted Voutomytis and was cured after Isaiah's timely and, by extension, divine intervention. The icon now constitutes the raison d'être for the Kykkos Monastery and has been kept for over four centuries, sealed in a silver-encased phylactery.

The current imposing, modern-looking monastery structure dates from no earlier than 1831. Nearly all of the beautiful mosaics and other cosmetic features of the monastery's walls and hallways are of recent design and execution, which in no way detracts from their beauty. The monastery grounds are open to the public and attract a steady stream of visitors year-round.

The most appealing part of a visit to Kykkos is the absolutely exquisite **Byzantine Museum** (☎ 2294 2736; admission CY£1.50; open 10am-6pm daily, 10am-4pm Nov-May), with its breathtaking collection of Byzantine and ecclesiastical artefacts. The museum interior is a work of art in itself and it could well take up a couple of hours of your time just to admire the rich and priceless items.

There is a small antiquities display on the left after you enter; a large ecclesiastical gallery with Early Christian, Byzantine and post-Byzantine church vestments, vessels and jewels; a small circular room with manuscripts, documents and books; and a rich display of icons, wall paintings and carvings in a larger circular chamber. Visitors are treated to appropriately soothing Byzantine church music.

A comprehensive *Visitors Guide* in English and other languages is available from the ticket office for CY£3.

Tomb of Archbishop Makarios III

If you have already made the trip out to Kykkos, it is worth the extra effort to visit the tomb of Archbishop Makarios III on Throni Hill, 2km beyond the monastery. The route is not too obvious; follow the road past the main entrance of the monastery and the car park until it bends right and heads upwards. There is a little parking area at the top with a mobile cafeteria. Take the road to the right to reach the tomb more efficiently.

The tomb is quite sombre and nondescript, a stone sepulchre overlaid with a black marble slab and covered by a rounded stone-inlaid dome. It cannot be approached directly and is permanently guarded by a couple of bored-looking soldiers. The tomb was apparently prepared in considerable haste, since Makarios died unexpectedly.

Further up the hill is the little **Throni Shrine** with an icon of the Virgin Mary. The views from here on a clear day are spectacular, with the long serpentine road leading to Kykkos from the east clearly visible snaking over the ridge tops.

Visitors might care to detour about 8km to **Kampos** (see Around Pafos in the Pafos & the

Frescoes, Church of Agios Ioannis Lambadistis

Shepherds and herds, east Troödos highlands

Ancient Kourion amphitheatre, Lemesos region

The glory of Kykkos Monastery, Troödos Mountains

Byzantine church of Agia Paraskevi in Geroskipou, near Pafos

Detail of ancient Roman mosaic floor, Pafos

View of the harbour, Pafos

West chapter), where there are two or three centrally located outdoor **tavernas** that are eager to attract the monastery trade, which is heavy from pilgrims on a Sunday afternoon.

The Solea Valley
Κοιλάδα Σολέας

The route through the Solea Valley to the north of the Troödos Massif is the fastest and most direct way into the area from Lefkosia. The Solea Valley parallels its less explored neighbour to the west – the Marathasa Valley – and is home to a number of attractive traditional villages and a clutch of frescoed churches. The valley served as the hide-out area for EOKA insurgents during the anti-British campaign of the 1950s. It is traversed by the Karyiotis River and is popular with weekend visitors from Lefkosia, as testified by the numerous restaurants and picnic areas dotting the sides of the valley.

The main village serving the region is Kakopetria. The village is actually off the main road itself, but through buses call into the village centre. It is possible to exit the valley via alternative mountain roads to both the east and west. While these routes are slower and unpaved in parts, they're often more picturesque.

GETTING THERE & AWAY
The valley is served by **Clarios Bus Co** (☎ 2245 3234) buses that run up to nine times daily between Lefkosia and Kakopetria in summer (CY£1.10), the first one departing from Lefkosia at 6.10am and the last one at 7pm. There are only two buses on Sunday in July and August (CY£1.90), leaving at 8am and 6pm. Seven buses leave Kakopetria for Lefkosia between 4.30am and 8am on weekdays, with two later services at 1.30pm and 2.30pm. In July and August there are departures on Sunday at 6am and 4.30pm only.

The 11.30am service from Lefkosia continues to Troödos village except on weekends. It returns from Troödos at 6.30am.

KAKOPETRIA ΚΑΚΟΠΕΤΡΙΑ
pop 1200
Kakopetria is the main village of the Solea Valley and here you'll find banks, petrol stations, restaurants and accommodation. As

such it attracts the lion's share of visitors, many of whom are Sunday picnickers to the Troödos from Lefkosia and who drop in to Kakopetria on the way back to the capital for a coffee and a stroll. It is a pleasant place, strung out along both banks of the Karyiotis River with a disproportionate share of restaurants and hotels.

The name derives from the words *kaki petra*, which mean 'wicked stone'. Legend has it that a line of stones along the ridge above the village brought good luck to newlyweds. One day, perhaps during an earthquake, some of the stones fell onto a hapless couple and killed them. The name of the village was thus born.

Apart from having a relaxing old-world atmosphere, the village is also handily placed for visits to two more of the Troödos' Byzantine church treasures. There are Laïki Bank and Bank of Cyprus ATMs in the village.

Places to Stay
Kakopetria offers about the only real sleeping options in the Solea Valley and the choices are good. There are about six hotels and a few rooms to let.

For starters, try **Ekali** (☎ 2292 2501, fax 2292 2503; e hekalihotel@cytanet.com.cy; Grigoriou Digeni 22; singles/doubles CY£28/44) which is a central, two-star hotel and has 30% discounts out of season.

The cosiest option is **Linos Inn** (☎ 2292 3161, fax 2292 3181; w www.linos-inn .com.cy; Palea Kakopetria 34; singles/doubles CY£28.50/38), a gorgeous little stone and wood hostelry in the old quarter. Rooms are decorated with old traditional furniture and have air-con and heating, four-poster bed and minibar; some have fireplaces and a Jacuzzi. There is even a sauna and bar for guests.

Enjoying superb views over the valley is the subtly classy **Mill Hotel** (☎ 2292 2536, fax 2292 2757; w www.cymillhotel.com; Mylou 8; singles/doubles from CY£21.50/43). Perched high up on the hillside overlooking the village, it has exceptionally comfortable rooms ranging from standard to suites. All rooms have valley views and are tastefully decorated in slate and wood.

Places to Eat
Eating out is best on the west bank of the river in the restored, folksy streets of the old village. Restaurants in the village centre are

fine, but the area can get crowded with tourists and the service becomes mediocre.

The **Village Pub** (mezes CY£6 – minimum 6 persons) has a range of vegetarian dishes such as lentils, mushrooms, onions and okra for between CY£2.50 to CY£4. You'll find it at the beginning of the street leading into the old village.

Linos Inn Taverna (see Places to Stay; open lunch & dinner) is perhaps the most atmospheric place to eat in the village. Menu choices include starters such as Cyprus plate (CY£2.75), consisting of taramasalata (a dip made of fish roe), cured ham, halumi cheese, smoked pork slices, koupepia (savoury rice wrapped in vine leaves), cucumber, tomatoes and olives, and extend to main course specialities such as ostrich (CY£7.80) and salmon (CY£7.50). There is a wide range of mix 'n' match mezedes ranging in price from CY£1.10 to CY£4.20.

Mill Restaurant in the hotel of the same name (see Places to Stay; open lunch & dinner; closed 20 Nov-20 Dec) is a very pleasant eating spot. Choices include the house speciality Maryland trout (CY£6.50) plus an imaginative choice of soups and omelettes. Reservations are usually required.

AROUND KAKOPETRIA
Agios Nikolaos tis Stegis
Άγιος Νικόλαος της Στέγης
The **Church of St Nicholas of the Roof** (donations welcome; open 9am-4pm Tues-Sat, 11am-4pm Sun) is the most easily accessible (with road signs) and potentially more interesting of the two churches. This rather odd-looking place of worship is prominently signposted from the Kakopetria and lies about 3km to the southwest of the village on the Pedoulas mountain road. It was named because of the large and heavy roof of this tall barn-like church that was commenced in the 11th century. A dome and narthex came later and the characteristic Troödos pitched roof was added in the 15th century as protection against the heavy snows that sometimes fall in the area.

As in other Troödos churches, the art of icon and fresco painting flourished here in the Middle Ages when Orthodoxy sought refuge from the then-dominant Latin church administration in Cyprus. The **frescoes** at Agios Nikolaos are the usual convolution of images and styles, but among those worth

seeking out is an unusual depiction of the **Virgin Mary breastfeeding Jesus**. Look out also for images of the **Crucifixion**, the **Nativity** and the **Myrrh Carriers**, showing an angel on top of Christ's empty tomb.

Photos (without flash) may be allowed, but the fussy caretaker may subtly suggest you make a donation to the collection box.

Panagia tis Podythou
Παναγία της Ποδύθου
A less commonly visited Unesco-listed church – or rather duo of churches – is this rather charming pair made up of **Panagia tis Podythou** (☎ 2292 2393; open upon request) and **Panagia Theotokou (Arhangelou)**, a couple of kilometres north of Kakopetria (the signpost is easy to miss). The main church was established in 1502 by Dimitrios de Coron, a Greek military officer in the service of James II, King of Cyprus at the time. Up to about the 1950s the church was occupied by monks. The church is rectangular with a semicircular apse at the eastern end. A portico, constructed at a later date, surrounds the church on three sides. The church is covered with the characteristic pitched roof with flat tiles and the floor inside is covered with baked terracotta tiles. The interior decoration of the church was never actually completed, yet frescoes cover the pediments of both the east and west wall. Two 17th-century frescoes on the north and south wall depicting **Apostles Peter and Paul** were never completed. The fresco style is of a Renaissance-influenced Italo-Byzantine painter, that uses vivid colours and a three-dimensional treatment of the subject matter.

The smaller and often overlooked Panagia Theotokou nearby is in fact more impressive, with quite vivid didactic-style panels, quite striking in their freshness even today. Dating from around 1514, the interior frescoes depict a rather fascinating panoply of images from the **life of Christ**.

Seek the caretaker of both churches at the kafenio (coffee shop) next to the Lambrou supermarket in Kakopetria. Bring a torch as neither of the churches has electric lighting.

PANAGIA FORVIOTISSA (ASINOU)
ΠΑΝΑΓΙΑ ΦΟΡΒΙΩΤΙΣΣΑ (ΑΣΙΝΟΥ)
This beautiful Unesco-listed church (☎ 9983 0329; admission free but donations welcome;

open 9.30am-12.30pm & 2pm-4pm Mon-Sat, 10am-1pm & 2pm-4pm Sun) is not in the Solea Valley, but is easily accessible from Kakopetria or Lefkosia. On the perimeter of the Adelfi Forest, 10km northeast (as the crow flies) from Kakopetria, the Panagia Forviotissa is reached by a circuitous route over the mountain ridge east of Kakopetria, or via a well-signposted fast route from the B9 from Lefkosia, via Vyzakia.

The church arguably boasts the finest set of Byzantine frescoes in the Troödos and if you feel that you have overdosed elsewhere, the calm rural setting of the Panagia Forviotissa makes for a delightful day out and can be combined with a picnic in the adjoining forest. The styles and motifs of the frescoed interior cross several artistic generations and are quite arresting.

Most of the interior images date from the 14th and 15th centuries and portray many themes found elsewhere in the Troödos Byzantine churches. However, it is the sheer vibrancy of the colours that make the Asinou frescoes so appealing.

Father Kyriakos of nearby Nikitari village (population 430) is the priest and caretaker of the church and, if he is not already tending to groups of Cypriot pilgrims at the church, he can be summoned on his mobile phone or found in the village itself – ask at the *kafenio*.

There is a pleasant forest hike to the Unesco-listed church of Panagia Forviotissa (Asinou) from the village of Agios Theodoros to the west, off the B9.

Pitsylia Πιτσυλιά

The widespread region of Pitsylia is the least well-known and visited segment of the Troödos Mountains. It stretches from where the E909 starts north of Troödos village to the Maheras Monastery in the east. Pitsylia is home to another clutch of frescoed Byzantine churches, an important Orthodox monastery, some pretty mountain villages and some challenging walks for longer-distance hikers.

The de facto centre of Pitsylia is the sprawling, amphitheatrically laid-out village of **Agros**. Other villages in the area are **Kyperounda** (population 1500), **Platanistasa** (population 170), **Alona** (population 130) and **Palehori** (population 410). The region encompasses a number of small north–south

valleys leading to the west–east ridge of the Troödos Massif and a number of smaller valleys on the southern side of the ridge.

GETTING THERE & AWAY
Transport into and out of the region is strictly functional and designed to get people to and from Lefkosia for work or business. For example, there is a Monday to Saturday bus from Agros to Lefkosia at 7am (CY£1) via Lagoudera and back at midday. Other colourful, old-fashioned local buses link most major Pitsylia villages with Lefkosia, but usually leave early in the morning and return to the villages in the early afternoon. Seats need to be booked, though, and visitors should not rely on them for planned day trips to the region.

This is an area where you need time and energy; hiking from one village to another and perhaps hitching to a better-served transport artery is probably your best bet.

HIKING
The CTO has created marked hiking trails in the Pitsylia region. With the exception of two short circular trails, they generally require an out-and-back approach, unless you are prepared to keep on hiking to the next village or transport link. Most are about 6km (or less), so will require a few hours trekking to complete. The trails take hikers through a combination of forests, orchards, mountain ridges, villages and mountain peaks and offer some of the best recreational hiking in Cyprus.

A short description of the trails in the region follows:

Trail 1: Doxasi o Theos to Madari Fire Station (3.75km, two hours) This is a panoramic ridgetop hike with excellent views. It begins about 2km from Kyperounda.

Trail 2: Teisia tis Madaris (3km, 1½ hours) A continuation of the above trail, it involves a circular cliff-top hike around Mt Madari (Adelfi; 1613m) with excellent views.

Trail 3: Lagoudera to Agros (6km, 2½ hours) It is a longish hike through vineyards and orchards with spectacular views from the Madari-Papoutsas ridge.

Trail 4: Panagia tou Araka (Lagoudera) to Stavros tou Agiasmati (7km, 3 hours) The longest hike, it links two of the most important Troödos Byzantine churches through a forest, vineyards and stone terraces.

Trail 5: Agros to Kato Mylos (5km, 2 hours, circular) This is an easy hike through cherry and pear orchards, vineyards and rose gardens.

Trail 6: Petros Vanezis to Alona (1.5km, 30 minutes, circular) It involves a short hike around the village of Alona, passing through hazelnut plantations.

Trail 7: Agia Irini to Spilies tou Digeni (3.2km, 1½ hours) This is an easy out-and-back hike to the secret caves of Digenis where EOKA resistance fighters hid during the insurgency of 1955–59.

The CTO pamphlet *Cyprus – Nature Trails* describes all the hikes in some detail and provides basic maps, but hikers would be advised to take along a more detailed map of the region.

AGROS ΑΓΡΟΣ
pop 840
Conveniently poised for hiking or driving forays into the surrounding hills is the decidedly breezy and pleasant village of Agros. While the village is generally a workaday home to its industrious residents, it is gradually shouldering the mantle of an alternative mountain resort to the better-known village of Platres to the west. This trend is reinforced by the existence of a communally owned and well-run resort hotel and by the emergence of a few thriving cottage industries making bottled fruit, smoked meats and products made from roses.

Pottery & Rose Products
An unusual yet thriving industry in the village is run by local entrepreneur Chris Tsolakis who runs a rose product and pottery business called **CNT** (☎ 2552 1893; fax 2552 1894; *www.rose-tsolakis.com; Anapafseos 12; open 8am-7pm year-round*). Visit the workshop and learn what can be made out of roses: rose and flower water, rose brandy, skin cleansers, candles, rose liqueur and even a rose-infused Cabernet Sauvignon red wine. Decorative pottery bottles and other pottery items are also made in the workshop.

The Agros Sweet Factory
Got a sweet tooth? Want to see how local fruits are bottled and jarred? Visit **Niki's Sweet Factory** (☎ 2552 1400; *prices CY£0.70-3*) where Niki Agathokleous and her eager team of workers make and bottle every conceivable form of fruit. Buy some orange marmalade, fig preserve or diabetic walnut sweet. Niki exports her product all over Cyprus and even as far as Australia.

The Sausage Factory
Less glamorous perhaps but no less tasty are the products made by the **Kafkalia Sausage Factory** (☎ 2552 1426; *prices CY£4.50-11 according to weight*). All products – which include *lountza* (pork loin), *hiromeri* (traditional smoked ham), *loukanika* (village sausages), *pastourmas* (spicy smoked beef) and bacon, are made on the premises. Ask to see the dark and hot smoke room next to the busy little shop.

Places to Stay & Eat
The best place to stay and eat in the region is at Agros' communally owned and run three-star hotel, the excellent and sprawling **Rodon** (☎ 2552 1201, fax 2552 1235; *www.sway page.com/rodon; Agros; singles/doubles low season CY£26/38, high season CY£32/50)*. The Rodon has excellent rooms and extensive guest facilities including a good restaurant, a bar, two pools and tennis courts. Manager Lefkos Christodoulou is a very keen advocate of green tourism and has worked hard to promote Agros as an alternative tourist destination. Ask for his helpful hiking trail maps.

Two places at the northeastern end of the long, snaking main village drag vie for lunchtime and evening customers. The **Agros Village Restaurant & Pub** (2552 1558; *open Mon-Sat; mains CY£3-4)* is probably marginally better than the nearby **Kilada Restaurant** (☎ 2552 1303; *grills CY£3.50- 4.50)*.

STAVROS TOU AGIASMATI
ΣΤΑΥΡΟΣ ΤΟΥ ΑΓΙΑΣΜΑΤΗ
This Unesco-listed Byzantine church is famous for its frescoes that decorate its gable roof, painted by Filippos Goul in 1494. Access to the church requires some forethought – you must obtain the key from the priest at Platanistasa village 5km away and, of course, return it.

The church is somewhat remote, hidden along a sealed side road off the Orounda–Platanistasa (E906), though it can be approached by a signposted but unsealed road from the next valley to the west through which the E907 Polystypos–Xyliatos road runs.

PANAGIA TOU ARAKA
ΠΑΝΑΓΙΑ ΤΟΥ ΑΡΑΚΑ

This more accessible and more frequently visited Unesco-listed church *(admission free but donations welcome; open 9am-6pm daily)* looks, from the outside, more like a Swiss cattle byre than a place of worship. Its enormous all-encompassing snow-proof roof and surrounding wooden trellis all but conceal the church within. The paintings inside are a wide selection of neoclassical works by artists from Constantinople. The vivid images on display run the usual thematic range, with the impressive Pantokrator in the domed tholos taking pride of place. Look out also for the **Annunciation**, the **Four Evangelists, Matthew, Mark, Luke and John**, the **Archangel Michael** and the **Panagia Arakiotissa**, the patron of the church. The unusual name of the church – *arakiotissa* means 'of the wild pea' – owes its origin to the vegetable that grows in profusion in the district.

If things are quiet here, it might be possible to take nonflash photos, but only if the watchful caretaker approves.

THE TROÖDOS MASSIF

Pafos & the West

For a long time the far western quadrant of Cyprus was considered to be the island's Wild West. Isolated both physically and culturally from the heartland of the country, the region gained a reputation for backwardness and introspection. Its people were considered canny, yet undereducated, and the Greek and Turkish dialects of the west were among the most difficult for an outsider to understand.

Nowadays, only Greeks live in this area, their Turkish Cypriot compatriots having reluctantly moved to the North in 1974. The region is no longer considered a backwater, and indeed it attracts an increasing share of the burgeoning tourist influx, as witnessed by the ranks of sumptuous resort hotels that stretch north and south from Pafos, the region's capital.

Pafos is a delightfully breezy town. Here you can combine both culture and entertainment in a conveniently sized package. You will find some of Cyprus' most stunning archaeological gems, such as its Roman mosaics and Tombs of the Kings cheek-by-jowl with the resort hotels and golden beaches. Cultivated bananas grow in profusion along the southwestern littoral, yet the Akamas Peninsula is one of the island's last unspoilt wildernesses and is home to flora and fauna species found only on Cyprus.

Pretty villages, untouched by time, litter the valleys of the hinterland and the vast Pafos Forest melts almost imperceptibly into the sombre tracts of the Tyllirian wilderness in the North. Small beach resorts that have not yet succumbed entirely to commercialisation await discerning travellers and there are abundant land and sea-based activities to suit every taste. What is more, the west has its own international airport and visitors may fly here directly from many European destinations. An investment of some time in the western region of Cyprus will be well rewarded.

Pafos Πάφος Baf

pop 40,000

While Lemesos is brash and Larnaka is demure, Pafos is quite user-friendly and is one

Highlights

- Explore the Tombs of the Kings, the ancient necropolis of Pafos
- Hike the wild and rugged Akamas Peninsula and look for the rare *Glaucopsyche Pafos* butterfly, the symbol of the region
- Glimpse the rare and endangered moufflon in Pafos Forest
- Walk in the cool shade of the Cyprus cedars of Cedar Valley
- Swim at some of the remotest beaches on the whole island

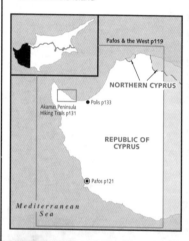

Pafos & the West p119

NORTHERN CYPRUS

Akamas Peninsula Hiking Trails p131

Polis p133

REPUBLIC OF CYPRUS

Pafos p121

Mediterranean Sea

of Cyprus' most liveable cities. The tourism boom has seen the capital of the west receiving considerably more of the tourist dollar than its sisters further east. Kato Pafos (Lower Pafos) is the port annex of Ano Pafos (Upper Pafos) and is home to the greatest number of archaeological sites in the area. It provides a lively and friendly ambience in its renovated port area where visitors, unlike elsewhere in Cyprus' ports, can actually swim. With its palm-tree lined boulevards, tasteful public and private buildings, Pafos is a downright pleasant place to spend a holiday. There are ample restaurants and watering holes and if you

PAFOS & THE WEST

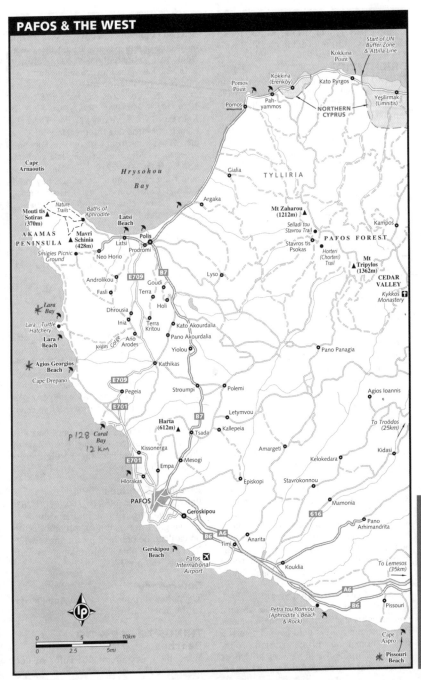

Start of UN Buffer Zone & Attilla Line
Kokkina Point
Kokkina (Erenköy)
Pomos Point
Pomos
Pah-yammos
Kato Pyrgos
Yeşilirmak (Limnitis)
NORTHERN CYPRUS

Hrysohou Bay
Cape Arnaoutis
Gialia
TYLLIRIA
Argaka
Mt Zaharou (1212m)
Kampos
Nature Trails
Baths of Aphrodite
Mouti tis Sotiras (370m)
Selladi tou Stavrou Trail
PAFOS FOREST
Latsi Beach
Stavros tis Psokas
AKAMAS PENINSULA
Mavri Schinia (428m)
Polis
Latsi
Prodromi
Horteri (Chorteri) Trail
Mt Tripylos (1362m)
CEDAR VALLEY
Smigies Picnic Ground
Neo Horio
B7
Lyso
Kykkos Monastery
Androlikou
E709
Goudi
Terra
Fasli
Holi
Dhrousia
Terra Kritou
Kato Akourdalia
Inia
Pano Akourdalia
Lara Bay
Ano Arodes
Yiolou
Lara : Turtle Hatchery
Ayias Gorge
Pano Panagia
Lara Beach
Kathikas
Agios Georgios Beach
E709
Agios Ioannis
Cape Drepano
Pegeia
Stroumpi
Polemi
E701
Letymvou
To Troödos (25km)
B7
Harta (612m)
Tsada
Kallepeia
p 128 Coral Bay 12 km
Kissonerga
Amargeti
Kidasi
Kelokedara
E701
Empa
Mesogi
Stavrokonnou
Hlorakas
Episkopi
Mamonia
PAFOS
616
Geroskipou
Pano Arhimandrita
B6
A6
Timi
Anarita
Gerskipou Beach
Pafos International Airport
Kouklia
To Lemesos (35km)
A6
Petra tou Romiou (Aphrodite's Beach & Rock)
B6
Pissouri
Cape Aspro
Pissouri Beach

0   5   10km
0   2.5   5mi

tire of the beach area you can always retire to Ano Pafos (known also as Ktima) for an afternoon's stroll or evening meal.

ORIENTATION

The two distinct sections of Pafos are 2km apart. Intercity buses and service taxis arrive at Ano Pafos and to get to Kato Pafos you can take local bus No 11, walk or take a taxi. Leoforos Apostolou Pavlou links the two parts of Pafos and Leoforos Georgiou Griva Digeni leads east out of Ano Pafos towards Lemesos. Leoforos Evagora Pallikaridi heads north out of Ano Pafos to Polis.

INFORMATION
Tourist Offices

The **Cyprus Tourism Organisation** (CTO; ☎ 2693 2841, Gladstonos 3; open 8.15am-2.30pm Mon-Sat & 3pm-6.30pm Mon, Tues, Thur & Fri) office is just down from the main square in Ano Pafos. There's another CTO office at the airport (☎ 2642 2833).

There are three **Infopoint** touch-screen electronic information booths in town. One is on the main square in Ano Pafos and the other two are on Posidonos in Kato Pafos: one near the Fort and the other on the main promenade. The information is in English, Greek and German.

There is a handy site at w www.paphos finder.com that lists a lot of useful services for visitors to the city.

Money

There are plenty of banks and accompanying ATMs in both Ano and Kato Pafos as well as between the two along Leoforos Apostolou Pavlou. Both the **Hellenic Bank** (Georgiou Griva Digeni) in Ano Pafos and the **National Bank** (Posidonos) in Kato Pafos have easy-to-find ATMs. The **Hellenic Bank** (Posidonos) in Kato Pafos, in addition to an ATM, has a foreign-exchange service that keeps long hours. There are other private exchange services in both parts of town. You can also change money at Pafos' international airport.

Post & Communications

The **main post office** (Nikodimou Mylona, Ano Pafos) is just west of the main square. Poste-restante mail is held here. There is a smaller branch post office on Agiou Antoniou in Kato Pafos. There is a **Cyprus Telecommunications Authority** (CYTA; Leo-

foros Georgiou Griva Digeni, Ano Pafos) office and public phones are everywhere; the most convenient phones are on the waterfront close to the harbour in Kato Pafos.

In Ano Pafos the most convenient Internet café is **Maroushia Internet** (☎ 2694 7240; 6 Kennedy Square; access per hour CY£3; open 10am-11pm Mon-Sat, 3pm-10pm Sun). In Kato Pafos you have more choice. There is a branch of **Maroushia Internet** (☎ 2694 7240) just off the waterfront with the same opening times as its Ano Pafos sister. The **Website tion C@fe** (☎ 2695 2220; Agiou Antoniou 12) is in Kato Pafos and so is smaller **Baywatch Internet Cafe** (Konstantias 1). Both open at about 10am, close around midnight and charge around CY£2 an hour.

Travel Agencies

Pafos has a branch of **Salamis Tours** (☎ 2693 5504, fax 2693 5505; Leoforos Georgiou Griva Digeni 44). It can issue cruise tickets for Greece and Egypt as well as air tickets to most destinations outside of Cyprus.

Bookshops

The **Moufflon Bookshop** (☎ 2693 4850; Kinyras 30, Ano Pafos; open 8.30am-1pm & 4pm-7pm Mon, Tues, Thur, Fri & Sun, 8.30am-2pm Wed & Sat) is an offshoot of the bookshop of the same name in Lefkosia. It has a good selection of foreign-language books, newspapers and magazines as well as many Lonely Planet titles.

Foreign-language newspapers can also be bought at **Stazo Trading** (Posidonos) on the waterfront and at the **Foreign Press Kiosk** on the main square in Ano Pafos.

Medical Services

Pafos General Hospital (☎ 2680 3100, 2680 3264; Ahepans) is out in the suburb of Anavargo. Information on private doctors on call can be obtained by ringing ☎ 1426. You can also obtain information on night pharmacies on ☎ 1406.

Emergency

The **police station** (☎ 1120) in Ano Pafos is on the main square.

THINGS TO SEE & DO
Beaches

While the waters around the Pafos area are as clean and blue as anywhere else, the open

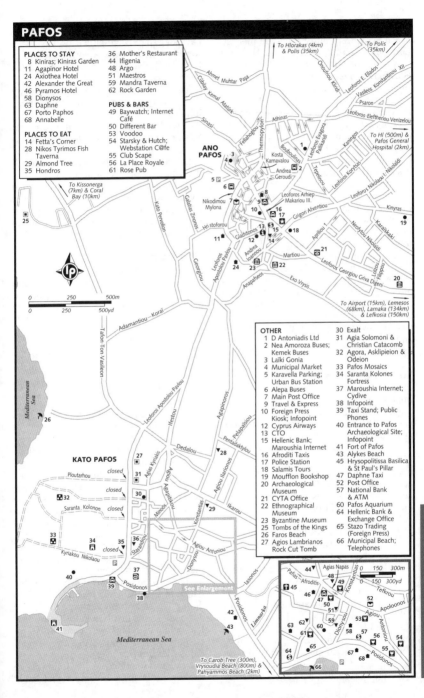

PAFOS

PLACES TO STAY
- 8 Kiniras; Kiniras Garden
- 11 Agapinor Hotel
- 24 Axiothea Hotel
- 42 Alexander the Great
- 46 Pyramos Hotel
- 58 Dionysos
- 63 Daphne
- 67 Porto Paphos
- 68 Annabelle

PLACES TO EAT
- 14 Fetta's Corner
- 28 Nikos Tyrimos Fish Taverna
- 29 Almond Tree
- 35 Hondros
- 36 Mother's Restaurant
- 44 Ifigenia
- 48 Argo
- 51 Maestros
- 59 Mandra Taverna
- 62 Rock Garden

PUBS & BARS
- 49 Baywatch; Internet Café
- 50 Different Bar
- 53 Voodoo
- 54 Starsky & Hutch; Webstation C@fe
- 55 Club Scape
- 56 La Place Royale
- 61 Rose Pub

OTHER
- 1 D Antoniadis Ltd
- 2 Nea Amoroza Buses; Kemek Buses
- 3 Laïki Gonia
- 4 Municipal Market
- 5 Karavella Parking; Urban Bus Station
- 6 Alepa Buses
- 7 Main Post Office
- 9 Travel & Express
- 10 Foreign Press Kiosk; Infopoint
- 12 Cyprus Airways
- 13 CTO
- 15 Hellenic Bank; Maroushia Internet
- 16 Afroditi Taxis
- 17 Police Station
- 18 Salamis Tours
- 19 Moufflon Bookshop
- 20 Archaeological Museum
- 21 CYTA Office
- 22 Ethnographical Museum
- 23 Byzantine Museum
- 25 Tombs of the Kings
- 26 Faros Beach
- 27 Agios Lambrianos Rock Cut Tomb
- 30 Exalt
- 31 Agia Solomoni & Christian Catacomb
- 32 Agora, Asklipieion & Odeion
- 33 Pafos Mosaics
- 34 Saranta Kolones Fortress
- 37 Maroushia Internet; Cydive
- 38 Infopoint
- 39 Taxi Stand; Public Phones
- 40 Entrance to Pafos Archaeological Site; Infopoint
- 41 Fort of Pafos
- 43 Alykes Beach
- 45 Hrysopolitissa Basilica & St Paul's Pillar
- 47 Daphne Taxi
- 52 Post Office
- 57 National Bank & ATM
- 60 Pafos Aquarium
- 64 Hellenic Bank & Exchange Office
- 65 Stazo Trading (Foreign Press)
- 66 Municipal Beach; Telephones

PAFOS & THE WEST

sea often develops a bit of a swell making beach activities a bit of a hit-and-miss affair, unless you like choppy seas. However they have all earned European Union (EU) Blue Flags for cleanliness, so you can swim freely at all the places listed below.

The **municipal beach** abutting Posidonos in central Kato Pafos, despite its proximity to a big built-up area, is very popular and the sea swimmable. A little more out of the way is **Faros Beach**, north of the archaeological site. Best reached by car or scooter, it's a little exposed and is comprised of sand and sandstone rocks and has a couple of onsite snack bars. Some 8km north of Kato Pafos is the large, generally undeveloped beach of **Kissonerga Bay**, backed by banana plantations. There are few facilities here but lots of open sand and rolling breakers.

Heading southeast from Kato Pafos, the first major beach is **Alykes** – no great shakes visually, but very handy. Further along are **Vrysoudia** and **Pahyammos** beaches; like Alykes, they win no prizes for aesthetics but the water is also clean and fine for swimming when there is no surf, and each has a range of facilities from umbrellas for hire to restaurants and toilets.

Tombs of the Kings

Pafos' most popular – and certainly most impressive – attraction is the sprawling site of the Tombs of the Kings (☎ 2694 0295; admission CY£0.75; open 8.30am-7.30pm May-Sept, 8.30am-5pm Oct-Apr). This World Heritage site is 2km north of Kato Pafos on a rocky, convoluted ledge overlooking the sea. It contains a set of well-preserved underground tombs and chambers used as a necropolis by residents of Nea Pafos during the Hellenistic and Roman periods from the 3rd century BC to the 3rd century AD. The name 'Tombs of the Kings' was coined to reflect the impressive appearance of the uncovered tombs and the heavy Doric style of the column pediments rather than any royal pedigree of the people buried here.

The seven discovered tombs are scattered over a wide area and all are accessible to the public. The most recently restored tomb is No 3 and is perhaps the most impressive, with a below-ground atrium surrounded by impressive Doric columns. Other tombs, accessible by stone stairways, have niches built into the walls where bodies were

stored. Most of the treasures of the tombs have long since been spirited away by grave robbers – notably the American consul of Larnaka, Luigi Palma de Cesnola, in the late 19th century.

The tombs are unique in Cyprus and owe their peristyle court structure to Egyptian influences. The ancient Egyptians believed that tombs for the dead should resemble houses for the living and this tradition is demonstrated amply here. A recently excavated Ptolemaic tomb in Cyprus bears all the hallmarks of this influence.

Allow at least two hours for the site and try to visit during the early morning as it can get very hot walking around the sprawling necropolis. To get here, jump on bus No 15 heading for Coral Bay from Kato Pafos.

Nea Pafos

Nea Pafos (New Pafos) is the name given to the sprawling **Pafos Archaeological Site** (☎ 2694 0217; admission CY£1.50; open 8am-7.30pm daily) which occupies the western segment of Kato Pafos. Nea Pafos refers to the Ancient City of Pafos, which was founded in the late 4th century BC. Palea Pafos (Old Pafos) was in fact Kouklia, southeast of today's Pafos, and the site of the Sanctuary of Aphrodite. Cyprus at the time of Nea Pafos was part of the kingdom of the Ptolemies, the Graeco-Macedonian rulers of Egypt whose capital was in Alexandria. Nea Pafos became an important strategic outpost for the Ptolemies and the settlement grew considerably over the next seven centuries.

The city was originally encircled by massive walls and occupied an area of about 950,000 sq metres, reaching several hundred metres east of today's Leoforos Apostolou Pavlou. The streets were laid out in a rectangular grid pattern and archaeological excavations have shown evidence of commercial and cultural activity over the life of the city. Nea Pafos was ceded to the Romans in 58 BC, but remained the centre of all political and administrative life of the whole of Cyprus, while reaching its zenith during the 2nd or 3rd century AD. It was during this time that Nea Pafos' most opulent public buildings were constructed, including those that house the now famous **Pafos Mosaics** (see later).

Nea Pafos went into decline following an earthquake in the 4th century that badly damaged the city, and many other cities in Cyprus. Subsequently, and for prevailing political and strategic reasons, Salamis in the east became the new capital of Cyprus and Nea Pafos was relegated to the status of a mere bishopric. It was at this time that the fine **Basilica of Hrysopolitissa** was built (see later in this chapter). Arab raids of the 7th century set the seal on the city's demise and neither Lusignan settlement (1192–1489), when the **Saranta Kolones Fort** and **Pafos Fort** were built (see later in this chapter), nor Venetian and Ottoman colonisation revived Nea Pafos' fortunes.

The current archaeological sites are being slowly excavated since it is widely believed that there are many treasures still to be discovered. Visitors can spend a busy half-day exploring the sites. The following sections detail the major sites in Kato Pafos. Access to the Pafos Archaeological Site, with all the following subdivisions, is via the one entrance at the western end of the large harbour car park.

Pafos Mosaics Pafos' second most popular attraction is an impressive collection of intricate and colourful mosaics in the southern sector of the archaeological park immediately to the south of the Agora. Discovered by accident during levelling operations in 1962, excavations carried out by the Department of Antiquities brought to light remains of a large and wealthy residence from the Roman period with exquisite coloured mosaics decorating its extensive floor area. Subsequently named the **House of Dionysos** (because of the large number of mosaics featuring Dionysos, the god of wine), this complex is the largest and most well known of the mosaic houses.

Look out for striking **mosaics** depicting Pyramos and Thisbe (Room 16), the Triumph of Dionysos (Room 4) and a series of panels depicting the Four Seasons (Room 4). Altogether, there are 34 rooms displaying a striking variety of themes. The mosaics are best viewed for their colours when given a sprinkling of water, but this treat is seldom afforded to mere tourists. Thus the colours are not as bright as they appear in the excellent official *Guide to the Pafos Mosaics* on sale for CY£3 at the ticket kiosk – recommended reading if you want a blow-by-blow account of the mosaics on view.

A short walk away are the smaller **Villa of Theseus** and **House of Aion**. The latter is a purpose-built structure made from recycled stones found on the site and housing a panel of 4th-century mosaics. The house was named after the pagan god, Aion, who is depicted in the mosaic display which itself is made up of five separate panels. Although the image of Aion has been damaged somewhat, the name Aion and the face of the god can be clearly seen.

The Villa of Theseus is most likely a 2nd-century private residence and is named after a mosaic representation of the hero Theseus fighting the Minotaur. The building occupies an area of 9600 sq metres and 1400 sq metres of mosaics have so far been uncovered. The round mosaic of Theseus and the Minotaur is remarkably well preserved and can be seen in Room 36. Other mosaics to look out for are those of Poseidon in Room 76 and Achilles in Rooms 39 and 40.

Allow at least two hours to see the three houses properly.

Agora, Asklipieion & Odeion The Agora (or forum) and Asklipieion date back to the 2nd century AD and constitute the heart of the original Nea Pafos complex. The Agora consists mainly of the Odeion, a semicircular theatre that was restored in 1970 but does not look particularly ancient. The Agora is discernible by the remains of marble columns that form a rectangle in the largely empty open space. What is left of the Asklipieion, the healing centre and altar of Asklepios – the god of medicine – runs east to west immediately on the southern side of the Odeion.

Saranta Kolones Fortress Not far from the mosaics complex, you will come across the remains of the medieval Saranta Kolones Fortress. *Saranta kolones* in Greek means 'forty columns', which once was a feature of the now almost-levelled structure. Little is known about the precise nature or history of the original fortress other than that the structure was built by the Lusignans in the 12th century and was subsequently destroyed by an earthquake in 1222. The structure had four huge corner towers and another four intermediary towers along the joining walls. A few desultory arches are the only real visual evidence of its original grandeur.

Fort of Pafos

Unlike the interesting fort and medieval museum at Lemesos, Pafos' fort *(admission CY£0.75; open 9am-6pm daily May-Sept, 9am-5pm Oct-Apr)* is rather dull, musty smelling and bereft of any arresting exhibits that may shed some light on its role in the city's earlier history. It boasts an attractive site – perched out on the edge of the new harbour – but its only real attraction is the view from the roof. The fort is in fact all that remains of an earlier Lusignan fort built in 1391; the rest of it was destroyed by the Venetians less than a hundred years later. Entry is via a drawbridge over a moat.

Agia Solomoni & Christian Catacomb

This fairly nondescript tomb complex just off Leoforos Apostolou Pavlou was the burial site of the Seven Machabee Brothers who were martyred during the time of Antiochus IV Epiphanes (around 174 BC). The entrance to the catacomb is marked by a collection of votive rags tied to a large tree outside the tomb. This ostensibly pagan practice is still carried out by Christian visitors today. The tomb was used as a church in the 12th century as can be witnessed by the still-visible frescoes.

Agios Lambrianos Rock Cut Tomb

A little further north on the side of **Fabrica Hill** are a couple of enormous underground caverns dating most likely from the early Hellenistic period. These are also burial chambers associated with the two saints Lambrianos and Misitikos. The interiors of the tombs bear frescoes that indicate their use as a Christian place of worship.

Hrysopolitissa Basilica & St Paul's Pillar

This fairly extensive site *(admission free)* – still being excavated – was home to one of Pafos' largest religious structures. What's left are the foundations of a **Christian basilica** (built in the 4th century) and they aptly demonstrate the size and magnificence of the original church; it was ultimately destroyed during Arab raids in 653. Green marble columns from this church lie scattered around the site and **mosaics** from the church floor are still visible. Further reincarnations

of the basilica were built over the years leading to the present small **Agia Kyriaki** church. The overall area is loosely roped off and signs request visitors to keep off, so you can't get a total picture of the remains.

What is visible on the western side of the basilica is the so-called **St Paul's Pillar** where St Paul was allegedly tied and scourged 39 times before he finally converted his tormentor, the Roman governor Sergius Paulus, to Christianity.

On the northwest side of the site is a tiny **early Christian basilica**, the entrance to which has almost been completely taken over by the gnarled root of an overgrowing tree.

Pafos Aquarium

The Pafos Aquarium *(☎ 2695 3920; Artemidos 1, Kato Pafos; adult/child CY£3.75/2, family pass CY£10; open 10am-9pm daily year-round)* has fishy specimens of all kinds on display and a fun family hour or two can easily be spent here.

Church of Agia Paraskevi

In Geroskipou, just east of Pafos, is the Byzantine church of Agia Paraskevi *(admission free; open 8am-1pm & 2pm-5pm)*. The church is unusual in that it has six domes. Inside you can view a number of 15th-century frescoes, many of which were restored in the 1970s.

Archaeological Museum

This small museum *(☎ 2694 0215; Leoforos Georgiou Griva Digeni, Ano Pafos; admission CY£0.75; open 9am-5pm Mon-Fri, 10am-1pm Sat & Sun)*, a bit out of the way in Ano Pafos, houses a varied and extensive collection of artefacts from the Neolithic period to the 18th century. Displayed in four rooms, the collection includes jars, pottery and glassware, tools, coins and coin moulds. Hellenistic and Roman artefacts include a limestone grave stele, marble statuettes, votive objects, pottery from the House of Dionysos (see the Pafos Mosaics earlier) and terracotta figures of dogs and stags. All in all, it is a collection for the admirer of archaeological minutiae without any outstanding items on display. It is worthy of a browse before visiting Ano Pafos' other two museums.

The Archaeological Museum is about 1km from the centre of Ano Pafos.

Byzantine Museum

This noteworthy museum (☎ 2693 1393; Andrea Ioannou 5; admission CY£1; open 9am-4pm Mon-Fri, 9am-1pm Sat) is south of the main square. It is worth visiting for its collection of icons from the 13th and 14th centuries, ecclesiastical vestments, church vessels, documents and copies of scriptures. The collection, while not outstanding, is interesting enough and contains a 9th-century icon of Agia Marina, thought to be the oldest known icon on the island and an unusual double-sided icon from Filousa dating from the 13th century.

Ethnographical Museum

Also in Ano Pafos, the privately owned and maintained Ethnographical Museum (☎ 2693 2010; Exo Vrysis 1; admission CY£1; open 9am-6pm Mon-Sat, 9am-1pm Sun) houses a varied collection of coins, traditional costumes, kitchen utensils, Chalcolithic axe heads, amphorae and other assorted items. There is more of the same in the garden, including a Hellenistic rock cut tomb. The CY£3 guidebook available at the entrance will help you sort out the exhibits in what can be a seemingly jumbled collection at times.

Agios Georgios Museum

Of possible interest to buffs of recent Cypriot history is this rather bizarre and nationalistic museum (Hlorakas; admission free; open 9am-6pm daily) where the caique, Agios Georgios, captained by EOKA rebel Georgios Grivas in November 1954 landed with a large supply of arms and munitions to start the uprising against British colonial rule. The spot where he landed in his boat is now a museum with the boat itself as the prime exhibit. Grivas and his band of rebels were finally arrested attempting another landing two months later. The museum's walls document their capture and subsequent trial and make for some fascinating browsing.

The site, known as 'Grivas Landing', is 4km north of Kato Pafos and is easily identified by the large Agios Georgios church, built to commemorate the event. Take the No 10 or No 15 Coral Bay bus to get there.

DIVING

The waters off Pafos are ideal for diving and one outfit, Cydive (☎ 2693 4271, fax 2693 5307; w www.cydive.com; Posidonos),

has taken full advantage of the opportunity. Single dives, including all equipment, cost CY£22 while a package of 10 dives costs CY£200. With around 30 sites to explore, some with evocative names such as 'Bubbles', the 'Wreck of the Achilleas', 'Stan's Dilemma' or the 'Valley of Caves', there are enough dives to fill a month or more.

ORGANISED TOURS

Exalt (☎ 2694 3803, fax 2694 6167; w www.cyprus-adventure.com; Agias Kyriakis 24), a Pafos-based outfit, runs a series of trekking and jeep-based expeditions out of Pafos to the Akamas Peninsula, the Avgas Gorge and the Troödos Mountains.

PLACES TO STAY

Accommodation in Pafos is plentiful with a huge array of hotels to soak up the large tourist/traveller presence. The majority is designed for package-tour groups, though all hotels will invariably fit you in if there is a vacancy. Many of the hotels not listed here are along the 'hotel strip' to the north or south of Kato Pafos and, apart from having a handy beach nearby, are normally totally self-contained with pools, restaurants and bars.

The only worthwhile camping ground nearby is at Coral Bay, 11km north of Pafos (see Beaches under Around Pafos later in this chapter).

Ano Pafos

The rather run-down HI Hostel (☎ 2693 2588; Eleftheriou Venizelou 37; dorm beds CY£4.50) is quite a way northeast of Ano Pafos. To get there, walk up Leoforos Evagora Pallikaridi, turn right into Leoforos Eleftheriou Venizelou and the hostel is 750m along here on the left.

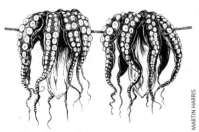

The local seafood is usually a good choice.

The two-star **Axiothea Hotel** (☎ 2693 2866, fax 2694 5790; Ivis Mallioti 2; singles/ doubles including breakfast CY£23/31.50) is a reasonable budget option. This hotel, on the high ground to the south of the CTO, has a glass-fronted bar and reception with wonderful views of the sea – perfect for sunset watching.

Kiniras (☎ 2694 1604, fax 2694 2176; W www.kiniras.cy.net; Arhiepiskopou Makariou III 91; singles/doubles including breakfast CY£32/49) is at the northern end of Gladstonos. The renovated, traditional pension provides rooms with private facilities and there's a very pleasant garden at the back with a good restaurant (see Places to Eat).

Fully renovated in 2001, the excellent three-star **Agapinor Hotel** (☎ 2693 3926, fax 2693 5308; W www.agapinorhotel.com.cy; Nikodimou Mylona 24-25; single/doubles including breakfast CY£32/46) caters to small groups of package tourist as well as walk-ins. There's a pool, evening restaurant, coffee shop and guest parking.

Kato Pafos

Here the selection of hotels can be bewildering. Most work the package-tour circuit so may not be used to walk-ins. The following places are used to walk-ins, though.

The one-star **Pyramos Hotel** (☎ 2693 5161, fax 2694 2939; e pyramos@cytanet.com.cy; Agias Anastasias 4; singles/doubles CY£22/34) is a decent budget place. It's central, basic and reasonable. There's a 20% discount in the off season.

The three-star **Porto Paphos** (☎ 2694 2333, fax 2694 1341; e porto@spidernet.com.cy; Posidonos; singles/doubles CY£43/62) is an older, well-established hotel closer to the sea. It's a very pleasant hotel with many facilities, including a pool, gymnasium, children's area and restaurant.

Daphne (☎ 2693 3500, fax 2693 3110; Alkminis 3; studios & apartments CY£53-55) is an A-class apartment hotel. You get a fully equipped, neat, self-catering studio or apartment for two to four people. The location is also very central.

Dionysos (☎ 2693 3414, fax 2693 3908; W www.dionysos-paphos.com; Dionysou 1; singles/doubles CY£56/82) is a comfortable three-star hotel that is also very central. You get well-appointed air-con rooms, a pool, restaurant and a 50% off-season discount.

A five-minute walk on the southeastern side of Kato Pafos is **Alexander the Great** (☎ 2696 5000, fax 2696 5100; W www.kanika -group.com/alexander; Posidonos; singles/ doubles including breakfast CY£62/88), which is a good resort-style hotel to stay if you want extra luxury. This four-star hotel has most of the facilities you probably need – pool, tennis, gymnasium, children's area, restaurant and bar – and is right on the beach. Discounts of 40% apply out of season.

Annabelle (☎ 2693 8333, fax 2694 5502; W www.thanoshotels.com; Posidonos; singles from CY£131, doubles to CY£174), a five-star hotel, is Pafos' best and most expensive hotel. Breakfast is included. Discounts of 30% apply out of season.

PLACES TO EAT

Pafos has a wide selection of eateries spread far and wide across both Ano and Kato Pafos, though the greater concentration is to be found in Kato Pafos and out along the hotel strip heading north. These establishments run the gamut from raucous British-style pubs to swish bars offering food and fast-food fish-and-chip joints to restaurants offering Mexican, Chinese and Indian food in addition to Cypriot staples.

Ano Pafos

You can always shop for yourself and stock up on picnic items at the **Municipal Market** near the covered bazaar area not far from Karavella Parking.

Fetta's Corner (☎ 2693 7822; Ioanni Agroti 33; mains CY£3-5) is ever popular and can provide a quick and cheap meal. It's open evenings only and locals tend to eat here.

Kiniras Garden (☎ 2694 1604; Arhiepiskopou Makariou 91; mains CY£6-12) is in a leafy and shaded garden that is part of the Kiniras Hotel (see Places to Stay). The rather inviting menu includes such mouth-watering BBQ items as chicken la Platres (CY£6.25), duck la Kythrea (CY£9) and 'Dream' (CY£12.50). There are vegetarian items on offer also.

Kato Pafos

Moving down to around the harbour you will find a much broader choice of places to eat.

Advertising itself as the oldest restaurant in Pafos is **Hondros** (☎ 2693 4256; Apostolou Pavlou 96; mains CY£3.95-4.95). The food is reliable, solidly Cypriot and good quality and features *mousakas*, meatballs, and, for vegetarians, aubergines in sauce.

Mother's Restaurant (☎ 2696 3474; *Apostolou Pavlou*), across the road from Hondros and set back from the street in the Basilica Centre, is a popular restaurant offering a wide selection of Cypriot dishes and a selection of vegetarian dishes from CY£2.45 to CY£3.70. Children have their own menu – a rarity in Cyprus.

There are many bland tourist restaurants along the waterfront. Most decent eateries are clustered around the backstreets.

Argo (☎ 2693 3327; *Pafias Afroditis 21; 3-course set dinner CY£6*) is a quaint restaurant favoured by locals. The service is impeccable and the oven-baked *mousakas* and *kleftiko* (Tuesday and Saturday only) are especially recommended.

Ifigenia (☎ 2694 3504; *Agamemnonos 2; set menu CY£5*), tucked away a block or two northwest of Argo, is a cosy family-run establishment with modestly priced home-cooked food as well as *mezedes*, meat and fish dishes.

One of Pafos' better-kept culinary secrets is the **Almond Tree** (☎ 2693 5529; *Konstantias 5; mains CY£5-10*), featuring a *nouvelle* Cypriot 'fusion' cuisine. Thai/Cypriot tastes titillate palates along with a smattering of stock Cypriot and international dishes.

Carob Tree (☎ 2696 5652; *Kleious 6; mains CY£4-8*) is considered by some to serve up the best Lebanese food in Cyprus. It's a ten-minute walk south of the main promenade area.

There's a Cypriot-international twist to dishes at **Maestros** (☎ 2693 2269; *Theoskepastis 5; mains CY£4.20-8.5*) where you can sample unusual starters such as potato skins in garlic sauce, or deep fried cheese in cranberry sauce. Try also succulent mussels marinated in onion, garlic, parsley, butter and wine sauce, if the starters aren't enough,

At **Mandra Taverna** (☎ 2693 4129; *Dionysou 4; mains CY£5.25-9*) a more mainland Greek atmosphere prevails. Dining is undertaken in a cool and shady courtyard with fountains and overhead fans and the food is of a high quality. The fish *mezes* (CY£9.95) is recommended.

Indian food is tops at the flashy-looking and appropriately named **Rock Garden**

(☎ 2691 2761; *Alkminis 7; mains CY£5-8*). One LP reader said the onion *bhajis* were 'out of this world'. Standard curries as well as a few house specialities feature. Reservations are recommended.

As you walk into the busy **Nikos Tyrimos Fish Taverna** (☎ 2694 2846; *Agapinoros 71; fish mezes CY£8*) you can smell the fresh fish. Caught daily from the owner's own boats, this is *the* place to come for the best fish in Pafos. Choose your fish from those on display (CY£3.75 to CY£8) or settle for an enormous fish *mezes* of 22 different dishes.

ENTERTAINMENT

Pafos is no slouch when it comes to entertainment. There are more clubs and pubs to the square kilometre packed into the centre of Kato Pafos than there are days in August.

Pubs & Bars

As far as drinking is concerned, you can choose from noisy pubs to classy watering holes. Avoid the noisy 'pubs' dominated by tourists along the waterfront and move to the backstreets. Most bars and pubs are clustered along lively Agiou Antoniou, known locally as Bar Street.

One of the classiest café-cum-bars is **La Place Royale** (☎ 2693 3995; *Posidonos*) right on the people-watching strip at the eastern end of Posidonos. This little oasis of glass, cane and wrought iron in a shaded paved patio is perfect for a prepub or club cocktail.

British-run and selling British beer, but OK, is the **Rose Pub** (☎ 2693 6946; *Alkminis 28*), a busy, bustling and generally good-fun place. There are lots of UK and Irish beers on tap (CY£2.30 a pint), snacks and large-screen TVs for the weekend football matches back in Blighty.

Gays drift towards **Different Bar** (☎ 2693 4668; *Agias Napas*) while **Baywatch** (*cnr Konstantias & Agias Napas*) is a busy bar nearby in a prime position for people-watching.

Clubs

There are about eight establishments touting themselves as after-midnight venues. The following were among the hotter of the bunch at the time of research.

Refurbished in 2002, **Club Scape** (*Agiou Antoniou*) now boasts two enormous bars (less queuing), a seated chill-out area and a new sound system. Be present for the weekly Carwash disco parties (prepare to be sudsed and rinsed!) and enjoy classic tracks from '70s disco and '80s pop as well as house, trance, UK garage and R'n'B.

Specialising in '70s funk, soul, jazz and disco, **Starsky & Hutch** (☎ 9983 8054; *Agiou Antoniou*) offers an alternative music scene to the perhaps by now over-exposed garage and house that permeates most clubs around the island.

Attracting more of a local crowd, **Voodoo** (☎ 9942 8143; *Agiou Antoniou*) is a classy club, dishing up permutations of Greek/European pop, jazz and funk. Dress standard is smart and the fun is sophisticated.

GETTING THERE & AWAY
Air
Pafos' international airport is 8km southeast of Pafos. Many charter flights and some scheduled flights arrive at and depart from here. There are also two **Cyprus Airways** offices (☎ 2693 3556; *Gladstonos 37-39, Ano Pafos • airport* ☎ 2642 2641).

Bus
The **Nea Amoroza/Kemek** (☎ 2693 6822; *Leoforos Evagora Pallikaridi 79*) bus companies operate to Polis, Lemesos and Lefkosia. The office is northeast of Ano Pafos' main square. There are two services per day to Lemesos (CY£2) and Lefkosia (CY£3) and around 10 buses a day to Polis (CY£1). There are also three other buses daily (except Sunday) to and from Pomos village (CY£1.10), northeast of Polis.

Alepa Bus Co (☎ 2693 1755; *Nikodimou Mylona 17*) also has daily buses at either 7.30am or 8am to Lefkosia and Lemesos. If you book in advance you can be collected from your hotel; otherwise buses leave from the bus station near Karavella Parking.

Service Taxi
Service taxis are operated by **Travel & Express** (☎ 07 77 474; *Evagora Pallikaridi 9*) in Ano Pafos. Sample rates are CY£2.85 to Lemesos, CY£5.85 to Larnaka (change at Lemesos) and CY£6.60 to Lefkosia (change at Lemesos).

GETTING AROUND
There are no buses to the airport. A regular taxi to the airport from Pafos will cost between CY£5 and CY£7.

The urban bus station in Ano Pafos is at Karavella Parking, behind the Nea Amoroza bus company office. From here buses leave for various local destinations. Bus No 10 runs every 20 minutes for Coral Bay and its beach (CY£0.50). Bus No 11 leaves every 10 to 15 minutes for Kato Pafos (CY£0.50).

Bus service No 15 runs via Kato Pafos linking Geroskipou Beach, 3km to the southeast of Kato Pafos, and Coral Bay, 12km to the north. This service is every 15 to 20 minutes and follows the coastal route and major hotel strip. The cost is CY£0.50.

Afroditi Taxis (*Georgiou Griva Digeni*) are handy for a quick lift if you are up in Ano Pafos, while **Daphne Taxi** (☎ 2624 4013; *cnr Pafias Afroditis & Agias Napas*) are easy to spot in Kato Pafos.

D Antoniades Ltd (☎ 2693 3301; *Leoforos Evagora Pallikaridi 111-113*) rents mountain bikes, motorcycles and mopeds.

Around Pafos

With a hire car or bicycle at your disposal, some time and a sense of curiosity you can spend a few pleasant days exploring the western Troödos foothills and villages, the wild and desolate Akamas Peninsula or the seldom-visited and sparsely populated Tyllirian wilderness of northwest Cyprus. While a conventional vehicle will take you to most destinations described here, you might be more satisfied hiring a small off-road vehicle to get to the out-of-the-way places. A scooter is great for pottering around beach resorts, but you will be severely short-changed if you attempt to tour the region on one. Many private tour companies run jeep 'safaris' out of Pafos and Polis, should you prefer to let others do all the hard work.

BEACHES
Coral Beach, 12km from Pafos, is a well-developed and busy stretch of attractive sand. If you like regimented loungers and symmetrical lines of umbrellas and large crowds, all of whom somehow seem to find a decent spot of sand to lie on, then Coral Beach is for you. There are several different stretches of the beach, all accessible from different parts of the approach road. The cafeterias on the beach are indifferent and serve mainly hamburgers and chips or varieties thereof.

Camping Feggari (☎ 2662 1534; tent & 1 person CY£2.50) is about the only worthwhile camping ground in the Pafos region. There are 47 sites and a snack bar.

ADONIS FALLS
Touted locally as the Adonis Falls, this refreshing 10-high waterfall splashes into the so-called Baths of Adonis, a small swimming hole just upstream from the Mavrokolymbos reservoir. The reservoir is signposted inland off the main Pafos–Coral Bay road, about 1km before Coral Bay. The owner of the 'baths' charges visitors CY£2 for the opportunity to splash around.

AKAMAS HEIGHTS VILLAGES
Travellers between Pafos and Polis have a choice of two routes: the faster inland (B7) road or the slower but more picturesque western road (E701/709) via the villages of the Akamas Heights. If you take the latter route from Pafos, the climb to the heights starts at the largish escarpment settlement of **Pegeia** (population 2360) from where you can branch northwest towards the southern approach to the Akamas Peninsula. Once you are up on the heights, you will come across a series of villages that enjoy a cooler climate, grow fine wine grapes and are prettier than most Cypriot villages. They also make a useful alternate base for travellers wishing to avoid the busy beach scene of the coast further south.

The villages also offer peace and quiet, great views, good wining and dining and relaxed, enjoyable touring. If you prefer to be based in either Pafos or Polis, the villages are accessible and easily visited, even for an evening meal.

There is a convenient rash of rather good agrotourist accommodation establishments scattered throughout the villages. These are without doubt the best options. There are more, but we list here just a sample of some of the better ones. For the full listing see ⓦ www.agrotourism.net.

Kathikas Κάθικας
pop 330
This is the most easily accessible village, famous for its vineyards and wine, and home to a couple of good restaurants.

Loxandras Inn (☎ 9960 8333, fax 2533 5739; ⓦ www.gmbds.com/lox.htm; 2-person

apartments CY£18-27) consists of two one-bedroom apartments and a studio built around a large open courtyard. All rooms have a kitchen and fridge, fireplace, central heating and a TV.

Two eateries pull in evening crowds from both Pafos and Polis. **Araouzos Taverna** (☎ 2663 2076; mains CY£4-7; open lunch & dinner except Sun evening) serves hearty and traditional oven-baked Cypriot dishes. Identify the owner from his portrait hanging over the door.

Imogen's Inn (☎ 2663 3269; mezes CY£6.50), close to Araouzos Taverna, offers similar home-cooked food. The mainstay of the menu is *mezes* – 20 plates split evenly between vegetarian and nonvegetarian. Among other items on offer is an Egyptian-influenced *foul mesdames* – beans in an egg-and-tomato sauce and accompanied by a cumin-laced salad. There is a special access ramp for wheelchair diners.

Pano Akourdalia & Kato Akourdalia
Πάνω Ακουρδάλια & Κάτω Ακουρδάλια
pop 25 & 30
From Kathikas you can detour onto the B7 via these two picturesque villages, where you have the option of staying overnight or taking a relaxing lunch.

Amarakos Inn (☎ 2663 3117, fax 2231 3374; ⓦ www.amarakos.com; Kato Akourdalia; singles/doubles CY£28/49) has spacious, air-con apartments in a wood and stone complex of buildings. There is a pool, children's facilities and an in-house restaurant (see Places to Eat).

Olga's Cottages (☎ 2276 1438, fax 2247 4988; ⓔ lakes@spidernet.com.cy; Kato Akourdalia; 2-3 person apartments CY£60) is a lovely 200-year-old stone residence that offers relaxed, self-contained accommodation.

The **Royal Oak** (Vasilikos Drys; ☎ 2663 3117; Kato Akourdalia; open noon-3pm, 7pm-11pm; mains CY£4-6) is conveniently part of the Amarakos Inn complex. This cosy old house-cum-restaurant serves up palate-pleasing fare such as grilled mushrooms and *afelia* (pork cooked in red wine) with cracked wheat or village sausages.

Other villages
If you proceed from Kathikas without detouring to Pano and Kato Akourdalia you

will be able to detour west off the main road towards the popular and much-visited villages of **Inia** (population 350) and **Dhrousia** (population 390), or east to **Terra Kritou** (population 90) and **Goudi** (population 160), both of which offer accommodation options.

Kostaris (☎ 2962 6672, fax 2627 2339; ⓦ *www.agrino.org/eleonora; Goudi; 2-person house CY£50*) has three beautiful wood and stone houses. This complex also has a swimming pool.

THE AKAMAS PENINSULA

This anvil-shaped chunk of western Cyprus, jutting almost defiantly out into the Mediterranean, is one of Cyprus' last remaining wilderness regions. The other is the Karpas (Kırpaşa) Peninsula in the far east of Northern Cyprus. There is at least one reason why the Akamas has remained relatively untouched: the British army has used the interior of the peninsula as a firing range for a long time and has never been too happy about travellers spoiling their games. While not strictly part of the Sovereign Base Area agreements of 1960, the Cypriot government has tacitly allowed the Akamas to be used for military purposes. This state of play has not sat well with conservationists whose lobbying and outspokenness has brought the controversial status of the Akamas into public consciousness. It could be argued that by isolating the peninsula for dubiously self-serving purposes – such as giving the British army room to play commandos – the wilderness is being preserved de facto. However, the spent and perhaps even unspent ordinance littering the land doesn't look too politically or environmentally sound.

Despite the odds, visitors can still traverse the Akamas as long as they are prepared to walk, ride a trail bike or bump along in suitably sturdy 4WD vehicles. Visitors with less stamina can do it the easy way on board tour boats that sail the Akamas coastline from Latsi, west of Polis. The peninsula can be approached from two sides: from the east via Polis, or from the south via the little village of Agios Georgios (see Beaches under Around Polis later in this chapter). Tracks linking the two entry points are very rough – perhaps deliberately so as to discourage traffic – and care should be taken if riding or driving, as much to avoid live firing ranges as to avoid becoming stuck in a big rut.

The peninsula's big attraction is the abundant flora and fauna that is a result of the Akamas being the easternmost point of the three major flora zones of Europe. Around 600 plant species are found here and 35 of them are endemic to Cyprus. There are also 68 bird species, 12 types of mammals, 20 species of reptiles and many butterflies, of which the native *Glaucopsyche Pafos* is the symbol of the region.

The only public transport to the area is the bus from Polis to the Baths of Aphrodite (see Getting There & Away under Polis for details).

Akamas Hiking Trails

Easily the most popular way to get a taste of the Akamas is to spend a few hours hiking one of the four listed trails that run through the northeastern sector of the peninsula. All can start and end at one of two points: the Baths of Aphrodite or the **Smigies** picnic ground, reached via an unsealed road 2.5km east of Neo Horio.

The most popular two trails are those that start and end at the Baths of Aphrodite. They are both longer than the Smigies trails and offer better views. The first of the trails is the aptly named **Aphrodite Trail**. This is a three-hour circular loop, 7.5km in length. It heads inland and upwards to begin with and this can be tiring on a hot day, so make an early start if you can. Halfway along the trail at the so-called **Castle of Rigena** you can see the ruins of a Byzantine monastery before heading up to the summit at the **Mouti tis Sotiras** (370m). At this point you head eastwards and down towards the coastal track, which will eventually lead you back to the car park.

The second hike, the **Adonis Trail**, shares the same initial path as the Aphrodite as far as the Castle of Rigena, but then turns left and southwards before looping back to the car park. Allow at least three hours for this trail which is also about 7.5km in length. Alternatively you can continue on to the Smigies picnic ground and end your hike there if you have arranged a pick-up beforehand.

Water is usually available at two points along the above trails: at the Castle of Rigena and Kefalovrysi. However, don't count on it in high summer. These trails in any case are best attempted in spring or autumn, or if you must do it in summer – when it can get extremely hot – just on sunrise.

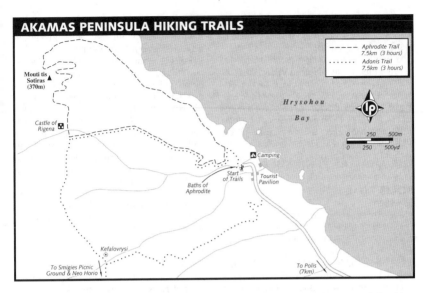

AKAMAS PENINSULA HIKING TRAILS

- - - - Aphrodite Trail
7.5km (3 hours)
.... Adonis Trail
7.5km (3 hours)

Mouti tis
Sotiras
(370m)

Hrysohou
Bay

Castle of
Rigena

Camping

Start
of Trails

Tourist
Pavilion

Baths of
Aphrodite

0   250   500m
0   250   500yd

Kefalovrysi

To Smigies Picnic
Ground & Neo Horio

To Polis
(7km)

The CTO produces a step-by-step, plant-by-plant description of these two trails in a booklet entitled *Nature Trails of the Akamas,* available from the main CTO offices. Numbers in the text refer to locations on the maps found on the last page and there is a detailed botanical glossary that describes the plants you are likely to spot. There is as yet no similar brochure for the two trails that commence from the Smigies picnic ground; the circular 5km, two-hour **Smigies Trail** and the circular 3km, 1½-hour **Pissouromouttis Trail**, both of which afford splendid views of Hrysohou Bay, Latsi and Lara Bay to the west.

Baths of Aphrodite

The grandly titled Baths of Aphrodite (Loutra tis Afroditis) sound more appealing than they actually look. Aphrodite, patron goddess of Cyprus, came to the island in a shower of foam and nakedness (according to Botticelli's painting of the event, at least) to launch a cult on the island that has remained to this day. Legend has it that Aphrodite came to this secluded spot 11km west of Polis to bathe after entertaining her lovers.

The baths are nothing more than a cool water pool in an open rock cave, fed by trickling water from rocks above. Cocooned in creepers, vines and assorted vegetation the baths look very tempting – especially

after a hard day's hiking around the Akamas. However, neither bathing in nor drinking of Aphrodite's fabled bath water is allowed and you will no doubt be jostling for elbow room with the many tourists who make the trip to see the baths and who perhaps leave nonplussed at all the fuss.

To get to the baths, follow the well-marked paved trail from the car park at the end of the sealed Polis road for 200m. If you're suitably inspired, you can continue up the path to start the Aphrodite Nature Trail, which conveniently starts and ends here (see earlier).

Avgas Gorge

Also known as the Avakas Gorge, this narrow split in the Akamas Heights escarpment is a popular hiking excursion. The gorge is reached by vehicle from the western side via Agios Georgios (see Beaches later). You can drive or ride more or less up to the gorge entrance, though low-slung conventional vehicles will have to take care. The hike up the gorge, which becomes a narrow defile with cliffs towering overhead, is easy and enjoyable. There is usually water in the gorge until at least June. The walk will take no longer than 30 to 40 minutes after which you must turn back, although some groups do press on upwards – with some difficulty – emerging on the escarpment ridge and then finding their way to the nearest village of Ano Arodes (not much use if your vehicle is at the gorge entrance).

If you have not taken a picnic with you, excellent food is available at **Viklari** (☎ *2699 6088; mains CY£4-5.50)*, close to the entrance of the Avgas Gorge – a great little eating oasis. It provides lunch (only) for hungry hikers. For CY£4 you get a delicious *kleftiko* BBQ and can relax at heavy stone tables while enjoying great views. Look for signs to the 'Last Castle' from the coast road and seek out jovial owner Savvas Symeou.

POLIS ΠΟΛΙΣ
pop 1890

There are not too many places left in Cyprus that haven't totally succumbed to the lure of the fast buck and overdevelopment, but Polis (or Polis Hrysochous) is one. Polis is on the wide Hrysohou Bay that runs along the northwest sweep of Cyprus from the tip of the Akamas Peninsula at Cape Arnaoutis to Pomos Point at the start of Cyprus' Tylliria wilderness. This small town is ideally situated for holidays that actually leave you time to relax.

Polis is an ideal base for hiking or mountain biking in the Akamas, swimming at a number of nearby beaches, touring the wine-making villages of the Akamas Heights or exploring the often wild and rarely visited northwest of Cyprus. Once the haunt of adventurous travellers from Germany, Britain and Scandinavia seeking an alternative holiday, Polis has gentrified somewhat these days. While it still caters primarily to the independent visitor, low-key development has crept in and provides, in turn, better accommodation possibilities and some of the best and most affordable dining to be had in the whole of Cyprus.

Orientation

The town is set back about 2km from the sea on a gradual rise and is fairly compact. Its centre is a pedestrianised zone from which most important streets radiate. Buses

The Cult of Aphrodite

Cyprus is indelibly linked to the ancient worship and reverence of the goddess Aphrodite (Venus in Roman mythology). She is known primarily as the Ancient Greek goddess of sexual love and beauty, though she was also worshipped as a goddess of war – particularly in Sparta and Thebes. While prostitutes often considered her their patron, her public cult was usually solemn and even austere.

The name is thought to derive from the Greek word *afros* meaning 'foam'. Cypriot legend has it that Aphrodite arose out of the sea off the south coast of Cyprus. She was enveloped in white foam produced by the severed genitals of Ouranos (Heaven), after his son Chronos threw them into the sea. The people of Kythira in Greece hold a similar view, and an enormous rock off the south coast port of Kapsali is believed by Kytherians to be the place where Aphrodite really emerged.

Despite being a goddess, Aphrodite was, nonetheless, disposed to taking on a few mere-mortal lovers, among whom the better-known were Anchises (by whom she became mother to Aeneas) and Adonis (who was killed by a boar while hunting). His death

TRUDI CANAVAN

Aphrodite

was later lamented by women at the festival of Adonia. It is said that Aphrodite retired to the Baths of Aphrodite to refresh herself after consorting with her mortal males.

The main centres of worship on Cyprus for the cult of Aphrodite were at Pafos and Amathous. Among her symbols were the dove, pomegranate, swan and myrtle. Greek art represented her either as an Oriental nude-goddess type, or as a standing or seated figure similar to all other goddesses. Ancient Greek sculptor Praxiteles carved a famous statue of Aphrodite and it later became the model for the Hellenistic statue of the goddess now known as the *Venus de Milo*.

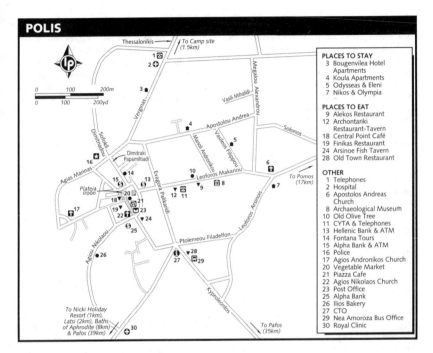

POLIS

PLACES TO STAY
3 Bougenvilea Hotel
  Apartments
4 Koula Apartments
5 Odysseas & Eleni
7 Nikos & Olympia

PLACES TO EAT
9 Alekos Restaurant
12 Archontariki
   Restaurant-Tavern
18 Central Point Café
19 Finikas Restaurant
24 Arsinoe Fish Tavern
28 Old Town Restaurant

OTHER
1 Telephones
2 Hospital
6 Apostolos Andreas
  Church
8 Archaeological Museum
10 Old Olive Tree
11 CYTA & Telephones
13 Hellenic Bank & ATM
14 Fontana Tours
15 Alpha Bank & ATM
16 Police
17 Agios Andronikos Church
20 Vegetable Market
21 Piazza Cafe
22 Agios Nikolaos Church
23 Post Office
25 Alpha Bank
26 Ilios Bakery
27 CTO
29 Nea Amoroza Bus Office
30 Royal Clinic

from Pafos arrive at the Nea Amoroza bus office on Kyproleontos on the south side of town – one of the two approach roads from Pafos. Restaurants and central accommodation are all within easy walking distance, though the camp ground is a fairly lengthy trek out to the beach area.

Information

The **CTO** (☎ 2632 2468; *Vasileos Stasioikou 2; open 9am-1pm & 2.30pm-5.30pm Sun-Tues, Thur & Fri, 9am-1pm Sat*) is central.

There are several ATMs scattered around town, as well as banks to exchange travellers cheques. The **Alpha Bank** (*Plateia Iroön*) on the main square, and the **Hellenic Bank** (*Leoforos Makariou*) are the most central.

There's a **Cyprus Telecommunications Authority office** (*CYTA; Leoforos Makariou*) and a clutch of phones on the same street, with more phones on the road to the camp ground. You can check your email at the **Piazza Cafe** (*open 10am-10pm daily; access CY£3 per hr*) prominently signposted off the pedestrian street.

Dr Dimitris Polydorou at the **Royal Clinic** (☎ 9962 2331; *Efessou 13*) is on call most

hours to assist travellers in need of medical assistance. The town's **hospital** (☎ 2632 1431; *Verginas*) is between the camp ground and the town centre.

Fontana Tours (☎ 2632 1555; *Apostolou Pavlou 147*) books air and other transport tickets and organises 'safari' tours and boat trips to the Akamas Peninsula. You can also organise hire cars here for between CY£14 and CY£46 per day, and accommodation from CY£17 for a basic room to CY£45 for an apartment for two to three people.

There are plenty of companies that rent mountain bikes, motorcycles and cars.

Things to See & Do

Polis is the kind of town where visitors prefer to stroll and unwind rather than actively seek out entertainment or cultural stimuli. Perhaps Polis' greatest drawcard is the proximity of the Akamas Peninsula with its hiking trails, fabled baths of the island's patron goddess and fine swimming at Latsi, 3km to the west.

Nonetheless, there is a pretty reasonable **Archaeological Museum** (☎ 2632 2955; *Leoforos Makariou; admission CY£0.75; open*

PAFOS & THE WEST

8am-2pm Mon-Wed & Fri, 8am-6pm Thur, 9am-5pm Sat) that offers you some cerebral distractions from strolling and dining. The exhibits are mainly grave finds from the nearby sites at Marion and Arsinoe.

There is an extremely old **olive tree** close to the museum, for those interested in such floral phenomena. The trunk of the tree is almost split in two but it is still producing olives after 600 years. The church of **Agios Andronikos** has in recent times revealed some of its Byzantine frescoes. Ask for the key from the CTO office.

The **beach** next to the camp ground is actually very decent. It's sandy, backed by the pines trees, has a beach restaurant and lifeguards to boot. It's a good place to make a day of it with your own picnic.

Special Events
In summer various free concerts take place in the Town Hall Square under the banner of 'Summer Evenings in Polis'. These range from traditional dancing, music and folkloric events to classical- and jazz- music concerts.

Places to Stay
About 2km north of Polis is a **camp ground** *(☎ 2632 1526; sites per tent/person CY£1.50/1)* surrounded by eucalyptus trees and right next to the beach. It's signposted from the town centre, is a fairly large site and is well shaded with good facilities.

Koula Apartments *(☎ 2632 1542; Apostolou Andrea 15; 2-person units CY£25)* offers clean and well-appointed self-contained units.

Odysseas & Eleni *(☎ 2632 1172, fax 2632 2279; Vasileos Filippou 8; 2-person units CY£25-30)* has fine apartments one block to the east. There is also a swimming pool for guests.

Nicos & Olympia *(☎ 2632 1274, fax 2632 1607; e nolympia@cytanet.com.cy; Arsinois 1; 2-person apartments CY£25)* is further out still. It is another small apartment complex that has a pool and air-con apartments.

Bougenvilea Hotel Apartments *(☎ 2632 2201, fax 2632 2203; Verginas 13; 2-person studios CY£30-32, breakfast CY£2)* is a lovely flower-covered complex with pleasant and airy studios. The price drops by up to 50% out of season.

A little out of town on the way to Latsi is the exceptionally comfortable and friendly

Nicki Holiday Resort *(☎ 2632 2226, fax 2632 2155; w www.nickiresort.com; apartments from CY£25).* The hotel is used to walk-ins and boasts a restaurant, snack bar and large pool. The rooms are spacious and have air-con, phone and TV with local and satellite channels. Nicki's Holiday Resort is open year-round.

Places to Eat
Polis leaves most other tourist resorts for dead when it comes to the quality and value-for-money of its eating establishments. Great bread and snacks can be had at the **Ilios Bakery** along Agiou Nikolaou.

For a quick snack and beer and a spot of people-watching, **Central Point Café** *(☎ 2681 5032; snacks CY£1-2.40)* probably has the edge over the other pedestrian-zone eateries in the main square. Sandwiches and pizzas are on offer at reasonable prices.

Tucked away where almost no-one notices is the budget-minded **Alekos Restaurant** *(☎ 2632 3381; Makariou 20; mains CY£3-4).* This is about the only local place where you fill find filling dishes such as black-eyed beans or garden beans with tomatoes and meat. There's a complimentary litre of house wine for each pair of diners.

Not far down the same street is the classy and atmospheric **Archontariki Restaurant-Tavern** *(☎ 2632 1328; Makariou 14; mains CY£4-9)* where the service is attentive, the food top-class. Dine in an old renovated stone house with a courtyard and try chicken stuffed with *halumi* cheese and mushrooms, or octopus *kathisto* – cooked in wine and oregano.

Arsinoe Fish Tavern *(☎ 2632 1590; Grigoriou Digeni; fish meals CY£4-6)* is an atmospheric place on the south side of the pedestrian zone housed in an old stone building and dining is alfresco. Fish is the speciality; try the succulent octopus.

Finikas Restaurant *(☎ 2632 3403; mains CY£5.60-8.50)* capitalises on its central location but it does have a reasonably inventive menu with items such as pork marsala and a vegetarian house special. The chef recommends the 'Finikas chicken'.

The **Old Town Restaurant** *(☎ 2632 2758; Kyproleontos 9; mains CY£7-10),* south of the Arsinoe, is discreet and relaxing. Dining takes place in a leafy, secluded garden with running water. Its specialities include wood-

MAP p 119

grilled chicken, chicken in a spicy yogurt sauce and duck breast in black-cherry sauce. There is also a children's menu.

Entertainment
Call the CTO office for details of events. Ticketed concerts, often given by top-name artists from Greece, take place in the Evkalyptionas (Eucalypt Grove) at the Polis camp site. These outdoor events can be magic on a hot summer night. Tickets cost between CY£7 and CY£10.

Getting There & Away
Two minibus companies go to Lefkosia (CY£5) and Lemesos (CY£3.50): **Lysos Minibus** (☎ 9941 4777) leaves at 5.30am Monday to Saturday (except Wednesday) and **Solis Minibus** (☎ 2635 2332, 9943 1363) leaves at 5am on Monday and Wednesday to Friday.

The office of **Nea Amoroza** (☎ 2632 1114) is on Kyproleontos, beside the Old Town Restaurant. Buses run more or less hourly to Pafos (CY£1, 40 minutes) and in summer it also has services to Latsi (CY£0.50) and the Baths of Aphrodite (CY£0.50) at 10am, noon and 3pm. They return 30 minutes later.

AROUND POLIS
By basing yourself in Polis you can explore the hinterland and do a bit of beach combing if you have a vehicle.

Beaches
Starting at Polis, the nearest stretch of sand is the one in front of the Polis camp site – fine if you don't want to move far from Polis or are camping there. Otherwise, the best beaches accessible from Polis are those on the eastern side of **Latsi**, a small fishing village 2km to the west of Polis. They tend to be mixed sand and pebble and somewhat exposed to the vagaries of the weather, but they are popular enough and well serviced with restaurants. You can reach Latsi by bus (see Getting There & Away under Polis). East of Polis, Hrysohou Bay stretches seemingly endlessly northwards, and while on the map the potential for finding a good, quiet beach looks promising, disappointment is in store. The beaches there tend to be scruffy and isolated, somewhat more exposed to the elements and interspersed with unwelcoming sandstone outcrops. Other than a well-

organised picnic ground close to the beach about 6km north of Polis, facilities for beachcombers are fairly sparse until you reach Pomos 11km further north (see later in this chapter).

On the western side of the Akamas Peninsula, things get better as you move southwards. **Lara Beach**, with its accompanying **turtle hatchery**, is really only accessible by 4WD vehicles from the south, ie, from Pafos. The beach is wild, exposed and totally undeveloped other than for a small beach taverna.

More easily accessible is **Agios Georgios Beach**, which can easily be reached by conventional vehicle from Polis (via Pegeia) or Pafos (via Coral Bay). It is a 100m stretch of shadeless sand and rock sharing the water with a little boat harbour, but beach umbrellas and loungers are for hire. There is a small beach cantina and a couple of restaurants up on the bluff overlooking the beach to feed hungry bathers. It's not a flashy beach, but it's quiet and clean and some people prefer it that way.

Tylliria Τυλλιρία

If the Akamas is Cyprus' last wilderness then the vast Tylliria region comes close to being Cyprus' last forgotten land. Comprising a swathe of sparsely populated, forested territory and a few desultory beach resorts nestled between Hrysohou and Morfou Bays, the Tyllirian wilderness is worth a day or two of exploring.

The only public transport in this area is the bus connecting Pomos with Polis and Pafos.

POMOS & PAHYAMMOS
ΠΟΜΟΣ & ΠΑΧΥΑΜΜΟΣ
If you head up the coast towards Tylliria from Polis the first stop of any consequence you will reach is the small village of **Pomos** (population 570). The settlement is rather strung out and is punctuated with a few perfunctory beach homes and restaurants and one or two places to stay. There is a rather good place to swim at **Kallinousa Beach**, a smallish, sheltered pebbly beach just beyond the little harbour of Pomos where you can rent umbrellas. The snorkelling is good here in the rocky sheltered bays. The handmade sign at the beach entrance says 'Relax to be happy'. Say no more.

PAFOS & THE WEST

If you decide to put down pegs in Pomos, consider renting an apartment at **Gabriel Beach Villas** (☎ 2696 2485; W *www.paphos beachvillas.com; 4-6 person villa CY£60)*. The villas are fully equipped and there is a private pool to service the four apartments. The villas are set back on their own about 500m inland from Kallinousa Beach.

Pahyammos (population 100) is next up, 5km further eastwards. Pahyammos means 'broad sand'. The beach is indeed very broad and sweeps around a large bay up to the UN watchtowers marking the beginning of a Turkish Cypriot enclave (see following). The beach is made up of darkish sand and there is no natural shade but the swimming is reasonable. There are no facilities whatsoever on the beach, but there are one or two places to eat in the rather strung out settlement of Pahyammos up on the main through road.

KOKKINA (ERENKÖY)

Tylliria really felt the pinch when it was effectively isolated from the rest of Cyprus following the Turkish invasion of 1974. The main access road from Morfou (Güzelyurt) into the region was closed and is only occasionally opened to allow passage by civilians from both the North and South on humanitarian visits. Paradoxically, a small parcel of territory known in Greek as **Kokkina** and in Turkish as **Erenköy** remains isolated in the same way, but in this case from the rest of Turkish-occupied Northern Cyprus, surrounded as it is by Greek Cypriot territory.

KATO PYRGOS ΚΑΤΩ ΠΥΡΓΟΣ
pop 1120

This remote beach resort is as far out of the way as you can get in the Republic, yet it attracts a regular summer clientele of Cypriots who come for its isolation, cheap accommodation and food, and laid-back ambience. Kato Pyrgos is like Cyprus used to be and many Cypriots come here just to get away from the rampant commercialism that they recognise has overwhelmed most of the more popular coastal resorts of their island.

The breezy village is strung out along a wide bay that runs from Kokkina Point to where the Attila Line meets the sea – a point frequently brought home by the chattering clatter of UN helicopters that regularly fly in and out of their nearby base. You can bathe at a number of locations along the bay, though the most popular spot seems to be the far eastern end close to the Line.

Places to Stay & Eat

The newish **Tylos Beach Hotel** (☎ 2652 2348, fax 2652 2136; Nikolaou Papageorgiou 40; singles/doubles including breakfast CY£20/40) is on the western side of the village overlooking the newly reconstructed harbour. The comfortable rooms all have TV and air-con.

Not too far away is the **Ifigeneia Hotel** (☎ 2652 2218; singles/doubles including breakfast CY£17/34) with decent air-con rooms and an in-house restaurant.

The **Pyrgiana Beach** (☎ 2652 2322, fax 2652 2306; singles/doubles CY£14/28) is quite

The Kokkina Enclave

Prior to 1974, the villages of Tylliria contained a sizable Turkish Cypriot population. During the EOKA-led anti-Turkish aggression of the early 1960s, Turkish Cypriots were gradually forced to leave their villages and eventually seek umbrage in the Turkish Cypriot port of Kokkina/Erenköy. This strategic piece of land had hitherto been used to ship in arms and supplies from Turkey for Turkish Cypriots. The village remained a Turkish Cypriot stronghold even after the 1974 invasion and despite being some 9km away from the cease-fire line (the Attila Line). However, the villagers have long since been shipped out of Kokkina/Erenköy to be resettled in the former Greek village of Yialousa, now renamed by the Northern Cyprus authorities Yenierenköy (New Erenköy) on the Karpas (Kırpaşa) Peninsula.

Kokkina/Erenköy presents an obstacle to easy passage between the coastal village of Pahyammos in west Tylliria and Kato Pyrgos in east Tylliria. Travellers must now traverse a sealed but narrow and winding inland road that bypasses the jealously guarded enclave. Even though it is possible to stop at one point and peer into what is now a Turkish military base, UN observers, who maintain the peace between edgy Greek and Turkish soldiers perched opposite each other on the heights may signal you to move along lest you unwittingly cause an 'incident'.

The Much-Maligned Cypriot Moufflon

Featured as a stylised graphic on the tail fin of Cyprus Airways' planes, the Cypriot Moufflon (*ovis orientalis ophion*), known as *agrino* in Greek, is Cyprus' de-facto national symbol. The moufflon is similar to a wild sheep and is native to the island of Cyprus. It has close cousins also on the islands of Sardinia and Sicily and in Iran. Today, Cyprus' moufflon population is limited to the dense forest of the Pafos Forest Reserve on the west side of the Troödos Mountains.

The moufflon were once treated as vermin and fair game for trigger-happy hunters, and by the 1930s there were only 15 alive in Cyprus. Since then an enlightened preservation programme has seen their numbers rise to around 10,000 animals today. The moufflon is a shy, retiring animal and will rarely be seen in the wild as it will have long disappeared into the forest before your arrival on the scene. The male moufflon sports enormous curved horns and, while not aggressive to humans, uses the horns in mating battles with its fellow males.

While numbers have reached stable levels, the moufflon is still considered an endangered species. The main danger nowadays comes from forest fires and poachers. In Sardinia an Italian biogenetics team in 2001 successfully cloned a Sardinian moufflon, thus setting the precedent for the preservation of other endangered species.

Moufflons can be seen today at the Stavros tis Psokas Forest Reserve where they are kept safe from depredation in a secure enclosure.

---

near the Ifigeneia and also has a restaurant specialising in fish (meals CY£4 to CY£6). Rooms have air-con, TV and harbour views.

Kato Pyrgos has a fair sprinkling of restaurants and tavernas. **Klimataria**, at the far eastern end, is right on the beach, has the cosiest feel and the food is pretty reasonable. Bank on CY£5 for a simple seaside meal with beer.

STAVROS TIS PSOKAS
ΣΤΑΥΡΟΣ ΤΗΣ ΨΟΚΑΣ

From Kato Pyrgos or Pahyammos you can strike southwards into the Tylliria hinterland. If taking this route, make sure to detour slightly to the popular forest resort of **Stavros tis Psokas**, also accessible from Pafos (51km) via a picturesque road, but still unsealed for a considerable distance. This vast picnic site is a forest station responsible for fire control in the Pafos Forest. The area is surprisingly popular among day-trippers and Cypriots wanting to 'get back to the woods'. In a small enclosure, signposted from the main parking area, you can get a glimpse of the rare and endangered native Cypriot **moufflon**, (see boxed text 'The Much-Maligned Cypriot Moufflon'). Move quietly and slowly if you want to see them as they get rather skittish at the approach of humans.

The Stavros tis Psokas forest station has a **Hostel** (☎ 2633 2144; *rooms per person around CY£12*) with cool rooms. The only way up here is under your own steam.

Hiking Trails

You can do some forest trekking from the Stavros tis Psokas forest station. There are two trails. The **Horteri Trail,** a 5km, two-hour circular hike, loops around the eastern flank of the Stavros Valley. The trail starts at the Platanoudkia Fountain about halfway along the approach road to the forest station from the Stavros Saddle (Selladi tou Stavrou) on the main through road. The hike involves a fair bit of upward climbing and can get tiring in the heat of summer, so tackle the walk early in the day if you can.

The second trail is the **Selladi tou Stavrou,** a 2.6km circular loop of the northern flank of the Stavros Valley. The start is prominently marked from the junction of the forest station approach road and the main through road (the Saddle). A longer alternative route (7km, 2½ hours) is to tackle the trail anti-clockwise and then branch south (right) to the heliport. From there you can walk along a forest road to the forest station proper.

The CTO's brochure *Cyprus – Nature Trails* describes these trails in more detail.

Kambos Κάμπος

Although technically part of the Kykkos Monastery sector of the Troödos, the pretty village of Kampos (population 430) is literally stuck out on the southern edge of the Tyllirian wilderness with, these days, only one road in and out. The road that leads

PAFOS & THE WEST

north from the village now comes to an ig-nominious end after 12km at the Attila Line and curious drivers must turn back. Still, you could do worse; Kampos is an ideal spot for lunch, especially if you have been visiting the Kykkos Monastery (see The Marathasa Valley in the Troödos Massif chapter). There is even one hotel should you decide to stay put for the night.

This part of Tylliria is now less isolated than it was, thanks to the completion of a good sealed road that leads across the Tyl-lirian hinterland and northern extent of the vast Pafos Forest linking the Kykkos Monastery with Kato Pyrgos and Pahyam-mos. Take it slow though; the road, while good, is *very* winding and tiring to drive. Most maps still show it as unsealed. It is a much shorter, if more challenging, route into the Tyllirian wilderness than the traditional road from the southeast via Polis.

WESTERN TROÖDOS

The sparsely populated area flanking the western foothills of the Troödos Mountains is home to few sights other than slow-moving villages, where traditions hold fast and the local Cypriot dialect is just that bit more im-penetrable. If you are looking for a route to Central Troödos from the west coast you can now easily follow a mixture of good sealed and unsealed roads into the mountains. The best route takes you to the Kykkos Monastery via the village of Pano Panagia.

Pano Panagia Πάνω Παναγιά

Fans of Cypriot political history may wish to make an excursion to the **birthplace of Makarios III**, Cyprus' famous son and once archbishop-president of Cyprus. Set in the western foothills of the Troödos Mountains, Pano Panagia (population 560) village is best approached from Pafos. Here you can visit the **Makarios Cultural Centre** (admis-sion free; open 9am-1pm & 2pm-5pm), which is less grandiose than the title would suggest. It contains some memorabilia from Makarios' life as politician and priest, and plenty of photos. Among the odder exhibits

are his priestly vestments, overcoat, dress-ing gown, shoes and slippers.

The **childhood house of Makarios** (ad-mission free; open 10am-1pm & 2pm-6pm daily) is perhaps of more interest. It is well signposted from the village centre. The quite large house contains photos and more memorabilia from the life of the younger Makarios. If the house is locked, obtain the key from the nearby Cultural Centre.

If you decide to spend the night in Panagia, you could try **Arhondiko tou Meletiou** (☎ 2693 5011, fax 2694 7395; Panagia; 2-3 person apartments CY£20) located right next to the house of Archbishop Makarios. Other options are the folksy **Stelios House** (☎ 2672 2343, fax 2672 2971; 2-person apartments CY£24), or the spacious apartments of **Palati tou Xylari** (☎ 9961 4673, fax 2233 9849; e palati@cytanet.com.cy; 2-person studios CY£25) or the twin apartments of **Liakoto** (☎ 2623 5597, fax 2624 2025; 2-person studios CY£20). All four places are part of the CTO-sponsored agrotourism scheme and represent good-value and high-quality accommodation.

A few simple tavernas on the main street provide adequate eating options.

Cedar Valley

If you are touring the western Troödos hin-terland, you can detour onto an unsealed road to visit the startlingly different Cedar Valley. This cool valley is home to a large number of the unusual indigenous Cypriot cedars (Cedrus brevifolia) – close cousins to the better-known Lebanese cedar. The val-ley is approached via a winding, unsealed forest road from Pano Panagia on the Pafos side of the Troödos Mountains, or along a signposted unsealed road from the Kykkos (eastern) side of the Troödos along the Kykkos–Stavros tis Psokas road. There is a picnic ground here and the opportunity to hike 2.5km to the summit of **Mt Tripylos**.

You'll need a vehicle to see these places as public transport is patchy or nonexistent. Alternatively you could join a tour from ei-ther Polis or Pafos (see earlier in this chap-ter for details of tour operators).

Larnaka & the East

The majority of visitors to Cyprus arrive at Larnaka international airport in Cyprus' southeast and their first impressions of the island are invariably formed by the drive from the airport to their hotel. Larnaka is the largest town in the area and it has played its part in Cypriot history. The streets of the present-day town are built over the ancient city of Kition. Lazarus, who was raised from the dead by Jesus, came to live in Larnaka and brought Christianity to Cyprus. An important Islamic shrine in honour of the aunt of Mohammed sits forlornly at the edge of a shimmering salt lake close to Larnaka airport.

The island's first documented settlers lived in round stone houses in the remarkable Neolithic settlement of Choirokoitia, west of Larnaka. Along the sweeping expanses of Larnaka Bay and clustered around the sandy coves of Cape Greco is the heart of Cyprus' blooming tourist industry.

At Agia Napa, on the far eastern edge of the South, travellers can witness a party that continues from April to November, yet within a few kilometres is a secluded beach where few visitors venture. Inland and away from the high life and occasional excesses of the coast you will find small, timeless villages more reminiscent of the Australian outback than Mediterranean Europe, where the potato is king, not the tourist dollar. It is in eastern Cyprus, though, that the poignant and painful division of the island is only too obvious. Travellers curious enough to stare across barbed wire fencing – the Attila Line – into the ghost town of Varosia (Maraş), abandoned by fleeing Greek Cypriots in 1974 and never resettled. Yet, against the odds, the east is home to one village where Greek and Turkish Cypriots still manage to live together in harmony – a reminder of how things used to be. The east offers its visitors both cerebral and corporal pleasures and a stay here will not easily be forgotten.

Larnaka Λάρνακα

pop 46,700

Larnaka is the first port of call for most visitors to Cyprus. However, unless you are booked to stay in Larnaka itself, you will

Highlights

- Peek over barbed wire into the ghost town of Varosia (Maraş), which was abandoned in 1974
- Bargain for an exquisite piece of handmade Lefkara lacework
- Lap up the relaxed lifestyle of Larnaka, the vibrant buzzing city of eastern Cyprus
- Party hard at Agia Napa, one of the Mediterranean's hottest nightlife venues
- Enjoy some of the best beaches and water sports in Cyprus at Protaras and Pernera

NORTHERN CYPRUS
Larnaka & the East p140

Agia Napa p151

REPUBLIC OF CYPRUS
Larnaka p143

Mediterranean Sea

more than likely be whisked off from the airport to your hotel with nary a glimpse of this most attractive of Cypriot cities.

Both a commercial port and yacht marina, Larnaka is also home to Cyprus' largest community of foreigners. Many Lebanese Christians took refuge here during that country's troubles in the '80s. Many never went home. Foreign governments in the past tended to use Larnaka as a base for their consulates in preference to inland and less easily accessible Lefkosia. Prior to 1974, the city was also home to a large Turkish Cypriot population which, following the division of the island by their mainland compatriots, was obliged to ruefully flee to the North.

LARNAKA & THE EAST

LARNAKA & THE EAST

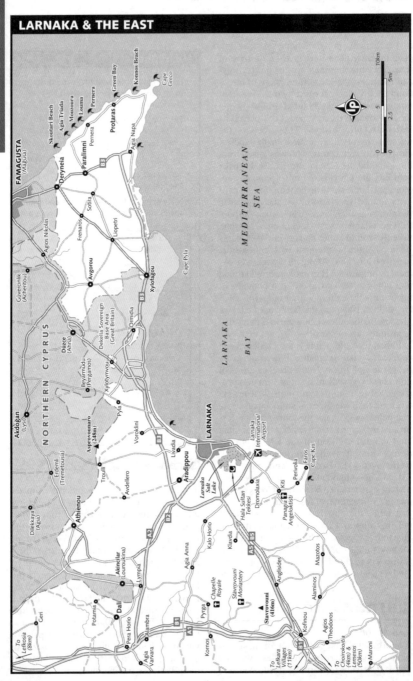

Larnaka is a resort destination and the town centre and the tourist strip to the north-east are equally popular choices for foreign visitors. There are not many gripping sites to tempt the amateur archaeologist or historian and the city is best enjoyed for its relaxed dining, easy ambience and warm – though occasionally humid and torrid – climate.

HISTORY

Larnaka was originally established as a Middle Bronze Age colony sometime between the 14th and the 11th centuries BC. It prospered as the port for export of copper and other metals mined in the Troödos Mountains and at Tamassos to the west. The city flourished well into Hellenistic times despite siding with the Persians in the Greek–Persian wars. Kimon of Athens arrived in 450 BC to subdue Kition, but died prematurely outside the city walls. His statue now graces the Larnaka promenade. Zenon of Kition, the Stoic philosopher and darling of the Athens intelligentsia, was born in Larnaka in 335 BC. His radical philosophies seem not to have pleased Zenon himself in the final analysis; he died by his own hand at the age of 98.

Lazarus brought Christianity to Larnaka and became its first bishop. When he died, he was buried in the vault of the church that now carries his name. Little more is known about Kition until at least the 14th century when it took the name of Salina because of the nearby salt lake. Larnaka in Greek means 'funerary chest' and it is likely that the city received this name as a result of ancient tombs discovered in the early days of its development in the 16th century.

Under the Ottomans, the city was an important port and became home to a growing number of dignitaries. Many of them were emissaries from foreign countries and a disquieting number of them engaged in amateur archaeology; much of Larnaka's archaeological wealth was secretly sequestered and spirited away during this time.

Over the period of British rule of 88 years, Larnaka gradually fell behind Famagusta (Ammohostos in Greek and Mağusa in Turkish) and Lemesos in importance. It only really received a demographic jolt following the influx of refugees from the North in 1974 and the development of its hitherto backwater airfield as the country's prime international airport.

ORIENTATION

Larnaka is a reasonably compact city and most major sites and facilities are within walking distance of transport terminals and central hotels. The city centre is encircled by Leoforos Grigoriou Afxentiou to the north, Leoforos Artemidos to the west, Leoforos Faneromenis to the south and in the east by Leoforos Athinon. Leoforos Athinon is a landscaped, paved street lined with palm trees and is usually called the Finikoundes (Palm Trees) Promenade. Within the rectangle formed by these major avenues is the main business and central tourist district. Immediately south of this area and adjoining the seafront is the former Turkish district, the beginning of which is marked by the Grand Mosque and Larnaka Fort.

Buses to/from Deryneia and Paralimni arrive at and depart from the bus stop opposite the police station. All other buses arrive at and depart from the bus stop on Leoforos Athinon opposite the Four Lanterns Sunotel. Service-taxi terminals are all close to the town centre.

INFORMATION
Tourist Offices

The **Cyprus Tourism Organisation** (*CTO* ☎ *2465 4322; Plateia Vasileos Pavlou; open 8.15am-2.30pm & 3pm-6.15pm Mon, Tues, Thur & Fri, 8.15am-1.30pm Sat*) office is two short blocks west of the Sun Hall hotel. There is also a **CTO** (☎ *2464 3576; open 8:15am-11pm daily*) at the airport. Flight information can be obtained on ☎ 2464 3000.

Money

There is an ATM and exchange facility at Larnaka airport that is open for all flights. However, it is in the departures area. Within the precinct of the city centre, there are plenty of banks for changing money and some of them are open afternoons. There are ATMs at the **National Bank of Greece** (*Zinonos Kitieos*) and **Hellenic Bank** in the same street, 200m further north on the opposite side.

Post & Communications

The main **post office** (*Plateia Vasileos Pavlou*) is close to the CTO office and poste restante mail is held here. There is also a smaller branch close to the church of Agios Lazaros.

There is a fair number of Internet cafés in town. An easy one to find is **Alto Internet**

Café (☎ 2465 9625; Leoforos Grigoriou Afxentiou; open 10am-2am; CY£4 per hour), close to the centre.

Travel Agencies

The Larnaka branch of **Salamis Tours** (☎ 2465 6464, fax 2465 0698; Leoforos Grigoriou Afxentiou 7) is in central Larnaka. As well as Israel or Egypt cruise tickets, you can take advantage of a wide range of other travel-related services.

Bookshops

Academic & General (☎/fax 2462 8401; Ermou 41) is the best place to go for English-language books, stationery and maps. The **Tofarides Bookshop** (☎ 2465 4912; Zinonos Kitieos 45-47) in the city centre is another excellent choice with a wide selection of English-language publications.

Laundry

You can get your clothes washed and pressed at **Artemis Laundrette** (Armenikis Ekklisias 12) or at the **White House Self-Service Laundry** (Shop 5, Helen Court). A full-service wash costs about CY£4, while a self-service wash and dry will cost around CY£2.

Toilets

There are signposted public toilets 100m east of the CTO office at the northern end of the city centre.

Medical Services

Larnaka's main public **hospital** (☎ 2463 0322; Leoforos Grigoriou Afxentiou) is northwest of the city centre. **Night pharmacy assistance** (☎ 1414) can also be contacted.

Emergency

The **police station** (☎ 2480 4040; cnr Leoforos Grigoriou Afxentiou & Leoforos Arhiepiskopou Makariou) is easy to find near the yacht marina.

THINGS TO SEE & DO
Church of Agios Lazaros & Byzantine Museum

This hard-to-miss church (☎ 2465 2498; admission free; open 8am-12.30pm & 3.30pm-6.30pm daily Apr-Aug, 8am-12.30pm & 2.30pm-5.30pm Sept-Mar), at the southern end of Larnaka, owes its existence to a rather interesting story. Tradition says that Jesus raised

Lazarus from the dead. Immediately after Lazarus was expelled by the Jews and came to Larnaka, he was ordained as a bishop by St Barnabas. He reportedly remained a bishop for 30 years. After he died (for the second time) he was buried where the current church stands. His relics did not stay entombed for very long after their discovery in 890, as they were transported to Constantinople and subsequently removed to Marseille in 1204.

The church structure itself is a mix of Latinate and Orthodox influences, the most obvious example being the prominent bell tower that is visible for some distance. The church was in fact used by both Catholic and Orthodox worshippers for some 200 years; this is affirmed by inscriptions in Latin, French and Greek that can be seen in the portico.

The **Tomb of Lazarus** is under the altar, accessible by stairs to the right, but in fact comprises just one of several sarcophagi in the catacomb, suggesting that the area was used as a general burial place.

In the courtyard of the church is the Byzantine Museum (☎ 2465 2498; admission CY£0.50; open 8.30am-1pm & 3pm-5.30pm Mon, Tues, Thur, Fri & Sun; 8.30am-1pm Wed & Sat), which houses a collection that supplants a previous ecclesiastical collection lost over the period 1964–74. During that time the original collection containing priceless relics and artefacts was housed in Larnaka Fort, which had come under Turkish administration following the insurgences of the early '60s. In 1974 the administration of the fort reverted once more to the Greeks, but the priceless treasures had apparently disappeared. All that is left of the original collection is the catalogue and the missing items are still being sought. The present collection was assembled in their place and it is still a fairly extensive and impressive display of Byzantine ecclesiastical artefacts, icons and church utensils. Many of the items on display have been donated by Russian clerics.

Pierides Archaeological Foundation Museum

This former private residence of the Pierides family houses an admirable collection of artefacts in this grandly named museum (☎ 2465 2495; Zinonos Kitieos 4; admission CY£1; open 9am-1pm Mon-Sat, 11am-1pm Sun year-round). The founder, Dimitrios Pierides, commenced this private collection in 1839 as a

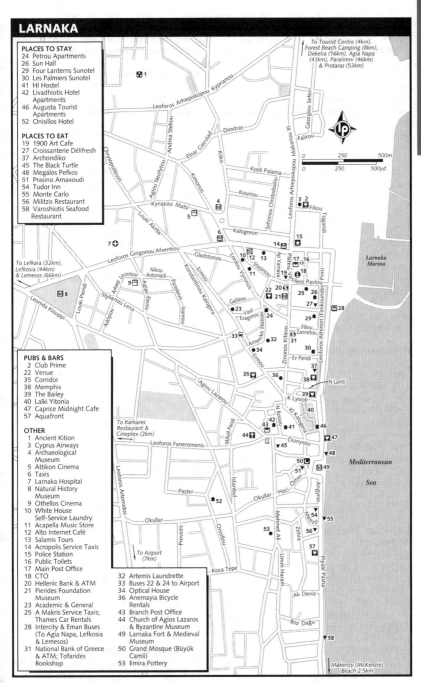

way to stave off the depletion of Cyprus' archaeological heritage by amateur archaeologists/diplomats, such as the infamous Luigi Palma di Cesnola. The US consul in Larnaka spirited away an enormous number of artefacts, which are now in New York's Metropolitan Museum. The Pierides Museum competes vigorously with the state-operated Archaeological Museum and features artefacts and finds from all over Cyprus. The exhibition includes a fairly comprehensive representation of Cypriot history from prehistoric times (7000–1500 BC), the Mycenaean/Achaean period (1400–1100 BC), the Iron Age (1050–54 BC), the Roman occupation, through to the later Byzantine, Crusader, Frankish, Venetian and Ottoman periods.

There are six rooms in the museum, each arranged chronologically. Look out for a terracotta of the **howling man** sitting on a stool in room 1. What use it originally served can only be guessed. Room 4 is devoted to a fascinating collection of **Roman glassware** and room 5 is given over to a display of **Cypriot folk art**, with weaving and embroidery, woodcarvings and traditional costumes.

Archaeological Museum

This museum (☎ 2463 0169; Kalogreon; admission CY£0.75; open 9am-2.30pm Mon-Fri, 3pm-5pm Thur Sept-June) is second best to its more illustrious partner, the Pierides Foundation Museum. There is a wide collection of predictable pottery, much of it Mycenaean, from Kition. There is a reconstructed **Neolithic tomb** from Choirokoitia, terracotta votive figures, Roman glassware and even folk art. Spread out over five rooms, the collection is worth a browse, though you may get a sense of deja vu if you have already visited the Cyprus Museum in Lefkosia.

Larnaka Fort & Medieval Museum

The fort (☎ 2463 0576; admission CY£0.75; fort & museum open 9am-7pm Mon-Fri) stands prominently at the water's edge dividing Larnaka's former Greek and Turkish sectors. Originally a Lusignan-era castle, the present structure is a result of remodelling by the Ottomans from around 1605, but is otherwise fairly unimpressive. There is little to see in the castle itself, but the upper floor contains a small Medieval Museum with various displays from Hala Sultan

Tekkesi and Ancient Kition. The open area inside the fort is occasionally used for concerts and other cultural events.

Ancient Kition

Much of present-day Larnaka is built over the original site of Ancient Kition (admission CY£0.75; open 9am-2.30pm Mon-Fri) so no real excavations are expected to be carried out unless Larnaka is demolished – an unlikely prospect. What is left of the ancient city is a small site known as **Area II**, a rather nondescript and essentially uninteresting site about 1km northwest of the city centre. A raised walkway takes you over what is left of the remains of Ancient Kition, where excavations sporadically continue. Labels or explanations are sparse, so unless you are an amateur archaeologist, the layout may not mean much to you.

Natural History Museum

This small but varied and interesting collection of exhibits (☎ 2465 2569; admission CY£0.20; open 10am-1pm & 4pm-6pm Tues-Sun 1 June-30 Sept; 10am-1pm & 3pm-5pm Tues-Sun 1 Oct-31 May) is dedicated primarily to the fauna, flora, geology, insect and marine life of Cyprus. Displayed in a series of eight rooms, the museum is very popular with school groups and is an excellent introduction to the natural history of the island, which would otherwise be very hard to witness.

The museum is a little out of the way off Leoforos Grigoriou Afxentiou in the Municipal Gardens at the western edge of town.

Grand Mosque

The Büyük Camii, or Grand Mosque, stands alone on the periphery of both the former Greek and Turkish quarters of Larnaka. Somewhat underused since 1974, the mosque is nonetheless the spiritual home to Larnaka's Muslim community. Originally built in the 16th century, and once called the Latin Holy Cross Church, the current building is the result of a 19th-century restoration. The mosque reluctantly accepts visitors, though not during prayer times, and you may also be able to climb the **minaret** for a small fee. The views are quite impressive.

ORGANISED TOURS

The CTO runs a couple of free, chaperoned walks from its office. This is a painless way

Monastery doorway, Pafos

Tombs of the Kings, Pafos

Fishing boat at Agios Georgios, Pafos region

Delightful Adonis Falls, Pafos region

VERONICA GARBUTT

Ancient Choirokoitia, Larnaka region

PAUL HELLANDER

Nightlife, Larnaka

PAUL HELLANDER

Tombs of the Kings, Pafos

OLIVER STREWE

Gnarled ancient olive tree

to get an introduction to the layout and attractions of Larnaka. The first one called *Larnaka – Its Past & Present* starts at 10am on Wednesday from the CTO. Call ☎ 2464 4322 for further information. The second one is called *Skala – Its Craftsmen* and leaves at 10am on Friday from Larnaka's Fort. Call ☎ 2463 0576 for further information.

SPECIAL EVENTS

In June each year – usually about 50 days after Orthodox Easter – the annual Kataklysmos Festival is held in most major coastal towns, but holds special significance for Larnaka. Kataklysmos means 'deluge' in Greek and is ostensibly a feast to celebrate the salvation of Noah from the Flood, but is often an excuse for people to throw water at one another and generally have fun. In Larnaka, Leoforos Athinon is given over to a nightly bazaar of stall holders selling snacks and trinkets interspersed with various concerts. During the day there are water-based activities such as windsurfing and kayak races as well as swimming competitions.

PLACES TO STAY

Larnaka offers a reasonable range of accommodation options spread out quite evenly across its downtown area as well as in the hotel stretch northeast of the town centre. Popular options are self-contained apartments, which are excellent value if there are at least two of you.

PLACES TO STAY – BUDGET & MID-RANGE

There are two budget options in Larnaka, as the accommodation scene is pitched firmly at the mid-range (family) apartment group and the top-end resort-hotel scene.

Forest Beach Camping *(☎ 2464 4514; 1 person & tent CY£2.50)* is 8km towards Agia Napa. The site is somewhat rundown but it is passable.

HI Hostel *(☎ 2462 1188; Nikolaou Rossou 27; dorm beds CY£3, family room CY£5)* is east of St Lazaros church and has mixed or single-sex dorms. It's small and facilities are minimal but there is a little kitchen and communal toilets and showers. HI cards are not required and there is no discount for holders.

The best mid-range options are hotel apartments where you can be self-contained and cook for yourself, but they are usually require a minimum stay of two days. Forward bookings are always a good idea.

Les Palmiers Sunotel *(☎ 2462 7200, fax 2462 7204; Leoforos Athinon 12; singles/doubles CY£22.50/38)* is a central, reasonable hotel, with 20% discounts in the off season.

Augusta Tourist Apartments *(☎ 2465 1802; Leoforos Athinon 102; 2-person apartment CY£22, air-con extra CY£2.50)* is a smallish, modern block of holiday apartments right on Leoforos Athinon. Apartments are very clean and neat and each sports a kitchen and TV.

Livadhiotis Hotel Apartments *(☎ 2462 6222, fax 2462 6406; e livadhiotishotapts@ cytanet.com.cy; Nikolaou Rossou 50; 2-person studios CY£17)* is similar to the Augusta but operates more like a hotel; it is also somewhat cheaper. These neat apartments are self-contained with kitchenette, phone and TV, and are also very centrally located.

About 500m west of the fort in a very quiet part of town is the cheery **Onisillos Hotel** *(☎ 2465 1100, fax 2465 4468; w www.oni sillos.com.cy; Onisillou 17; singles/doubles CY£25/33)*. Room rates at this friendly, two-star hotel include breakfast and the rooms come with bathroom, air-con and phone.

Very central, close to the beach and with handy car parking at the rear are **Petrou Apartments** *(☎ 2465 0600, fax 2465 5122; w www.petrou.com.cy; Armenikis Ekklisias 1; 2-person apartment CY£14-25)*. These large, self-catering apartments all have air-con, TV and phone.

PLACES TO STAY – TOP END

Both these hotels are within the city centre.

Four Lanterns Sunotel *(☎ 2465 2011, fax 2462 6012; e crown@cytanet.com.cy; Leoforos Athinon 19-24; rooms CY£48-77)* is a three-star hotel with comfortable accommodation at the northern end of Leoforos Athinon.

Sun Hall *(☎ 2465 3341, fax 2465 2717; Leoforos Athinon 6; rooms CY£62.50-82)* has earned some high praise from travellers. This four-star hotel is equally well-equipped, and offers a 25% off-season discount.

There is also a cluster of four-star hotels on the Larnaka-Dekelia road 8km northeast of Larnaka along the tourist strip.

PLACES TO EAT

While you will find some excellent dining choices out on the tourist strip heading out towards Deryneia, recommendations here are limited primarily to establishments within the city centre itself.

For a quick snack or promenade breakfast, look no further than the French-influenced delicatessen and patisserie **Croissanterie Délifresh** (*Leoforos Athinon; breakfast from CY£1.70*) at the northern end of the seafront. Croissants, cakes, decent coffee – you name it, it's all here.

For a quick lunch or evening snack, seek out **Prasino Amaxoudi** (*☎ 2462 2939; Agias Faneromenis*), sitting cheek-by-jowl with the Grand Mosque in the old Turkish quarter. Here you'll get good-value, freshly prepared souvlaki or döner kebab for CY£2, or *halumi* pitta sandwiches for around CY£1.50.

The **1900 Art Cafe** (*☎ 2462 3730; Stasinou 6; open 9am-2pm & 6pm-midnight Wed-Mon; snacks CY£1-2*) is located in an old house. This cosy eatery offers good company, coffee and good-value snacks including several options for vegetarians

The quirky **Black Turtle** (*☎ 2465 0661; Mehmet Ali 11; live music Wed & Sat; mezedes CY£6.50-8*) is a great little *mezes* taverna that features live music when only *mezedes* are served. Don't be put off by the turtle shells on the wall; the owner is really a turtle lover.

Megalos Pefkos (*☎ 2462 8566; Angyras 7; open lunch & dinner; fish dishes CY£4-8*) is at the southern end of Leoforos Athinon. This place is perhaps marginally the best of a clutch of fish taverns on this small street. Swordfish is often the best buy, but there are plenty of other dishes on offer. You dine in a pleasant waterside setting.

Archondiko (*☎ 2465 5905; Leoforos Athinon 24; mezedes per person CY£6.50*) is a well-known restaurant housed in an old mansion. This is a great place to watch the parade of skateboarders and hair-braiders while *mezedes* are probably the best meal choice.

The stretch of beachfront south of the castle is less touristy and home to a few other places worth seeking out.

Monte Carlo (*☎ 2465 3815; Piyale Pasha 28; open 7.30pm-midnight; meat/fish mezedes CY£6.50/7.75*) sits right on the water's edge and is a great place to dine in peace and watch the sea. Set menus are a good choice at CY£4.90.

Militzis Restaurant (*☎ 2465 5867; Piyale Pasha 42; open lunch & dinner; mains CY£4-5*) is across the road from the Monte Carlo and a little further south. It's best at pro-

viding traditional oven-cooked dishes; try the delicious lamb *ofto lysiotiko* (CY£4.25).

Lovers of Guinness can hardly miss the sign outside **Tudor Inn** (*☎ 2462 5608; Lala Mustapha Pasha 28a; open dinner only; steaks CY£10*), off Piyale Pasha. Apart from serving up pints of the famous Irish brew, the Tudor Inn serves a decent steak – try the steak in blue cheese sauce. Noncarnivores are catered for with a vegetarian plate for CY£5.50.

Perhaps the flashiest, and certainly the busiest, is the always-popular **Varoshiotis Seafood Restaurant** (*☎ 2465 5865; Piyale Pasha 7; fish dishes CY£7-8*). The tables look out directly over the water and the service, like the food, is spot on. Wash your meal down with excellent house wine.

A bit out of town but worth the effort is **Kamares Restaurant** (*☎ 2436 4400; Hrysoupoleos 24a; mains CY£5-6*) facing the impressive Kamares aqueduct, which is romantically floodlit at night. Few tourists get this far out but the quality of the food is excellent. Try *karaolia* (land snails) or *kouloumbra* (kohlrabi) for a taste of something special. There is live music on Friday and Saturday. Take a cab to get there and direct your driver towards the nearby Cineplex cinema complex (see Cinemas later).

ENTERTAINMENT

Larnaka is a very pleasant place to watch people over a beer or a coffee. Tourists make their own fun in the long tourist strip 8km northeast of the city, while locals and city-oriented travellers hang out along Leoforos Athinon and the little streets inland from the sea. You will not find the rowdy, packed element of the tourist centres of Agia Napa or Lemesos here; fun is sought more sedately.

Pubs & Bars

The small Laïki Yitonia, just back from the centre of Leoforos Athinon, holds a swathe of mainly forgettable bars and discos. While this strip is unquestionably popular with visitors, the locals tend to avoid it.

The Bailey (*☎ 2462 1000; Leoforos Athinon 36*) is a big, brash Irish pub (yes, yet another one!) right in the middle of Leoforos Athinon. The various draft Irish beers are inevitably good, though service can get a bit flaky when the crowds pour in.

Aquafront (*☎ 2462 5904; Piyale Pasha 54*), in the Turkish quarter, is a place where sea-lovers can sip cocktails and spirits. Happy hour is from 7pm to 9pm and there is a BBQ meal on Wednesday for CY£4.

Caprice Midnight Cafe *(Leoforos Athinon)*, at the southern end of Leoforos Athinon, is a great spot for an evening pint or a vodka and coke while taking in the sea views.

Clubs

Most of the local club scene is in Agia Napa, a 30-minute drive to the east. Nonetheless, Larnaka holds its own with at least ten thriving clubs in and around town, and regular beach parties are held at various points along the long Larnaka Bay during summer.

Corridor *(☎ 9967 6134; Karaoli & Dimitriou 8)* is probably the most lively club in town and is pitched at a local Greek clientele. Expect mostly Greek pop music with some UK dance sounds thrown in for good measure. It is usually closed in high summer.

Club Prime *(☎ 9943 7222; Filiou Tsigaridi 2-4)*, like all good clubs, is somewhat hidden in a side street off Leoforos Makariou. This is Larnaka's newest and most hi-tech venue with an impressive sound and light system. The music choice is broad-ranging and top-class DJs keep the revellers happy.

Memphis *(☎ 9963 8986; Leoforos Athinon 76)* was refurbished in 2002 and is now very plush and lives up to its reputation as the best club in town. It attracts clubbers from all over Cyprus. Look out for its summer beach parties.

Venue *(☎ 9961 7262; Thermopylon 8)* usually caters for special events or parties and features house, Greek and Euro pop and an overlay of UK dance.

Cinemas

There are a number of cinemas scattered around Larnaka, with all foreign-language films subtitled into Greek. Admission normally costs around CY£3 to CY£4 per person.

The most modern movie theatre complex is **Cineplex** *(☎ 2481 9022 8.30am-5.30pm Mon-Fri or ☎ 2436 2167 5pm-10.30pm Mon-Fri; w www.kcineplex.com; Peloponisou 1)*, which is a five- to 10-minute taxi ride west of the city centre near the Kamares aqueduct.

Two smaller and older theatres, both fairly central, are the **Attikon** *(☎ 2465 2873; Kyriakou Matsi 5)* and the **Othellos** *(☎ 2465 7970; Agias Elenis 13)*.

SHOPPING

Pottery is a good buy in Larnaka. Head out to **Emira Pottery** *(☎ 2462 3952; Mehmet Ali 13)* in the old Turkish quarter, which is a good place to see it being made and to buy an item to take home.

Acapella *(☎ 2466 4165; Lordou Vyronos 50)* is the best place for CD music purchases. **Optical House** *(☎ 2465 5436; Ermou 95-97)*, in the town centre, has discount optical items that are a good buy. They will test your sight for free.

GETTING THERE & AWAY
Air

Larnaka international airport is 7km from the city centre. Most flights to Cyprus arrive and depart from here. There are a couple of **Cyprus Airways** offices *(☎ 2462 6666)*; one on Leoforos Arhiepiskopou Makariou 21 and one at the airport *(☎ 2464 3313)*.

Bus

The stop for **Intercity** *(☎ 2464 3492)* buses to Lefkosia (CY£1.50; four to five buses daily Monday to Saturday) and Lemesos (CY£1.70, three to four buses Monday to Saturday), and **Eman Buses** *(☎ 2372 1321)* to Agia Napa (CY£1, nine buses Monday to Saturday, four buses on Sunday), is almost opposite Croissanterie Délifresh on Leoforos Athinon.

Buses for Lefkara (CY£0.95, one bus daily Monday to Saturday), Kiti (CY£0.50, 12 buses Monday to Saturday), Perivolia and Faros (CY£0.50, three to six buses daily Monday to Saturday) all leave from Plateia Agiou Lazarou, near Agios Lazaros church.

Taxis & Service Taxis

Travel & Express *(☎ 2466 1010; cnr Papakyriakou & Marsellou)* run service taxis to major destinations. There is a second office at Kimonos 2.

A couple of smaller outfits still operate. **Acropolis** *(☎ 2465 5555; Leoforos Arhiepiskopou Makariou)* is opposite the police station, and **A Makris** *(☎ 2465 2929)* is on the north side of the Sun Hall hotel. Rates are CY£2.60 to Lefkosia and CY£3.10 to Lemesos.

Regular taxis will take you wherever you want. Sample fares are the airport CY£5, Lefkosia CY£12, Lemesos CY£16 and Troödos CY£30.

Yacht

Larnaka has an excellent private **marina** (☎ 2465 3110, fax 2462 4110; e larnaka .marina@cytanet.com.cy) offering a wide range of berthing facilities for up to 450 yachts. These include telephone, fax and telex services, repair facilities, laundry, showers, lockers, post office boxes and a minimarket and provisions store. The marina is an official port of entry into Cyprus.

GETTING AROUND
To/From the Airport

Bus No 22 or 24 from Ermou and Plateia Palion Finikoundon go to the airport (CY£0.50). The first bus is at 6.20am and the last at 7pm in summer, 5.30pm in winter. A private taxi costs around CY£5.

Bus

A Makris buses run every 30 minutes from the north side of the Sun Hall hotel to the tourist hotel area on the road to Agia Napa (CY£0.80 return).

Car & Motorcycle

Thames Car Rentals (☎ 2465 6333) is next door to A Makris and rents cars. There are also several car-rental booths at the airport. You can hire motorcycles or mopeds from **Anemayia** (☎ 2464 5619; Larnaka-Dekelia Road); ring for free delivery. The cost is about CY£5 for three hours.

Bicycle

Bicycles can be hired at **Anemayia** (☎ 2465 8333 or 9962 4726; Zinonos Kitieos 120 • Kimonos 2), which has its office in the middle of the city. Call for free delivery, which is promised within 10 minutes. Prices range from CY£4 to CY£6 for daily rental.

Around Larnaka

The sights in the west of the Larnaka region can also easily be visited as day trips from Lemesos or even Lefkosia. Limited public transport does not make it easy to get to the sights, so you are once again you'll have to rely on your own wheels or inventiveness.

GETTING AROUND

Other than bus Nos 6 and 7, which will take you to both the Hala Sultan Tekkesi and Kiti from Larnaka, transport options for the other sights are thin on the ground. Taking a bus to Lefkara will require an overnight stay there. Your own transport is the only way to get around. Even hitching – always a touch-and-go option – is tricky because much of the travelling involves using the motorways and the need to get off at different exits. See Getting There & Away in the Larnaka section for more details.

BEACHES

Swimming is definitely not one of the highlights of the Larnaka coastline. While Cypriots and foreigners alike swim quite contentedly at either of Larnaka's artificially constructed city beaches, or at the less congested beaches off the hotel strip to the northeast, none is particularly enticing. That said, **Makenzy (McKenzie) Beach**, 2.5km south of Larnaka, is the best local beach. The beach and water fronting Leoforos Athinon is quite clean, and the water is shallow and shelves gently, making it ideal for children.

Serious beach-lovers should consider moving further east to Agia Napa or Protaras for a more enjoyable swim. To the southwest, the minor resorts of **Cape Kiti** and **Perivolia** offer pebbly, narrow and rather exposed beaches, but compensate for less-than-idyllic strips with some decent tavernas, which could make for a pleasant lunchtime excursion.

HALA SULTAN TEKKESI

On the western side of the Larnaka salt lake is one of Cyprus' most important Islamic pilgrimage sites. It is a mosque (admission free, donation expected; open 9am-7.30pm daily, 9am-5pm Oct-Apr) surrounded by date palms, cypress and olive trees, and looks very much the part of a desert oasis in stark juxtaposition to the arid salinity of the adjoining salt lake. It was founded in 674 when Umm Haram, the reputed aunt of Mohammed, fell from a mule, broke her neck and died. She was buried on the site of the current Tekke (meaning Muslim shrine) and her tomb and subsequent mosque have become important places of worship for Muslims. Hala Sultan means 'Great Mother' in Turkish and refers to Umm Haram.

The Tekke stands empty for most of the year, except during visits by curious tourists and Muslim visitors from the Middle East.

However, as part of a limited access agreement, Turkish Cypriots from the North may visit the Tekke twice a year on goodwill pilgrimages. In reciprocation, Greek Cypriots may, twice a year, visit the monastery of Apostolos Andreas in the North. However, in 2002 this agreement was halted for political reasons, but may well recommence when North-South relations begin to look up once more.

A rather bored-looking curator gives visitors a quick tour and historical spiel, and takes them over to the tomb and sarcophagus of Hala Sultan herself. The interior is maintained as a working mosque with a layer of prayer mats covering the floor, so remove your shoes before entering.

Local bus No 6 will drop you off at the approach road to the Tekke, and from there it is a 1km walk.

LARNAKA SALT LAKE

Arriving at Larnaka's international airport in summer, you can hardly miss the vast expanse of white salt bordering the airport perimeter, less than a few hundred metres from the runway. This is Larnaka's salt lake where, in winter, you can see colonies of flamingos and other migratory birds. In summer, the lake slowly dries up, leaving a thin film of salt. In the Middle Ages, salt mining was carried on here, but pollution from aircraft exhaust in modern times has rendered the salt commercially useless. Signs warn potential adventure-drivers in 4WDs to keep off, and walkers are not particularly encouraged as the sticky salt-encrusted mud can easily ensnare vehicles and walkers.

KITI KOITH
pop 3140

In Kiti village, 7km southwest of Larnaka, you will find the domed, cruciform 11th-century church of **Panagia Angeloktisti** (admission free, but donations welcome; open 9.30am-noon & 2pm-4pm Mon-Sat summer). Literally meaning 'built by angels', this church is a reincarnation of an earlier structure from the 5th century (of which only the apse remains) that has now been incorporated into the current building. Visitors come for the 6th-century **mosaics**, which have survived from the original apse but were only discovered in 1952. In a striking depiction, you can see the Virgin Mary,

The spectacular Hoopoe passes through Cyprus on its annual migratory path.

with baby Jesus in her arms and the angels Gabriel and Michael standing next to her.

The church is a place of worship, so time your visit to avoid a service – unless you choose to participate, which you are at liberty to do. On Sunday it is open for regular services. Bus Nos 6 and 7 from Larnaka run hourly to and from Kiti.

CHAPELLE ROYALE

Just off the Lefkosia–Lemesos motorway (A1), and close to the village of Pyrga, is Chapelle Royale (Royal Chapel; admission CY£0.75; open dawn-dusk daily), a small Lusignan shrine dedicated to Agia Ekaterini (St Catherine). Established by the Latin King Janus in 1421 (the last of Cyprus' Crusader kings), the church is quite unassuming, but inside you can see an interesting set of French-influenced **wall frescoes**, not all of which are in good condition. You should be able to make out paintings of the Last Supper, the Raising of Lazarus, the Washing of Christ's Feet and the Ascension. Note that the inscriptions are in French – not Greek – as this was the official language of Lusignan Cyprus.

The church is best combined with a visit to Stavrovouni and Lefkara.

STAVROVOUNI MONASTERY
ΜΟΝΗ ΣΤΑΥΡΟΒΟΥΝΙΟΥ

High up in the hills (668m) above the Lefkosia–Lemesos motorway (A1) is the impressive Stavrovouni Monastery (open 8am-noon & 3pm-6pm Apr-Aug, 8am-noon &

2pm-5pm Sept-Mar), the oldest monastery in Cyprus. Reached by a steep winding road, it is only worth making the trip up here if you are male. Women are not allowed to enter the monastery, though the superb views from the monastery grounds over the Mesaoria and the Troödos Mountains may be enough reason to make the trip. Colin Thubron documented his stay in the monastery during his walking trek around Cyprus in 1972, in the book *Journey into Cyprus,* in which he describes the monastery as a 'lodestar for pilgrims in the wake of the Crusades'.

The origins of the monastery – the name means 'mountain of the cross' – date back to 327 when it was allegedly founded by the Empress Helena, mother of Constantine the Great, while on her way to Jerusalem. She is said to have erected a wooden cross containing a nail from the cross of Jesus. A small piece of Empress Helena's cross is now preserved in a silver cross in the church.

The monastery is a working religious community consisting of a few young monks who live to follow their ascetic principles, not to entertain visitors. If you come to visit (and are male), arrive during visiting hours only. Leave your camera behind as photos are not allowed. If you are a genuine or professed pilgrim you may be invited to stay.

CHOIROKOITIA

Archaeology buffs and early-history lovers should make the trip out to the fascinating Neolithic site of Choirokoitia (☎ 2432 2710; admission CY£0.75; open 9am-7.30pm Mon-Fri, 9am-5pm Sat & Sun May-Sept, 9am-5pm daily Oct-Apr), 32km southwest of Larnaka. It is perhaps best combined with a day trip to either Lemesos or Lefkara (see following). Dating from around 6800 BC, this Unesco World Heritage site is perhaps one of the earliest permanent human settlements in Cyprus. The original Choirokoitians lived in round, mud huts and practised a relatively sophisticated lifestyle for the time. It is thought that they came from Anatolia or the coast of present-day Lebanon. The original settlement was built on an easily defensible hillside, surrounded by a large perimeter wall. Inside the wall around 60 houses have been found, identified by the remains of their circular walls. Reconstructions of the houses have been built at the foot of the hill and, although they look a bit out of place, it is worth

seeing them since it is difficult to imagine the buildings from their scant remains.

Visitors view the various sections of the site via steps and a series of walkways that overlook the key points of the settlement. Signs give a clear description of the main features of each area, and the walkway finishes at the top of the hill where the best remains are to be found.

There is ample parking and a snack bar with refreshments.

LEFKARA ΛΕΥΚΑΡΑ
pop 1040

One of Cyprus' most famous exports is its exquisite lace, and most of it comes from the pretty mountain villages of **Pano Lefkara** and **Kato Lefkara**. Reached by a fast road from the Lefkosia–Lemesos motorway (A1), or by a winding and picturesque road from Choirokoitia via Vavla, Lefkara – the two settlements' more common name – is an excellent day's outing from Lefkosia, Lemesos or Larnaka. The story goes that, in the Middle Ages, the women of Lefkara took up lacemaking to supplement family incomes while the men were away working at sea or on the plains. More enterprising stay-at-home husbands took up making silverware. Leonardo da Vinci is said to have taken some lace to Italy and ever since, travellers and lace-lovers the world over have being doing the same.

The villages are pretty enough even if you are not keen on frilly patterns or intricately designed tablecloths. A wander around their picturesque streets is almost certain to guarantee an invitation to 'see my lace' from the many women who sit at doorways, whiling away their hours in a seemingly relaxing hobby. In reality, the competition to sell can be intense. The lace is of high quality and exquisite, but not necessarily dirt cheap. Bargain hard if you want a particular piece, or try in the nearby villages, some of which also sell Lefkara lace. Bear in mind that the lace on display outside the shops is not the good, handmade stuff. You will only find this inside the shop away from the depredations of the sun and dust.

For visitors interested to learn more, there is the **Museum of Traditional Embroidery & Silver-Smithing** (☎ 2434 2326; admission CY£0.75; open 9.30am-4pm Mon-Thur, 10am-4pm Fri & Sat) where you can get a better insight into these two flourishing trades.

There is a Hellenic Bank ATM in the village as well as a smattering of restaurants. There is only one place to stay and that is the **Agora** (☎ 2434 2901, fax 2434 2905; e hotel agora@hotmail.com; singles/doubles CY£35/54) – a central, two-star place that is quite decent and offers a 15% off-season discount. It also sports a handy restaurant where dinner will cost an extra CY£7.

Assuming you've arrived by car, there is one restaurant not far away that is worth seeking out. It is the **Platanos** (☎ 2434 2160; Kato Drys) in a small village about a 10-minute drive from Lefkara. The specialty is *ttavas lefkaritikos*, which is a kind of lamb and onion stew. Dine under a large plane tree *(platanos)* and unwind with the excellent wine and local dishes.

There is only one daily bus (CY£0.95, Monday to Saturday) to and from Lefkara and Larnaka. It leaves Lefkara at 7am and returns from Larnaka at 1pm.

Agia Napa Αγία Νάπα

pop 2680

From its humble beginnings as a small, insignificant fishing village, Agia Napa now shoulders the mantle of Cyprus' prime sun-and-fun tourist resort. Famagusta's Varosia beach strip and former prime resort was locked behind barbed wire and oil barrels following the North's takeover in 1974. Agia Napa is not everyone's cup of tea and 90% of people visiting here are overseas

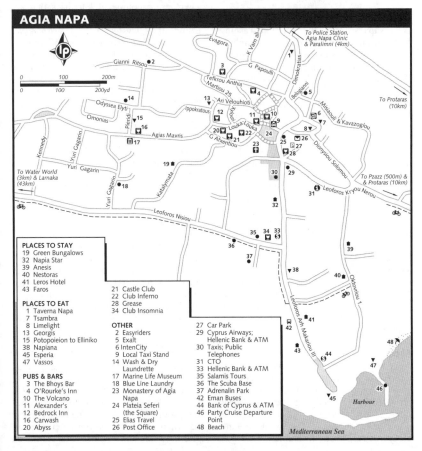

AGIA NAPA

0   100   200m
0   100   200yd

To Police Station, Agia Napa Clinic & Paralimni (4km)

To Protaras (10km)

To Water World (3km) & Larnaka (43km)

To Pzazz (500m) & & Protaras (10km)

Mediterranean Sea

Harbour

PLACES TO STAY
19 Green Bungalows
32 Napia Star
39 Anesis
40 Nestoras
41 Leros Hotel
43 Faros

PLACES TO EAT
1 Taverna Napa
7 Tsambra
8 Limelight
13 Georgis
15 Potopoieion to Elliniko
38 Napiana
45 Esperia
47 Vassos

PUBS & BARS
3 The Bhoys Bar
4 O'Rourke's Inn
10 The Volcano
11 Alexander's
12 Bedrock Inn
16 Carwash
20 Abyss

21 Castle Club
22 Club Inferno
28 Grease
34 Club Insomnia

OTHER
2 Easyriders
5 Exalt
6 IntenCity
9 Local Taxi Stand
14 Wash & Dry Laundrette
17 Marine Life Museum
18 Blue Line Laundry
23 Monastery of Agia Napa
24 Plateia Seferi (the Square)
25 Elias Travel
26 Post Office

27 Car Park
29 Cyprus Airways; Hellenic Bank & ATM
30 Taxis; Public Telephones
31 CTO
33 Hellenic Bank & ATM
35 Salamis Tours
36 The Scuba Base
37 Adrenalin Park
42 Eman Buses
44 Bank of Cyprus & ATM
46 Party Cruise Departure Point
48 Beach

tourists on packages, intent on specific and limited pleasures – drinking, eating and sunning themselves. That said, it is unquestionably popular. Restaurants, hotels and bars are still sprouting up like mushrooms in a dark cave, and the unfettered growth of the town has hardly abated in more recent years.

The beach, while crowded, is good and the nightlife never stops. If you are under 30 years of age, you may want to think twice about coming here for a holiday. If you turn up in the high season (from mid-July to mid-August), accommodation will be hard to find. While hoteliers are more used to package-tour visitors, most places will cater for individuals if room is available. If you are not staying here, at least visit the place once to see what all the fuss is about.

ORIENTATION

Agia Napa is strung out, rather like washing to dry, from east to west along the shoreline. Leoforos Nisiou is the main east-west street, and arrivals from Larnaka commonly enter Agia Napa along here. Running north-south at the eastern end of Nisiou is the other main artery, Leoforos Arhiepiskopou Makariou. Heading east is Leoforos Kryou Nerou. Agia Napa's main point of focus is Plateia Seferi, known universally as 'the Square'. Several of the streets leading off the Square are pedestrianised. Buses arrive at the southern end of Leoforos Arhiepiskopou Makariou near the harbour. Long-distance service taxis arrive and depart from a stand close to the Square. The police station is north of the Square at the junction of Dimokratias and the Larnaka–Protaras ring road.

INFORMATION
Tourist Offices

The **CTO** (☎ 2372 1796; *Leoforos Kryou Nerou 12; open 8.15am-2.30pm & 3pm-6.30pm Mon, Tues, Thur & Fri, 8.15am-2.30pm Wed & Sat*) is about 200m southeast of the main Square.

Money

Agia Napa is exceptionally well equipped with banks, ATMs and exchange offices that are open at all hours of the day. ATMs are provided by the **Hellenic Bank** (*Leoforos Arhiepiskopou Makariou*) with another branch just north of the Square. There is also a **Bank of Cyprus** ATM near the harbour.

Post & Communications

The **post office** (*D Liperti*) is about 100m east of the main Square. Convenient **public phones** (*Leoforos Arhiepiskopou Makariou*) are next to the long-distance service taxi stand 100m south of the Square.

The easiest Internet Café to find is **InTenCity** (☎ 2372 2233; w *www.intencity.net; Dionysiou Solomou; CY£2.20 per hour; open 10am-2am*), a large, modern, air-conditioned place with 26 stations.

Travel Agencies

Elias Travel (☎ 2372 5070, fax 2372 5072; e *eliastravel@cytanet.com.cy; Eleftherias*) is a reputable travel agency next to the Square.

Laundry

There are a couple of laundries that are fairly close to the town centre. **Wash & Dry Laundrette** (*Odyssea Elyti 23; wash & dry CY£1; open 8am-7pm Mon-Sat*), 500m west of the Square, is a do-it-yourself place.

Blue Line Laundry (*Yuri Gagarin; open 8am-7pm Mon-Sat*), 600m southwest of the Square, is a service laundry where you drop your gear off and pick it up 24 hours later.

Medical Services

The nearest **hospital** (☎ 2382 1211; *Paralimni*) is about a 15-minute taxi ride away. The **Agia Napa Clinic** (☎ 2372 3222), also known as the Olympic Napa, is another option for medical care. Information on **out of hours pharmacies** (☎ 192) is also available.

ADRENALIN PARK

What Agia Napa lacks in culture it sure makes up for in sheer exhilarating, gut-wrenching thrills and spills. This smallish park is dominated by fairly expensive super rides. You have to try one of them at least once. At around CY£12 for a few minutes of adrenalin-pumping excitement, these rides may not cure your hangover, but they'll give you an experience to remember.

First up, and the oldest, is the **Skycoaster** (☎ 9989 1251; *admission CY£12; open 3pm-1am daily*). Strapped into a canvas harness (up to three persons at a time), you are hoisted 33 metres into the air and, at the given signal, you release a ripcord. At this point you drop to the ground like a stone. The good thing is that within a second or so you are grabbed by your hoist line and commence an enormous swinging arc upwards and outwards and then back again – several times. It's all adrenalin-pumping fun and worth every penny. However, riding the Skycoaster is peanuts when compared to the thrill of the next ride.

The **Slingshot** (☎ 9964 0608; admission CY£12) is a super ride in which you are strapped, two at a time, into an open orb attached to two huge metal cords. The cords are tightened then released and you are slung 100m high in 1.3 seconds at up to 6Gs. The Slingshot is touted as the 'highest, fastest ride in the world'. Videos of your terror and T-shirts are available for CY£8.

Ever fancied free-fall parachuting? Try it in the **Aerodium** (CY£20) next to the Skycoaster. Pull on a flying suit and step onto an enclosed trampoline net and wait for the wind – lots of it – coming up from a powerful wind generator below. Spread your arms to catch the wind and fly. An instructor guides you through the techniques. If that's not enough, climb **The Wall** nearby (CY£5 per climb). Connected to a safety harness, you climb a specially made tower. If you fall off, try again.

Have a go on at least one of the rides – preferably before you have dinner and certainly not as a means to mix your cocktails.

MARINE LIFE MUSEUM
This little, private museum (☎ 2372 1179; Agias Mavris 25; adult/child 6 & over/child under 6 CY£1/0.50/free; open 9am-2pm Mon, Tues, Thur & Sat & 3pm-6pm Mon & Thur) is hidden away in the lower ground floor of the modern Agia Napa town hall. While not earth-shatteringly arresting, it does provide some relief from the hype and hedonism of most of Agia Napa's nightlife. If you are into marine biology, fossilised shells, stuffed fish, sharks, turtles and sea birds then drop in for a quick visit. The display is fairly limited, but well laid out and documented.

MONASTERY OF AGIA NAPA
ΜΟΝΗ ΑΓΙΑΣ ΝΑΠΑΣ
The beautifully cloistered monastery is incongruously sited next to the pub and club scene of the adjoining Square. Best visited in the early morning, after the revellers have gone to bed, the monastery is an oasis of calm amid the crass commercialism of Agia Napa's entertainment scene.

Built in around 1570 by the Venetians, the monastery is named after the 'holy handker-chief' that was used by St Veronica to wipe the face of Jesus as he carried his cross to Calvary. It is a remarkably well-preserved monastery and was indeed used as such up until 1790. Visitors enter from either the north or south side. Outside the south gate is a prominently labelled enormous sycamore fig tree, which is said to be over 600 years old. A cool, marble fountain is the centrepiece of the courtyard and dates from 1530. It is covered by a large dome mounted on four pillars.

The church itself, on the west side of the courtyard, is sunken somewhat lower than the courtyard level and is rather dark and gloomy inside. The monastery is ringed by a stout protective wall designed initially to keep marauding pirates at bay, but now ostensibly serving a better purpose in keeping inebriated foreign visitors at a respectable distance from its hallowed ground.

WATER WORLD
If you just want the water and not the sand, head 3km west out of Agia Napa for **Water World** (☎ 2372 4444; w www.waterworld waterpark.com; Agias Theklis 18; adult/child CY£12.90/6.50; open 10am-6pm daily Apr-Oct), supposedly Cyprus' best water theme park. Here you can tube, twirl, splash and slide to your heart's content. Queues can be long in peak season.

BEACHES
Once all the throngs of sun revellers have moved on, Agia Napa's beach is predictably good. However, the beach is usually very crowded and strewn from end to end with umbrellas and beach loungers, but everyone seems to be able to find a spot for themselves somewhere.

If you're looking for a bit of solitude, hire a scooter and move on to Cape Greco, Konnos or Green Bay beaches south of Protaras (see Beaches under Protaras & Pernera later in this chapter).

BOAT CRUISES
A large number of boat cruises operate out of Agia Napa's crowded little harbour. Most head out for trips around Cape Greco to the beaches of Protaras and Pernera, advertising their destination as 'Famagusta'. All must turn back before reaching Famagusta of course, since this city is under the control of the Turkish military.

'Party' cruises typically cost CY£4/2 per adult/child. They include music and drinks (extra cost) on board and stops for swimming. One such operation is **Party Cruise** (☎ 9963 7233) on the harbour; ask for Nikos. Cruises depart at 11.30am and return at 4pm daily. An evening night cruise runs every Tuesday, Wednesday and Sunday departing at 10.30pm and returning at 1.30am. Men pay CY£5 – the women go free.

DIVING

The waters around Agia Napa and Cape Greco up to Famagusta are perfect for diving. The sea is calm, warm and clear and a few operators are set up to cater for divers. **The Scuba Base** (☎ 2372 2441; w *www.the scubabase.com; Leoforos Nisiou 17a)* is a reputable local company that organises programmes ranging from an introduction to snorkelling to advanced open-water courses.

ORGANISED TOURS

Pafos-based **Exalt** (☎ 2372 4390, fax 2372 4393; w *www.cyprus-adventure.com; Belogianni 10)* runs a challenging 12-hour sea and land excursion around Agia Napa.

PLACES TO STAY

At least 90% of visitors come to Agia Napa with prebooked accommodation, and if you turn up between mid-July and mid-August without a booking you may have trouble finding a bed. Accommodation ranges from unlicensed rooms (normally a rarity in Cyprus) to five-star hotels. Most hotels will welcome independent travellers if there is space. Prices are cheaper in the off season, but many hotels only operate from March to October.

At the bottom of the scale, in price at least is small and homey **Leros Hotel** (☎ 2372 1126, fax 2372 1127; w *www.customers.wel cometocyprus.com/leros; Leoforos Arhiepiskopou Makariou 41; singles/doubles including breakfast CY£17.50/28).* It has decent rooms and sports a small pool and bar.

Anesis (☎ 2372 1104, fax 2372 2204; 1 Oktovriou 7; singles/doubles including breakfast CY£29/40) is a hotel with good air-con rooms. Internet access is available for guests.

Nestoras (☎ 2372 2880, fax 2372 2881; e *nestor@logos.net.cy; 1 Oktovriou 8; singles/ doubles including breakfast CY£29.50/42),* diagonally opposite the Anesis, offers even better accommodation.

Napia Star (☎ 2372 1540, fax 2372 1671; e *blueseasonshotels@cytanet.com.cy; Leoforos Arhiepiskopou Makariou 12; singles/ doubles CY£24/48)* is a three-star place closer to the action and offers comfortable rooms, a restaurant and bar.

Faros (☎ 2372 3838, fax 2372 3839; e *faroshot@spidernet.com.cy; Leoforos Arhiepiskopou Makariou; singles/doubles including breakfast CY£43/62)* is nearer to the harbour with superior rooms and a pool.

Green Bungalows (☎ 2372 1511, fax 2372 2184; e *anastassiadesa@cytanet.com.cy; Katalymata 19; 2-person apartment CY£31; open Apr-Oct)* is a superior B-class apartment hotel. This place offers cosy apartments and breakfast from CY£2.

PLACES TO EAT

Without guidance, eating in Agia Napa can be a bit of a hit-and-miss affair. The big fast-food chains are all close to each other and there is an eating place almost every 50m or so. Many pander only to tourists, but others pull in a knowledgeable local clientele as well. In general, prices are somewhat higher than elsewhere on Cyprus though not outrageously so. Try those described below for starters, but follow your nose and gut instinct if you see something that takes your fancy.

Vassos (☎ 2372 1884; Leoforos Arhiepiskopou Makariou 51; fish mezes CY£8) has been around since 1962, so has a well-tried and successful formula; fresh fish and good service. It looks a rather large, impersonal place during the day, but it's right on the harbour and makes for romantic evening dining.

Closer to the water, and boasting slightly more upmarket decor and a marginally better location, is **Esperia** (☎ 2372 1635; fish mezes CY£8.75). Enormous fish and meat dishes sell for similar prices as at Vassos.

Napiana (☎ 2372 2891; Leoforos Arhiepiskopou Makariou 29) is a busy establishment closer to central Agia Napa with exceptionally attentive service. Steaks are the big seller here with the rich *chateaubriand* for two at CY£8.50 per person.

Taverna Napa (☎ 2372 1280; Dimokratias 15; mains CY£5-8; open dinner only), a little way north of the main action, rates well with the locals. It's a cosy little taverna with a broad range of Cypriot and Greek dishes.

Georgis (☎ 2372 1838; Ippokratous 9; flambé steaks CY£6-8; open dinner only) specialises in flambé dishes and generally gets good reviews from the local dining community. Vegetarian dishes are also available at around CY£2.

Meals at **Limelight** (☎ 2372 1650; Dionysiou Solomou 10; fish platter CY£12.95) centre around the open BBQ where steaks, lobster, fish and chicken are cooked. The house speciality is succulent suckling lamb or pig.

Dine in a shaded courtyard at **Tsambra** (☎ 2372 2513; Dionysiou Solomou 9; pork dishes CY£6-7) where pork specialities are the selling point. Try special pork fillet, sauteed in butter, braised in a pot and served with cream mushrooms and onions.

Potopoieion to Elliniko (☎ 2372 2760; Theodosi Pieridi 2; minimum charge CY£7.50), tucked away where normally only Cypriots find it, is a Greek-style mezedopoleio where mezes dishes accompany the zivania, ouzo or wine that you choose to savour. There's usually some live music happening too.

ENTERTAINMENT

If you have come to Agia Napa, you are probably here to drink – and this is the place to do it. Bars and music rock on until around 2am, then it's time to hit the clubs. The central area within 200m of the Square is a riotous confusion of noise, karaoke, disco beats and clinking glasses. There are almost 20 bars and 15 clubs to choose from and nightlife never stops.

Pubs & Bars

For people-watching, choose the balconies of the pubs on the Square. **The Volcano** (☎ 2372 1049; Georgiou Seferi 2) is in a great location with its all-seeing upstairs balcony, while at the top of the Square, you'll find **Alexander's** (☎ 2372 1898; Georgiou Seferi 17) with an all-encompassing view of the action. It's a definite voyeur's favourite.

Bedrock Inn (☎ 2372 2951; Agias Mavris), just a two-minute walk further towards the beach from the Hard Rock, is a grotesque Fred Flintstone and Barney Rubble–style karaoke palace that really pulls in the crowds.

To be sure, there's an Irish pub or two in Napa. **O'Rourke's Inn** (☎ 2372 3357; Tefkrou Anthia 13) serves top Gaelic ales, offers live music and organises beach parties, while **The Bhoys Bar** (☎ 2372 2572; Tefkrou Anthia 20) offers more of the same as well as Irish sporting events on TV.

Clubs

Nightclubs come and go each year, but at the time of research these were some of the hottest nightspots in Napa. Most of these clubs open after 1am with admission costing between CY£5 and CY£10.

Abyss (☎ 2372 5066; W www.clubabyss.co.uk; Grigoriou Afxentiou 17), comprising a large room, three floors and an outdoor chill-out zone, is one of the biggest clubs in town and has a mix of house, R'n'B, old school and garage. Look out for foam parties.

Club Inferno (☎ 2372 3400; Louka Louka) was refurbished in 2002 and sports a 4-way sound system and DJ Richie P from Shagwells in London. Richie plays the best of the '70s to '90s music. Dress up for the Austin Powers theme night.

Club Insomnia (☎ 2372 5554; Leoforos Nisiou 4; open 4am-7am) is a place where nightaholics can always seek predawn solace and more drinks. Advertising 'quality chill-out time' and 'happy sunshine music', Club Insomnia is for serious all-nighters.

Grease ☎ 2372 4240; W www.3ds.com.cy/grease; Leoforos Arhiepiskopou Makariou) features classic tunes from the '70s to the '90s plus the soundtrack hits from the movie. Relive teenage bliss and dress up like Sandy and Danny. Rydell High is not out yet.

Pzazz (☎ 2372 2266; Kryou Nerou 10) was completely refurbished in 2002 and packs lots of the same. With top DJs from the UK the club promotes itself as the town's most prestigious venue.

Housed in a mock castle, **Castle Club** (☎ 9962 3126; Grigoriou Afxentiou) comprises three separate areas – two dance and one chill-out space – and the music mix is the ever-popular formula of house, R'n'B, old school and garage.

Two London DJs take the party goers through a mix of hits from the '70s and '80s at **Carwash** (☎ 2372 1388; Agias Mavris 24). The sound and light system is impressive, and in the words of management, Carwash 'is more like a party than a club'.

GETTING THERE & AWAY

The bus is the best and only budget way to get to Agia Napa. There are nine direct buses to/from Larnaka (CY£1) in summer and one daily bus to Lefkosia (CY£2) at 8am (returning at 3pm). There are more or less hourly (on the hour) buses to Paralimni and Protaras

(CY£0.50). All buses leave from the bus stop between the Square and the harbour.

Private taxis (from the taxi stand close to the Square) vary, with rates from CY£13 to the airport, CY£19 to Lefkosia, and CY£40 to Troödos. There are no service taxis.

Cyprus Airways (☎ 2372 1265; *Leoforos Arhiepiskopou Makariou 17*) has an office here.

GETTING AROUND
There's no public transport in Agia Napa as such, and other than taking a taxi; hiring a scooter or motorbike is the best option. **Easyriders** (☎ 2372 2438, fax 2372 4035; e *easyriders@easyriders.com.cy; Gianni Ritsou 1*) rents wheels from 50cc scooters (CY£10 per day) to Kawasaki or Suzuki 800cc heavies (CY£25 per day). There is a second hire outlet at Dimokratias 17.

Around Agia Napa

Agia Napa is a convenient base for a number of pleasant half- or one-day trips around the east of Cyprus. On most summer days, squadrons of bare-backed scooter riders throng the coastal roads around Agia Napa. You can seek out another beach, visit the villages of the hinterland, see what the Brits are up to on one of their Sovereign Base Areas, or peer over into the ghost town of Varosia from vantage points on the Attila Line.

GETTING AROUND
No public transport other than the Protaras–Paralimni–Larnaka bus is going to help you much here. The cheapest option is to hire a scooter in either Protaras or Agia Napa. Rates vary, but are usually very reasonable. Make sure you choose a scooter with some power in its engine; it is a fair haul across the backblocks of the Paralimni region. A scooter is the best option for beach hopping along the Pernera–Protaras coastal strip.

A car is the best way to see the region in comfort. Rates from smaller companies in Protaras or Agia Napa are usually better than those offered by big-name hire-car companies. A group of four should be able to hire a small 4WD open-top jeep fairly cheaply.

As the whole area is reasonably flat, cycling is an ideal way of getting around the Kokkinohoria. There is a cycle track between Agia Napa and Cape Greco.

CAPE GRECO
Die-hard lovers of lands' ends will no doubt head for Cape Greco, about 7km from Agia Napa or 4km from Protaras. It's hardly a safari though. A good road, narrow in parts, leads in and out of the area. Unfortunately, you can't get to the end of the Cape itself. As on Mt Olympus in the Troödos, the Brits have requisitioned the last piece of ground to install a radar ground station that is firmly fenced off from the public. However, all is not lost. Some of the best swimming can be had here if the weather is not too windy. From the shabby car park, walk north towards the little bay and clamber down onto the rocks. A few rock platforms support swimmers who really don't want to be part of the Protaras beach scene. The water is absolutely idyllic here. A coastal walking and cycling track will take you to the cape from Agia Napa in about 3½ hours, or from Konnos Beach in about one hour. Bicycles should have solid tyres as the track is stony in parts.

PARALIMNI ΠΑΡΑΛΙΜΝΗ
pop 11,100 (including Protaras & Pernera)
Paralimni has reluctantly taken over from Famagusta as the capital of the eastern section of Cyprus. While you will have little reason to come here other than out of curiosity, or if you are touring the area by scooter, it is a pleasant little town, seemingly a universe away from the hustle and bustle of the tourist scene. There is a pleasantly paved central square with two versions of the church of Agios Georgios (new and old) and a sprinkling of restaurants and shops.

DERYNEIA ΔΕΡΥΝΕΙΑ
pop 1850
People usually come to Deryneia to peer into no-man's land and stare at the firmly closed 'border' that separates Northern Cyprus from the South. During the second invasion by the Turks of the North in August 1974, the Turkish army encircled and occupied the deserted holiday resort centre of Varosia (Maraş in Turkish). Troops moved towards Deryneia and halted abruptly just below the rise on which the town is located, and which now gives it its unparalleled but politically charged view into Northern Cyprus.

There are at least two viewing platforms from which to look into the North. **Annitas**, the top platform (☎ 2382 3003; *ad-*

mission CY£0.50), is the better of the two, and is essentially a private apartment block that had the luck/misfortune to be the last building in the South that was not occupied. From the top-floor platform, you can see the Greek Cypriot barracks, the blue-and-white UN building and, further still, the cream-coloured Turkish Cypriot post with the Turkish and Turkish Cypriot flags flying defiantly. Both flags are now safely protected by barbed wire after two violent and fatal incidents in 1996 (see the boxed text 'The Deryneia Martyrs').

Graphic videos and wall posters in the little viewing platform cafeteria will describe events that shocked and still linger in the collective memory of Greek Cypriots. Binoculars are handed out to visitors as part of the entrance ticket. The stark cityscape to the right and north of Deryneia is Varosia; it is, to all intents and purposes, dead and abandoned and has been left in the way it was occupied in 1974. Only rats and a few Turkish military details now inhabit its overgrown streets.

THE DEKELIA BASE

As part of the hard-won deal between the nascent Republic of Cyprus and the UK in 1960, the British were granted rights to two major Sovereign Base Areas (SBAs), as well as access to a series of retained sites scattered around the country where satellite ground stations and radio listening stations were located. The Dekelia SBA is the second of the two major base areas taken over 'in perpetuity' by the canny Brits. (See the Lemesos & the South Coast chapter for details about Akrotiri.)

The area comprises a sizable chunk of eastern Cyprus and runs from Larnaka Bay to the current Attila Line border with the North. In reality, the Dekelia SBA cuts off the Paralimni district from the rest of the Republic of Cyprus, since the SBAs are deemed to be foreign territory. In practice, there are no 'border' controls, although formidable grey iron gates on the road at the SBA entrances prove that British territorial integrity could be invoked at any time should circumstances prove

The Deryneia Martyrs

On 11 August 1996 a Berlin-to-Cyprus peace ride by motorcyclists from around Europe ended at the Greek Cypriot village of Deryneia, which adjoins the Attila Line that divides Northern Cyprus from the Republic of Cyprus. Among the riders that day was a young Greek Cypriot from Protaras by the name of Tasos Isaak. Newly married, his young wife was pregnant with their first child.

At the protest that marked the end of the ride, and in memory of the continuing occupation of the North by Turkish forces, a melee developed, with clashes between Greek Cypriots and Turkish Cypriots in the UN buffer zone that separated the two communities. During the running clashes with Turks from the North – many of whom, it is widely believed, belonged to the paramilitary organisation the Grey Wolves from the Turkish mainland – Tasos Isaak was inexplicably cut off from his fellow demonstrators. He was set upon by thugs carrying wooden clubs and iron bars.

Before the astonished eyes of demonstrators and at least one photographer, Isaak was beaten deliberately and viciously to death. He was unarmed and dressed only in jeans and a shirt. Turkish police stood by and watched. Isaak's lifeless body was later recovered by UN personnel.

Three days later, after Isaak's funeral, a crowd once more gathered at the Deryneia checkpoint to protest against this unprovoked and unwarranted death. Among the protesters this time was Solomos Solomou, a 26-year-old friend of Isaak, who was enraged at the death of his friend. Despite repeated attempts to hold him back, Solomos eluded the UN peacekeepers and slipped across the no-man's land to one of the flagpoles carrying the Turkish Cypriot flag. Cigarette in mouth, he managed to climb halfway up the flagpole before being struck by five bullets that came from the Turkish Cypriot checkpoint building, and possibly from bushes sheltering armed soldiers. Solomos' bloody slide to death down the flagpole was captured dramatically on video, and is replayed endlessly at viewing points that today overlook the tragic site of the Deryneia murders.

The memories live on vividly in the minds of Greek Cypriots. The graphic photos of Isaak and Solomos, as well as that of an old man caught picking mushrooms in the buffer zone and subsequently shot, are displayed on the Greek side of the Ledra Palace Hotel crossing in Lefkosia. Security is tight at Deryneia now, but tensions run ever high. Life and death here can be as fragile as a Damoclean thread.

necessary. The British government has stated that it is prepared to cede back a large chunk of this SBA if Cyprus becomes reunified.

You are not supposed to 'tour' the SBA and photographs are a no-no. You can't actually enter the base installations themselves without passes and permits, but you can freely drive around the territory itself. Although the British military play it very low-key and rarely make themselves visible to casual travellers, the installations at Dekelia are a crucial intelligence-gathering apparatus. They continue to play a role in monitoring radio traffic in the Middle East, and keeping a watch on regional military activity with sophisticated over-the-horizon (OTH-B) radar units.

The Attila Line is less rigorously monitored here since there is no UN buffer zone as such. Turkish Cypriots from the North may come and go freely and move around within the SBA; many do so in order to visit the sole Turkish-Greek village left in Cyprus at Pyla (see later in this chapter). The informal border-crossing points at Pergamos (Beyarmudu) and Agios Nikolaos, while not open to casual visitors, are in total contrast to the tense atmosphere perceptible at the Ledra Palace Hotel crossing point in Lefkosia. Visitors should be extra vigilant about inadvertently wandering into the North, though, as there have been documented cases of southerners or foreigners being arrested and held by Northern authorities after straying across the sometimes indistinct Line.

These days, travellers heading to Agia Napa and Protaras from Larnaka are neatly diverted around (though still through) the SBA by the motorway which, by the end of 2002, had finally reached as far as Agia Napa, safely on the east side of Dekelia.

THE KOKKINOHORIA
ΤΑ ΚΟΚΚΙΝΟΧΩΡΙΑ

The Kokkinohoria villages are to Cyprus what Idaho is to the USA – they both produce famous potatoes. Kokkinohoria means 'Red Villages' and they are so-called not because of their political allegiances, but for the colour of the rich earth over which these once backwater but now prospering villages are built. The red soil of the Agia Napa hinterland is striking and appears almost suddenly, soon after the village of Ormidia in the Dekelia SBA. Coupled with a rash of wind-powered water pumps that litter the rolling landscape,

this part of Cyprus is in many ways geographically akin to the outback of Australia.

Potatoes and also *kolokasi* (a kind of root vegetable similar to the Pacific Islands' taro) grows profusely in the mineral-rich soil. Up to three crops of potatoes are cultivated annually here – no doubt contributing significantly to Cypriots' predilection for chips with everything. The main villages are **Xylofagou**, **Avgorou**, **Frenaros**, **Liopetri** and **Sotira** and, while they offer little to the tourist per se, other than a glimpse of rural Cyprus or the occasional excellent country taverna, they are great to get around on a scooter and are in total contrast to the coastal resorts to the east and south. Signposting in the Kokkinohoria is pretty poor at times so make sure you have a decent map to avoid going around in circles.

PYLA ΠΥΛΑ PİLE
pop 1370

The unlikely village of Pyla is the only place in Cyprus where Greek and Turkish Cypriots still live together in harmony. Admittedly, that harmony is reinforced by the presence of the UN peace-keeping contingent and a watchful Turkish military lookout post on the ridge high above the village, but it works. Pyla is in the UN buffer zone and, unlike elsewhere in Cyprus, this buffer zone area is open to all and sundry. That means Cypriots from both the North and the South.

The main feature of the village, illustrating the continuing peaceful coexistence of Turk and Greek, is the village square, where on one side a red-and-white Turkish Cypriot coffee shop eyes up a blue-and-white Greek Cypriot *kafenio* on the other side. Overlooking the middle of the square is the 'referee's' chair positioned prominently outside the UN watchtower and occasionally occupied by an Irish or Argentinean soldier in a blue beret.

Greeks and Turks live in mixed neighbourhoods and by all accounts mind their own business and get on with living normally. Cross-cultural mixing is low-key and not obvious to casual observers. The Greeks are somewhat peeved that they carry the burden of local taxes and utility costs, while the Turks pay nothing and get the benefit of access to both the North and the South. This is the only place in the South, other than in the Dekelia SBA, that you will see Northern Cyprus–registered cars. Look for the thin red band around the licence plates, or the give-away Turkish script on the plate frame. Many Turkish Cypriot residents of Pyla run two cars – one North-registered and the other South-registered, thereby getting the best of both worlds. Photography is not allowed.

If you don't want to backtrack to the Larnaka motorway, take the winding road out of Pyla signposted to Pergamos, entering the SBA about 1km outside the village. From here you can cut across the SBA to the motorway for Agia Napa.

PROTARAS & PERNERA
ΠΡΩΤΑΡΑΣ & ΠΕΡΝΕΡΑ
pop 11,100 (including Paralimni)
Protaras and Pernera are two separate communities but are in effect now linked by the ever-growing strip of hotels and restaurants that connect this long snaking coastal resort. Protaras–Pernera is a slightly watered-down version of Agia Napa, and more geared to couples and families. It is another beach resort area, but is more spread out, has a better range of beaches and tends to give visitors more breathing space. That said, Protaras–Pernera is geared almost exclusively to the resort crowd with sprawling hotels, lawns and swimming pools. While day visitors are welcome, they may feel a little left out. There seem to be enough restaurants and bars to compensate, though finding one that is beyond simply adequate can take some doing – most offer unimaginative meals served by uninspired, non-Cypriot waiting staff.

Orientation & Information
The 'centre' of the Protaras–Pernera community as such hinges upon the main high street running through the centre of Protaras. Here is the greatest concentration of shops, restaurants, bars and hotels. As this is primarily a tourist and not a residential area, little happens here outside of the tourist season. It is approximately 4km from the northern end of Pernera to the southern end of Protaras.

Beaches
There are some top-class beaches along this strip. While they do not compare to the postcard-pretty beaches of Greece, they are the best the Republic has to offer.

Skoutari Beach Starting from the far northern end, you will find this beach comprising 50m of hard-packed sand, scruffy rocks and crumbling cliffs. The bay is sheltered and the snorkelling is good here. There are a few restaurants nearby.

Agia Triada Beach Second along, and used mainly as a boat launching area, this diminutive beach has shallow water, the sand is a little coarse and cars tend to be parked along its 200m curving length. Ice-cream sellers are the only source of nourishment.

Mouzoura Beach Blink and you'll miss this next beach. It's fairly small and popular with Cypriot sunbathers. Its 100m length sports a good but narrow sand strip and some shade under the trees at the southern end. The sand drops away quickly so it might not be suitable for nonswimmers or young children. There are ample parking facilities, at least one good restaurant and a large hotel for people who choose to base themselves here.

Louma Beach Further south is the busy beach zone and the northern extension of Protaras called Pernera. The 400m curving strand of Louma Beach is protected by an artificial bay. The sand is fine, the water is clean and shelves gently, and there is shade under the trees at the northern end.

Water sports are catered for by **Baywater Water Sports**, which offers banana tube rides (CY£3), paragliding (CY£14 a flight), water-skiing lessons (CY£15) or 15 minutes on a jet ski (CY£15). Sun loungers and umbrellas rent for CY£1.25 each.

Pernera Beach Skipping a fairly lengthy section of coast with few swimming options, the next busy beach is this one, which is a smaller version of Louma Beach. It is a curvy 200m long and has good soft sand, but little shade. However, the water is also shallow and shelves suddenly. Five restaurants surrounding the beach compete for trade.

The **TABA Diving centre** (☎ 2483 2680) offers single dives for CY£18 or double dives for CY£30.

Protaras Beach Bypassing a series of open rocky coves, mostly backed by the lawns of large resort hotels, you arrive at the most popular and frequented of all the beaches on this strip. Protaras Beach is long and sandy, studded with umbrellas and served by a multitude of water sports. The various spots along the beach are approached by access roads from the main Protaras high street inland.

The most popular part is **Fig Tree Bay** at the southern end, so-named for the single fig tree that stands guard back from the beach.

Green Bay Beach To avoid the crowds and almost get away from it all, keep going. Not so prominently signposted is this neat swimming spot at the far southern end of the beach strip. It is the first obvious beach you will come to if approaching Protaras from Agia Napa. There are two parts to the beach: a sandy strip with umbrellas and loungers to rent on the north side and some little sandstone platforms 100m further south where, if you get in early enough, you can claim a very pleasant spot. Bring your own picnic.

Konnos Beach About 2km south of Green Bay, this gorgeous, sandy strand is signposted 1km off the main road to Cape Greco. It's sheltered, looks oh-so inviting and is home to **Mike's Water Sports** (☎ 9960 5833). Take a parachute ride (CY£15), a ski tow (CY£15), a beginner's ski lesson (CY£15) or hire a jet ski for CY£1 per minute.

Places to Stay
Without exception, all hotel options are clustered along the Pernera–Protaras strip. Most are resolutely geared to package-tour visitors and the choice is enormous, with over 90 places on offer. These range from two- to five-star hotels and A- and B-class hotel apartments. Budget accommodation is thin on the ground, with virtually no backpacker scene to speak of. Bookings are recommended in the high season, and would-be travellers are advised to get hold of the free CTO *Guide to Hotels and Other Tourist Establishments* that gives a full listing.

Aeolos (☎ 2383 2810, fax 2372 2809; Louma Beach; rooms CY£24-45) is one place that you might look at. It has several A-class hotel apartments, but it is not listed in the CTO guide. This spotless establishment is right on the beach and offers well-equipped rooms for up to four people.

The three-star **Cavo Maris** (☎ 2383 2043, fax 2383 2051; e cavo@cytanet.com.cy; singles/doubles from CY£46/74) has a couple of pools, a pleasant beach, restaurants, bars and night-time activities. It is at the southern end of Protaras, near Green Bay Beach. A 30% discount often applies even in season.

Places to Eat
Eating options are as plentiful as the accommodation possibilities. While hotels all tend to be of uniform quality, some restaurants can be downright bad. Choose prudently.

Mouzoura Beach Restaurant (☎ 2382 3333; Vryssoudion 79; mains CY£4.50-5.50) is a large-scale eatery, but it tends to draw a predominantly Cypriot crowd, ensuring that the food is better than average. Good pork chops and tender *kalamari* are recommended.

Nautilus Inn (☎ 2383 1042; light meals CY£2-2.50) is a cheap and excellent pub-restaurant in central Pernera. It's on the main road away from the beach. Jacket potatoes with chilli are filling, draught Guinness or Kilkenny is CY£2.40 a pint and there are eight varieties of bottled Belgian lager.

Cordon Bleu Flambé Restaurant (☎ 2383 1511; flambé dishes CY£3.95-9.25) has been recommended by travellers. Opt for a two-course special (CY£4.95), or try a mouth-watering escalope cordon bleu supreme of chicken maison for about the same price.

Island Oasis Bar & Restaurant (☎ 9949 2144; mains CY£5-7) is reputed to do the best steaks and ribs around. This popular eatery is a family-oriented place with a good kids menu and play area. It is in the heart of Pernera.

Olympus (☎ 2383 2262; mains CY£4.50-5.50) is a Greek-style taverna with charcoal-cooked meats and veggie options. It's at the southern end of Protaras' main high street.

Anemos (☎ 2383 1488; Fig Tree Bay, Protaras; mains CY£4-6) is a large, Cypriot, family-style restaurant with a large selection of nonvegetarian and vegetarian options. For CY£4.75 vegetarians can feast on fried vegetables, *halumi* cheese, mushrooms and rice. There's a good selection of Hrysorogiatissa wines for around CY£6.

Entertainment
Bars and pubs abound, though you'll need to go to Agia Napa for the club scene. Try these two watering holes to kick off your crawl.

South African–run **Africanos** (☎ 2383 1841; Hotels Rd, Protaras) allows you to 'hear yourself drink' according to the owner. Enjoy bar snacks, surf the Internet, enjoy '60s, '70s and Blues classics and unwind.

Homers (Protaras) is a full-on, spacious British-style pub, with all the trappings: karaoke, live entertainment, Sky Sports and even Sunday lunch (CY£4 to CY£5). It's near Agios Ilias church.

Northern Cyprus

North Nicosia (Lefkoşa)

Lefkosia Λευκωσία
pop 39,000

Overshadowed by its busier and better-known half to the south, North Nicosia (Lefkoşa, as it's known in Turkish) is the quieter half of the world's last divided capital. North Nicosia is seen by some as a backwater and by others, living south of the Green Line that divides the troubled city, as a poignant reminder of the bitter division that has kept Turkish North Nicosians apart from Greek Lefkosians, even before the events of 1974. Despite the odds and the continuing sense of ignominy, North Nicosia carries on with life the best it can and bestows a warm welcome upon the gradual trickle of travellers who make the effort to visit.

Easily visited on a day trip across the Green Line from Greek Lefkosia (South Nicosia), or from the northern resort of Kyrenia (Girne), North Nicosia offers a glimpse into the past of an old city that has changed little since 1974. Visitors can see hammams (Turkish bathhouses) and ancient markets, visit dusty backstreets where timeworn artisans still ply their traditional crafts and trades, as well as explore a slowly developing modern city that is seeking to create its own identity while still being shunned by the international community.

The streets of the city are safe and uncrowded, though busy traffic can occasionally make navigating the narrow streets of the Old City a little unnerving. The Old City can be seen easily in half a day and while most visitors come and depart on the same day, there is pleasant accommodation and fine dining for the adventurous few who wish to sample life on the 'other' side of the infamous Green Line.

HISTORY

Up until 1963 Lefkoşa, not surprisingly, shares much of the same history as its dismembered southern sector. For more details of this period, see the Lefkosia chapter.

The capital was effectively divided into Greek and Turkish sectors in 1963, when violence against Turkish Cypriots by Ethniki Organosi tou Kypriakou Agona (EOKA; National Organisation for the Cypriot Struggle) insurgents forced them to retreat

Highlights

- Wander through the narrow streets of the Old City and watch traditional artisans at work
- Enjoy a refreshing Turkish steam bath and massage at the Büyük Hammam
- Admire the striking Ottoman and Lusignan buildings in North Nicosia

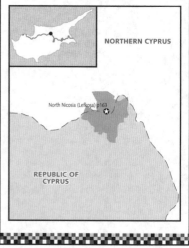

into safe enclaves or ghettos. The Green Line, as it has become known, was established when a British military commander divided up the city on a map with a green pen. The name Green Line has remained ever since. The Turkish military invasion – most Turkish Cypriots saw it as a rescue operation – of 1974 formalised the division between the two halves of the city. A wary truce was brokered by the blue-bereted members of the UN peacekeeping forces, who had been guarding the Green Line since the sectarian troubles of 1964. Despite sporadic negotiations between both sides and the occasional offers of intervention by foreign would-be guarantor powers, the reunification of the city still looks far off.

ORIENTATION

The Old City is easy to navigate. If you get lost, head for the Venetian Walls, which you

NORTH NICOSIA (LEFKOŞA)

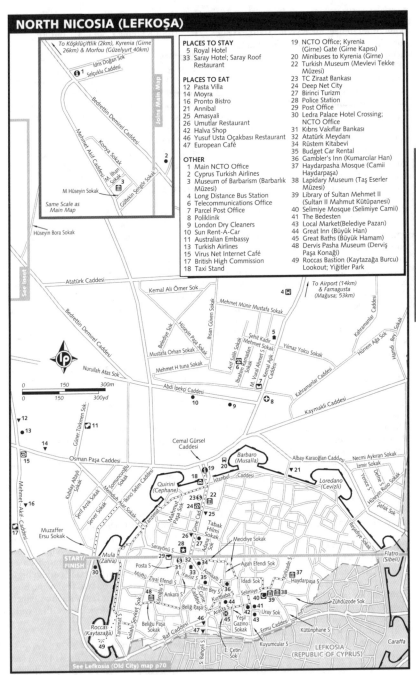

PLACES TO STAY
5 Royal Hotel
33 Saray Hotel; Saray Roof Restaurant

PLACES TO EAT
12 Pasta Villa
14 Moyra
16 Pronto Bistro
21 Annibal
25 Amasyali
26 Umutlar Restaurant
42 Halva Shop
46 Yusuf Usta Oçakbası Restaurant
47 European Café

OTHER
1 Main NCTO Office
2 Cyprus Turkish Airlines
3 Museum of Barbarism (Barbarlık Müzesi)
4 Long Distance Bus Station
6 Telecommunications Office
7 Parcel Post Office
8 Poliklinik
9 London Dry Cleaners
10 Sun Rent-A-Car
11 Australian Embassy
13 Turkish Airlines
15 Virus Net Internet Café
17 British High Commission
18 Taxi Stand
19 NCTO Office; Kyrenia (Girne) Gate (Girne Kapısı)
20 Minibuses to Kyrenia (Girne)
22 Turkish Museum (Mevlevi Tekke Müzesi)
23 TC Ziraat Bankası
24 Deep Net City
27 Birinci Turizm
28 Police Station
29 Post Office
30 Ledra Palace Hotel Crossing; NCTO Office
31 Kıbrıs Vakıflar Bankası
32 Atatürk Meydanı
34 Rüstem Kitabevi
35 Budget Car Rental
36 Gambler's Inn (Kumarcılar Han)
37 Haydarpasha Mosque (Camii Haydarpaşa)
38 Lapidary Museum (Taş Eserler Müzesi)
39 Library of Sultan Mehmet II (Sultan II Mahmut Kütüpanesi)
40 Selimiye Mosque (Selimiye Camii)
41 The Bedesten
43 Local Market(Belediye Pazan)
44 Great Inn (Büyük Han)
45 Great Baths (Büyük Hamam)
48 Dervis Pasha Museum (Derviş Paşa Konaği)
49 Roccas Bastion (Kaytazağa Burcu) Lookout; Yiğitler Park

NORTH NICOSIA (LEFKOŞA)

can easily follow in order to reach the main point of reference, the Kyrenia (Girne) Gate (or Girne Kapısı in Turkish). Running south from the Kyrenia Gate is Girne Caddesi, which leads onto Atatürk Meydanı, the main square, identifiable by a large portrait of Kemal Atatürk. Around here you will find banks, shops and hotels. To the east of the square are the Korkut Effendi and Selimiye districts where most of North Nicosia's sights are found. To the immediate south, near the Green Line, is a small pedestrianised area with shops and restaurants. In the west of the Old City are Karamanzade and Arabahmet districts.

Day visitors to North Nicosia will arrive to the west of the Old City via the Ledra Palace Hotel, at the UN-controlled checkpoint between Northern Cyprus and the Republic. From here it is a 10-minute walk to the Kyrenia Gate. Arrivals by service taxi or minibus will alight close to the Gate itself, while long-distance bus arrivees will find themselves about 800m northeast of the Gate. The New City spreads some distance north from Kyrenia Gate with Bedrettin Demirel Caddesi leading northwest to Kyrenia and Kemal Aşik Caddesi leading northeast to Famagusta (Mağusa).

Maps
The North Cyprus Tourist Organisation (NCTO) produces the reasonably useful *City Plan of Lefkoşa* in both English and Turkish. These should be available at the Ledra Palace Hotel NCTO office. Otherwise you will have to ask at one of the NCTO offices in North Nicosia. Commercially produced maps of Cyprus available in your local bookshop at home sometimes have city maps that include North Nicosia. Maps of Lefkosia published by the CTO in the South do not show street details of North Nicosia.

INFORMATION
Tourist Offices
The **NCTO** has two convenient offices *(Kyrenia Gate; open 9am-5pm Mon-Fri, 9am-2pm Sat • Ledra Palace Crossing; open 9am-5pm Mon-Sat, 9am-2pm Sun)* with maps and brochures on Northern Cyprus.

If you don't find the information you want at these two offices, you can always make the 2km trek out to the main **NCTO Office** *(☎ 227 9112, fax 228 5625; Bedrettin*

Demirel Caddesi). It's a long walk, so take a taxi from Kyrenia Gate (TL1 million).

Money
You can change your money into Turkish lira (TL) at any of the money-changing facilities just past the Ledra Palace Hotel passport-control booth. ATMs for credit cards can be found at the **TC Ziraat Bankası** at the northern end of Girne Caddesi, or at the **Kıbrıs Vakıflar Bankası** *(Atatürk Meydanı)*. Both change foreign currency as do private exchange offices nearby.

Post & Communications
The main **post office** *(Sarayönü Sokak)* is just west of Atatürk Meydanı. The **telecommunications office** *(Arif Salih Sokak; open 8am-midnight daily)* is in the New Town, west of the Telecom tower.

There are public telephone booths scattered throughout the Old City, all of which use prepaid phonecards. You may purchase phonecards from post offices.

The easiest internet outlet to find is the central **Deep Net City** *(☎ 227 9669; Girne Caddesi 73)*. This busy place is open 24 hours a day and access costs TL1 million per hour.

Another place is the **Virus Net Internet Café** *(☎ 0533 868 8086; Osman Paşa Caddesi C35)*, open 24 hours, where access to the Net at one of their modern computers is TL750,000 per hour.

Travel Agencies
Birinci Turizm *(☎ 228 3200, fax 228 3358; ⓦ www.birinciturizm.com; Girne Caddesi 158a)* issues ferry tickets to Turkey and airline tickets, and also offers a range of other travel-related services.

Bookshops
Visitors to **North Nicosia** should not miss the **Rüstem Kitabevi** *(☎ 228 3506; Girne Caddesi 22)* bookshop opposite Saray Hotel. The owners preside over organised chaos with books, old and new, piled ceiling high. In among the chaos you will find some English titles to take your fancy such as paperback versions of Frederick Forsyth novels.

Laundry
London Dry Cleaners *(☎ 227 8232; Abdi İpekçi Caddesi 30)* in the New City will do a service wash as well as dry clean your clothes.

Walking Tour of North Nicosia

For more details of the sights seen along the way, see the individual entries later in this chapter.

A self-paced walking tour is most conveniently started and finished at the **Ledra Palace Hotel crossing**, especially if you are visiting North Nicosia on a day trip from the South. From the checkpoint, walk 100m and turn right onto Memduh Asar Sokak and you will almost immediately cross into the **Old City**. Turn right along Zahra Sokak and walk past a line of old houses now undergoing renovation. These are the same houses that you can see from the Greek Cypriot side of the Ledra Palace Hotel crossing. Note the rusting oil barrels and gun placements on the Greek Cypriot side. Enter the small **Yiğitler Park** further along to your right that sits atop the **Roccas Bastion (Kaytazağa Burcu)** and stare out through the fence down into Greek Cypriot Lefkosia. This is the only point along the whole of the Attila and Green Lines where Turkish and Greek Cypriots can eyeball each other at such close quarters.

From the Roccas Bastion head eastwards into the Old City along narrow streets with tastefully restored houses of the **Arabahmet neighbourhood**. Make a left turn along Salahi Sevket Sokak and then right into Beliğ Paşa Sokak to visit the **Dervish Pasha Museum**, a small ethnographical collection housed in an old Turkish mansion. Follow Beliğ Paşa Sokak until it leads you into the **pedestrianised zone** in the centre of the city. Note the **restaurants and cafés** for lunch later. Follow Araşta Sokak past the **Büyük Hammam** (steam baths) and detour briefly to see the two Turkish caravanserais, the **Great Inn (Büyük Han)** and the **Gambler's Inn (Kumarcılar Han)**, which are both nearby. Continue a further 100m until you arrive at the locked Ottoman bazaar called the **Bedesten**, across the street from which is the local market, the **Belediye Pazarı**. Hard to miss is the uncompleted former Lusignan cathedral of Agia Sofia, now the **Selimiye Mosque**, incongruous with its soaring minarets attached after the Ottoman conquest.

If you have time, seek out the **Library of Sultan Mahmut II** close by. Further east are the **Lapidary Museum** and the **Haydarpasha Mosque**, which was originally the 14th-century church of St Catherine. Retrace your steps westwards along Idadi and Mecidiye Sokak and make for the main square of **Atatürk Meydanı**, from which it is a short stroll north along Girne Caddesi to the Mevlevi Tekke, originally home of the Whirling Dervishes (the mystic Islamic sect), but now the **Turkish Museum**. At the northern end of Girne Caddesi you will see Kyrenia Gate, cut off from its protective walls when the British created a throughway for vehicular traffic.

From the Kyrenia Gate it is a brisk 10-minute stroll inside the **Venetian Walls** back to the Ledra Palace Hotel crossing, or the pedestrian zone for lunch. Allow a leisurely two hours for the walk and extra time to see the sights

Medical Services

North Nicosia's main hospital is the **Burhan Nalbatanoğlu Devlet Hastahanesi** (☎ 228 5441). There is also the **Poliklinik** (☎ 227 3996; Kemal Aşik Caddesi) where foreigners can seek medical treatment.

Emergency

The **police station** (☎ 228 3311) is on Atatürk Meydanı. For emergencies, call ☎ 155.

Dangers & Annoyances

North Nicosia is a safe city at any time of the day and visitors should feel no concern about walking the streets. At night the Old City can become rather quiet and visitors may feel intimidated walking alone along dimly lit and sometimes narrow streets. Avoid them if you feel uncomfortable. The areas abutting the Green Line look threatening with large black-and-red signs that clearly forbid photography or trespassing in the buffer zone.

On the Roccas Bastion (Kaytazağa Burcu) at the western end of the Old City limits, where you can look over into Greek Lefkosia, do not take photographs. Watchful soldiers stationed not so obviously on the bastion may accost you and even confiscate your camera.

THINGS TO SEE & DO
Dervish Pasha Museum

This small ethnographical museum (Derviş Paşa Konaği; Beliğ Paşa Sokak; admission TL2 million; open 9am-7pm daily June–mid-Sept,

9am-1pm & 2pm-4.45pm mid-Sept–May) is North Nicosia's equivalent of Lefkosia's Dragoman Hatzigeorgakis house. The building is an old mansion that was built in 1807 and belonged to a wealthy Turkish Cypriot, Derviş Paşa, who published Cyprus' first Turkish-language newspaper. The house was turned into an ethnographic museum in 1988. Household goods, including an old loom, glassware and ceramics, are displayed in former servants' quarters on the ground floor. Upstairs is a rich display of embroidered Turkish costumes and, in the far corner, a sumptuous *selamlık* – a retiring room for the owner of the mansion and his guests – replete with sofas and hookah.

Büyük Hammam

The Büyük Hammam *(Tarihi Büyük Hammam; ☎ 228 4462; M İrfanbey Sokak 9; open 7.30am-10.30pm daily)* is a world-famous working Turkish bath frequented by male and female locals and tourists. The entrance is via an ornate low door, sunk six feet below street level. The door was originally part of the 14th-century Church of St George of the Latins. Inside you may be able to see a nail that marks the point where in 1330 the waters of the Pedieos River (Kanlı Dere) rose and drowned about 3000 Lefkosians. A refreshing steam bath and a massage (male masseurs only) cost TL20 million.

Great Inn & Gambler's Inn

The Great Inn *(Büyük Han; admission TL200,000; open 9am-2pm daily June–mid-Sept, 9am-1pm & 2pm-4.45pm mid-Sept–May)* is a rare surviving example of a Middle Age caravanserai. In the Middle Ages, travellers and traders could find accommodation at these *hans* (inns), as well as a place to stable their horses, trade their goods and socialise with fellow travellers. The Great Inn was built in 1572 and is built around a central courtyard. Some 67 rooms look out onto the courtyard from two storeys. The structure is slowly being converted to a museum and may still be closed when you visit. You can peer through a gap in the wooden gates and see the courtyard and the accompanying restoration work.

Just to the north, on Agah Efendi Sokak, is the better-preserved and now functioning Gambler's Inn *(Kumarcılar Han; admission TL1*

million; open 9am-2pm daily June–mid-Sept, 9am-1pm & 2pm-4.45pm mid-Sept–May)* – a late 17th-century caravanserai. Shops now occupy the outer perimeter and the Department of Antiquities has offices inside. There is also a quiet courtyard.

Local (Municipal) Market

Unlike the former Ottoman Bazaar of the Bedesten across the road, this is a working and functioning produce market *(Belediye Pazarı; open 6am-3pm Mon-Sat)* where you can also buy clothes and knick-knacks. While there is nothing architecturally or historically noteworthy about the building, it is a great place to stock up on picnic items and take photographs of wonderfully coloured displays of fruit and vegetables.

Bedesten

The ruined and usually locked Bedesten *(St Nicholas of the English; open 8am-1.45pm & 2pm-4.45pm Mon-Sat June–mid-Sept, 8am-12.45pm mid-Sept–May)* was originally a small Byzantine church built in the 6th century and augmented in the 14th century by a Catholic church. During the 82-year rule of the Venetians in Cyprus it became the church of the Orthodox Metropolitan. After the Ottomans took Lefkosia in 1570 the church was used variously as a grain store and general market, but was basically left to disintegrate. Today you can peer through the fencing and still make out the layout of the original churches. The complex, on Selemiye Meydanı, is earmarked for eventual restoration, so access to the site can be erratic at times. The north doorway has some splendid-looking **coats of arms** originally belonging to noble Venetian families who may have been supporters of the Orthodox Church which, despite the Catholic dominance of religious life in Cyprus, was nonetheless allowed to continue about its business.

Medieval tombstones from various parts of Cyprus are currently kept in a section of the Bedesten and may be viewable if restoration work isn't taking place.

If you ask, the attendant at the Library of Sultan Mahmut II will show you the Bedesten and also the Lapidary Museum. The admission fee for the library also lets you into the Lapidary Museum and the Bedesten (see later).

Selimiye Mosque

North Nicosia's most prominent landmark – clearly visible from the South also – is the Selimiye Mosque *(Selimiye Camii; admission free; open daily)*. This strange-looking building, a cross between a Gothic church and mosque, has an interesting history. Work started on the church in 1209 and progressed slowly. Louis IX of France, on his way to the Crusades, stopped by in 1248 and gave the building process a much needed shot in the arm by offering the services of his retinue of artisans and builders. However, the church required another 78 years before it was completed and finally consecrated in 1326 as the **Church of Agia Sofia**.

Up until 1570, the church suffered subsequent depredation at the hands of the Genoese and the Mamelukes, and severe shaking from two earthquakes in 1491 and 1547. When the Ottomans arrived in 1570, they stripped the building of its Christian contents and added two minarets between which the Turkish Cypriot and Turkish flags now flutter.

Today the Selimiye Mosque is a working mosque – albeit an odd-looking one with strong French Gothic style – and you can go inside. Observe the usual etiquette when visiting a mosque: dress conservatively, take your shoes off, observe silence and don't take photos if prayers are in progress. The Gothic structure of the interior is still apparent despite Islamic overlays such as the whitewashed walls and columns and the re-orientation of the layout to align it with Mecca. Note the ornate west front with the three decorated doorways, each of a different style. Look out also for four **marble columns** relocated from Ancient Salamis and now placed in the apse off the main aisles.

The mosque opens following no set times. If it's closed try to time your visit to one of the five Muslim prayer sessions.

Library of Sultan Mahmut II

The Library of Sultan Mahmut II *(Sultan II Mahmut Kütüpanesi; Haydarpaşa Sokak; admission TL1.5 million; open 9am-2pm June–mid-Sept, 9am-1pm & 2pm-4.45pm mid-Sept–May)* is housed in an octagonal building erected in 1829. The library contains some 1700 books and the interior is decorated with a calligraphic frieze in blue and gold. Some of the books are up to 700 years old and the more valuable tomes are displayed in special cases.

The same ticket also gives you access to the Bedesten and the Lapidary Museum.

Lapidary Museum

A visit to the **Lapidary Museum** *(Taş Eserler Müzesi; Kirilzade Sokak; open 9am-2pm June–mid-Sept, 9am-1pm & 2pm-4.45pm mid-Sept–May)* is usually included in a visit to the Library of Sultan Mahmut II. This is a 15th-century building containing a varied collection of sarcophagi, shields, steles, columns and a Gothic window rescued from a Lusignan palace that once stood near Atatürk Meydanı.

Haydarpasha Mosque

The mosque *(Camii Haydarpaşa; Kirilzade Sokak; admission free; open 9am-1pm & 2.30pm-5pm Mon-Fri, 9am-1pm Sat)* was originally built as the 14th-century Church of St Catherine but now functions as an art gallery. It is the second most important Gothic structure in North Nicosia after the Selimiye Mosque. The outside and inside sculptures of the structure are quite ornate, sporting gargoyles, dragons, shields and human heads.

Turkish Museum

The Turkish Museum *(Mevlevi Tekke Müzesi; Girne Caddesi; admission TL2.5 million; open 7.30am-2pm Mon-Fri & 3.30pm-6pm Mon)* is a former 17th-century monastery of the mystic Islamic sect known as the Whirling Dervishes. Their spiritual philosophy is based

Atatürk banned the Whirling Dervishes.

MICK WELDON

on Sufism and the Dervishes were followers of a 13th-century poet known as Jelaluddin Mevlana Rumi. They flourished for 700 years in Turkish life until they were banned by Atatürk in 1925. Their public persona is most commonly exemplified by their strange, slow-whirling trance-like dance. In this they slowly whirl in a circular fashion, one palm held upwards and the other downwards to symbolise man's position as a bridge between Heaven and Earth.

The Dervishes have long since left the Tekke and this fine old building is now a museum displaying Dervish artefacts as well as photographs, embroidery, calligraphy, illuminated Qurans and other Turkish Cypriot memorabilia.

Museum of Barbarism

While the Turkish Cypriots may have taken down the gruesome posters and photographs to greet arrivals at the Ledra Palace Hotel crossing, they have not forgotten the atrocities committed by Greek Cypriots and in particular EOKA thugs against the Turkish Cypriot community. The Museum of Barbarism (Barbarlık Müzesi; M İrhan Sokak 2; admission TL2 million; open 8am-2pm daily) is in a quiet suburb to the west of the Old City and takes a bit of seeking out. On 24 December 1963 a mother and her children, along with a neighbour, were shot dead in their bath by EOKA gunmen. The bloodstained bath is retained as one of the exhibits in this rather macabre museum. There are other photodocumentary displays, particularly of Turkish Cypriots murdered in the villages of Agios Sozomenos and Agios Vasilios.

GO KARTING

If you fancy yourself as a bit of a Formula 1 whiz, go to Zet Karting (☎ 0533 866 6173, fax 228 3530; w www.zetkarting.com; Lefkoşa-Güzelyurt Anayolu; open 4pm-midnight June–mid-Sept, noon-8pm mid-Sept–June, closed Mon) and pretend you are Michael Schumacher. A large and very professional-looking series of circuits has been built on the side of the North Nicosia–Morfou (Güzelyurt) road, 7km from the main Gönyeli roundabout on the northern outskirts of North Nicosia. You can rent carts from TL5 million per 10 minutes for the junior 300m course to TL15 million for 10

minutes on the 1,200m professional circuit. Unwind in the Z1 Bar or Z1 Cafeteria.

PLACES TO STAY

Most of the budget hotels are around the Selimiye Mosque area and in the streets east of Girne Caddesi. They all have dorm-style rooms where a bed costs around UK£4 to UK£6, but they are pretty dire places. We don't particularly recommend any of them. Better to fork out a bit more to sleep in some comfort.

The three-star Saray (☎ 228 3115, fax 228 4808; e saray@northcyprus.net; Atatürk Meydanı; singles/doubles UK£27/41) is the best hotel in the Old Town and is very central.

The three-star Royal Hotel (☎ 228 7621, fax 228 7580; e ichangar@kktc.net; Kemal Aşik Caddesi; singles/doubles UK£30/44) is a comfortable international-standard hostelry popular with travellers on business. All rooms are fully serviced and have minibar, phone, satellite TV and even a phone in the bathroom.

PLACES TO EAT

Eating in North Nicosia doesn't offer too many choices, unlike Kyrenia, which is positively overflowing with many high-quality eateries. Lunch-time diners are better off checking out a couple of places on Girne Caddesi, or sticking to a clutch of eateries in the centre of the Old City near the Green Line. Evening dining is more of a problem since the Old City is fairly subdued after dark. There is a scattering of restaurants to the northwest of the Old City, usually hard to find and best reached by taxi; they are open evenings.

Inside the Walls In Araşta Sokak opposite the Bedesten is a shop that makes delicious halvah on the premises. Nearby is the Belediye Pazarı, a large, covered market selling fresh produce.

On Girne Caddesi there are two friendly low-key kebab restaurants fairly close to each other. Amasyali (☎ 228 3294; Girne Caddesi 186; döner TL1.5 million) is open all day and serves up staples such as döner kebabs to eat in or take away. Diagonally across the street is Umutlar Restaurant (☎ 227 3236; Girne Caddesi 51; kebabs TL1.5 million), which dishes up a similar menu of kebab-style dishes.

On the pedestrianised zone close to the Green Line you will come across a cluster of restaurants. They are all pretty similar in quality and service.

Yusuf Usta Oçakbası Restaurant (☎ 228 9852; S Bahçeli Sokak 2; meals TL10-12 million) is the first you will come across while the **European Café** (☎ 227 715, S Bahçeli Sokak 8; kebab meal TL9 million) is a little closer to the barricades. Filling meals of kebabs and salad with ice cold beer at either place go down a treat after a tiring day.

A bit more upmarket is the **Saray Roof** (☎ 227 3115; fixed menu meals TL12 million), a top-floor restaurant at the Saray Hotel. You can enjoy a fine evening view with your meal. The cuisine is Turkish and European.

New City To the northwest of the city wall is a group of popular dining options.

About 100m north of the British High Commission is **Pronto Bistro** (☎ 228 6542; Mehmet Akif Caddesi; large pizza TL8 million) where you can enjoy great pizzas as well as a selection of Tex-Mex dishes and even a few Chinese and Indian dishes.

Further north, **Pasta Villa** (☎ 228 4878; Mehmet Akif Caddesi 56; pasta dishes TL7-10 million) is a busy little pasta restaurant. It does half-decent pizzas as well.

Moyra (☎ 228 6800; Osman Paşa Caddesi 32; meals TL14 million) is a pleasant restaurant offering traditional Cypriot steaks and kebabs.

Just outside the walls on the northern side of the Old City is **Annibal** (☎ 227 1835; Saraçoğlu Meydanı; kebabs TL9-11 million), a long-established kebab house that is probably worth a look-in.

ENTERTAINMENT

Turkish Cypriots themselves admit that nightlife in their capital is not all that hot, at least in the Old City. If it's noise and fun you are looking for, forget it or go to Kyrenia. Entertainment North Nicosia–style is mainly taken in restaurants or at home – not much use for travellers. Resign yourself to a pleasant meal and a drink back at your hotel bar rather than pin your hopes on the high life.

SHOPPING

North Nicosia does not have the wide range of shops and goods that Kyrenia does, but you can find inexpensive jewellery and optical items such as spectacles that can even be ordered and made for you in 24 hours. Be wary of fake Rolexes and other designer gear that is sold openly – often as 'genuine imitations' – and don't expect too many bargains

NORTH NICOSIA (LEFKOŞA)

Turkish-Cypriot Cuisine

It is said in some circles that there exist only three really great cuisines in the world: Chinese, French and Turkish. While this assertion may be arguable, there is no doubting that the quality and simplicity of Turkish-Cypriot cuisine is unmatched by most cuisines in the Western world today.

Turkish-Cypriot cuisine owes its heritage to a mixture of Mediterranean and Middle Eastern influences. In addition to being the refined product of centuries of experience, Turkish-Cypriot cuisine has a very pure quality. The variety and simplicity of the recipes and the quality and freshness of the ingredients guarantee delicious meals. While derived heavily from the mainland Turkish culinary influences, the food of Northern Cyprus does have its own subtle variants.

Local food uses an abundance of locally grown or produced products such as olive oil, tomatoes, yogurt, meat and fish. Fresh or dried herbs are used in large quantities, but spices – particularly hot ones – are not as apparent as in cuisines further east. The most common type of food that travellers will come across in the North is the *meze*, a hearty dining odyssey that needs a hefty appetite (see the boxed text 'Eating Meze in Cyprus' in the Lemesos chapter). Meat features prominently in Turkish-Cypriot cuisine with *şiş kebab* – succulent chunks of lamb skewered with peppers and onions and grilled over charcoal – featuring regularly. Pork is not eaten as it is in the South.

Vegetarians will find many enticing options with aubergines, okra, peas, beans, lentils and even taro root featuring in imaginative dishes. Rice (*pilav* in Turkish) is a more genuine alternative to the ever-present potato chips – a British habit shared equally by Cypriots in the South.

Turkish sweets and cakes are justifiably famous and many use cream and honey as prime ingredients. Western taste buds may find them a little too sweet at times. *Afiyet olsun!*

on imported goods. Local or Turkish-made items are usually good value, but don't expect to bargain – it is not part of the shopping scene. If you are on a day-trip from the South, forget about shopping – you cannot take it back across the Line with you and the Greek Cypriot police will tell you as much before you cross over.

GETTING THERE & AWAY
Air
Ercan airport is about 14km east of North Nicosia and is linked to the city by an expressway. There are scheduled flights to London and several destinations in Turkey. All charter flights operate from Ercan *(Tymvou; ☎ 231 4703)*, though occasional flights are diverted to Geçitkale (Lefkoniko) military airport *(☎ 227 9420)*, nearer to Famagusta (Mağusa), when Ercan is being serviced.

The two airlines serving Northern Cyprus are based in North Nicosia. Their addresses are as follows:

Cyprus Turkish Airlines (Kıbrıs Hava Yolları, ☎ 227 3820) Bedrettin Demirel Caddesi
Turkish Airlines (Türk Hava Yolları, ☎ 227 1061) Mehmet Akif Caddesi 32

Bus
The long-distance bus station is on the corner of Atatürk Caddesi and Kemal Aşik Caddesi in the New Town. Buses to major towns leave from here. You may prefer the bus to the sometimes hair-raising rides in service taxis or *dolmuş* (minibuses).

Car & Motorcycle
Drivers and riders will enter North Nicosia via one of two main roads that lead directly to the Old City. If you come from Famagusta or Ercan airport you will enter North Nicosia via Mustafa Ahmet Ruso Caddesi and then Kemal Aşik Caddesi. This road leads directly to Kyrenia Gate. Arriving from Kyrenia you will enter North Nicosia via Tekin Yurdabay Caddesi and eventually Bedrettin Demirel Caddesi, which also leads towards Kyrenia Gate.

If you are entering North Nicosia from Southern Cyprus, the easiest way into to the Old City is to turn immediately right after passing the Ledra Palace Hotel crossing and enter via Memdah Asar Sokak. Turn left onto Tanzimat Sokak as soon as you cross

the moat and you will reach the Kyrenia Gate after about 200m.

Parking is usually not a problem, though finding a place in the Old City may get tricky if you arrive late in the morning on a working day. If you arrive early you can easily park on Girne Caddesi.

Service Taxi & Minibus
Minibuses to local destinations and further afield start from various *termini* (stations) outside the Venetian Walls and also from İtimat bus station just outside Kyrenia Gate. Destinations include Kyrenia (TL1 million) and Famagusta (TL1.5 million). Service taxis also leave from this bus station.

GETTING AROUND
To/From the Airport
Buses to Ercan airport leave from the **Cyprus Turkish Airlines office** *(☎ 227 1240; Bedrettin Demirel Caddesi)*. They depart two hours before any flight and cost TL2 million. A taxi from Kyrenia Gate will cost TL16 million.

Buses
While there are public buses in North Nicosia they tend to mainly service the suburbs outside of the Old City. They are only really useful if you need to get to the Cyprus Turkish Airlines office or the main office of NCTO (both on Bedrettin Demirel Caddesi), or a hitching spot, on a traveller's budget. Buses leave from near Kyrenia Gate.

Car
For car hire, try **Budget Car Rental** *(☎ 228 2711, fax 228 6125; M İrfan Bey Sokak)* or **Sun Rent-A-Car** *(☎ 227 2303, fax 228 3700; W www.sunrentacar.com; Abdi İpekçi Caddesi 10)*. If you are coming from the South, call ahead (see the boxed text 'North-South Dialogue' in the Facts for the Visitor chapter for tips) and see if the company will meet you at the Ledra Palace Hotel crossing. Rates start at around UK£14 per day but are usually negotiable.

Taxi
There are plenty of taxi ranks, though the most convenient and easy to find is at Kyrenia Gate. A ride to anywhere in town should cost no more than TL1 million, though as a tourist you may be asked for more, say, TL1.5 million. Above that you are probably

being ripped off. Ask the driver for the rate before getting into the taxi.

Among the more reliable taxi companies in North Nicosia are **Ankara Taxi** (☎ 227 1788), **Özner Taxi** (☎ 227 4012), **Terminal Taxi** (☎ 228 4909) and **Yılmaz Taxi** (☎ 227 3036).

When you cross into North Nicosia from the South you will almost certainly be approached by tourist cab drivers offering to take you on tours of the North. They would prefer to give you the full treatment for around CY£30, but in practice you can ask to be taken to wherever you like, such as Kyrenia for the day, and pay less accordingly. These drivers are not rapacious – though they are keen for your custom – and they will often act as unofficial and at times informative guides. This is the best solution if you want a taste of the North without the hassles of organising it yourself.

NORTH NICOSIA (LEFKOŞA)

Kyrenia & the North Coast

The sight of the diminutive and picturesque harbour of Kyrenia (Girne) is unforgettable to most first-time visitors. There are few (if any) places like it in Cyprus. Kyrenia is a visual gem, backed by tall Gothic mountains and overlooking an azure sea leading across to the coast of Turkey, some 90km away. Retired British civil servants long ago discovered the beauty of the North and many settled here after years of service in scattered lands throughout the former British Empire, preferring the milder clime of Kyrenia to the cold and rain of the UK. Kyrenia's most famous colonial son Lawrence Durrell lived in Bellapais (Beylerbeyi), his idyllic life documented in his slow-paced nostalgic novel *Bitter Lemons of Cyprus*.

Augustinian monks settled here in the 12th century and built a monastery, the incongruous ruins of which still dominate the surrounding landscape. Fairytale castles were built by a displaced French dynasty on the lofty crags of the Kyrenia (Girne) Range and their stark remains can still be explored. Life for visitors to the North is still slow-paced and relaxed yet accommodation is plentiful and reasonably priced, and high-quality restaurants abound. Picnicking and hiking in the Kyrenia Range is another ideal way to spend a week or so in this timeless sun-drenched sector of Cyprus. The north coast can be fast yet subtle – it requires your time and attention and it won't disappoint.

Kyrenia (Girne)
Κερύνεια

pop 22,000

Kyrenia is the North's jewel and many Greek Cypriots still remember the town wistfully in their songs and poems, as many of them lived here prior to 1974. Politics aside, Kyrenia is a beautiful town on the north coast of Northern Cyprus, no more than a 30-minute drive from the centre of North Nicosia (Lefkoşa). It constitutes the nucleus of the North's tourist industry and here and along the surrounding coastline you will find more hotels, restaurants and bars per square kilometre than anywhere else in the North.

Kyrenia is inextricably identified with its pretty, horseshoe-shaped harbour, around which nestle restaurants, hotels, bars and shops. The harbour has long since ceded its role as the main port of the town; now it is far too small to service any craft other than tourist boats and small yachts that crowd its cluttered quays. Two kilometres to the east, a large purpose-built harbour now receives commercial and passenger shipping, mainly from Turkey.

Apart from its harbour, Kyrenia is known for its immense Byzantine castle that was once used as a prison by the British. It's now home to the Kyrenia Shipwreck Museum, which preserves one of the oldest shipwrecks ever recovered from the sea.

Writer Lawrence Durrell appreciated the beauty of Kyrenia in the early 1950s when he bought a house in the village of Bellapais nearby in the Kyrenia Range foothills. Many British visitors followed suit and today Kyrenia is home to a thriving British expat community who boast their own church and cultural and social club.

HISTORY

The history of Kyrenia is closely linked to the fortunes of its castle. Before the building of the castle, little is known about the town. It is thought that it was settled by mainland Greeks around 1000 BC. Kyrenia was certainly one of the 10 city kingdoms of Ancient Cyprus, but there is little left to document the town's earlier history. Arab raids of the 7th and 8th centuries AD levelled what there was of the settlement. It was only in the late 12th century, when the Byzantines built the castle, possibly over the remains of an earlier existing Roman fort, that Kyrenia's fortunes took an upward turn.

The Lusignans had a hand in the development of the castle and it was used by them both as a residence and as a prison. Over the period of their 82 years of tenure, the Venetians extended the castle and built the bulbous seaward bulwark that can be seen today. During the Ottoman rule, Kyrenia functioned primarily as a port – effectively the only port on the north coast. During British rule, the town became a favourite place for retiring excolonial British civil servants.

Almost all Greeks and many British retirees fled in 1974 following the Turkish invasion when the beaches to the west of Kyrenia were used as the prime beachhead for the landing of Turkish forces. More than 25 years later, Kyrenia has recovered from the turbulence and supports a modest but growing tourist influx mainly from Britain, Germany and Turkey.

ORIENTATION

Kyrenia is spread out over a wide area, but the central Old Town – where most travellers hang out – is fairly compact. Taxis and minibuses arrive at and depart from along Ecevit Caddesi and stop near the main square (Belediye Meydanı), which is about 200m immediately south of the Old Harbour. To the west of Belediye Meydanı runs Ziya Rızkı Caddesi along which you will find shops and money-exchange offices. To the southeast runs Mustafa Çağatay Caddesi, which takes you to the New Harbour and the ferry to/from Turkey.

Long-distance buses arrive at the station on Bedrettin Demirel Caddesi at the junction with İnönü Caddesi, 1km south of the centre. If you arrive by car, there is a handy free car park immediately to the east of Belediye Meydanı.

Maps

The North Cyprus Tourist Organisation (NCTO) issues a free *City Plan of Girne* in English and Turkish. While it is lacking in detail for the streets of the Old Town, it does give a good overall view of Kyrenia and most of the main regional destinations on a smaller inset.

INFORMATION
Tourist Offices

The **NCTO office** *(open 8am-6pm daily)* is at the west end of the Old Harbour. The **Kyrenia Society** *(Mersin Caddesi; open 10am-noon daily)* may be a good place to drop by to see if there are any worthwhile events taking place. Its office is behind the post office. If no-one is there, its notice board will display details of upcoming events or excursions.

Money

There are two ATMs that take credit cards. The **Türk Bankası** *(Ziya Rızkı Caddesi)* is near Belediye Meydanı and further west is the **İş Bankası** *(cnr Ziya Rızkı Caddesi & Atatürk Caddesi)*. There are also several efficient money-exchange offices along Ziya Rızkı Caddesi. Look out for **Yazgın Döviz** *(☎ 228 6673)* or the **Gesfi Exchange** *(Kordon Boyu 40)* opposite the Dome Hotel.

Post & Communications

The main **post office** *(Mustafa Çağatay Caddesi)* is about 150m southeast of Belediye Meydanı. The **telephone communications office** is directly opposite the post office.

There are at least two Internet cafés in town. The best is **Cafe Net** *(☎ 815 9259;*

KYRENIA (GIRNE) & THE NORTH COAST

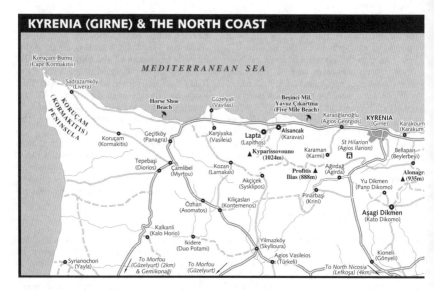

KYRENIA & THE NORTH COAST

Efeler Sokak; access TL1.5 million per hr; open 10am-midnight daily) where there are 12 terminals. English-speaking owner Mehmet Çavuş serves up hot and cold drinks and jacket potatoes, and runs a small book exchange. Mehmet can also arrange for you to take out an Internet account in Northern Cyprus if you plan to stay any length of time.

The other Internet café is **Bati Net Cafe** *(☎ 0542 873 1047; Ziya Rızkı Caddesi; access TL1 million per hr; open 10am-11pm daily)* west of Belediye Meydanı. This modern centre also has 14 terminals.

Travel Agencies
Two agencies issue tickets for ferries to Turkey: **Fergün Denizcilik Sirketi** *(☎ 815 3866; Mustafa Çağatay Caddesi 6/2c)* and **Ertürk Turizm** *(☎ 815 2308, fax 815 1808; İskenderum Caddesi)* towards the New Harbour. Ferry tickets are also issued at the New Harbour.

Bookshops
The **Green Jacket Bookshop** *(☎/fax 815 7130; Temmuz Caddesi 20)*, west of the centre near the Astro Supermarket, is the place to go for foreign-language books. There's a varied range of travel and Cyprus-specific books, and a decent selection of Lonely Planet guides to the region.

Toilets
There are public toilets on the breakwater, on the western side of the Old Harbour.

Medical Services
Kyrenia's local hospital is the **Akçiçek Hastahanesi** *(☎ 815 2254; Mustafa Çağatay Caddesi)*, which is about 500m southeast of the post office.

THINGS TO SEE & DO
Kyrenia Castle & Shipwreck Museum
The looming hulk of Kyrenia Castle *(Girne Kalesi; admission TL7 million; open 9am-6.45pm daily)* effectively dominates the scene in Kyrenia. It sits protectively overlooking the Old Harbour on the east side with a further bay to the east of the castle. The castle was built by the Byzantines and, while it might have staved off the Ottoman invasion of 1570, the Venetians quickly surrendered the castle when they saw how quickly Lefkosia had been overrun.

A visit to Kyrenia would be incomplete without a trip to the castle. It comprises a large rectangular structure punctuated with four fortified bastions at each corner. Visitors are guided around the ramparts via routes marked by handrails. You are advised to stick to the marked routes since some sections are rather precipitous. The views to the west

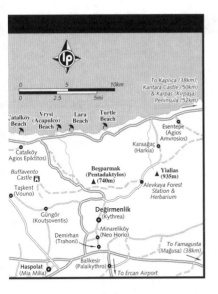

overlooking the harbour are very picturesque. Photographers should get there before 10am to take advantage of the angled light.

Within and off the central courtyard are the rooms and chambers that made up the living quarters and former prison sections of the castle. On the east side of the courtyard, you can enter the temperature-controlled chamber containing the Kyrenia Shipwreck, the oldest shipwreck ever recovered from the waters around Cyprus. This wooden-hulled cargo boat sank just off Kyrenia in approximately 300 BC and was discovered in 1967 by a local diver. Based on its freight, which consisted mainly of almonds, grain, wine and millstones from Kos, the crew most likely traded along the coast of Anatolia as far as the islands of the Dodecanese in Greece.

Antechambers display samples of the boat's cargo and photographs detailing the delicate salvage operation that was carried out to prevent the disintegration of the Aleppo pine wood from which the boat was constructed. The boat is displayed in a dim chamber where you can examine the structure and layout of this remarkable marine archaeological find in considerable detail.

Folk Art Museum
This small collection (*Halk Sanatları Müzesi; admission TL1.5 million; open 9am-5pm June–mid-Sept*) along the harbourfront (Girne Limanı) contains a predictable but interesting collection of old household utensils, furniture and fabrics. Look out for the impressive wooden wine press on the ground floor.

Diving
Scuba diving is well organised in Kyrenia with **Scuba Cyprus** (☎ 822 3430, fax 822 3429; Karaoğlanoğlu) offering PADI and BSAC diving courses. It is based at the Santoria Holiday Village, 2km west of Kyrenia. **Blue Dolphin Scuba Diving** (☎ 0542 851 5113; W www.bluedolphin.4mg.com) is based in the Jasmine Court Hotel but has a contact stand on the Old Harbour. 'Try' dives cost UK£20 while two regular dives cost UK£35.

Boat Cruises
Kyrenia harbour is chock-a-block full of small boats offering picnic and swimming excursions down the coast. All offer much the same formula: for UK£20 you will get cranked up disco music to cruise by, swimming and snorkelling, followed by an onboard BBQ lunch (drinks extra). Most leave at 10.30am and return at 4.30pm, and take up to 28 passengers. One outfit, **Aphrodite Boat & Fishing** (☎ 0533 868 0943; e fantasia@ superonline.com), offers all the above but only takes 10 passengers and is much more intimate. Ask for owner Musa Aksöy around the stand on the harbourfront.

Mountain Treks
British expat Barry Hurst runs a series of half- and full-day excursions to the Kyrenia mountain range with **Cyprus Mountaineering Kyrenia** (☎ 0542 859 4542; W www.cyprus mountaineering.com). For UK£25 you can walk, scramble and climb the rocky peaks and crags of the rugged Kyrenia Range. A restaurant lunch is included. Look for him in or near Boaters Café on the harbour.

Another British expat, Tony Hutchinson, along with a group of other trekking enthusiasts have pioneered a mountain trekking trail from Koruçam Burnu (Cape Kormakitis) in the west to Zafer Burnu (Cape Apostolos Andreas) in the far east of Northern Cyprus. This long and challenging trek can be completed in about 10 days, walking around 22km per day. See the website of **Kyrenia-Range-Walks** (W www.kyrenia-range -walks.com) for details.

KYRENIA & THE NORTH COAST

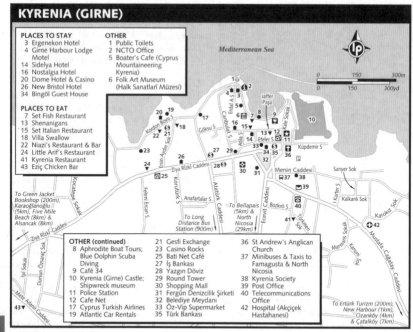

KYRENIA (GIRNE)

PLACES TO STAY
3   Ergenekon Hotel
4   Girne Harbour Lodge
    Motel
14 Sidelya Hotel
16 Nostalgia Hotel
20 Dome Hotel & Casino
26 New Bristol Hotel
34 Bingöl Guest House

PLACES TO EAT
7   Set Fish Restaurant
13 Shenanigans
15 Set Italian Restaurant
18 Villa Swallow
22 Niazi's Restaurant & Bar
24 Little Arif's Restaurant
41 Kyrenia Restaurant
43 Eziç Chicken Bar

OTHER
1   Public Toilets
2   NCTO Office
5   Boater's Cafe (Cyprus
    Mountaineering
    Kyrenia)
6   Folk Art Museum
    (Halk Sanatlari Müzesi)

Mediterranean Sea

Jaffer
Paşa

Küpdemir S

Sanyer Sok

Mersin Caddesi

To Green Jacket
Bookshop (200m),
Karaoğlanoğlu
(5km), Five Mile
Beach (8km) &
Alsancak (8km)

To Bellapais
(5km) &
North
Nicosia
(29km)

To Long
Distance Bus
Station (900m)

Kalkanlı Sok

To Ertürk Turizm (200m),
New Harbour (1km),
Ozanköy
& Çatalköy (7km)

To Hospital (Akçiçek...)

OTHER (continued)
8   Aphrodite Boat Tours;
    Blue Dolphin Scuba
    Diving
9   Café 34
10 Kyrenia (Girne) Castle;
    Shipwreck museum
11 Police Station
12 Cafe Net
17 Cyprus Turkish Airlines
19 Atlantic Car Rentals

21 Gesfi Exchange
23 Casino Rocks
25 Bati Net Café
27 İş Bankası
28 Yazgın Döviz
29 Round Tower
30 Shopping Mall
31 Fergün Denizcilik Şirketi
32 Belediye Meydanı
33 Öz-Vip Supermarket
35 Türk Bankası

36 St Andrew's Anglican
    Church
37 Minibuses & Taxis to
    Famagusta & North
    Nicosia
38 Kyrenia Society
39 Post Office
40 Telecommunications
    Office
42 Hospital (Akçiçek
    Hastanesi)

Aqua Fun for Kids

Junior travellers and parents will be pleased
to know that there is water-based fun to be
had at **Octopus Aqua Park** (☎ 853 9674;
*Beşparmak Caddesi, Çatalköy; open 8am-5pm
daily*), 8km east of Kyrenia. Here young visitors can climb, swing, slide and bounce on
watery and dry apparatus while their parents
can relax at the pool bar or restaurant.

Flower Walks

Tony & Maureen Hutchinson (☎ 0542 854
4329, fax 721 3013; ⓦ www.walksnorchids
northcyprus.com; *Hisarköy*), long-term residents of Northern Cyprus, organise orchid
and wild flower walks during March and
April on Tuesday, Thursday and Saturday.
The cost is UK£13 and includes lunch.

PLACES TO STAY

Kyrenia is well supplied with high-quality
accommodation, though much of it is to the
west and east of the town centre. The following options are more central.

The **Bingöl Guest House** (☎ 815 2749;
*Efeler Sokak; singles/doubles including break-
fast UK£4/10*) on the main roundabout is rea-

sonable and central. The owner speaks good
English an the rooms all have bathrooms.

Not far away, **Sidelya Hotel** (☎ 815 6051,
fax 815 6052; *Nasır Güneş Sokak 7; singles/
doubles including breakfast UK£6/9*) is a better choice. The owner, Yusuf Atman, also
speaks English and offers very neat and tidy
rooms.

A little old-fashioned, but OK, is **New
Bristol Hotel** (☎ 815 6570, fax 815 7365; *Ziya
Rızkı Caddesi 114; singles/doubles UK£15/19*),
which is a fairly pleasant place to stay.

Girne Harbour Lodge Motel (☎ 815 7392,
fax 815 3744; *Cambulat Sokak 46; singles/
doubles including breakfast UK£16/32*),
around to the west side of the harbour, is a
spacious and airy, old-fashioned hotel. The
rooms all come with bathrooms.

One of the better options is the friendly
and well-positioned **Ergenekon Hotel**
(☎ 815 4677, fax 815 6010; ⓦ www.ergene
kon-hotel.com; *Girne Limanı; singles/doubles
including breakfast UK£20/30*), run by the
affable Norwegian owner Kaya Wiese. The
hotel overlooks the western harbour, is
open all year and has very airy and comfortable rooms.

Sheep on the road with a backdrop of a huge Turkish-Cypriot flag, Kyrenia (Girne) region

The old harbour of Kyrenia (Girne)

Drying tobacco, Karpas (Kırpaşa) Peninsula

Street in North Nicosia (Lefkoşa)

View of Golden Beach, Karpas (Kırpaşa) Peninsula

Fields of flowers near the Attila Line, Famagusta (Mağusa)

Green olives

Ancient Salamis, one of Cyprus' old city states, near Famagusta (Mağusa)

Nostalgia Hotel (☎ 815 3079, fax 815 1376; Cafer Paşa Sokak 7; singles/doubles UK£20/33) is located in a narrow street parallel to the harbourfront. It is a tastefully designed hotel with rooms all bearing names of Turkish Cypriot historical figures. One room even has a four-poster bed. All rooms have TV, phone and air-con.

Dome Hotel (☎ 815 2453, fax 815 2772; e domehotel@northcyprus.net; Kordon Boyu Sokak; singles/doubles including breakfast UK£55/70) is one of Kyrenia's best and longer-standing hotels. Rooms come with many facilities. There is a large seawater swimming pool to relax in.

PLACES TO EAT
Kyrenia is equally well supplied with many fine restaurants. The most obvious choices are those on the harbourfront, but with perhaps one exception, these tend to be uniformly bland and pitch their menus at the passing tourist crowd; British staples such as steak and chips or hamburgers are common offerings. Still, the view is pleasant and there is hardly a better place in town to while away a lunch hour, or partake of a romantic evening meal with a bottle of wine and a plate of kebabs. Serious diners tend to head out west towards Karaoğlanoğlu (Agios Georgios) or even out east to Çatalköy.

In Town
Really a fast-food joint, **Eziç Chicken Bar** (☎ 815 2617; Mete Adanır Caddesi; open 10am-midnight; Kentucky-style chicken TL5 million) is nonetheless far enough away from the centre to be overlooked by most travellers and is popular with locals. Chicken dishes and sandwiches are the best meals and prices are cheap. It also offers a takeaway service and some mean-looking cakes such as diet-cracking ekmek kadayıfı (honey and cream fyllo wedges), or vişneli kek – too wicked to describe!

The no-nonsense **Little Arif's Restaurant** (☎ 852 0281; Ziya Rızkı Caddesi; full kebab TL5 million) is a bit of an institution and is also excellent value. Pitched almost exclusively at a local clientele, this eatery is unpretentious and cheap. It's in a side street off Ziya Rızkı Caddesi.

Quietly old-fashioned, with a limited, but select menu of home-cooked recipes, is the most pleasant **Kyrenia Restaurant** (Paşabahçe Restaurant; ☎ 815 1799; Türkmen Caddesi 2; open lunch & dinner; mains TL8-10 million). Run by a distinguished elderly couple, this restaurant oozes simplicity laced with culinary rusticity. The chicken in mushroom and onion sauce is highly recommended.

There is an Irish pub and eatery in Kyrenia too! Head for the minuscule **Shenanigans** (☎ 815 4521; Cafer Paşa Sokak; open 5pm-late; mains TL10 million), a cosy place for a meal and a drink. While it cannot yet serve draught Guinness, it does sell the near-perfect, canned and widgeted variety. Tuck into sausage, mash and gravy, or steak and Guinness pie and pretend that you are back in the UK.

Niazi's Restaurant & Bar (☎ 815 2160; Kordon Boyu Sokak; open 11am-midnight; full kebab TL10 million), diagonally opposite Dome Hotel, has achieved something approaching cult status among kebab lovers. Most clients would claim that Niazi's does the best kebabs. Certainly the big centrally positioned kebab rotisserie looks very professional and the food is definitely top notch. Bookings are necessary in the evenings.

New in mid-2002, the oh-so-classy **Villa Swallow** (☎ 815 3128; Ersin Aydın Sokak 16; open noon-3pm & 6pm-midnight; set BBQ TL20 million) leads the pack in dining chic. Savour paper-wrapped prawns with a sweet chilli and mango dip or lemon and pepper goujons (small, fried strips of fish). Tuesday is South African braai (BBQ) night while Friday is 'Fish Feast' night.

Set Fish Restaurant (☎ 815 2336; Girne Limanı; baked dish TL15 million) is one of the few harbourfront restaurants that gets the locals' approval. Fish dominates the menu and, although prices are a little higher than elsewhere, the ambience is unmatched, especially on a warm, balmy evening. Under the same management is the nearby **Set Italian Restaurant** (☎ 815 6008; Girne Limanı; pasta & pizzas TL8-10 million) – ostensibly Italian, but offering a mixed menu of Turkish as well as European dishes. Dining is undertaken in a pleasant, shaded courtyard.

Out of Town
If you have decided to head out towards Karaoğlanoğlu, **Address Restaurant & Brasserie** (☎ 822 3537; Ali Aktaş Sokak 13; mains TL11-16 million) is one to look out for. It's considered one of North Cyprus' best restaurants and is situated on a little point

overlooking the sea. The menu is European-based and includes mostly fish, pasta and meat. The orange and tarragon chicken (TL13.5 million) is a good dish to try.

Another established eatery is **Altınkaya I** (☎ 821 8341; Yavuz Çıkarma Plaji; mains TL10 million), further west and also overlooking Yavuz Çıkarma Beach on the way to Lapta (Lapithos). This place is a little way out but handy for lunch after the beach. Fish and *meze* are its specialities.

Heading east of Kyrenia, two restaurants are worth a mention. **Erol's Bar & Restaurant** (☎ 815 3657; Ozanköy; kleftiko TL10 million) serves up excellent grilled lamb, chicken and sea bream. There are great views over the village of Ozanköy. Wednesday is *kleftiko* (oven-baked lamb) night.

About 2.5km further east is **Anı** (☎ 824 4355; Zeka Adil Caddesi, Çatalköy; fish dishes TL10-20 million), where the locals all come to eat fish. Many consider it the best fish restaurant in Cyprus.

Self-catering
If you're planning a picnic or a mountain walk, stock up on necessities at **Öz-Vip Supermarket** (☎ 815 3972; Efeler Sokak). It's well-stocked with all your favourites including baked beans and Spam.

ENTERTAINMENT
The bars and cafés on the waterfront are all much of a muchness when it comes to variety. **Café 34** (☎ 815 3056; Girne Limanı; open 4pm-2am), however, is one of the more 'in' bars with the local crowd, while serious clubbers head for the **Mare Monte Disco** out in Alsançak, west of Kyrenia.

At night, the **Villa Swallow** (see Places to Eat; ☎ 815 3128; Ersin Aydın Sokak 16; beer TL3 million, cocktails TL7 million) is the classiest bar in town with about a dozen wicked cocktails and the whole range of Absolut vodkas.

If you really want to dispose of surplus cash, there is an oversupply of casinos in Kyrenia. These are not necessarily the black-tie and tux establishments you might imagine, but glorified gaming-machine, get-rich-quick dens of iniquity for gambling-deprived Turkish mainlanders. Still, if you want to try your luck at blackjack, chemin de fer or roulette, or to simply exercise your finger on the gaming machines, try **Dome**

Casino (☎ 815 9283; Kordon Boyu Sokak) for starters, or if that doesn't pull you a pile, move to the **Casino Rocks** (☎ 815 9333; Kordon Boyu Sokak) where a tie and tux are not out of place.

SHOPPING
There is a small shopping mall with boutiques and brand-name imported goods off Ziya Rızkı Caddesi as well as a wide range of tourist shops that sell everything from snorkelling gear to leather goods. **Round Tower** (☎ 815 6377; Ziya Rızkı Caddesi; open 10am-5.30pm) is a small art and crafts shop with a selection of tasteful goods such as pottery, rugs and paintings in the restored Lusignan-era Round Tower in the central area of Kyrenia.

GETTING THERE & AWAY
The long-distance bus station is on Bedreddin Demirel in the south of the New Town. Minibuses (*dolmuş*) to Famagusta (Mağusa; TL2 million) and North Nicosia (TL1 million), as well as service taxis to North Nicosia (TL1 million), all depart from Belediye Meydanı.

There are express boats to Taşucu in Turkey at 9.30am daily (three hours) from the New Harbour, east of town. There's also a slower daily ferry that takes about seven hours. One-way tickets cost TL41.5 million and TL33.5 million, respectively, and can be bought from the passenger lounge at the port or from **Fergün Denizcilik Şirketi** (☎ 815 2344; Mustafa Çağatay Caddesi 6/2c). During peak season there is also a twice-weekly express ferry to Alanya in Turkey (4½ hours, UK£20).

Cyprus Turkish Airlines (☎ 815 2513; Philecia Court, Suite 3, Kordon Boyu Sokak) has an office just west of the Old Harbour.

GETTING AROUND
Kyrenia is small enough for visitors to get around on foot. Should you need to travel further afield, there is a large number of car-hire outlets. Try **Atlantic Car Rentals** (☎ 815 3053, fax 815 5673; e mchavush@yahoo.co.uk), based in a wing of the Dome Hotel complex. Its rates range from UK£10 per day for a small Renault to UK£45 per day for an Isuzu Trooper.

There are service taxis from Kyrenia to destinations including Ercan airport (TL20 million), North Nicosia (TL12 million), Bellapais (TL7 million) and St Hilarion (TL2.5 million).

The North Coast

Given its position, Kyrenia is ideal for day trips to any part of Northern Cyprus. The distances are generally manageable and with only one or two exceptions can all be covered easily by a conventional vehicle. There is great variety on offer with excellent beaches, mountain-top castles, villages in the Kyrenia Range foothills and the desolate stretches of the northwest corner of Northern Cyprus. The road leading west of Kyrenia is fast and smooth, while heading east it is slow, winding, often bumpy and very rural.

GETTING AROUND
No public transport serves the area around Kyrenia so it will have to be service or private taxis, a hire car or pedal power. The area does provide for some of the best cycling in Northern Cyprus. Other than some climbing in the Kyrenia Range escarpment, the east–west routes are generally flat and well serviced by facilities such as places to eat and beaches to swim at. There's a fine place to stay in the village of Kaplıca, 63km east of Kyrenia. There are more options available if riding to the west.

BEACHES
Kyrenia's best swimming beach lies to the west of the town and is known as **Five Mile Beach**. Known in Turkish as both Beşinci Mil and Yavuz Çıkarma, the beach is a pleasant spot and is protected from the open sea by a rocky islet easily reached by paddling. Watch out for tricky currents on the open water side; a few bathers have been caught out and swept away. There are water sports available and umbrellas and sun loungers for hire, though there is not much natural shade. The rather phallic-looking monument on the road overlooking the beach is a monument to the Turkish army that used this beach to launch their invasion/rescue operation in 1974. A restaurant, **Altınkaya I**, overlooks the beach (see Places to Eat under Kyrenia earlier in the chapter).

East of Kyrenia, you will find a series of quieter and less developed beaches – with one notable exception – that are more suited to seekers of solitude. The first worth a mention is **Çatalköy Beach** 7km from Kyrenia. It is reached via a signposted road from the main road. Look for Seamus O'Flynn's pub, turn here and continue for 1.5km; Turn right at the junction. The beach is a narrow curve of sand in a pretty little protected bay. There are beach loungers to rent and a diving platform. The popular **Körfez Restaurant** (☎ 824 4354) at the beach keeps bathers fed and watered.

Next along is the private **Vrysi Beach**, now looked after by the large three-star **Acapulco Holiday Village** (☎ 824 4110, fax 824 4455), which caters for package tourists but takes in casual guests. Admission to the complex is TL2.5 million and the beach offers many facilities. It's OK if you don't mind paying to park and swim. Popular with expats is **Lara Beach** (also known as Vakıflar Beach), 3km further along and signposted just before the large power station. There is no charge to park and swim. The somewhat scruffy dark sand beach is nonetheless generally clean and there are spotless toilets and changing rooms. A small **snack bar** serves beach goers.

Finally, 19km from Kyrenia is **Turtle Beach**, also known as Alagadi Beach, where the Society for the Protection of Turtles (SPOT) has a small monitoring station affectionately called the 'Goat Shed'. The twin, sandy beaches here are generally undeveloped and are strictly speaking total turtle territory. Swim elsewhere if you can. The beach is closed from 8pm to 8am from May to October. See also the boxed text 'A Tale of two Turtles' in the Famagusta & Karpas Peninsula chapter. Better still, have a meal at the locally-lauded **St Kathleen's Restaurant** (☎ 0533 861 7640) nearby on the main road. Their *meze*, grills and fish dishes – *tsipura* (bream) is a good choice – are reputed to be excellent and good value for money.

HIKING
The NCTO produces a small brochure called *Mountain Trails*, available free from NCTO offices. It describes at least two walks in the Kyrenia Ranges that you may want to investigate. However, the brochure is not detailed enough for serious hikers, so you are advised to seek local advice and use a good map. Better still, join one of the organised local tours (see Mountain Treks

under Kyrenia earlier) and let others do the hard work of map reading.

Ağirdağ to Geçitköy

This is a fairly long hike that would need to be done in sections and perhaps broken over a few days, or taken as discrete hiking sections altogether. The hike runs west along the southern flank of the Kyrenia Range starting from the village of Ağirdağ on the Kyrenia–North Nicosia road and ending up at Geçitköy on the Kyrenia–Morfou (Güzelyurt) road. The trail can be broken or joined at Lapta. Most sections are of two- to three-hour lengths.

BELLAPAIS (BEYLERBEYI)

The greater majority of visitors on day trips out of Kyrenia will head for the beautiful hillside village of Bellapais off the main Kyrenia road. The village is the site of an impressive but quite incongruous abbey and is the former home of British writer Lawrence Durrell, who lived here prior to and during the EOKA uprising against British rule in Cyprus. The village is quite twee and touristy but makes for a very pleasant excursion. It can get crowded in the middle of the day so choose your visiting time carefully.

Arriving drivers should note that there is a large car park 70m past the monastery down to the left. Try to avoid parking in the already cluttered main street.

Bellapais Abbey

This impressive **Augustinian Monastery** (admission TL4.5 million; open 9am-7pm daily June–mid-Sept, 9am-5pm mid-Sept–May) is the reason most people visit Bellapais. Near the end of the 12th century the Augustinian monks, who had fled Palestine following the fall of Jerusalem to the Saracen Selahaddin Eyyubi in 1187, came here. They established a monastery by the name of *Abbaye de la Paix* (Abbey of Peace) from which the corrupted version of the name Bellapais evolved. The original structure was built between 1198 and 1205, yet the major construction work of the monastery that we see today was undertaken between 1267 and 1284 during the reign of King Hugh III. The cloisters and the large refectory were added during the reign of King Hugh IV (1324–59).

When Cyprus was taken by the Ottomans the monastery was put under the protection

of the Orthodox Church – which apparently wasn't enough to prevent villagers and later the British overlords from using the stone for other purposes.

What is left today is a mixture of completion and destruction, with some parts of the monastery in an excellent state of preserve. The **refectory** to the north side of the cloister is frequently used for gatherings and events. From here there are splendid views across to the sea and the sea plains below. Less well-preserved is the **kitchen court** on the west side, where all that remains are a few walls and a rather precarious section of wall onto which the more daring can scramble for a better view. The now dim and dank church is in generally good condition and remains much as it was in 1976 when the last Greek Orthodox faithful were obliged to leave.

The cypress-lined 14th-century **cloister** is the monastery's most poignant section and is almost complete, apart from the western side where it has fallen down or been pulled apart and now looks out onto a restaurant (see Places to Stay & Eat following) where diners can gaze over *meze* onto the open cloister courtyard.

Get your entry ticket from the not-so-obvious ticket booth set back a little to the left as you enter. You may exit the way you came, or directly into the restaurant forecourt.

Home of Lawrence Durrell

Bellapais is now almost equally famous for its literary son, Lawrence Durrell, who lived in the village in the early 1950s. The near-idyllic, mixed-community days described in his book *Bitter Lemons of Cyprus* have long since gone, but the novel has become almost *de rigueur* reading for visitors to Cyprus. The **Tree of Idleness** under which Durrell's characters spent many an indolent hour still remains, these days more likely shading tourists clutching cold beers. Durrell's house is still a private residence, but a yellow plaque over the main door marks the spot where he spent his bohemian days.

To reach the house, head inland along the street to the right of the Huzur Ağaç Restaurant and walk about 200m more or less straight and upwards. You will come across the house on your left. Ask if you lose your way – not difficult in the winding, narrow alleyways.

A Tale of Two Trees

When writer and novelist Lawrence Durrell took up residence in Bellapais between 1953 and 1956, he little realised the minor controversy he would leave behind almost 50 years after he first described life in the then blissfully bucolic mixed community. His now-famous book *Bitter Lemons of Cyprus* describes the trials and tribulations of purchasing and renovating a house in the village, as well as the intrigues and gossip of village life in general. On a more sombre note, he sounded the alarm bell for the troubles that were to ultimately befall Cyprus not too many years ahead.

Among the villagers' favourite activities was to spend many an hour in idle conversation under the so-called 'Tree of Idleness' which dominated the main square. Throughout the whole of the text of *Bitter Lemons of Cyprus* he never once mentioned what kind of tree it was. A plane tree? A mulberry tree? An oak tree?

Today there are two trees that vie for the title of 'Tree of Idleness'. One is a leafy mulberry tree overshadowing the coffee shop next to the Monastery ticket office. The other contender, and not 20 metres distant, is a Japanese pagoda tree casting shade over the eponymous Huzur Ağaç (Tree of Idleness) Restaurant. In fairness, both trees could qualify for the role pretty well; both have their ardent supporters and draw an idle crowd of onlookers who like to sit and drink coffee or a cold beer just as the villagers would have done in Durrell's day. So, pick your tree, order a coffee and engage in idle chatter. It's all the same in the end.

Special Events
Every year during May and June the **Bellapais Music Festival** (☎ *0542 854 6417;* e *kktcb@north-cyprus.net*) takes place in and around Bellapais Abbey. The Festival consists of concerts, recitals and even brass-band performances within the refectory of the Abbey. Prominent posters advertising the events are on display around town and in Kyrenia and elsewhere.

Places to Stay & Eat
Bellapais is close enough to Kyrenia to be easily accessible, yet far enough away to feel like somewhere different. There are a few places to stay worth investigating.

The Abbey Inn (☎ *815 9444, fax 815 9446; singles/doubles UK£19/24*), close to the monastery, is a good option. This cosy hotel offers 10 double rooms and a small swimming pool. It's run by the same owners as the Huzur Ağaç (Tree of Idleness) Restaurant.

Hotel Bellapais Gardens (☎ *815 6066, fax 815 7667;* e *bgarden@cypnet.com; singles UK£30-45, doubles UK£60-90, breakfast UK£4.50*) is the best place to stay. The very homely hotel has a great view, a swimming pool and in-house restaurant.

High up at the back of the village near Lawrence Durrell's house are the two self-catering studios of **Garden of Irini** (☎ *0523 865 8262;* w *www.pagemagic.net/Irini; studio UK£28*). Each studio has a kitchen, small

lounge, bathroom with shower *and* bath – and a fireplace for winter. Owners Deirdre Guthrie and Justin McClean also run a small restaurant, **Guthrie's Bar** (☎ *0523 865 8262; open 10.30am-6.30pm daily; lunch UK£3.50*). Lunch is usually soup and sandwiches. In the evenings you can book a private dinner party (UK£15.50 per person fully inclusive) for up to eight people and dine in a shady, secluded courtyard.

There are a couple of other restaurants worth checking out also.

Kybele (☎ *815 7531; meals TL16 million*) has the most atmosphere, is right next to the Abbey and commands the best views. While the food is good and service very attentive, you can also just enjoy a drink in the cool, welcoming gardens and enjoy the soothing piped ecclesiastical music.

Huzur Ağaç Restaurant (☎ *815 3380; fixed menu TL12 million*) is across the road from Kybele. Most patrons seem to prefer a cool beer under the famous tree, but the food is pretty decent too.

ST HILARION CASTLE
ΑΓΙΟΣ ΙΛΑΡΙΩΝ
Children will love exploring the almost magical fairytale remains of the castle (*kalesi*) of St Hilarion (☎ *0533 161 276; admission TL4.5 million; open 9am-4.45pm daily*). It has just enough hidden rooms, tunnels, overgrown gardens and steep staircases

and paths to leave parents gasping for breath and the children asking for more.

This lofty aerie is named after a monk called Hilarion, who fled persecution from the Holy Land. He lived and died in a cave on the mountain that overlooks the plain of Kyrenia and protects the pass between Kyrenia and North Nicosia. During the 10th century, the Byzantines built a church and monastery over the tomb of Hilarion. Earlier the site's strategic position saw it used mainly as a watch tower and beacon during the Arab raids of the 7th and 8th centuries. This was an important link in the communication chain between Buffavento and Kantara castles further east. In 1191 Guy de Lusignan decided to take control of St Hilarion by besieging and dislodging the self-styled Byzantine emperor of Cyprus, Isaak Komninos. Over this time St Hilarion was extensively expanded and used both as a military outpost and a summer residence for the Lusignan court until the arrival of the Venetians.

The Venetians neglected the castle and it fell into disrepair. It only saw practical use again in 1964 when Turkish Cypriot Turk Müdafaa Teskilati (TMT) activists were able to take control of the castle and fend off EOKA-inspired attacks. It has been in Turkish Cypriot hands ever since and a covetously protected Turkish military base on the ridge below the castle is testament to its status once more as a militarily strategic location.

The site is in three main parts, though this is not immediately obvious to the visitor, so seamlessly do the stones and ruined buildings blend into the rocky landscape upon which it has been grafted. Visitors enter by the **barbican** and the main gate into the **lower enceinte**, which was used as the main **garrison** and **stabling area**. A meandering path leads you up to the **middle enceinte**, which was originally protected and sealed off by a drawbridge. Here are the remains of a **church**, more **barrack rooms** and a four-storey **royal apartment**. There is also a large **cistern** for the storage of vital water.

Access to the **upper enceinte** of the castle is via a windy and steep track, thankfully paved and renovated in more recent years with the assistance of a London boys' home. You enter the upper castle via a **Lusignan gate** guarded by a **Byzantine tower** and reach an overgrown central courtyard. Around the courtyard are more

royal apartments, kitchens and **ancillary chambers**. A final breath-sapping climb takes you to **Prince John's tower** where, as legend has it, Prince John of Antioch, convinced that two Bulgarian bodyguards were planning to kill him, had them thrown over the steep cliff to their death.

The view from the top is stunning and on a clear day you can see the **Taurus Mountains** in Turkey, more than 100km away. To the west you can look down on the village of Karaman (Karmi). Kyrenia to the north, some 730m lower in elevation and several kilometres away, looks very small and insignificant.

Come early if you can; the climb to the top is tiring and can be quite difficult on a hot day. There is a small **snack bar** in the car park.

BUFFAVENTO CASTLE

If Kantara Castle (see the Famagusta & Karpas Peninsula chapter) is considered the most romantic of the trio of castles and St Hilarion the most interesting, then this lofty fortress *(Buffavento Kalesi; admission free; open dawn to dusk)* has to be the most fun to get to. This majestic castle, whose appropriate name means 'buffeted by the winds', perches precariously 940m above the sea overlooking the Mesarya Plain to the south. In medieval times it was known as the Castle of the Lion, but its origins are less prosaic and little is known about its early history. It dates back at least to 1191 when Richard the Lionheart took it over from the daughter of the Byzantine emperor Isaak Komninos. The Lusignans used the castle as a prison and beacon tower as it was in line of sight with both Kantara Castle to the east and St Hilarion Castle to the west.

The attraction of the castle is its remoteness and the views from the ruins, especially on a clear day when the winds aren't buffeting it. While the castle isn't in the best condition, there are still a couple of covered chambers in the lower castle, and a renovated stairway now allows access to the upper parts. Unlike Kantara castle, the walkways are well protected and the views from the very top are truly magnificent.

The castle is divided into two main sections: the **lower** and the **upper enceinte** and it occupies a relatively small area on the rocky peak where it was constructed. The castle was built in such a way that no further fortifications were needed other than the outer walls of the main buildings, since there is no other way in other than through the main entrance.

Getting to the castle is half the fun. It is prominently signposted off the Beşparmak Pass as Buffavento Kalesi. From here it is a 5km, 15-minute drive along a dirt track to the small parking area below the castle. The walk up should take between 30 and 40 minutes. It is fairly steep but gradual. Good footwear is necessary and a walking stick or trekking poles are useful.

KYRENIA TO KAPLICA

The meandering narrow coastal road from Kyrenia towards Kantara Castle runs eastward through a Cyprus that has basically remained unchanged since the 1960s. It makes for an excellent full day's excursion with the promise of a scramble around craggy Kantara Castle at the end of it (see the Famagusta & Karpas Peninsula chapter for details).

The route passes some beaches (see earlier) then narrows to basically a one-vehicle road shortly after the hard-to-miss power station (16km) and continues for a further 45km before you turn inland to Kantara Castle at the village of Kaplıca (Davlos). The road passes successively through small rural communities, which cultivate stands of olive and carob trees or tend small market gardens that can be seen for kilometre after kilometre along the first section of the drive.

Later, the land becomes more dry and barren and the road passes within metres of the sea for long stretches at a time. Look out for the long-abandoned **carob warehouses** still standing sentinel from a time when this fairly unknown natural commodity in the West was a source of great wealth to Cyprus.

Kaplıca (Davlos) Δαυλός

You will see the first sign to Kantara Castle (Kantara Kalesi) at about 7km before Kaplıca. Ignore it: it is a longer route and, besides, you will miss out on the opportunity for a pre-castle swim at **Kaplıca Beach** shortly before the junction to Kaplıca village, which lies a kilometre or so up the hillside. This wonderfully sandy strand is the only decent place to swim along this long lonely stretch. The beachside **Kaplıca Beach Restaurant & Hotel** (☎ 387 2032, fax 387 2031; Kaplıca Plaj) will feed you and give you a place to stay should you wish to break your journey.

Turn right at the signposted junction for Kaplıca village and eventually you will see Kantara castle perched precipitously high up above the coastline on a rocky spur. For details of the castle, see the Famagusta & Karpas Peninsula chapter.

ALEVKAYA HERBARIUM

A worthwhile visit can be made along the back road of the Pentadaktylos spur of the Kyrenia Range to the **Alevkaya Herbarium** (admission free; open 8am-4pm daily), a forest station on the mountain ridge between Esentepe (Agios Amvrosios) and Değirmenlik (Kythrea). The herbarium is home to samples of most of the endemic Cypriot flora and includes some 1250 native-plant species.

The Odd Carob

The carob (ceratonia siliqua) is a leguminous evergreen tree native to the coastal regions of the Mediterranean basin. It grows in abundance in Cyprus and was once one of the island's most valuable crops. Its dark-green leaves are quite distinctive and the trees can often be found interspersed with the lighter-green olive trees along Cyprus' north coast.

The long, bean-like pods are not used directly for human consumption, though you can eat the dark-brown, dried pods raw – they taste rather like chocolate. They are instead used to produce seed gums and 'kibble' (fruit pulp without seeds). Many products are also made from kibble for human consumption including sweets, biscuits and drinks. The kernels are made into a carob-bean gum and germ meal. The gum from the seeds is used in the food-processing industries in soups, sauces and a large range of manufactured dairy products. Carobs are polygamous, meaning they can have either a male flower, a female flower or flowers can be hermaphrodite (both male and female). Stop and examine these odd trees and their curious fruit as you drive around the island. Eat a pod or two if you are bold enough. The carob is actually not so odd after all.

On display are many dried and preserved specimens, as well as the fresh variety. The display developed out of a collection made by English botanist Deryck Viney, whose book *Illustrated Flora of North Cyprus* (see Flora in Facts About Cyprus) documented the country's varied botanical treasure trove.

If you arrive outside opening times someone will normally let you in. To get there, go along a signposted forest road off the south side of Pentadaktylos Pass, or from the northern coastal road signposted via Karaağaç (Harkia) or Esentepe.

LAPTA (LAPITHOS) ΛΑΠΗΘΟΣ

The beautiful village of Lapta is popular as a day trip for its proximity to Kyrenia as well as for its views, fine restaurants and cool, leafy atmosphere. Forest fires devastated much of the Kyrenia Range escarpment in the mid-1990s, but fortunately Lapta managed to escape much of the ruination and still retains an old-world charm.

Lapta was one of the original city kingdoms of Cyprus and was a regional capital under Roman rule. Its abundant water and protected position have made it a favourite choice for foreign residents over many years. Greeks and Turks lived here in harmony until 1974. Today it is home to a scattering of expats, mainland Turks and original Turkish Cypriot villagers. The village is spread out and is best visited on foot, particularly its leafy lanes.

The rather splendid **Ayia Anastasia Resort** (☎ 821 8961, fax 821 8966; 🅦 www .lapethos.com; Maresal Fevzi Cakmak Caddesi; singles/doubles UK£12/18) is built in and around a former church on the top of a mountain overlooking Lapta. All rooms are spacious and have telephones and satellite TV. There are two swimming pools and two in-house restaurants; perfect if you don't feel like moving around.

There are a couple of restaurants worth checking out. **Başpınar** (☎ 821 8661; Sunday lunch specials TL9 million) has the best view from the top of the village and offers cool, shaded dining under plane trees. There are à-la-carte dishes and ready-made local dishes of the day such as lamb or goat casserole in a clay pot. Look for the prominent signs as you enter the village. It's a long winding drive up.

The **Hill Top Restaurant** (☎ 821 8889; mains TL8-12 million) is a little further down

the hill and is also well signposted. Though not quite as popular as the Başpınar, it is probably less taxing for walkers to reach and the food is very similar with Sunday lunch specials on offer.

KORUÇAM (KORMAKITIS) PENINSULA ΑΚΡΩΤΗΡΙ ΚΟΡΜΑΚΙΤΗ

The bare northwestern tip of Northern Cyprus is known as the Koruçam Burnu (Kormakitis Peninsula) and, apart from being yet another 'land's end' in the same sense as Cape Greco and Cape Arnaoutis in the South, or Zafer Burnu (Cape Apostolos Andreas) in the East, it is also home to one of Cyprus' least-known religious communities (see the boxed text 'The Maronites of Koruçam'). A trip to the cape makes for a pleasant excursion from Lapta. There is at least one decent beach on the way with a popular grill and fish restaurant. Or you can take a picnic and enjoy your solitude at the cape itself.

A sealed road now runs almost to the cape. It is best tackled as a loop starting from the northern end of Kyrenia–Morfou road at the junction just after the village of Karşıyaka (Vasileia). Look for the sign to Sadrazamköy (Livera).

Shortly after the turn-off is the neat little **Horse Shoe Beach,** with its eponymous **Horseshoe Beach Restaurant** (☎ 851 6664; grills TL7-8 million), which gets very busy at weekends with locals on a day out for a snorkel or swim followed by a lazy lunch of grilled fish or meats.

The coastal road onward is winding but well maintained and you will reach the rather scruffy settlement of Sadrazamköy after 11km. Here, a rather curious box-like resort settlement in typical mainland-Turkish style has sprung up on the western edge of the village.

The road from here to the cape is a 3.5km dirt track – lumpy in parts, but driveable in a conventional vehicle. There is nothing at the end but bare rocks, a couple of abandoned buildings and a solar-powered shipping beacon. A small rocky islet lies offshore to which a determined couple were spotted wading, while loaded down with picnic gear, for the ultimate land's end Sunday lunch. This is also Cyprus' closest point to Turkey, which lies 60km across the sea.

Head back via the picturesque inland loop road through Koruçam village and take

The Maronites of Koruçam (Kormakitis)

The **Maronites** are an ancient Christian sect from the Middle East. They split from the prevailing Orthodox theory of Christianity that God was both Man and God. The Maronites, in contrast, followed the Monophysite religious line that states that God could only be viewed as one spiritual persona. Persecuted by the Orthodox, they first sought refuge in Lebanon and Syria, and came to Cyprus in the 12th century in the wake of the Crusaders whom they had helped as auxiliaries in the Holy Land campaign.

Today the Cypriot Maronites cling to a tenuous existence in the main village of Koruçam (Kormakitis) where they still maintain a church. Over the years, the once-vigorous congregation has gradually left and barely one hundred Maronites remain in the country to keep the old traditions and religion alive. While primarily Greek speakers, they have managed to tread the fine line between political and religious allegiances with some degree of success. For that they are able to move between the North and South with a greater degree of freedom than the few Greeks remaining in the Karpas (Kırpaşa) Peninsula to the east.

note of the huge Maronite **Church of Agios Georgios**, built in 1940 from funds raised by the villagers. There is a small **coffee shop** in the village and, if you speak Greek, you may get into conversation with the Greek-speaking Maronites here.

The last leg back to the Kyrenia–Morfou road is along a rather poorly maintained road through a military area. There are a couple of prominent military checkpoints and you may be stopped. Join the main highway at Çamlibel (Myrtou) from where you can loop back to Kyrenia, cut south to Morfou or veer southeast to North Nicosia.

The Northwest

The landscape stretching east and west of North Nicosia is a vast, flat brown region called the Mesarya. The name is derived from the Greek 'Mesaoria', which means 'between the mountains'. In summer it looks desolate and uninviting, in winter it comes alive with greenery and wild flowers. Being fairly flat, it's easy to drive or ride around. The western Mesarya has more places of interest than in the east and the following sights make for an alternative tour of the North away from the beach scenes of the north and east coasts.

The northwestern quadrant of Northern Cyprus loosely covers the territory south of the Kyrenia Range and westwards to the agricultural town of Morfou, Morfou Bay (Güzelyurt Körfezi), the one-time mining port of Gemikonağı (Karavostasi), the pretty

hill village of Lefke (Lefka) and two obscure but worthwhile archaeological sites of Soloi and Vouni in the far west.

Distances are relatively short and the whole excursion can be made into a loop, returning to North Nicosia via the Koruçam Peninsula and Kyrenia, or vice versa.

GETTING AROUND

There are regular daily buses to Morfou from North Nicosia (TL1 million, every 30 minutes) and onward bus transport to Gemikonağı and Lefke (TL5 million) every 30 minutes from Morfou. You may be able to charter a taxi from North Nicosia or Kyrenia for a round trip and this may work out more economical if there are at least two of you. Overall though, getting around is better conducted under your own steam, especially if you want to see Soloi and Vouni.

MORFOU (GÜZELYURT) ΜΟΡΦΟΥ
pop 15,000
The once-busy city of Morfou (known less commonly as Güzelyurt by Turkish Cypriots) was once the centre for Cyprus' lucrative citrus industry. Sunzest, the company owned by renegade and runaway Cypriot businessman, Asil Nadir, used to produce vast quantities of orange juice for the export market. The factory now languishes in receivership and the potentially lucrative citrus industry has taken a severe downturn.

This is bittersweet news to the Greek Cypriots who were particularly aggrieved when the citrus groves were lost to Turkish forces in 1974. Most were proudly owned by

Greek Cypriots and when meeting someone who has been to the North they invariably ask after the health of their beloved groves.

You can hardly miss the citrus groves; they start shortly before the village of Şahinler (Masari) and stretch all the way to the sea. Watered by a series of underground aquifers, they are beginning to feel the pinch. This is a result of a drop in the level of the aquifer reserves and of a rise in the salinity of the underground water, as well as from a sometimes less-than-loving approach to their cultivation and maintenance. In fairness, though, this visible degradation is no doubt due, to some degree, to the disruption brought about by Sunzest's demise.

In better days, in the earlier half of the 20th century, oranges were shipped by train from Morfou to Famagusta for exportation overseas. Why facilities were never developed for their export at the nearer port of Gemikonağı is odd. Incidentally, the train route from Morfou to North Nicosia ceased passenger services in 1932, though it continued to take on freight until 1951. The line has long since fallen into disrepair (see the boxed text 'Once Upon a Train').

Morfou today offers scant interest for the tourist. Travellers may content themselves with wandering around a low-key, rather tatty-looking agricultural town with a few narrow, winding streets, small shops and life totally unfazed or dependent upon tourism. The bus station is on the south side of town. Follow Ecevit Caddesi from the bus station for 800m to reach the town centre.

The Orthodox church of **Agios Mamas**, once visited by the Greek Cypriot faithful for the reputed miraculous qualities of a strange liquid that emanated from the tomb of the patron saint at irregular intervals, is usually firmly closed. It competes for attention with a splendid-looking new mosque that has been built, in seeming defiant juxtaposition, across the square.

If you choose to stay in Morfou, there is the fairly central one-star, 13-room **Güzelyurt Otel** (☎ *714 3412, fax 714 5085;* e *guzelyurt@northcyprus.net; Bahçelievler Bulvarı; singles/doubles UK£10/14).* It is a basic but reasonable hotel. All rooms have air-con, a phone and TV. There is a bar and a laundry service.

For a meal, an LP reader suggested **Şah** (☎ *714 3064),* not far from the Church of Agios Mamas on the north side of town. *Meze* here is supposed to be excellent.

GEMİKONAĞI (KARAVOSTASI)
ΚΑΡΑΒΟΣΤΑΣΗ
From Morfou the good highway barrels westwards towards Morfou Bay, passing

Once Upon a Train

Few people today would realise that Cyprus once boasted a rail system. For over 50 years, trains ran the length of the island traversing the vast Mesarya (Mesaoria) plain and linking the western port of Gemikonağı (Karavostasi) with the main port of Famagusta (Mağusa) in the east.

The Cyprus Government Railway was 60km in length and there were stations about every 3km to 4km. Between Famagusta and Lefkosia there were two passenger trains a day in each direction and the trip took two hours travelling at a speed of between 32km/h and 48km/h – hardly an express service. To travel the extra 38km to Morfou took another two hours. The branch line to Gemikonağı was used mainly for freight.

Standard-gauge steam engines were fuelled by coal imported from England, or the Admiralty Yards in Port Said in Egypt. The water used in the engines had to be softened chemically so as not to damage the boilers and all lighting was with acetylene lamps. While the engines ran like clockwork, the main problem was the maintenance of bridges, which could be washed away by sudden and unusual winter torrents.

Freight ultimately came to be more important than passenger traffic, but even the trains could not compete with the emergence of diesel-powered trucks that came onto the scene in the mid-1940s. The last train left Lefkosia for Famagusta on 31 December 1951 and the Cyprus steam era came to a sad end. There are few signs of the old railway line today, the most visible being a stretch of line and an old steam engine in a park about 1km north of Morfou, and a railway tunnel near the Land Gate in Famagusta.

even more citrus groves. Bathing at the bay is no real treat. The beaches are exposed, pebbly and rather thin, though you can take a dip at one or two obvious spots along the way as long as the sea is not too choppy. Prior to 1974, inhabitants of the Troödos foothills in the South would make the short trip to Morfou Bay to swim. Now the most convenient beach for them is over 100km away at Larnaka.

The once-flourishing port of Gemikonağı dominates the bay and you will spot the long-abandoned and slowly disintegrating jetty before you actually catch sight of the port itself. The town was once home to a large American-run mining enterprise that for many years mined the now scarred hinterland immediately south and east of town. That industry ceased after 1974 and the town has taken on a backwater appearance, not unlike the town of Kato Pyrgos further along the coast at Tylliria in the Republic.

Nonetheless, the town still supports a small local tourist industry and a few restaurants. Small beaches to the west of Gemikonağı testify to the area's pull on the few visitors who prefer alternative dining and bathing options to the often crowded and more expensive spots elsewhere in the North. Gemikonağı is one place in the region to base yourself for a day or two.

There is one accommodation choice. The one-star **Soli Inn Hotel** (☎ 727 7575, fax 727 8210; e soliinn@northcyprus.net; singles/ doubles including breakfast UK£31/41) is comfortable and situated by the sea on the west side of the town. Rooms all have a TV and fridge and there is a pool for guests.

For a meal, head for the nearby and excellent **Mardin Restaurant** (☎ 727 7527; mains TL5-6 million) where the dining is waterside. The service is very attentive and the food is top notch. The Adana kebabs are recommended.

BEACHES
From Gemikonağı to the border with the Republic, some 12km to the west, are a series of small, sandy and pebbly beaches. First up is the prominently signposted **Zafer Gazinosu Beach**. It's mainly a pebble beach with some imported sand retained for those who prefer it. There is a wooden diving and swimming pier, changing rooms and toilets, as well as an attendant bar and restaurant.

From here you are better advised to ignore the subsequent, rather scrappy beaches to the west and head for **Asmalı Beach** fronting the border village of Yeşilırmak (Limnitis). This is a clean, pebble beach with four restaurants catering to those who make it this far out. Of curious interest is an enormous grapevine. Planted in 1947 this enormous vine completely covers the outside dining area of the Asmalı Beach Restaurant at the western end.

At the eastern end is **Green River Bar** (☎ 0533 855 8331; meals TL6 million), run by Turkish/Cockney–speaking Erdal (Eddie). Apart from dishing up large meals of kebabs, fish or kleftiko (lamb or goat wrapped in foil), he also offers a small, shaded area with seats and tables (TL5 million entry) for independent picnickers.

LEFKE (LEFKA) ΛΕΥΚΑ
From Gemikonağı a road runs off at right angles to the hillside village of Lefke. The turn-off is not well signposted, but it is hard to miss. The village is an easy 10-minute drive along a fast, straight road and is the unlikely home for a hardy bunch of British expats. The village derives its name from the Greek word lefka (meaning 'poplar'). There are seemingly more palm trees than poplars these days, but Lefke's position amid riotous greenery and rolling hills does give the village a pleasant feel, and it is not surprising that its foreign residents stay here despite its de facto status of isolation. The practical tragedy is that access to the vast hinterland of Tylliria and the Pafos Forest is no more than 2km away, but is as firmly closed to Lefkans as lovely Lefke and its access to the sea is to Cypriots on the other side of the Attila Line. The only way out is back the way you came.

ANCIENT SOLOI
A good reason for venturing further west is to visit two archaeological sites. The first, Ancient Soloi (Soli Harabeleri; admission TL4.5 million; open 9am-7pm daily), one of the 10 ancient city kingdoms of Cyprus. Soloi traces its origin back to an Assyrian tribute list (700 BC) where the original city was referred to as Si-il-lu. In 580 BC King Philokyprios moved his capital from Aepia to Si-il-lu on the advice of his mentor and Athenian philosopher, Solon. Philokyprios promptly renamed the citadel Soloi in honour of Solon. In 498 BC Soloi, along with

most of the other city kingdoms of Cyprus (Amathous being the exception), rose up against the Persians but was ultimately captured and languished until Roman times when it flourished once again, thanks to the rich copper mines nearby. As happened in other parts of Cyprus, Soloi suffered looting and sacking at the hands of Arab raiders in the 7th century AD.

The site consists of two main parts: the basilica nearest the entrance to the site and the theatre along a short path up a hill south of the basilica. The remains of a royal palace can also be found on the acropolis next to the theatre, though it is believed that this dates from a later period.

The **basilica** is now covered with a large, open-walled, tin-roofed structure that protects the remains and the archaeologists who are still working sporadically on excavations. St Mark received baptism here from St Auxibius and the first church is thought to have been built in the second half of the 4th century. As is the case with most archaeological remains, it is difficult to imagine the size and extent of the church, which by all accounts was an impressive structure. What is immediately obvious are the remains of the **decorated floors**. Notable among those visible is a mosaic of a swan surrounded by floral patterns and four small dolphins nearby. The heavy roof over the sanctuary has spoiled the view of the mosaics as the light has been reduced.

The **Roman theatre** has been restored considerably as much of the original stonework was carted away by the British to rebuild the dockside of Port Said in the late 19th century.

As such, it does little for the imagination, but in its time the theatre could accommodate up to 4000 spectators. Nearby, the now-famous Roman statuette of **Aphrodite of Soli** was discovered. This is now in the Cyprus Museum in Lefkosia.

ANCIENT VOUNI

Viewed in the early morning or late afternoon, this rather surreal and 'what's-it-doing-here?' site is a bit of a mystery. The hilltop location of Ancient Vouni *(Vouni Sarayı Kalıntıları; admission TL3.5 million; open 10am-4.30pm daily)* is simply superb and is reached along a narrow road off the main highway. Look for the black-and-yellow *Vouni Sarayı* sign pointing north and up the hill. Go up the hill to the car park and ticket office at the very top.

The site, ostensibly supporting a palace or large complex of buildings, dates back to the 5th century BC. The palace was built by the leaders of the pro-Persian city of Marion (today's Polis) following the failed revolt of the Ionian Greeks against the Persians. The details of this incident were described by Herodotus in Book V of his *Histories*. Built to keep watch over the activities of nearby pro-Greek Soloi, the palace consisted of a discernible megaron, private rooms and steps leading down to a courtyard under which is a cistern. A curious guitar-shaped stone still stands and seemingly supported a windlass. The palace was burned down in 380 BC and never re-established. Today the site stands forlornly on its magnificent hilltop commanding some of the best views of the region.

Famagusta & the Karpas Peninsula

The wide sweep of Famagusta (Mağusa) Bay and the sprawling flat Mesarya (Mesaoria) hinterland were home to some of Cyprus' most important ancient settlements. The Bronze Age city of Enkomi (Alasia) existed during the 17th century BC, while Mycenaean tombs from the 9th century BC support the description of a flourishing culture detailed by Homer in the *Iliad*, and the illustrious kingdom of Salamis prospered in the 6th century BC. In addition to these, the Venetian city of Famagusta was perhaps the most opulent and wealthy in the eastern Mediterranean with its numerous churches. In post-independence Cyprus and until 1974, Famagusta was the jewel in the crown of the country's tourist industry, its golden beaches attracting sun-starved visitors from all over Europe. Famagusta today is a quiet town for people who like it that way. Sun-seekers head for the beaches in the north because those to the south have been out of bounds since 1974.

Like a finger pointing searchingly to the Asian mainland, the wild and inviting Karpas (Kırpaşa) Peninsula is the quietest and most undeveloped part of the country. Beyond the scattered village of Dipkarpaz (Rizokarpaso), travellers will be hard pressed to find electricity, yet the island's most exquisite beach lies here. At the tip of the peninsula is a monastery that is dear to the Greek Cypriot Orthodox population. Many make the twice-yearly pilgrimage from the Republic to the monastery; which, despite the politics of division on the island, allows Cypriots from both sides to mingle for a fleeting few hours.

If time moves slowly elsewhere in Cyprus, in this region it has almost stood still.

Famagusta (Mağusa)
Αμμόχωστος

pop 30,000

The booming tourist industry in Famagusta of the 1960s and early '70s came to an end in August 1974 when the Turkish army swept into the city and the vast tourist en-

Highlights

- Admire the Gothic architecture of the imposing Lala Mustafa Paşa mosque in Famagusta (Mağusa)
- Reflect on the grandeur of the ancient kingdom of Salamis
- Swim at the most beautiful beach in Cyprus on the isolated Karpas (Kırpaşa) panhandle
- Climb the romantic, abandoned Kantara Castle high up in the Kyrenia (Girne) Mountains
- Meander around the rambling backblocks of the Karpas Peninsula where time has stood still

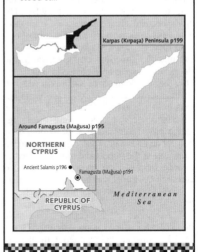

Karpas (Kırpaşa) Peninsula p199

Around Famagusta (Mağusa) p195

NORTHERN CYPRUS

Ancient Salamis p196 ● Famagusta (Mağusa) p191

REPUBLIC OF CYPRUS

Mediterranean Sea

clave of Maraş (Varosia in Greek) – Famagusta's Miami Beach – was closed down. It has remained closed to this day. Despite the setback the citizens of Famagusta (officially called Gazimağusa in Turkish – though usually called Mağusa – or Ammohostos in Greek) have picked themselves up, dusted off the debris of a bitter conflict and once more welcome visitors to this lively town on the far east coast of Northern Cyprus.

189

For most people, Famagusta means Old Famagusta – the original walled city that is now within the large Venetian Walls that surround and protect it. New Famagusta, once home to its Greek population, has expanded considerably, but offers little to attract the casual visitor.

The Old Town presents a curious cityscape to the first-time visitor. From the top of the Venetian Walls it looks almost bombed out or unfinished – an image not altogether untrue, since much of the damage from its turbulent past has never been repaired and, in some cases, buildings were never finished. It is, however, a pleasant place to spend a day or two. Famagustans are very welcoming of visitors, there are enough sites to keep the culturally attuned fascinated, and there are good quality hotels and restaurants to support a low-key tourist presence.

HISTORY

Famagusta was founded by Ptolemy Philadelphus of Egypt in the 3rd century BC. The city's original Greek name was Ammohostos, which means 'buried in the sand'. For a long time, the town played second fiddle to Salamis, the illustrious city kingdom just to the north. Despite an increase in population after the abandonment of Salamis in AD 648, Famagusta remained obscure and unimportant until the fall of Acre in 1291, when Christians fleeing the Holy Land took refuge in the city. From this sudden demographic boost, Famagusta grew exponentially and became one of the richest and most lavish cities in the eastern Mediterranean. Many religious communities built churches and it is said that, at one stage, there were as many churches in the town as there were days in the year.

The fortunes of Famagusta took a tumble in 1372 when the Venetians and the Genoese had a dispute that resulted in the seizure of the town by the Genoese. This provoked an exodus of the city's wealthy and more illustrious citizens. The fortunes were never regained even after the town was recaptured by the Venetians 117 years later. It was after this time that the huge walls and bastions were constructed, but even this belated measure did not prevent the capture of Famagusta by the Ottomans in 1571 following a bloody 10-month siege. Much of the damage caused during that siege is what you see today. The Turks have remained in residence of the Old Town – known as the Kaleici in Turkish – ever since.

ORIENTATION

Famagusta is not a difficult town to navigate as most of your movements will be within or near the Old Town. Long-distance buses arrive at the Otobüs Terminali on Gazi Mustafa Kemal Bulvarı, on the west side of the Old Town. Minibuses and service taxis arrive at İtimat bus station, a small parking lot 400m further southeast, just off Yirmisekiz Ocak Meydanı – a large square capped by an enormous black statue of Atatürk – the major landmark in the New Town and impossible to miss.

Across from Yirmisekiz Ocak Meydanı is the Land Gate, the easiest way into the Old Town. There is a handy car park just to the right as you enter the Old Town via the Gate. İstiklal Caddesi is a pedestrian street and the main thoroughfare running through the Old Town to Namık Kemal Meydanı, the square in front of Lala Mustafa Paşa Mosque.

Arrivals by ferry from Turkey will dock at the port to the east of the Old Town.

Maps

The North Cyprus Tourist organisation (NCTO) issues a free *City Plan of Gazimağusa* in English and Turkish. While it's lacking in detail for the streets of the Old Town it does give a good overall view of the city. Most of the main regional destinations are included on a smaller inset. You can get a copy from any office of the NCTO.

INFORMATION
Tourist Office

The local **Tourist Information Office** (☎ 366 2864; Fevzi Çakmak Bulvarı; open 8am-5pm Mon-Sat) is just south of the Old Town walls. It has a limited amount of material.

Money

Inside the Old Town, the **İş Bankası** on the main square opposite Lala Mustafa Paşa Mosque has an ATM that accepts major credit cards. Money-exchange offices nearby on İstiklal Caddesi keep extended office hours.

Post & Communications

The post office (☎ 366 2250; Fazıl Polat Paşa Bulvarı) and the main **Telecommunications**

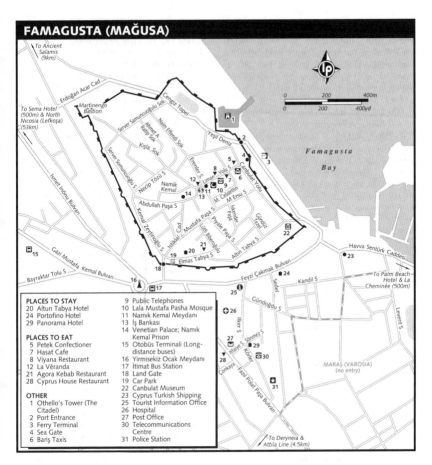

FAMAGUSTA (MAĞUSA)

To Ancient Salamis (9km)
Erdoğan Acar Cad
To Sema Hotel (500m) & North Nicosia (Lefkoşa) (53km)
Martinengo Bastion
Server Samuncuoğlu Sok
Cengiz Topel
Ahmet A Ratip Sok
Naim Effendi Sok
Yeşil Deniz
Kişla Sok
Server Samuncuoğlu S
İsmet İnönü Bulvarı
Necip Tözü S
Erenler S
Liman Yolu S
Canbulat Yolu
Namik Kemal
Kemal Zeytinoğlu S
Abdullah Paşa S
İstiklal Cad
Mustafa Paşa S
Pyiale Paşa S
M. Celalettin
M Ersu S
İskender Paşa
Gündiz Tepesi
Gazi Mustafa Kemal Bulvarı
Lütfi Biberoğlu
Altın Tabya S
Bayraktar Tolu S
Elmas Tabya S
Feyzi Çakmak Bulvarı
Kandil S
Sedel
Gündoğdu S
İlker S
Havva Sentürk Caddesi
To Palm Beach Hotel & La Cheminée (500m)
Levent S
Sönmez S
İlker S
İhtaye S
Körler S
Conkaya
Fazıl Polat Paşa Bulvarı
To Deryneıa & Attila Line (4.5km)
MARAŞ (VAROSIA) (no entry)

Famagusta Bay

0   200   400m
0   200   400yd

PLACES TO STAY
20 Altun Tabya Hotel
24 Portofino Hotel
29 Panorama Hotel

PLACES TO EAT
5 Petek Confectioner
7 Hasat Cafe
8 Viyana Restaurant
12 La Véranda
21 Agora Kebab Restaurant
28 Cyprus House Restaurant

OTHER
1 Othello's Tower (The Citadel)
2 Port Entrance
3 Ferry Terminal
4 Sea Gate
6 Barış Taxis

9 Public Telephones
10 Lala Mustafa Pasha Mosque
11 Namık Kemal Meydanı
13 İş Bankası
14 Venetian Palace; Namık Kemal Prison
15 Otobüs Terminali (Long-distance buses)
16 Yirmisekiz Ocak Meydanı
17 İtimat Bus Station
18 Land Gate
19 Car Park
22 Canbulat Museum
23 Cyprus Turkish Shipping
25 Tourist Information Office
26 Hospital
27 Post Office
30 Telecommunications Centre
31 Police Station

Centre (☎ 366 5332; İlker S Körler) are both south of the Old Town. There is a clutch of phonecard telephones on Liman Yolu Sokak adjacent to the Lala Mustafa Pasha Mosque

Emergency
Both the **hospital** (☎ 366 2876; Fazıl Polat Paşa Bulvarı) and the main **police station** (☎ 366 5310; İlker Körler Caddesi) are south of the Old Town.

THINGS TO SEE & DO
When you look from the top of Othello's Tower on the northeastern corner of the Venetian Walls, you could be excused for thinking that the Old Town sights consist solely of ruins. Indeed much of Famagusta looks much like bombed-out cities must

have done in Germany and England during WWII. Broken churches and other medieval buildings punctuate the skyline, while low houses and winding streets make up the rest of this laid-back and crumbling sector of what was once Cyprus' most lavish and important city. A full day is recommended to take in the city leisurely on foot.

Venetian Walls
These squat, sprawling defence walls define the extent of the **Old Town**. The walls were built to their present size in the early 16th century and cover a surprising amount of territory resolutely encircling the city on all four sides. The walls seem quite low – in reality 15m high and up to 8m thick in parts – an image perhaps exaggerated by their

length. While they were built for defence purposes, they ultimately failed to keep the Ottomans at bay. The Ottomans took the town and, despite wreaking considerable havoc and damage within, the walls themselves escaped relatively unscathed.

Like their counterparts in North Nicosia (Lefkoşa), the Old Town's walls were punctuated with 15 **bastions** around the roughly rectangular layout. While it is impossible to walk the length of the walls due to the existence of the military at various points, you can get a decent enough feel for them at the southern end near the **Land Gate** on the Ravelin (or Rivettina) Bastion. It was at this point that the Turks first breached the fortifications.

From the Ravelin Bastion the walls head northwards passing four minor bastions, the **Diocare, Moratto** and **Pulacazara** culminating in the steeply pitched **Martinengo** bastion. This in turn leads seawards passing the **Del Mezzo, Diamante** and **Signoria** bastions where it cedes into the impressive citadel, or Othello's Tower.

Further along, the **Sea Gate** on the eastern side originally opened directly to the sea, but today the wharfs of the modern port have extended the land bridge considerably. At the southeast extremity is the **Canbulat** bastion, in which a Turkish hero, General Canbulat Bey, died in the siege of Famagusta. This corner of the walls now houses the Canbulat Museum (see later) before looping back to the Land Gate via the **Composanto, Andruzzi** and **Santa Napa** bastions.

Othello's Tower (The Citadel)
This rather grandly but perhaps mistakenly named citadel *(Othello Kalesi; admission TL4.5 million; open 9am-4.45pm daily)* was built as an extension to the main walls of the Old Town on the northeast seaward side. It was constructed in the 12th century during Lusignan rule in order to protect the harbour and the Sea Gate entrance further south. In 1492, during the time of Venetian rule, the citadel was further reinforced by its transformation into an artillery stronghold in much the same way Kyrenia (Girne) Castle was fortified. Above the impressive entrance to the citadel you can spot the **Venetian Lion** inscribed with the name of the architect, Nicolò Foscarini. It is believed that Leonardo da Vinci gave advice on the refurbishment when he visited Cyprus in 1481.

The citadel consists of various towers and corridors leading to the artillery chambers, a large courtyard bordered on one side by a refectory and, above that, living quarters, both dating back to the Lusignans. The connection between the citadel and Othello is derived from the time of the British rule in Cyprus. Shakespeare's play of the same name is set 'in a seaport in Cyprus' and the 'moor' connection may be a misunderstanding of the name of the then Venetian governor of Cyprus Cristoforo Moro (r. 1506–08), whose name means Moor. The convenient name has since stuck permanently.

Other than wandering around the dusty corridors and the corroded sandstone walls where there is not all that much to see, the main attraction is climbing up to the ramparts and sampling the good views over the town, which are best enjoyed in the early morning or evening.

Lala Mustafa Pasha Mosque
This enormous mosque, or *camii* in Turkish *(Cathedral of Agios Nikolaos; admission TL2 million)*, which dominates the skyline of the Old Town, was built between 1298 and 1326. It is the finest example of Lusignan Gothic architecture in Cyprus and was modelled on the Cathedral of Rheims in France. Many believe it outshines its sister church in North Nicosia, the Agia Sophia. The Cathedral of St Nicholas was the centrepiece of Famagusta's Lusignan heyday, and the last Lusignan king, Jacques II, and his infant son, Jacques III, were buried here.

The church was damaged considerably during the siege of Famagusta by the Ottomans and, during this time, the twin towers of the church were destroyed. Afterwards, the Ottomans added a rather incongruous minaret, emptied the floor tombs and stripped the innards of all Christian accoutrements and turned it into the Lala Mustafa Pasha mosque.

The west-facing facade is particularly impressive and easier to admire in totality now that the area in front of the mosque is a pedestrian zone. Three gracious portals point towards a six-paned window, which is decorated with a circular rose. The inside has been whitewashed in typical Islamic fashion, but the soaring architectural lines are easy to follow. Visits are allowed when prayers are not being conducted.

Venetian Palace & Namık Kemal Museum

There is very little left of what was once a **Venetian Palace** in the area immediately to the west of Namık Kemal Meydanı. Known originally as the **Palazzo del Provveditore**, the palace now consists of some desultory cannon balls and a few arches supported by columns removed from Salamis. The one remaining structure that is still whole is the former **prison** *(admission TL1 million; open 7.30am-2pm daily & 3.30pm-6pm Mon)* of Namık Kemal (1840–88) who was one of Turkey's best-known poets and playwrights. He was imprisoned here for six years after writing a play that was considered offensive to the Sultan of the time. The square between the prison and the Lala Mustafa Pasha Mosque is named in his honour.

Canbulat Museum

The tomb of **Canbulat Bey**, who was an Ottoman hero, contains a small museum *(Canbulat Yolu; admission TL2 million; open 9am-5pm Mon-Sat)* at the southeastern corner of the Venetian Walls. During the siege of Famagusta, he ran his horse and himself into a gruesome protective device consisting of a wheel with spikes. He destroyed the device and both himself and his horse in the process, thus precipitating the downfall of the then Venetian-held city.

The museum is a rather tired collection of cultural and historical artefacts and a display detailing the 1974 campaign to liberate the enclaved Turks of the Old Town.

Maraş (Varosia) Βαρόσια

The sight of the barricaded Maraş district (known as Varosia in Greek) in southern Famagusta is one of this city's more haunting legacies and is a lingering reminder of the dark days of 1974. Prior to that time, Maraş was a thriving community of Greeks who also owned and ran most of the hotels in what was Famagusta's Riviera overlooking some of the island's best resort beaches. Panic-stricken by Turkish advances into the north in July and August 1974, Maraş' residents fled in fear, taking with them little more than the clothes they wore. Most of them believed that they would be returning within a few days when the emergency was over. As it happened, the Turkish army just walked in unimpeded and took an abandoned city. To this day Maraş has remained uninhabited and abandoned.

Visitors cannot enter the area and are indiscreetly discouraged from doing so by barbed wire fences and metal drums blocking the streets. Inside, shops, houses and hotels have lain untouched for 30 years. A Toyota car dealership apparently still has 1974 models, frozen in time, locked in the showroom windows. Visitors with their own vehicles can drive down the western side of Maraş, alongside the fence and peer into the past. You are not supposed to stop and stare and photography is forbidden. The perimeter road will take you almost as far as the Deryneia checkpoint. Here you encounter a military zone just before the checkpoint and it is probably advisable to turn around by this time.

Beaches

The best and most convenient beach in town is in front of Palm Beach Hotel (see Places to Stay following) where nonguests can use the beach. Look for the little 'To the Beach Club' sign south of the hotel, hard up against the Maraş barricades.

PLACES TO STAY

Accommodation pickings in Famagusta are not rich as most visitors tend to stay in resort hotels along the fringes of the bay to the north.

Altun Tabya Hotel *(☎ 366 5363; Altun Tabya Sokak; singles/doubles including breakfast UK£13/16)*, inside the city walls, is a pleasant place to stay. Follow the signs from the Land Gate. All rooms have bathrooms.

Panorama Hotel *(☎ 366 5880, fax 366 5990; İlker S Körler; singles/doubles UK£13/18)* is in a run-down section of the New Town (south of the tourist office). It's friendly, but breakfast is not included in the room rate.

Portofino Hotel *(☎ 366 4392, fax 366 2949; ⓦ www.portofinohotel.cyprus.com; Fevzi Çakmak Bulvarı 9; singles/doubles UK£13/19, breakfast UK£3.20)*, to the south of the Old Town, was radically renovated in 1999 and offers comfortable accommodation.

Sema Hotel *(☎ 366 1222, fax 366 1032; ⓔ semahotel@northcyprus.net; Gazi Mustafa Kemal Bulvarı; singles/doubles UK£17/25)* is a modern three-star option on the west side of the city on the road out to Lefkoşa. Rooms have air-con and TV, and there are two restaurants within the hotel.

Palm Beach Hotel (☎ 366 2000, fax 366 2002; e bilfer@management.emu.edu.tr; Deve Limanı; singles/doubles including breakfast UK£51/64) is the top of the lot in town. It's hard up to the Maraş closed zone and one of the few hotels to escape the sealing off of the ghost city immediately to the south. This well-appointed five-star hotel has most facilities you would expect from a top-class establishment.

Salamis Bay Conti Resort Hotel (☎ 378 8201, fax 378 8209; e salamisbay@north cyprus.net; singles/doubles UK£51/64) is 8km north of Famagusta. It's a luxurious five-star place that underwent renovation in 1999. It's slightly cheaper for rooms without a sea view.

PLACES TO EAT

For a cool beer and a quick snack, make for **La Véranda** (☎ 367 0153; Namık Kemal Meydanı; hamburger, chips & beer TL5.5 million) on the northern side of the square in front of Lala Mustafa Pasha Mosque, or walk east towards the port from La Véranda along Liman Yolu Sokak and look for the cool and leafy **Hasat Cafe** on your right.

Viyana Restaurant (☎ 366 6037; Liman Yolu Sokak 19; grilled meatballs, salad & beer TL10 million), in the same street and diagonally opposite the Hasat Cafe, is where you can get excellent food served attentively in a vine-covered courtyard. The scrumptious köfte (grilled meatballs) dish is very filling.

At the eastern end of Liman Yolu Sokak is the wonderful **Petek Confectioner** (☎ 366 7104; Yeşil Deniz Sokak 1; 'Petekburger' & Coke TL5 million) where you can drink tea, eat cakes and Turkish delight or have a tasty, burger-laced lunch while reading foreign magazines such as Newsweek.

Agora Kebab Restaurant (☎ 366 5364; Elmas Tabya Sokak 1; set kebab meals TL5 million) is on the south side of the Old Town and is quite unassuming. It specialises in oven-cooked kebabs, done in the prominent oven at the front of the restaurant.

Cyprus House Restaurant (☎ 366 4845; Fazıl Polat Paşa Bulvarı; mains TL6-8 million) is in the New Town and has a beautiful outside dining area. It's about 400m southeast of Yirmisekiz Ocak Meydanı. The kebab dishes are highly recommended and at night you might get a belly dancer thrown in for good measure.

La Cheminée (☎ 366 4624; Kemal Server Sokak 17; mains TL7-10 million) is hard up against the ugly road blocks of the Maraş area and very close to the Palm Beach Hotel. French cuisine is the order of the day here, and you will find prices are mid-range to somewhat more expensive than many other places.

GETTING THERE & AWAY
Bus
The main bus station is **Otobüs Terminali** (Gazi Mustafa Kemal Bulvarı); services go to North Nicosia, Kyrenia and Yenierenköy via Boğaz. Minibuses for North Nicosia (TL1 million) go frequently from the **İtimat bus station** on the south side of Yirmisekiz Ocak. Also from here, minibuses for Kyrenia leave every half hour or so (TL1.5 million).

Sea
Ferries to Mersin in Turkey leave from the port east of the Old Town on Tuesday, Thursday and Sunday. They depart at 10pm and the trip takes 12 hours. One-way tickets cost TL50 million (students TL37.5 million) per person and TL65 million per car. Departure tax is included in the price. The ticket agents are **Cyprus Turkish Shipping** (☎ 366 5786, fax 366 7840; e cypship@superonline .com; Bulent Ecevit Bulvarı).

GETTING AROUND
There are a few private taxi companies that operate in and around Famagusta. **Barış Taxis** (☎ 366 2349) operates a fleet of modern air-conditioned Mercedes taxis around the city and further afield. Tariffs are generally fixed, but make sure you know the fare before accepting a ride. There's a taxi stand in the Old Town, near the Sea Gate.

There are no public buses within the city, but all the major sights and services are within walking distance anyway.

Around Famagusta

Most of the sites around Famagusta are conveniently clustered within a 9km to 10km radius north of town. If you have a car, though, you can strike out further north and west to the rarely visited northern Mesarya villages of Geçitkale (Lefkoniko) and İskele (Trikomo). You can also base yourself at

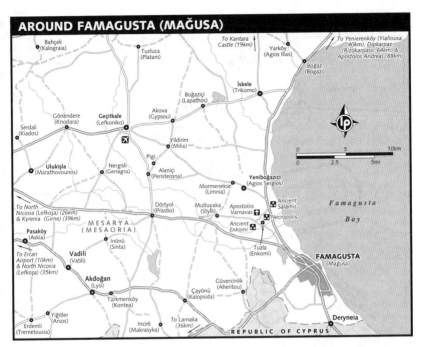

AROUND FAMAGUSTA (MAĞUSA)

Bahçeli (Kalograia)
Tuzluca (Platani)
To Kantara Castle (19km)
Yarköy (Agios Ilias)
To Yenierenköy (Yiallousa, 40km), Dipkarpaz (Rizokarpaso, 64km) & Apostolos Andreas (88km)
Boğaz (Bogazi)
İskele (Trikomo)
Boğaziçi (Lapathos)
Gönendere (Knodara)
Geçitkale (Lefkoniko)
Akova (Gypsou)
Serdali (Kiados)
Yıldırım (Milia)
Pigi
0   5   10km
0   2.5   5mi
Ulukışla (Marathovounos)
Nergisli (Genagra)
Alaniçi (Peristerona)
Yeniboğazici (Agios Sergios)
Mormenekşe (Limnia)
Famagusta Bay
To North Nicosia (Lefkoşa) (26km) & Kyrenia (Girne) (39km)
Dörtyol (Prastio)
Mutluyaka (Stylli)
Apostolos Varnavas
Ancient Salamis
MESARYA (MESAORIA)
Ancient Enkomi
Necropolis
Pasaköy (Askia)
İnönü (Sinta)
To Ercan Airport (10km) & North Nicosia (Lefkoşa) (35km)
Vadili (Vatili)
Tuzla (Enkomi)
FAMAGUSTA (Mağusa)
Akdoğan (Lysi)
Güvercinlik (Aheritou)
Türkmenköy (Kontea)
Çayönü (Kalopsida)
Yiğitler (Arsos)
Erdemli (Tremetousia)
İncirli (Makrasyka)
To Larnaka (36km)
Deryneia
REPUBLIC OF CYPRUS

any one of a scattering of hotels north of Famagusta, or at the little low-key resort of Boğaz (Bogazi).

GETTING AROUND

The closeness of the sites to Famagusta makes it feasible to hire a taxi and get around economically. A return taxi from Famagusta to Ancient Salamis will cost about UK£8. There are buses between Famagusta and Yenierenköy that stop at Boğaz and pass near Salamis, but taking them would limit your options a lot.

Cycling is also a good way of seeing the sites mentioned here. However, there is nowhere to rent cycles in Famagusta.

BEACHES

There is a decent beach with restaurant facilities at the Ancient Salamis site north of Famagusta. From there on are some excellent beaches all the way to Boğaz.

ANCIENT SALAMIS

Salamis (*Salamis Harabeleri; admission TL4.5 million; open 8am-6pm daily June–mid-Sept, 9am-1pm & 2pm-4.45pm mid-Sept–May*) is one of Cyprus' prime archaeological sites and should not be missed by visitors to the North. It is extensive and a minimum of half a day should be allowed for a visit. Salamis is 9km north of Famagusta and is signposted – not very prominently – to the seaward side of the Famagusta–Boğaz highway.

Ancient Salamis was one of the 10 city kingdoms of Cyprus and was first mentioned on an Assyrian stele in 709 BC where it was listed as paying a tribute to Assyrian ruler Sargon II. Its period of major importance came during the 6th century BC under kings Evalthon and Evagoras when Salamis issued its own money and nurtured a thriving philosophical and literary scene, with Greek poets as regular visitors to the royal court.

The Persians destroyed Salamis in 306 BC and it was placed under Ptolemaic rule from 294 BC until 58 BC, at which point the Romans took control and Salamis flourished once again. For three centuries the city's fortunes waxed and waned and in AD 350 the city was renamed Constantia and declared an episcopal see. Constantia suffered the same depredation of the 7th- and 8th-century Arab raids as the rest of Cyprus,

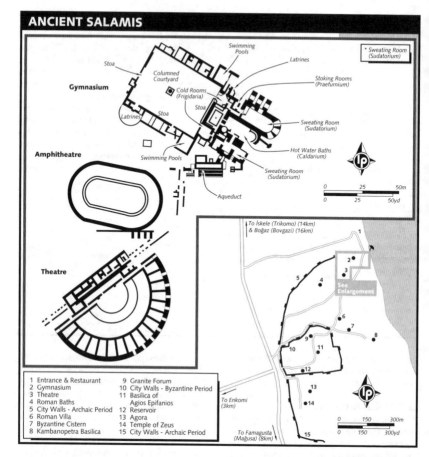

ANCIENT SALAMIS

1 Entrance & Restaurant
2 Gymnasium
3 Theatre
4 Roman Baths
5 City Walls - Archaic Period
6 Roman Villa
7 Byzantine Cistern
8 Kambanopetra Basilica
9 Granite Forum
10 City Walls - Byzantine Period
11 Basilica of Agios Epifanios
12 Reservoir
13 Agora
14 Temple of Zeus
15 City Walls - Archaic Period

and remained largely abandoned and forgotten from that time onwards. Much of the stone from the ancient city was carted away by Famagusta to build its own city. Archaeological explorations of the ancient site started in 1880 and are still continuing.

Today, visitors can see a fair amount of walls and columns, though you will need a map to make sense of the jumbled layout. Look out for the **gymnasium** and the **baths** that served as an exercise ground and were built close by the columned courtyard, and which today provide most of the visual clues of the glory days of Salamis. The **theatre**, dating from the time of Augustus (31 BC–AD 14), could hold 15,000 spectators in its day. Earthquakes in the 4th century destroyed much of the theatre and its stone

was removed for building projects elsewhere. Today it has been restored to some degree and occasionally hosts summer events. The **Roman Villa**, originally a two-storey structure south of the theatre, was made up of a reception hall and central inner courtyard with columned portico. The nearby **Kambanopetra Basilica** was built in the 4th century and consisted of a columned courtyard. A mosaic floor is visible inside. The **Basilica of Agios Epifanios** was the largest basilica in Cyprus and was built during the episcopacy of Epifanios (386–403).

There is a decent beach nearby and a handy restaurant for lunch. For accommodation, the Salamis Bay Conti Resort Hotel (see Places to Stay in the Famagusta section) is nearby.

CHURCH OF APOSTOLOS VARNAVAS

While the Turks have been accused of a fair amount of desecration of Orthodox religious sites – and justifiably so in many cases – they have at least made an effort to maintain an air of solemnity and normality with this important Orthodox church (☎ 378 8331; church & museum admission TL4.5 million; open 9am-7pm daily). It is in the Mesarya hinterland, 9km northwest of Famagusta and close to Salamis.

The church is dedicated to one of St Paul's good friends. Despite his name, Varnavas (Barnabus) was never an official apostle, but he is mentioned for his missionary work in the Acts of the Apostles. He was born in Cyprus and carried out his missionary work here. The original church was built over the site of his tomb, which was discovered by Anthemios the bishop of Constantia (Salamis), following a revelationary dream. The current structure dates from the 18th century, though it does incorporate parts of the 5th-century original church.

The church is used as an **icon museum** today and has a wide selection of well-preserved Orthodox icons. There is also a small **archaeological museum** in the courtyard buildings containing an extensive selection of finds from Salamis and nearby Enkomi.

NECROPOLIS OF SALAMIS

Close to Salamis are a couple of sights worth seeing that won't cause you to detour

Orthodoxy & Islam

While Turkish and Greek Cypriots may be separated by physical, man-induced barriers, they at least share the same God – even if they worship Him via two different religions.

Cyprus is home to two major religious faiths: Eastern Orthodoxy and Sunni Islam. Much smaller religious groups such as the Maronites and the Jews also practise their faith on the island. Orthodoxy came to Cyprus with St Barnabus, companion and cotraveller of Apostle Paul in AD 45, while Islam arrived with the Ottoman conquerors in 1570.

Eastern Orthodoxy is a community of Christian churches that arose when the Greek-speaking Eastern section of the Latin-speaking Church of Rome split from Rome in what was known as the Great Schism in 1054. Orthodoxy means 'the right belief' and its adherents do not recognise the jurisdiction of the Catholic Pope. Instead, they recognise only the Patriarch of Constantinople as their leader. Other than dogmatic differences and an entrenched sense of separateness from Rome, the Eastern Orthodox Church is in many ways similar to the Catholic Church with which it has most in common.

However, much of the church liturgy is steeped in tradition and conservatism and little has changed since the Schism. Church services are redolent with formality and ceremony and often last up to three hours. Yet, at the same time, they are informal family affairs, with participants wandering in and out of the service at will, often exchanging small talk and gossip with other churchgoers. This is in stark contrast to the strict observances of behaviour in the Catholic Church, yet it has a more liberal approach to liturgy.

Islam is a monotheistic religion that came out of what is today's Saudi Arabia in the early 7th century. Islam is an Arabic word meaning 'submission to God' and Muslims strive to submit their individual wills to the will of God alone. The religion of Islam was named in honour of its final prophet, Mohammed, after he was witness to a series of revelations about the one true God, Allah. These revelations are written up in the Islamic holy book, the Quran, and the dictates of the Quran constitute the basis for Islamic beliefs today.

Turkish Cypriots and mainland Turks who have settled in Northern Cyprus follow the Sunni branch of Islam – the traditional 'Orthodox' Islam that constitutes the majority in the Islamic world. However, Islamic life in Cyprus is far from the chador-shrouded world of Saudi Arabia or the strictures of Afghan Taliban Islam. Most Turkish Cypriots, while taking their religion seriously enough, are fairly liberal in the implementation of Islamic laws. Women dress much more freely than their Islamic sisters elsewhere and alcohol is commonly available. Mosques can be seen in both Northern Cyprus and the Republic, while previously Christian churches have been recycled into mosques – a solution that is practical yet occasionally bizarre.

too much. Known more commonly as the **Royal Tombs** *(Salamis Mezarlık Alanı; ☎ 378 8331; admission TL3.5 million; open 9am-7pm daily)*, these are a scattering of 150 graves spread out over a wide area. This historic cemetery, dating back to the 7th and 8th centuries BC, confirms the account of Mycenaean tombs described by Homer in the *Iliad*. Kings and various other nobles were buried with all their favourite worldly goods, food and drink, even their favourite slaves, in order to make their afterlife a little easier. In one particularly gruesome reminder of the practices, two hapless horses were sacrificed after transporting a king to his tomb (No 79), where their agonised skeletons have been exposed to the public gaze. Most tombs have been looted over the years by unknown grave robbers, though at least three did yield enough treasure to make it to the Cyprus Museum in Lefkosia.

Further to the south and marked by a lone eucalyptus tree are the **Cellarka tombs**, also included in the admission price. These are smaller rock-cut tombs that were used for less noble members of the royal community. Each tomb has a flight of steps leading down to the burial area in which the remains of the deceased were placed in stone urns pending their decomposition. After this, the bones were removed and the chambers were reused.

The tombs are south of Salamis on the road to the Monastery of Apostolos Varnavas and are prominently signposted.

ENKOMI (ALASIA)
ΕΓΚΩΜΗ (ΑΛΑΣΙΑ)

Heading further west from the Necropolis of Salamis you will come across the ancient Bronze Age city of Enkomi *(Enkomi Ören Yeni; admission TL3 million; open 9am-5pm daily)*, which dates back as far as 1800 BC. Most activity at the site, however, seems to have taken place during the Late Bronze Age period (1650–1050 BC) when Enkomi was a large copper-producing centre.

The name Alasia derives from Akkadian cuneiform slabs found in Tel el-Amarna in Egypt in which the Pharaoh of the time received promises from the King of Alasia of copper in return for silver and other luxury items. Other script evidence and a careful juxtaposition of data suggest that Alasia was either Cyprus as a whole or possibly just Enkomi itself.

The remains of the present site date from around 1200 BC and possibly beyond when a rectangular grid layout was established with fine public buildings erected. After this time, the arrival of the Mycenaeans on the island ensured the ultimate demise of Enkomi. Its inland harbour silted up and it is thought that the last residents moved to the coast where they founded Salamis.

The site is fairly extensive and requires a bit of walking to get around, but there is a helpful leaflet handed out at the ticket office with a map of the site and a compact review of its history.

ICON MUSEUM OF İSKELE

If you are heading up to Kantara Castle or cutting across the northern Mesarya plain back to Lefkoşa from Boğaz, you can easily make a brief stop at the little crossroads village of İskele (Trikomo), the birthplace of Greek EOKA leader Georgos Grivas. Here is the Panagia Theotokou, which has now been converted into an **Icon Museum** *(İskele İkon Müzesi; admission TL2 million; open 9am-7pm daily)* with a small collection of 12th- to 15th-century wall paintings and more recent icons from the 1950s and '60s.

The building is a 12th-century single-sided domed church with arched recesses in the side walls. In the recesses you can see paintings of the **Virgin Mary of the Annunciation** as well as the **Prayer of Joachim and Anna** who embrace each other as a girl peers curiously from behind a curtained window.

In the belfry outside the church you can spot a marble inlay taken from the original iconostasis of the church. The church is on the western edge of the village and is easy to spot.

BOĞAZ (BOGAZI) ΜΠΟΓΑΖΙ

Boğaz makes a convenient stop for travellers around the Karpas Peninsula. It is a small fishing village about 24km north of Famagusta and the last beach halt before an excellent sealed road heads inland to the peninsula proper. There is a little harbour, south of which is a stretch of developed beach with straw beach umbrellas and sun loungers for those few tourists on package holidays that base themselves in the low-key hotels in the village. For some reason, Russians seem to have taken a shine to Boğaz and you are just as likely to hear Russian spoken in any of the beachside tavernas as you will hear German speakers, who make up the bulk of the remaining clientele. It is a pleasant enough place to stay for a day or two, though there is little to do other than swim, read and eat.

Places to Stay & Eat

There are at least two decent places to stay in Boğaz. The **Boğaz Hotel** (☎ 371 2559, fax 371 2557; w www.bogazhotel.com; singles/ doubles including breakfast UK£12/24) is a comfortable three-star hotel with good-value rooms, all of which have fridges and air-con.

The nearby **Exotic Hotel** (☎ 371 2885, fax 371 3220; e exoticmirillo@superonline.net; singles/doubles including breakfast UK£28/ 35) doesn't quite have the same beachside location as the Boğaz, but is more modern. Rooms have satellite TV, minibar, phone and safe.

Dining is probably best undertaken at the **Boğaz Fish Restaurant** (☎ 371 2559 ext 103; fish dishes UK£4.50-6.50), which is right on the beach. Here you'll find a good selection of fish; the seafood platter (UK£4.50) is a good option.

The Karpas (Kırpaşa) Peninsula

The long swathe of the Karpas (also known as Karpasia and the Turkish version, Kırpaşa) Peninsula was virtually untouched by the traumatic events of 1974 and remains a timeless land of rolling fields, vast beaches, scattered settlements and the best sunsets in Cyprus. The peninsula is Cyprus' panhandle and it reaches eastwards to Syria as if seeking to look elsewhere. It is little visited, undeveloped, quite remote and untouched by mass tourism. The government has plans to turn the area into a vast nature reserve, which is just as well since colonies of turtles nest on the broad expanse of its southern beaches. In any case, electricity has not yet reached beyond the village of Dipkarpaz (Rizokarpaso). Adventurous travellers who do stay on the panhandle often make do with oil lamps or generator-powered lighting.

Twice a year, Greek Cypriot pilgrims from the South are normally allowed to make the long trip to the tip of the panhandle to visit the Monastery of Apostolos Andreas

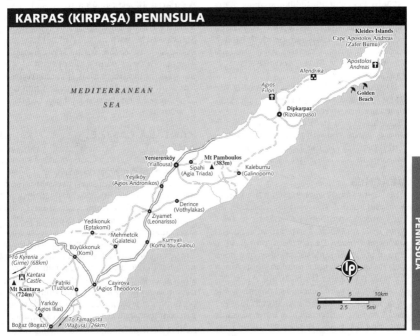

KARPAS (KIRPAŞA) PENINSULA

while, in return, Turkish Cypriots are allowed to visit the Hala Sultan Tekkesi in the South (see Around Larnaka in the Larnaka & the East chapter).

Other than the village of Dipkarpaz, which was once home to a thriving Greek Cypriot community and now home to only a few score elderly Greeks, the only other village of any size is Yenierenköy (Yiallousa). There is a very helpful tourist office here, which was set up in the hope of generating a greater number of travellers to the region. The area, with its rolling hills, is ideal for cyclists, ramblers and lovers of wild flowers. The displays of wild flowers in the spring are magic. See the special section 'Wild Flowers of Cyprus' for details of the flora here.

Things are looking up all along the peninsula and you will no longer be caught out without a place to sleep or eat.

GETTING AROUND

The only public transport is the bus from Famagusta to Yenierenköy. Your own transport is necessary to get around this region, unless you are prepared to pay for taxis. The main road into the peninsula as far as Yenierenköy is excellent, though signs to some of the sites are lacking in clarity and prominence. A taxi shared between two or three people on a day basis may work out much the same as hiring a car and, if you are on a day trip from the South, you may have already hired a taxi.

Distances on the Karpas Peninsula are quite long and you will need to plan your time carefully if you want to get around to all sights. If you are coming from the South on a day trip, you will need to make a very early start. Be at the Ledra Palace Hotel crossing in North Nicosia by at least 8am.

BEACHES

The island's best beaches are on the Karpas Peninsula and if you visit the Karpasia for only one reason then it should be to feast your eyes on the vast expanse of sand and dunes at **Golden Beach (Nangomi Bay)**, a duo of postcard-fantastic swathes of golden yellow sand with not a hotel in sight. About 5km short of Zafer Burnu (Cape Apostolos Andreas), the twin beaches sit on either side of a scrubby headland and stretch for several kilometres. Reached by quite passable sand and dirt roads, the beaches sport only

minimal facilities – a trio of beach restaurants with fairly basic shack-like huts for accommodation (see Zafer Burnu later for details). If you want to get away from it all and you love sand and rolling dunes, then this is the place.

It is unlikely that Golden Beach is going to see any development in the future since a new nature reserve is on the drawing board. This is good news for the **turtles** that nest on these two beaches and on other beaches on the north side of the panhandle, and for fans of nature who like it just the way it is.

HIKING

The NCTO produces a small brochure called *Mountain Trails*, available free from NCTO offices. The following is the second of the two walks in the Kyrenia Range that you may care to investigate. However, the brochure is not detailed enough for serious hikers, so you are advised to seek local advice and use a good map.

Contact the **Association of Mountaineering** (☎ 0542 851 1800; e mustafacemal@hot mail.com) for full details.

Kantara to Alevkaya

This hike is fairly long, over 40km, linking Kantara Castle and the Alevkaya Forest Station and herbarium (see Around Kyrenia in the Kyrenia & the North Coast chapter). The hike follows mainly forest trails along the spine of the Beşparmak (Pentadaktylos) Range. It passes through or near a number of villages along the way and can be taken in sections.

KANTARA CASTLE

Another of the trio of Cyprus' Lusignan Gothic castles, Kantara Castle (Kantara Kalesi; admission TL3.5 million; open 9am-7pm daily), is the furthest east, the lowest in elevation and the best preserved. Its documented history dates back to 1191 when Richard the Lionheart seized it from Isaak Komninos, the Byzantine emperor of Cyprus. Kantara was used as a beacon station to communicate with Buffavento to the east. Its significance faded in the 16th century when Venetian military strategists began to depend more on firepower than elevation for protection and the ports of Famagusta, Larnaka and Kyrenia gained importance at the expense of the once-crucial mountain fortresses.

The Tale of Two Turtles

Turtles have been around on our planet for perhaps 200 million years – far longer than humans. There are eight species of turtles in the world and two of them live in the Eastern Mediterranean.

The green turtle *(chelona mydias)* and the logger-head turtle *(caretta caretta)* have long lived in the Mediterranean basin and in particular on the island of Cyprus. It is estimated that the greatest proportion of the endangered green turtle lives in Cyprus – on both sides of the island – with a disproportionate number making the beaches of the north coast and the Karpas Peninsula their favoured nesting grounds. The loggerhead turtle – classified 'vulnerable' by conservationists – also nests on these often pristine coastlines.

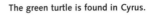

The green turtle is found in Cyrus.

Gradual human encroachment into their territory has meant that, over the years, the chances of survival of these lumbering marine animals has decreased. Visitors to Cyprus' beaches should be aware that their presence at the wrong time (at night) disrupts the breeding cycle and contributes to their gradual disappearance.

In Northern Cyprus, Alagadı Beach 19km east of Kyrenia is one of the prime breeding grounds. Golden Beach on the Karpas Peninsula and large swathes of the vast Famagusta Bay are also popular breeding grounds as is the largely untouched northern tract of the Karpas Peninsula.

When visiting a turtle beach, do so with caution and care. Some beaches such as Alagadı Beach are closed between dusk and dawn and have the breeding areas staked out with protective cages. Place beach umbrellas as near to the water as possible to avoid crushing unhatched eggs. Do not use torches at night when hatchlings are emerging and take only official 'turtle tours' if you are really keen to observe them.

Enjoy your turtles but remember; they were here long before you.

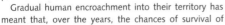

Today, you can see a quite well-preserved northern section of the castle with towers and walls still resolutely standing. You enter the castle by the outer entrance, which leads into a now rather overgrown **barbican**. Two squat towers, the **north tower** and the **south tower**, guard the inner entrance at which point you enter the castle proper. Inside the castle you are able to make out the **garrison**, **latrines**, and a **cistern**.

The highest point of the castle complex is the **lookout tower** from which flares would be lit to alert the residents of the castles to the west of any impending danger. At the southwestern end you can find more garrisons and the **postern gate** used to catch would-be attackers by surprise.

A useful map and potted history is given out with your ticket and you should allow an hour or so to make a relaxed tour and enjoy the views. Parents should keep small children under tight rein as there are some

pretty serious unfenced drops, rough scrambling and uncapped holes to contend with. The view from the roof of the eastern tongue of the North Tower is stupendous, but not for the vertiginously challenged as it is narrow and completely unfenced.

You can see the sea on both sides of the Karpas Peninsula and, on a clear day, the coast of Turkey or even Syria. Kantara is best reached from Boğaz and is at least a 45-minute drive. From Kaplıca on the coast, the ascent route to Kantara is narrow but quite driveable and there are regular passing places along the way. If driving from Kyrenia, allow at least 1½ hours to drive to the castle in comfort. There is no public transport that reaches the castle.

YENİERENKÖY (YIALLOUSA)
ΓΙΑΛΛΟΥΣΑ
This is another village once populated by Greeks and now resettled with the former

residents of Erenköy (Kokkina) in the South's Tylliria region (see Around Pafos in the Pafos & the West chapter).

The **Tourist Information Office** (☎ 374 4984; open 10am-6pm June–mid-Sept, 9am-1pm & 2pm-5pm mid-Sept–May) is run by the enthusiastic, English-speaking Suat Hüseyin Oğulları. Suat knows a lot about the Peninsula and readily shares his passion with visitors. He has created a large wall map of the Karpas Peninsula showing the better known sites as well as a few that he has discovered himself. Ask about the large 'undiscovered' **cave tombs** between Avtepe (Elisi) and Kuruova (Koroveia) or the **sandstone caves** near Kaleburnu (Galinoporni).

The **Theresa Hotel** (☎ 374 4266, fax 374 4009; w www.theresahotel.com; singles/doubles UK£10/15) is 7km east of Yenierenköy on the northern side of the panhandle. Catering for 36 guests, this is a small place that is ideal for hikers and nature lovers. All rooms have bathroom and fan. The hotel also has an in-house restaurant.

SIPAHI (AGIA TRIADA)
ΑΓΙΑ ΤΡΙΑΔΑ

The small and rather strung-out village of Sipahi (Agia Triada) is home to a small community of some 134 Karpas Greeks who, despite the political odds and like their brethren in Dipkarpaz (Rizokarpaso), cling tenuously to life in the peninsula. The village is also home to a rather well-preserved set of mosaics in the now-ruined **Basilica of Agia Triada** (admission TL1.5 million; open 9am-5pm daily) dating from around the 5th Century. While little is left of the main structure, the extensive flooring is intricately patterned with abstract mosaics, and Greek inscriptions at both the northern and southern ends of what was once the nave reveal that the church was financed partially by a certain deacon Iraklios and by three other men who did so in response to a personal vow.

The site is at the eastern end of the village and is best approached from the Dipkarpaz end of Sipahi.

AGIOS FILON & AFENDRIKA

Standing in silent sentinel on a rather deserted coastline, some 5km north of Dipkarpaz, is the well-preserved shell of **Agios Filon** (free admission; no set opening hours), a 12th-century church built over an earlier 5th-

century Christian basilica. Abstract mosaics from the earlier basilica can be viewed outside the standing walls of the later church.

The site is that of **Carpasia**, an ancient site of some importance during the Hellenistic period and the Middle Ages. A **Roman harbour** was also sited here and the remains of the mole can be seen out to sea. A further 7km eastwards will bring you to **Afendrika** (free admission; no set opening hours), a rather desultory site that was once one of the six major cities of Cyprus in the 2nd century BC. What's left is a set of contiguous ruins comprising three churches – **Agios Georgios** from the 6th century, and **Panagia Hrysiotissa** and **Panagia Asomatos** from around the 10th century. Nearby are a **necropolis** and the remains of a **citadel**.

MONASTERY OF APOSTOLOS ANDREAS

Twice a year, 15 August and 30 November, coachloads of Greek Cypriots cross the Green Line at the Ledra Palace Hotel in Lefkosia to make the long trek to this monastery (Manastır; admission free but donations accepted; no set opening hours), near the tip of the Karpas Peninsula. These are the only times when the Turkish Cypriot authorities allow any large numbers of Greeks to their side of the island and the visit is undertaken with great fanfare and seriousness. The object of their pilgrimage is to visit this site where miracles are reputed to take place.

The current main church dates from 1740, though additions have been made in later years to the whole monastery complex. The monastery gained a reputation for miracles as far back as the time of St Andrew – the patron saint of sailors – who reputedly restored the sight of a ship's captain after arriving here from Palestine. Attested miracles range from curing blindness, lameness and epilepsy to granting personal wishes. In the years prior to 1974, the monastery made a good living out of the pilgrims' (monetary) votive offerings. Today, with mass visits taking place only twice a year, revenue is down and the monastery's fortunes look ever bleaker, operating as it does under the watchful eye of the Turkish Cypriot administration and with only a couple of Greek caretakers to look after the place.

In between pilgrimages, visitors may still come to the monastery during the day to be guided by one of the caretakers after being signed in by a Turkish Cypriot guardian. Your contribution to the upkeep of the church will always be appreciated.

ZAFER BURNU (CAPE APOSTOLOS ANDREAS)

If you have come this far and have a penchant for lands' ends then you simply must make the extra effort to reach the point where Cyprus begins, or ends. From the monastery, it's a further 5km along a reasonable dirt road to the easternmost tip of Cyprus. There is little to see but the sea on both sides and the cluster of little rocky islets known collectively as the **Kleides** (Keys). If you have a jeep, you can take a rough northern track from here back to Dipkarpaz, though the going can get rough in wet weather.

Places to Stay & Eat

Most places are on or near Golden Beach (see Beaches earlier in this section). All places are pretty low-key and range from basic to quite comfortable.

Clustered close to one another on Golden Beach are three low-key, prebackpacker joints for the really nature-keen. These are really back-to-basics places consisting of little more than a bed-in-a-box, a laid-back cafeteria-cum-restaurant, trees for shade, and sand – oodles of the stuff – stretching for kilometres.

Best of the bunch – and most remote – is **Hasan's Turtle Café & Restaurant** (☎ 0533 864 1063, fax 372 22 90; single/double cab-ins including breakfast UK£6/12), signposted off the main road and located down a spiralling sandy track amid shady trees and sand dunes. The English-speaking Hasan Korkmaz – known in some quarters as the Turtle man of Nangomi – runs seven fairly tiny huts and a generator-powered restaurant. Bring a torch and lots of books and seriously chill out.

Located cheek by jowl are the other two of the trio. **Tekin Place** (☎ 0533 863 7365) and **Golden Beach Bar & Restaurant**, a kilometre or so further west. Both are prominently signposted from the main road and offer similar, basic deals as Hasan.

Near Turtle bay, on the south side of the peninsula, is **Blue Sea Hotel** (☎ 372 2393, fax 372 2255; Dipkarpaz; singles/doubles UK£10/15). Built on a rocky spur with ample shade from its shoreline trees, this is another good centre for hikers and lovers of nature. The hotel's restaurant serves up fresh fish caught by the hotel owner.

A kilometre or so past the Monastery of Apostolos Andreas is the get-away-from-it-all **Seabird** (☎ 372 2012; Apostolos Andreas; singles/doubles UK£8/13), which is really more of a seasonal restaurant with a few basic rooms to rent.

For a meal with a golden view, the **Big Sand Restaurant** camping and picnic corner, just before the Monastery of Apostolos Andreas, offers good views from high up overlooking the magnificent beach scene. Expect no more than reasonably priced meat and fish grills.

Language

GREEK

Most Cypriots in the Republic speak English and nearly all road signs are in Greek and English. Since mid-1995 the Republic has converted all place names into Latin characters according to the official system of Greek transliteration, which has resulted in some place names being changed (see the boxed text 'What's in a Name?' in the Facts about Cyprus chapter). Greek may still be spoken by some Turkish Cypriots who formerly lived in the South, though they may be understandably reluctant to speak it in public. Greek is also spoken by small numbers of Greeks enclaved in villages in the Karpas (Kırpaşa) Peninsula and by Maronites living on the Koruçam (Kormakitis) Peninsula in the North.

For a more in-depth guide to Greek, get a copy of Lonely Planet's compact and comprehensive *Greek phrasebook*.

Pronunciation

Cypriot Greek pronunciation treats some consonants differently with κ and χ being pronounced as 'tch' and 'sh' respectively (see the boxed text 'Talking Cypriot' on this page). Greek Cypriots tend to talk slower than their mainland brethren, but speech modulation and word syncopation, especially in rural areas, may make understanding Cypriot Greek difficult. The Pafos region is well known for the difficulty of its local accent.

All Greek words of two or more syllables have an acute accent, which indicates where word stress falls. For instance, άγαλμα (statue) is pronounced *aghalma*, and αγάπη (love) is pronounced *aghapi*. In the transliterations used in this language guide, bold lettering indicates word stress. Note also that **dh** is pronounced as 'th' in 'then'; **gh** is a softer, slightly guttural version of 'g'.

Essentials

Hello.

*ya***sas**	Γειά σας.
*ya***su** (informal)	Γειά σου.

Goodbye.

*an***dio**	Αντίο.

Yes.

ne	Ναι.

Talking Cypriot

Visitors to Cyprus are unlikely to encounter any serious language difficulties since many people in the North and the South speak English as a matter of course. However, if you have a smattering of Greek or Turkish and wish to fine tune your linguistic skills, there are a few pointers you should be aware of. Talking Cypriot is not as simple as it might seem.

In the South the Cypriots speak Greek, but it's not the same as what you'll hear in Greece. To an ear familiar with the standard language, Cypriot Greek sounds harsh and even incomprehensible. Consonants are palatalised so that the guttural 'ch' becomes 'sh', 'k' becomes 'tch' and the vocalised 'b' becomes 'p'. Many other phonetic variations distinguish Cypriot Greek. The vocabulary has its own set of words not heard outside Cyprus, though both standard Greek terms as well as Cypriot versions will be familiar to most Cypriots. Speakers of Greek from the mainland are known as *kalamarades* or penpushers – a hangover from the days when the only educated speakers of the language in Cyprus were from Greece.

Turkish Cypriots have their own dialect, which is distinguished from Turkish spoken on the mainland by a number of peculiarities. These include a slurred, lazy mode of articulation, and the use of verb forms not used in standard Turkish, as well as a whole lexicon of Cyprus-specific words.

Neither Greek nor Turkish Cypriots will expect a visitor to be able to speak their respective languages – let alone the Cypriot variants. However, an hour or so spent practising the contents of the short language section in this book will go a long way to breaking the ice and to demonstrating to your new Cypriot friends your interest in their country.

No.

*o***hi**	Όχι.

Please.

*paraka***lo**	Παρακαλώ.

Thank you.

*efharis***to**	Ευχαριστώ.

Excuse me. (before a request)

*me synho***rite**	Με συγχωρείτε.

The Greek Alphabet & Pronunciation

Greek	Pronunciation Guide		Example		
A α	a	as in 'father'	αγάπη	*aghapi*	love
B β	v	as in 'vine'	βήμα	*vima*	step
Γ γ	gh	like a rough 'g'	γάτα	*ghata*	cat
	y	as in 'yes'	για	*ya*	for
Δ δ	dh	as in 'there'	δέμα	*dhema*	parcel
E ε	e	as in 'egg'	ένας	*enas*	one (m)
Z ζ	z	as in 'zoo'	ζώο	*zoo*	animal
H η	i	as in 'police'	ήταν	*itan*	was
Θ θ	th	as in 'throw'	θέμα	*thema*	theme
I ι	i	as in 'police'	ίδιος	*idhyos*	same
K κ	k	as in 'kite'	καλά	*kala*	well
Λ λ	l	as in 'leg'	λάθος	*lathos*	mistake
M μ	m	as in 'man'	μαμά	*mama*	mother
N ν	n	as in 'net'	νερό	*nero*	water
Ξ ξ	x	as in 'ox'	ξύδι	*ksidhi*	vinegar
O o	o	as in 'hot'	όλα	*ola*	all
Π π	p	as in 'pup'	πάω	*pao*	I go
P ρ	r	as in 'road'	ρέμα	*rema*	stream
		a slightly trilled r	ρόδα	*rodha*	tyre
Σ σ/ς	s	as in 'sand'	σημάδι	*simadhi*	mark
T τ	t	as in 'tap'	τόπι	*topi*	ball
Υ υ	i	as in 'police'	ύστερα	*istera*	after
Φ φ	f	as in 'find'	φύλλο	*filo*	leaf
X χ	h	as the 'ch' in Scottish *loch*, or	χάνω	*hano*	I lose
		like a rough 'h'	χέρι	*heri*	hand
Ψ ψ	ps	as in 'lapse'	ψωμί	*psomi*	bread
Ω ω	o	as in 'hot'	ώρα	*ora*	time

Combinations of Letters

The combinations of letters shown here are pronounced as follows:

Greek	Pronunciation Guide		Example		
αι	e	as in 'bet'	αίμα	*ema*	blood
ει	i	as in 'police'	είδα	*idha*	I saw
οι	i	as in 'police'	οικόπεδο	*ikopedho*	land
ου	u	as in 'mood'	πού	*pou*	who/what
μπ	b	as in 'beer'	μπάλα	*bala*	ball
	mb	as in 'amber'	κάμπος	*kambos*	forest
γγ	ng	as in 'angle'	αγγελία	*angelia*	classified
γκ	g	as in 'God'	γκάζι	*gazi*	gas
γξ	ks	as in 'minks'	σφιγξ	*sfinks*	sphynx
ντ	d	as in 'dot'	ντουλάπα	*doulapa*	wardrobe
	nd	as in 'bend'	πέντε	*pende*	five
τζ	dz	as in 'hands'	τζάκι	*dzaki*	fireplace

The pairs of vowels shown above are pronounced separately if the first has an acute accent, or the second a dieresis, as in the examples below:

γαϊδουράκι	*gaidhouraki*	little donkey
Κάιρο	*kairo*	Cairo

Some Greek consonant sounds have no English equivalent. The υ of the groups αυ, ευ and ηυ is generally pronounced 'v'. The Greek question mark is represented with the English equivalent of a semicolon ';'.

What's your name?
pos sas lene?   Πώς σας λένε;
My name is ...
me lene ...   Με λένε ...
How much is it?
poso kani?   Πόσο κάνει;

Language Difficulties

Do you speak English?
milate anglika?
Μιλάτε Αγγλικά;
Does anyone here speak English?
milai kanis anglika?
Μιλάει κανείς Αγγλικά;
I (don't) understand.
(dhen) katalaveno
(Δεν) καταλαβαίνω.
Please write that down.
parakalo grapste mou to
Παρακαλώ, γράψτε μου το.

Getting Around

Where is the bus stop?
pou ine i stasi tou leoforiou?
Που είναι η στάση του λεωφορείου;
Where is the taxi stand?
pou ine i stasi tou taxi?
Που είναι η στάση του ταξί;
I want to go to (Agia Napa).
thelo na pao stin Ayia Napa
Θέλω να πάω στην Αγία Νάπα.
Can you show me on the map?
borite na mou to dhixete sto harti?
Μπορείτε να μου το δείξετε στο χάρτη;
Go straight ahead.
piyenete efthia
Πηγαίνετε. ευθεία.
Turn left.
stripste aristera
Στρίψτε αριστερά.
Turn right.
stripste dexia
Στρίψτε δεξιά.
near/far
konda/makrya
κοντά/μακρυά

When does the ... leave/arrive?
pote fevyi/ftanee to ...?
Πότε φεύγει/φτάνει το ...;

ferry/boat	*ferribot*	φερρυμπώτ
city bus	*to astiko*	το αστικό
intercity bus	*leoforio*	λεωφορείο
next	*epomeno*	επόμενο
first	*proto*	πρώτο
last	*telefteo*	τελευταίο

Signs – Greek

ΕΙΣΟΔΟΣ	**Entry**
ΕΞΟΔΟΣ	**Exit**
ΩΘΗΣΑΤΕ	**Push**
ΣΥΡΑΤΕ	**Pull**
ΓΥΝΑΙΚΩΝ	**Women** (toilets)
ΑΝΔΡΩΝ	**Men** (toilets)
ΝΟΣΟΚΟΜΕΙΟ	**Hospital**
ΑΣΤΥΝΟΜΙΑ	**Police**
ΤΡΟΧΑΙΑ	**Traffic Police**
ΑΠΑΓΟΡΕΥΕΤΑΙ	**Prohibited**
ΕΙΣΙΤΗΡΙΑ	**Tickets**
ΝΕΚΡΗ ΖΩΝΗ	**Buffer Zone**

I'd like a ... ticket.
tha ithela ena isitirio ...
θα ήθελα ένα εισιτήριο ...
one-way
mono   μονό
return
me epsitrofi   με επιστροφή

Accommodation

I'd like ...
thelo ena ...   Θέλω ένα ...
a cheap hotel
ftino xenodohio   φτηνό ξενοδοχείο
a clean room
katharo dhomatio   καθαρό δωμάτιο
a camp site
kamping   κάμπιγκ

single	*mono*	μονό
double	*dhiplo*	διπλό
room with a	*dhomatio*	δωμάτιο
bathroom	*me banio*	με μπάνιο
key	*klidhi*	κλειδί

How much is it ...?
poso kani ...?   Πόσο κάνει ...;
per night
ti vradhya   τη βραδυά
for ... nights
ya ... vradhyez   για ... βραδυές

May I see it?
boro na to dho?   Μπορώ να το δω;
Where is the
bathroom?
pou ine to banio?   Πού είναι το μπάνιο;

Around Town

I'm looking for ...
psahno ya ...   Ψάχνω για ...

the bank
  *tin **trapeza***   την τράπεζα
a hotel
  ena xenodohio   ένα ξενοδοχείο
a market (vegetable)
  ti laeeki aghora   τη λαϊκή αγορά
the police
  tin astynomia   την αστυνομία
the post office
  to tahydhromio   το ταχυδρομείο
a public toilet
  mia toualeta   μια τουαλέττα
a telephone
  ena tilefono   ένα τηλέφωνο
the tourist office
  to touristiko   το τουριστικό
   grafio   γραφείο

the beach
  tin plaz   την πλαζ
the bridge
  ti yefyra   τη γέφυρα
the castle
  to kastro   το κάστρο
the church
  tin ekklisia   την εκκλησία
the hospital
  to nosokomio   το νοσοκομείο
the mosque
  to dzami   το τζαμί
the old city
  tin palya poli   την παλαιά πόλη
palace
  to palati   το παλάτι
the ruins
  ta arhea   τα αρχαία
the square
  tin platia   την πλατεία

Health

I'm ...
  ime ...   Είμαι ...
diabetic
  dhiavitikos/dhiavitiki (m/f)
  διαβητικός/διαβητική
epileptic
  epiliptikos/epiliptiki (m/f)
  επιληπτικός/επιληπτική
asthmatic
  asthmatikos/asthmatiki (m/f)
  ασθματικός/ασθματική

I'm allergic ...
  ime alergikos/alergiki ... (m/f)
  Είμαι αλλεργικός/αλλεργική ...

Emergencies

Help/Emergency!
  voithya!   Βοήθεια!
Call a doctor!
  fonaxte ena   Φωνάξτε ένα
  yatro!   ιατρό!
Call the police!
  fonaxte tin   Φωνάξτε την
  astynomia!   αστυνομία!
Go away!
  fiye!   Φύγε!

to antibiotics
  sta andiviotika   στα αντιβιωτικά
to penicillin
  sthn penikillini   στην πενικιλλίνη

antiseptic
  andisiptiko   αντισηπτικό
aspirin
  aspirini   ασπιρίνη
condom
  profylakatiko/   προφυλακτικό/
  kapota   καπότα
contraceptive
  andisylliptiko   αντισυλληπτικό
diarrhoea
  dheeareea   διάρροια
medicine
  farmako   φάρμακο
nausea
  naftia   ναυτία
sunblock cream
  andieeliaki   αντιηλιακή
  krema   κρέμα
tampon
  tambon   ταμπόν

Time & Dates

What time is it?
  ti ora ine?   Τι ώρα είναι;

It's ...   *ine ...*   Είναι ...
1 o'clock   *mia i ora*   μία η ώρα
2 o'clock   *dhio i ora*   δύο η ώρα
7.30   *efta ke misi*   εφτά και μισή
am   *to pro-i*   το πρωί
pm   *to apoyevma*   το απόγευμα

Sunday   *kyriaki*   Κυριακή
Monday   *dheftera*   Δευτέρα
Tuesday   *triti*   Τρίτη
Wednesday *tetarti*   Τετάρτη
Thursday   *pempti*   Πέμπτη

Friday	*paraskevi*	Παρασκευή
Saturday	*savato*	Σάββατο
January	*ianouarios*	Ιανουάριος
February	*fevrouarios*	Φεβρουάριος
March	*martios*	Μάρτιος
April	*aprilios*	Απρίλιος
May	*maios*	Μάιος
June	*iounios*	Ιούνιος
July	*ioulios*	Ιούλιος
August	*avghoustos*	Αύγουστος
September	*septemvrios*	Σεπτέμβριος
October	*oktovrios*	Οκτώβριος
November	*noemvrios*	Νοέμβριος
December	*dhekemvrios*	Δεκέμβριος

Numbers

0	*midhen*	μηδέν
1	*enas*	ένας (m)
	mia	μία (f)
	ena	ένα (n)
2	*dhio*	δύο
3	*tris*	τρεις (m & f)
	tria	τρία (n)
4	*teseris*	τέσσερεις (m & f)
	tesera	τέσσερα (n)
5	*pende*	πέντε
6	*exi*	έξη
7	*epta*	επτά
8	*ohto*	οχτώ
9	*enea*	εννέα
10	*dheka*	δέκα
20	*ikosi*	είκοσι
30	*trianda*	τριάντα
40	*saranda*	σαράντα
50	*peninda*	πενήντα
60	*exinda*	εξήντα
70	*evdhominda*	εβδομήντα
80	*oghdhonda*	ογδόντα
90	*eneninda*	ενενήντα
100	*ekato*	εκατό
1000	*hilii*	χίλιοι (m)
	hiliez	χίλιες (f)
	hilia	χίλια (n)

one million
  ena ekatomyrio ένα εκατομμύριο

GREEK FOOD

breakfast	*pro-ino*	πρωϊνό
lunch	*mesimvrino*	μεσημβρινό
dinner	*vradhyno*	βραδυνό

May I see the menu, please?
  boro na dho to menou parakalo?
  Μπορώ να δω το μενού, παρακαλώ;

I'm a vegetarian.
  ime horotofagos
  Είμαι χορτοφάγος.
I don't eat meat.
  dhen tro-o kreas
  Δεν τρώω κρέας.

ashtray	*tasaki*	τασάκι
the bill	*loghariazmos*	λογαριασμός
cup	*flitzani*	φλυτζάνι
fork	*piruni*	πηρούνι
glass	*potiri*	ποτήρι
knife	*macheri*	μαχαίρι
plate	*piato*	πιάτο
spoon	*kutali*	κουτάλι

Staples

bread	*psomi*	ψωμί
butter	*vutiro*	βούτυρο
cheese	*tiri*	τυρί
eggs	*avgha*	αυγά
honey	*meli*	μέλι
olive oil	*eleoladho*	ελαιόλαδο
olives	*elies*	ελιές
pepper	*piperi*	πιπέρι
salt	*alati*	αλάτι
sugar	*zachari*	ζάχαρη

Meat, Fish & Seafood

beef	*vodhino*	βοδινό
chicken	*kotopulo*	κοτόπουλο
goat	*katsiki*	κατσίκι
hare	*laghos*	λαγός
lamb	*arni*	αρνί
liver	*sikoti*	σηκώτι
pork	*chirino*	χοιρινό
sausages	*lukanika*	λουκάνικα
veal	*moschari*	μοσχάρι
seafood	*thalasina*	θαλασσινά
baby squid	*kalamaraki*	καλαμαράκι
mussels	*midhia*	μύδια
octopus	*chtapodhi*	χταπόδι
sardines	*sardheles*	σαρδέλλες
swordfish	*ksifias*	ξυφίας
whitebait	*maridha*	μαρίδα

Fruit & Vegetables

apples	*mila*	μήλα
apricots	*verikoka*	βερίκοκα
bananas	*bananes*	μπανάνες
figs	*sika*	σύκα
fruit	*fruta*	φρούτα
grapes	*stafilia*	σταφύλια
lemon	*lemoni*	λεμόνι

oranges	*portokalia*	πορτοκάλια
peaches	*rodhakina*	ροδάκινα
pear	*achladhi*	αχλάδι
prickly pear	*papou-tsosyka*	παπου-τσόσυκα
strawberries	*fra-ules*	φράουλες
watermelon	*karpuzi*	καρπούζι

broad beans	*kukia*	κουκιά
green beans	*fasolakia*	φασολάκια
cabbage	*lachano*	λάχανο
carrots	*karota*	καρότα
cauliflower	*kunupidhi*	κουνουπίδι
cucumber	*anguri*	αγγούρι
fennel	*anitho*	άνιθο
garlic	*skordho*	σκόρδο
mushrooms	*manitaria*	μανιτάρια
ocra	*bamies*	μπάμιες
onion	*kremidhi*	κρεμμύδι
peas	*arakas*	αρακάς
potatoes	*patates*	πατάτες
spinach	*spanaki*	σπανάκι
tomatoes	*domates*	ντομάτες
vegetables	*lachanika*	λαχανικά
chick peas	*revithia*	ρεβύθια
rice	*rizi*	ρύζι

Regional Specialities – Greek

afelia (αφέλια) – pork cooked in red wine and crushed coriander seeds

borekia (μπουρέκια) – small pies stuffed with cheese/mince/spinach

commandaria (Κομμανδαρία) – fortified red wine originally produced by the Knights Hospitaller at Kolossi castle

feta (φέτα) – salty white goat's cheese

flaunes (φλαούνες) – cheese tartlets made with chalumi cheese

halumi (χαλούμι) – firm goat's or ewe's milk cheese

humus (χόμμος) – chick pea and garlic dip

karaolia (καραόλια) – snails; a *mezes* delicacy

kleftiko (κλέφτικο) – oven-baked lamb

kolokasi (κολοκάσι) – a root vegetable similar to taro

kontosuvli (κοντοσούβλι) – large chunks of lamb cooked on a spit

kupepia (κουπέπια) – Cypriot word for stuffed vine leaves

lountza (λούντζα) – spicy ham made from cured, smoked pork fillet

musakas (μουσακάς) – baked dish made from layers of minced meat, aubergines, spices and a cheese topping

ofto (οφτό) – similar to *kleftiko* but individually packed in foil

seftalia (σεφταλιά) – short, fat sausages made of minced meat and spices

stifadho (στιφάδο) – rich beef and onion stew

taramosalata (ταραμοσαλάτα) – a dip made of fish roe

ttaavas (ττάβας) – savoury stew of beef or lamb, herbs and onions

yemista (γεμιστά) – any of a variety of stuffed vegetables

DRINKS

bottled water	*emfialomeno nero*	εμφιαλωμένο νερό
tap water	*nero tis vrisis*	νερό της βρύσης
juice	*himos*	χυμός
tea	*tsai*	τσάι
coffee	*kafes*	καφές
iced coffee	*frappe*	φραππέ
milk	*ghala*	γάλα
beer	*byra*	μπύρα
wine	*krasi*	κρασί
red	*kokino*	κόκκινο
white	*aspro*	άσπρο
retsina	*retsina*	ρετσίνα

(pine-resinated wine)

| ouzo | *uzo* | ούζο |

(aniseed-flavoured spirit)

| zivania | *zivania* | ζιβανία |

(strong spirit made from grape leftovers)

TURKISH

Ottoman Turkish was written in Arabic script, but this was phased out when Atatürk decreed the introduction of Latin script in 1928. The Turkish spoken in Cyprus differs somewhat from that spoken on the mainland, both in pronunciation and vocabulary. In big cities and tourist areas, many locals know at least some English and/or German. For a more in-depth look at Turkish, get a copy of Lonely Planet's compact and comprehensive *Turkish phrasebook*.

Pronunciation

The letters of the new Turkish alphabet have a consistent pronunciation; they're reasonably easy to master, once you've learned a few basic rules. All letters except ğ (which is silent) are pronounced, and there are no diphthongs.

Vowels

A a   as in 'shah'
E e   as in 'fell'
İ i   as 'ee'
I ı   as 'uh'
O o   as in 'hot'
U u   as the 'oo' in 'moo'
Ö ö   as the 'ur' in 'fur' (with pursed lips)
Ü ü   as the 'ew' in 'few' (with pursed lips)

Consonants

Ç ç   as the 'ch' in 'church'
C c   as English 'j'
Ğ ğ   not pronounced – it draws out the preceding vowel
G g   as in 'go'
H h   as in 'half'
J j   as the 's' in 'measure'
S s   as in 'stress'
Ş ş   as the 'sh' in 'shoe'
V v   as the 'w' in 'weather'

Essentials

Hello. — *Merhaba.*
Goodbye/ — *Allaha ısmarladık/*
  Bon Voyage. — *Güle güle.*
Yes. — *Evet.*
No. — *Hayır.*
Please. — *Lütfen.*
Thank you. — *Teşekkür ederim.*
That's fine/ — *Bir şey değil.*
  You're welcome.
Excuse me. — *Affedersiniz.*
Sorry. (Excuse me/ — *Pardon.*
  Forgive me.)
How much is it? — *Ne kadar?*

Language Difficulties

Do you speak — *Ingilizce biliyor*
  English? — *musunuz?*
Does anyone here — *Kimse Ingilizce biliyor*
  speak English? — *mu?*
I don't understand. — *Anlamiyorum.*
Please write that — *Lütfen yazın.*
  down.

Getting Around

The Turkish names for North Nicosia, Famagusta and Kyrenia are Lefkoşa, Mağusa and Girne respectively.

Where is the bus — *Otobüs durağınerede?*
  stop?
I want to go to — *(Lefkoşa)'e gitmek*
  (Lefkoşa). — *istiyorum.*

Signs – Turkish

Giriş	**Entrance**
Çikiş	**Exit**
Açik/Kapali	**Open/Closed**
Polis/Emniyet	**Police**
Yasak(tir)	**Prohibited**
Tuvalet	**Toilets**
Yeşil Hat	**Buffer Zone**

Can you show me — *Haritada gösterebilir*
  on the map? — *misiniz?*
Go straight ahead. — *Doğru gidin.*
Turn left. — *Sola dönün.*
Turn right. — *Sağa dönün.*
far/near — *uzak/yakın*

When does the ... — *... ne zaman kalkar/*
leave/arrive? — *gelir?*
  bus — *otobüsü*
  ferry/boat — *feribot/vapur*

next — *gelecek*
first — *birinci/ilk*
last — *son*

I'd like a ... ticket. — *... bileti istiyorum.*
  one-way — *gidiş*
  return — *gidiş-dönüş*

Accommodation

Where is a cheap — *Ucuz bir otel nerede?*
  hotel?
What is the — *Adres ne?*
  address?
Please write down — *Adresıyazar mısınız?*
  the address.
Do you have any — *Boş oda var mı?*
  rooms available?

I'd like ... — *... istiyorum.*
  a single room — *tek kişilik oda*
  a double room — *Ikıkişilik oda*
  a room with a — *banyolu oda*
    bathroom
  to share a dorm — *yatakhanede bir yatak*
  a bed — *bir yatak*

How much is it — *Bir gecelik nekadar?*
  per night?
May I see it? — *Görebilir miyim?*
Where is the — *Banyo nerede?*
  bathroom?

Around Town

I'm looking for the/a ...	... arıyorum
bank	bir banka
... embassy	... büyükelçiliğini
market	çarşıyı
police	polis
post office	postane
public toilet	tuvalet
telephone centre	telefon merkezi
tourist office	turizm danışma bürosu

beach	plaj
bridge	köprü
castle	kale/hisar
church	kilise
hospital	hastane
island	ada
mosque	cami(i)
old city	tarihişehir merkezi
palace	saray
ruins	harabeler/kalıntılar

Health

I'm ...	Ben ...
diabetic	şeker hastasıyım
epileptic	saralıyım
asthmatic	astımlıyım

I'm allergic to ...	... alerjim var.
antibiotics	antibiyotiğe
penicillin	penisiline

antiseptic	antiseptik
aspirin	aspirin
condom	prezervatif
contraceptive	gebeliğiönleyici
diarrhoea	ishal/diyare
medicine	ilaç
nausea	bulantı
sunblock cream	güneş blok kremi
tampon	tampon

Time & Dates

What time is it?	Saat kaç?
today	bugün
tomorrow	yarın
in the morning	sabahleyin
in the afternoon	öğleden sonra
in the evening	akşamda

Monday	Pazartesi
Tuesday	Salı
Wednesday	Çarşamba

Thursday	Perşembe
Friday	Cuma
Saturday	Cumartesi
Sunday	Pazar

January	Ocak
February	Şubat
March	Mart
April	Nisan
May	Mayıs
June	Haziran
July	Temmuz
August	Ağustos
September	Eylül
October	Ekim
November	Kasım
December	Arlık

Numbers

0	sıfır
1	bir
2	iki
3	üç
4	dört
5	beş
6	altı
7	yedi
8	sekiz
9	dokuz
10	on
11	on bir
12	on iki
20	yirmi
21	yirmibir
22	yirmiiki
30	otuz
40	kırk
50	elli
60	altmış
70	yetmiş
80	seksen
90	doksan
100	yüz
200	ikiyüz
1000	bin
2000	ikibin
one million	bir milyon

TURKISH FOOD

breakfast	*kahvaltı*
lunch	*öğleyemeği*
dinner	*akşamyemeği*
I'd like the set menu, please.	*Fiks menü istiyorum, lütfen.*
Is service included in the bill?	*Servis ücretıdahil mi?*
I don't eat meat.	*Hiç et yemiyorum.*
bill/cheque	*hesap*
fork	*çatal*
glass	*bardak*
knife	*bıçak*
plate	*tabak*
spoon	*kaşık*

Staples

bread	*ekmek*
butter	*tereyağı*
cheese	*peynir*
eggs(s)	*yumurta(lar)*
honey	*bal*
olive oil	*zeytinyağı*
olives	*yzeytin*
pepper	*kara/siyah biber*
rice	*pirinç*
salt	*tuz*
soup	*corba*
sugar/sweets	*şeker*

Meat, Fish & Seafood

Aegean tuna	*trança*
anchovy	*hamsi*
bluefish	*lüfer*
crab	*yengeç*
fish	*balık*
mussels	*midye*
sardine	*sardalya*
shrimp	*karides*
swordfish	*kılıç*
beef	*sığır*
boiling chicken	*tavuk*
kidney	*böbrek*
liver	*ciğer*
meat	*et*
pork	*domuz*
roasting chicken	*piliç*
veal	*dana*

Fruit & Vegetables

apple	*elma*
apricot	*kayısı*
banana	*muz*
fig	*incir*
fruit	*meyva/meyve*
grapes	*üzüm*
lemon	*limon*
orange	*portakal*
peach	*şeftali*
pear	*armut*
prickly pear	*frenk inciri*
watermelon	*karpuz*
cabbage	*lahana*
capsicum/pepper	*biber*
carrot	*havuç*
cauliflower	*karnabahar*
cucumber	*salatalık*
garlic	*sarmısak*
green beans	*taze fasulye*
okra	*bamya*
onion	*soğan*
peas	*bezelye*
potato	*patates*
spinach	*ıspınak*
tomato	*domates*
vegetable	*sebze*

Regional Specialities – Turkish

börek – flaky, fried pastry filled with white cheese or meat
hellim – firm goat's or ewe's milk cheese
küp kebab – oven-baked lamb
musaka – baked dish made from layers of minced meat, aubergines, spices and a cheese topping
pide – flat, unleavened bread
raki – strong aniseed-flavoured spirit
zivania/zivaniya – strong Cypriot spirit made from the leftovers of grapes after crushing (see also *raki*)

TURKISH DRINKS

water	*su*
mineral water	*maden suyu*
fruit juice	*meyva suyu*
lemonade	*limonata*
ice	*buz*
milk	*süt*
yogurt drink	*ayran*
tea	*çay*
coffee	*kahve(si)*
coffee & milk	*Fransız*
Turkish coffee	*Türk kahvesi*
beer	*bira*
... wine	*... şarap*
white	*beyaz*
red	*kırmızı*

Glossary

For items dealing with Cypriot cuisine, see the Language chapter.

(Fr) = French; (Gr) = Greek; (Tr) = Turkish

agios (m), agia (f) – saint (Gr)
ano – upper, eg, Ano Pafos (Gr)
Attila Line – furthest point of advancement of the Turkish army following their 1974 invasion of Cyprus. It now separates Northern Cyprus from the Republic of Cyprus.

baglam/baglamas – very small, bouzouki-like stringed instrument (Tr/Gr)
barbican – gate house of castle
bedesten – covered market (Tr)
belediye – town hall (Tr)
bouzouki – stringed lute-like instrument associated with *rembetika* music (Gr/Tr)
burnu – cape (Tr)
bulvarı – boulevard, avenue (Tr)
Byzantine Empire – Hellenistic, Christian empire lasting from AD 395 to 1453, centred on Constantinople (İstanbul)

caddesi – road (Tr)
camii – mosque (Tr)
commandery – a district under the control of a commander of an order of knights
CTO – Cyprus Tourism Organisation, The South's official tourism promotion body
CTP – Cumhuriyetçi Türk Partisi (Republican Turkish Party; Tr)
Cypriot syllabary – a writing system based on symbols representing syllables. Used in Cyprus from the 6th to the 3rd centuries BC
CYTA – Cyprus Telecommunications Authority (South)

DISY – Dimokratikos Synaspismos (Democratic Coalition; Gr)
dolmuş – shared (literally 'stuffed') taxi (Tr)
DP – Demokrat Partisi (Democratic Party; Tr)
dragoman – 'interpreter' (Turkish *tercüman*), or liaison officer between the Ottoman and Orthodox authorities

enceinte – enclosed area within a castle
enosis – union (with Greece); the frequent demand made by many Greek Cypriots prior to 1974 (Gr)

entrepot – commercial centre for import and export (Fr)
EOKA – Ethniki Organosi tou Kypriakou Agona (National Organisation for the Cypriot Struggle), nationalist guerrilla move- ment that fought for independence from Britain
EOKA B – post-independence reincarnation of EOKA, which mostly fought Turkish Cypriots
ethnarch – leader of a nation (Gr)
exohiko kentro – country tavern; large restaurant specialising in catering for diners usually from the city (Gr)

foo-koo – Cypriot BBQ, usually low and designed for rotating spit. The name derives from sound made while blowing on the charcoal to get it to light (Gr)
frescoes – painting made on fresh lime plaster so as to absorb the pigments

garigue – low open scrubland with many evergreen shrubs, low trees, aromatic herbs, and bunchgrasses found in poor or dry soil in the Mediterranean region (Fr)
Green Line – section of the Attila Line that divides Greek Cypriot Lefkosia from Turkish Cypriot North Nicosia (Lefkoşa)

hammam – public bathhouse (Tr)
hastanesi – hospital (Tr)

kafenio – coffee shop (Gr)
kalesi – castle (Tr)
kartzilamas – folk dance (Turkish *karşilama*)
kato – lower, eg, Kato Pafos (Gr)
KKTC – Kuzey Kıbrıs Türk Cumhuriyeti (Turkish Republic of Northern Cyprus; Tr)
KOT – Kypriakos Organismos Tourismou (see CTO); the official tourist organisation of the South
körfezi – bay (Tr)
KTHY – Kıbrıs Türk Hava Yolları (Cyprus Turkish Airlines; Tr)
Kypriako – the 'Cyprus issue'; politically sensitive and never forgotten by Greek Cypriots and Greeks alike (Gr)

Laïki Yitonia – 'popular neighbourhood'; renovated old areas now designated as urban tourist centres

leoforos – avenue (Gr)
Lusignan – Cypriot dynasty founded by French nobleman Guy de Lusignan in 1187 and which lasted until 1489
machiolation – an opening in the floor of a gallery or roof of a portal for discharging missiles upon assailants below
Mamelukes – slave soldiers who won political control of several Muslim states during the Middle Ages
maquis – thick scrubby underbrush of Mediterranean shores and especially of the islands of Corsica and Cyprus (Fr)
Maronites – ancient Christian sect from the Middle East
megaron – ancient Greek and Middle Eastern architectural form consisting of an open porch, a vestibule and a large hall with a central hearth and throne
Mesaoria – the large plain between the Kyrenia (Girne) and Troödos Mountains (Turkish Mesarya)
meydanı – square (Tr)
meze(s), mezedes (pl) – literally 'appetiser'; used in Cyprus to mean dining on lots of small plates of appetisers
mezedopolio – small restaurant specialising in *mezedes* (Gr)
moni – monastery or convent (Gr)
moufflon – endangered indigenous wild sheep of Cyprus (Fr)

narthex – railed-off western porch in early Christian churches used by women and also penitents (Gr)
nea, neo(s) – new; common prefix to place names (Gr)
NCTO – (North Cyprus Tourist Organisation) Northern Cyprus' tourism-promotion body

odos – street (Gr)
Ottoman Empire – Turkish Empire founded in the 11th century AD that ruled Cyprus from 1570 to 1878. The Ottoman Empire was abolished in 1922

panagia – church (Gr)
panigyri – feast or festival (Gr)

Pantokrator – the 'Almighty'; traditional fresco of Christ painted in the dome of Orthodox churches (Gr)
paşa – Ottoman title roughly equivalent to 'Lord' (Tr)
periptero – street kiosk selling newspapers, drinks and small items (Gr)
PIO – Public Information Office (South)
pitta – flat, unleavened bread (Gr)
plateia – square (Gr)
Ptolemies – Graeco-Macedonian rulers of Egypt in 4th Century BC

rembetika – Greek equivalent of American blues music, believed to have emerged from 'low-life' cafés in the 1870s (Gr)

saz/sazi – long necked stringed instrument
sokak – street (Tr)
sufi – adherent of the Sufi variant of Islam (Tr)

taksim – partition (of Cyprus); demanded by Turkish Cypriots in response to Greek Cypriots' calls for *enosis* (Tr)
taverna – traditional restaurant that serves food and wine (Gr)
tekkesi – gathering place of the Sufi; mosque (Tr)
tholos – the dome of an Orthodox church (Gr)
THY – Türk Hava Yolları, Turkish Airlines (Tr)
TMT – Turk Müdafaa Teskilati, Turkish (underground) defence organisation (Tr)
TRNC – Turkish Republic of Northern Cyprus (see KKTC; Tr)

UBP – Ulusal Birlik Partisi (National Unity Party; Tr)
Unesco – United Nations Educational, Scientific and Cultural Organisation
UNFICYP – United Nations Forces in Cyprus, UN body responsible for peacekeeping in Cyprus

yeni – new; common prefix to place names (Tr)

Thanks

Many thanks to the travellers who used the last edition and wrote to us with helpful hints, useful advice and interesting anecdotes.

Panagiotis Antonopoulos, Neil Barker, Claudine Belayche, Rick Besijn, Michel & Clément Betout, Caterina Bolognese, Christos Christou, Michael Counsell, JP Crawford, Geneviève Croguennec, David Crosier, Jane d'Arcy, Heiko Degenhardt, Rachel Dodds, Caghan Elsiz, Debroah Filcoff, Joyce Finn, Beth & David Frederikssen-Jones, Carlos R Gajardo, Celia Gale, Father David Gilchrist, Ben Godfrey, Meahan Grande, EA Green, Jill Green, John Hanks, Dr Ralph Hebden, AJ Hellard, John Hird, Jan & Mirjam Hissink, Simon Ho, Volkmar E Janicke, Hywel Jones, Sam Kelly, Thecle Kentfield, Aid Lavin, Alanna Lee, Paul Lester, Juha Levo, Stacey Ann Levy, Luther Link, David & Sally Martin, Patricia McCoy, RS Merrillees, Markella Mikkelsen, Wayne Mitchell, Andrew Mitchinson, Greard Munier, John Murphy, Kate Murray, Alan Nadin, Byron Odriscoll, Andrew J Orchard, Graham Pallett, Matthew Panayiotou, Seth Parks, Carol Peddie, Jane Perry, Zoli Pitman, Sean Plamondon, Fleur Porter, Dave Ratford, Kathryn Read-Bolam, Anna Richter, Michael Rogan, Yoav Rogovin, Jens Roth, Jeff Sale, Stritof Samo, Mari Schmidt, Suzy Scorer, Amos Shirman, Kerry Smallman, Ivan Stockley, Samo Stritof, Brian Tlongan, J Toth, Peter Turcot, Chris Underwood, Marjolein Verwie, Kenny Wheeler, John White, Alwyn Williams

LONELY PLANET

Guides by Region

L onely Planet is known worldwide for publishing practical, reliable and no-nonsense travel information in our guides and on our Web site. The Lonely Planet list covers just about every accessible part of the world. Currently there are 16 series: Travel guides, Shoestring guides, Condensed guides, Phrasebooks, Read This First, Healthy Travel, Walking guides, Cycling guides, Watching Wildlife guides, Pisces Diving & Snorkeling guides, City Maps, Road Atlases, Out to Eat, World Food, Journeys travel literature and Pictorials.

AFRICA Africa on a shoestring • Botswana • Cairo • Cairo City Map • Cape Town • Cape Town City Map • East Africa • Egypt • Egyptian Arabic phrasebook • Ethiopia, Eritrea & Djibouti • Ethiopian Amharic phrasebook • The Gambia & Senegal • Healthy Travel Africa • Kenya • Malawi • Morocco • Moroccan Arabic phrasebook • Mozambique • Namibia • Read This First: Africa • South Africa, Lesotho & Swaziland • Southern Africa • Southern Africa Road Atlas • Swahili phrasebook • Tanzania, Zanzibar & Pemba • Trekking in East Africa • Tunisia • Watching Wildlife East Africa • Watching Wildlife Southern Africa • West Africa • World Food Morocco • Zambia • Zimbabwe, Botswana & Namibia
Travel Literature: Mali Blues: Traveling to an African Beat • The Rainbird: A Central African Journey • Songs to an African Sunset: A Zimbabwean Story

AUSTRALIA & THE PACIFIC Aboriginal Australia & the Torres Strait Islands •Auckland • Australia • Australian phrasebook • Australia Road Atlas • Cycling Australia • Cycling New Zealand • Fiji • Fijian phrasebook • Healthy Travel Australia, NZ & the Pacific • Islands of Australia's Great Barrier Reef • Melbourne • Melbourne City Map • Micronesia • New Caledonia • New South Wales • New Zealand • Northern Territory • Outback Australia • Out to Eat – Melbourne • Out to Eat – Sydney • Papua New Guinea • Pidgin phrasebook • Queensland • Rarotonga & the Cook Islands • Samoa • Solomon Islands • South Australia • South Pacific • South Pacific phrasebook • Sydney • Sydney City Map • Sydney Condensed • Tahiti & French Polynesia • Tasmania • Tonga • Tramping in New Zealand • Vanuatu • Victoria • Walking in Australia • Watching Wildlife Australia • Western Australia
Travel Literature: Islands in the Clouds: Travels in the Highlands of New Guinea • Kiwi Tracks: A New Zealand Journey • Sean & David's Long Drive

CENTRAL AMERICA & THE CARIBBEAN Bahamas, Turks & Caicos • Baja California • Belize, Guatemala & Yucatán • Bermuda • Central America on a shoestring • Costa Rica • Costa Rica Spanish phrasebook • Cuba • Cycling Cuba • Dominican Republic & Haiti • Eastern Caribbean • Guatemala • Havana • Healthy Travel Central & South America • Jamaica • Mexico • Mexico City • Panama • Puerto Rico • Read This First: Central & South America • Virgin Islands • World Food Caribbean • World Food Mexico • Yucatán
Travel Literature: Green Dreams: Travels in Central America

EUROPE Amsterdam • Amsterdam City Map • Amsterdam Condensed • Andalucía • Athens • Austria • Baltic States phrasebook • Barcelona • Barcelona City Map • Belgium & Luxembourg • Berlin • Berlin City Map • Britain • British phrasebook • Brussels, Bruges & Antwerp • Brussels City Map • Budapest • Budapest City Map • Canary Islands • Catalunya & the Costa Brava • Central Europe • Central Europe phrasebook • Copenhagen • Corfu & the Ionians • Corsica • Crete • Crete Condensed • Croatia • Cycling Britain • Cycling France • Cyprus • Czech & Slovak Republics • Czech phrasebook • Denmark • Dublin • Dublin City Map • Dublin Condensed • Eastern Europe • Eastern Europe phrasebook • Edinburgh • Edinburgh City Map • England • Estonia, Latvia & Lithuania • Europe on a shoestring • Europe phrasebook • Finland • Florence • Florence City Map • France • Frankfurt City Map • Frankfurt Condensed • French phrasebook • Georgia, Armenia & Azerbaijan • Germany • German phrasebook • Greece • Greek Islands • Greek phrasebook • Hungary • Iceland, Greenland & the Faroe Islands • Ireland • Italian phrasebook • Italy • Kraków • Lisbon • The Loire • London • London City Map • London Condensed • Madrid • Madrid City Map • Malta • Mediterranean Europe • Milan, Turin & Genoa • Moscow • Munich • Netherlands • Normandy • Norway • Out to Eat – London • Out to Eat – Paris • Paris • Paris City Map • Paris Condensed • Poland • Polish phrasebook • Portugal • Portuguese phrasebook • Prague • Prague City Map • Provence & the Côte d'Azur • Read This First: Europe • Rhodes & the Dodecanese • Romania & Moldova • Rome • Rome City Map • Rome Condensed • Russia, Ukraine & Belarus • Russian phrasebook • Scandinavian & Baltic Europe • Scandinavian phrasebook • Scotland • Sicily • Slovenia • South-West France • Spain • Spanish phrasebook • Stockholm • St Petersburg • St Petersburg City Map • Sweden • Switzerland • Tuscany • Ukrainian phrasebook • Venice • Vienna • Wales • Walking in Britain • Walking in France • Walking in Ireland • Walking in Italy • Walking in Scotland • Walking in Spain • Walking in Switzerland • Western Europe • World Food France • World Food Greece • World Food Ireland • World Food Italy • World Food Spain **Travel Literature:** After Yugoslavia • Love and War in the Apennines • The Olive Grove: Travels in Greece • On the Shores of the Mediterranean • Round Ireland in Low Gear • A Small Place in Italy

LONELY PLANET

Mail Order

Lonely Planet products are distributed worldwide. They are also available by mail order from Lonely Planet, so if you have difficulty finding a title please write to us. North and South American residents should write to 150 Linden St, Oakland, CA 94607, USA; European and African residents should write to 10a Spring Place, London NW5 3BH, UK; and residents of other countries to Locked Bag 1, Footscray, Victoria 3011, Australia.

INDIAN SUBCONTINENT & THE INDIAN OCEAN Bangladesh • Bengali phrasebook • Bhutan • Delhi • Goa • Healthy Travel Asia & India • Hindi & Urdu phrasebook • India • India & Bangladesh City Map • Indian Himalaya • Karakoram Highway • Kathmandu City Map • Kerala • Madagascar • Maldives • Mauritius, Réunion & Seychelles • Mumbai (Bombay) • Nepal • Nepali phrasebook • North India • Pakistan • Rajasthan • Read This First: Asia & India • South India • Sri Lanka • Sri Lanka phrasebook • Tibet • Tibetan phrasebook • Trekking in the Indian Himalaya • Trekking in the Karakoram & Hindukush • Trekking in the Nepal Himalaya • World Food India **Travel Literature**: The Age of Kali: Indian Travels and Encounters • Hello Goodnight: A Life of Goa • In Rajasthan • Maverick in Madagascar • A Season in Heaven: True Tales from the Road to Kathmandu • Shopping for Buddhas • A Short Walk in the Hindu Kush • Slowly Down the Ganges

MIDDLE EAST & CENTRAL ASIA Bahrain, Kuwait & Qatar • Central Asia • Central Asia phrasebook • Dubai • Farsi (Persian) phrasebook • Hebrew phrasebook • Iran • Israel & the Palestinian Territories • Istanbul • Istanbul City Map • Istanbul to Cairo • Istanbul to Kathmandu • Jerusalem • Jerusalem City Map • Jordan • Lebanon • Middle East • Oman & the United Arab Emirates • Syria • Turkey • Turkish phrasebook • World Food Turkey • Yemen **Travel Literature**: Black on Black: Iran Revisited • Breaking Ranks: Turbulent Travels in the Promised Land • The Gates of Damascus • Kingdom of the Film Stars: Journey into Jordan

NORTH AMERICA Alaska • Boston • Boston City Map • Boston Condensed • British Columbia • California & Nevada • California Condensed • Canada • Chicago • Chicago City Map • Chicago Condensed • Florida • Georgia & the Carolinas • Great Lakes • Hawaii • Hiking in Alaska • Hiking in the USA • Honolulu & Oahu City Map • Las Vegas • Los Angeles • Los Angeles City Map • Louisiana & the Deep South • Miami • Miami City Map • Montreal • New England • New Orleans • New Orleans City Map • New York City • New York City City Map • New York City Condensed • New York, New Jersey & Pennsylvania • Oahu • Out to Eat – San Francisco • Pacific Northwest • Rocky Mountains • San Diego & Tijuana • San Francisco • San Francisco City Map • Seattle • Seattle City Map • Southwest • Texas • Toronto • USA • USA phrasebook • Vancouver • Vancouver City Map • Virginia & the Capital Region • Washington, DC • Washington, DC City Map • World Food New Orleans **Travel Literature**: Caught Inside: A Surfer's Year on the California Coast • Drive Thru America

NORTH-EAST ASIA Beijing • Beijing City Map • Cantonese phrasebook • China • Hiking in Japan • Hong Kong & Macau • Hong Kong City Map • Hong Kong Condensed • Japan • Japanese phrasebook • Korea • Korean phrasebook • Kyoto • Mandarin phrasebook • Mongolia • Mongolian phrasebook • Seoul • Shanghai • South-West China • Taiwan • Tokyo • Tokyo Condensed • World Food Hong Kong • World Food Japan **Travel Literature**: In Xanadu: A Quest • Lost Japan

SOUTH AMERICA Argentina, Uruguay & Paraguay • Bolivia • Brazil • Brazilian phrasebook • Buenos Aires • Buenos Aires City Map • Chile & Easter Island • Colombia • Ecuador & the Galapagos Islands • Healthy Travel Central & South America • Latin American Spanish phrasebook • Peru • Quechua phrasebook • Read This First: Central & South America • Rio de Janeiro • Rio de Janeiro City Map • Santiago de Chile • South America on a shoestring • Trekking in the Patagonian Andes • Venezuela **Travel Literature**: Full Circle: A South American Journey

SOUTH-EAST ASIA Bali & Lombok • Bangkok • Bangkok City Map • Burmese phrasebook • Cambodia • Cycling Vietnam, Laos & Cambodia • East Timor phrasebook • Hanoi • Healthy Travel Asia & India • Hill Tribes phrasebook • Ho Chi Minh City (Saigon) • Indonesia • Indonesian phrasebook • Indonesia's Eastern Islands • Java • Lao phrasebook • Laos • Malay phrasebook • Malaysia, Singapore & Brunei • Myanmar (Burma) • Philippines • Pilipino (Tagalog) phrasebook • Read This First: Asia & India • Singapore • Singapore City Map • South-East Asia on a shoestring • South-East Asia phrasebook • Thailand • Thailand's Islands & Beaches • Thailand, Vietnam, Laos & Cambodia Road Atlas • Thai phrasebook • Vietnam • Vietnamese phrasebook • World Food Indonesia • World Food Thailand • World Food Vietnam

ALSO AVAILABLE: Antarctica • The Arctic • The Blue Man: Tales of Travel, Love and Coffee • Brief Encounters: Stories of Love, Sex & Travel • Buddhist Stupas in Asia: The Shape of Perfection • Chasing Rickshaws • The Last Grain Race • Lonely Planet ... On the Edge: Adventurous Escapades from Around the World • Lonely Planet Unpacked • Lonely Planet Unpacked Again • Not the Only Planet: Science Fiction Travel Stories • Ports of Call: A Journey by Sea • Sacred India • Travel Photography: A Guide to Taking Better Pictures • Travel with Children • Tuvalu: Portrait of an Island Nation

LONELY PLANET

You already know that Lonely Planet produces more than this one guidebook, but you might not be aware of the other products we have on this region. Here is a selection of titles that you may want to check out as well:

Athens Condensed
ISBN 1 74059 350 2
US$11.99 • UK£5.99

Greece
ISBN 1 86450 334 3
US$19.99 • UK£12.99

Europe Phrasebook
ISBN 1 86450 224 X
US$8.99 • UK£4.99

Greek Islands
ISBN 1 74059 050 3
US$19.99 • UK£11.99

Athens
ISBN 1 86450 295 9
US$12.99 • UK£8.99

World Food Greece
ISBN 1 86450 113 8
US$13.99 • UK£8.99

Turkey
ISBN 1 74059 362 6
US$24.99 • UK£14.99

Istanbul
ISBN 1 74059 044 9
US$15.99 • UK£9.99

World Food Turkey
ISBN 1 86450 027 1
US$11.99 • UK£6.99

Mediterranean Europe
ISBN 1 74059 302 2
US$27.99 • UK£16.99

Rhodes & Dodecanese
ISBN 1 86450 117 0
US$15.99 • UK£9.99

Crete
ISBN 1 74059 049 X
US$15.99 • UK£9.99

Available wherever books are sold

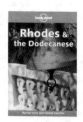

Index

Abbreviations

(FR) – Forest Reserve   (WF) – Wild Flowers of Cyprus

Text

Bold indicates maps.